THE SIGNAL BOX

A Pictorial History

and Guide to Designs

Frontispiece A large station in the heyday of mechanical signalling. Manchester Victoria East box was built by The Railway Signal Company for the Lancashire & Yorkshire Railway in 1889.

National Railway Museum

THE SIGNAL BOX

A Pictorial History

and Guide to Designs

Signalling Study Group

Oxford Publishing Company

First published 1986
Second impression 1998

ISBN 0-86093-224-9

Published by Oxford Publishing Co

an imprint of Ian Allan Publishing Ltd, Terminal House, Station Approach, Shepperton, Surrey TW17 8AS.
Printed by WBC Book Manufacturers Ltd, Waterton Industrial Estate, Bridgend, Mid Glamorgan CF31 3XP.

Code: 9810/A1

Publisher's note
Readers will appreciate that this book was first published in 1986 and that, in a number of cases, rationalisation and modernisation may have overtaken information which was correct at the time.

To the memory of John Saxby and all his rivals

Contents

Notes for the Reader

(1) Abbreviations

Railway Companies:

A (N&SW) D&R	Alexandra (Newport & South Wales) Docks & Railway Co.
B&E	Bristol & Exeter
B&M	Brecon & Merthyr
BP&GV	Burry Port & Gwendraeth Valley
BR	British Railways
BR (ER)	British Railways, Eastern Region
BR (LMR)	British Railways, London Midland Region
BR (NER)	British Railways, North Eastern Region
BR (SR)	British Railways, Southern Region
BR (ScR)	British Railways, Scottish Region
BR (WR)	British Railways, Western Region
Cal	Caledonian
Cam	Cambrian
C&WJ	Cleator & Workington Junction
CK&P	Cockermouth, Keswick & Penrith
CLC	Cheshire Lines Committee
CV&H	Colne Valley & Halstead
District	Metropolitan District
DN&S	Didcot, Newbury & Southampton
E&WYU	East & West Yorkshire Union
FY&N	Freshwater, Yarmouth & Newport
GC	Great Central
GE	Great Eastern
GN	Great Northern
GNoS	Great North of Scotland
GSW	Glasgow & South Western
GW	Great Western (do not confuse with GWCo = Gloucester Wagon Co.)
H&B	Hull & Barnsley
IoW	Isle of Wight
IoWC	Isle of Wight Central
L&B	Lynton & Barnstaple
L&MM	Llanelly & Mynydd Mawr
L&Y	Lancashire & Yorkshire
LBSC	London, Brighton & South Coast
LCD	London, Chatham & Dover
LDEC	Lancashire, Derbyshire & East Coast
LNER	London & North Eastern
LNW	London & North Western
LMS	London Midland & Scottish
LSW	London & South Western
LT	London Transport
LT&S	London, Tilbury & Southend
M&C	Maryport & Carlisle
M&GN	Midland & Great Northern Joint
Met	Metropolitan
Mid	Midland
MSJ&A	Manchester South Junction & Altrincham
MS&L	Manchester, Sheffield & Lincolnshire
MSWJ	Midland & South Western Junction
NB	North British
N&B	Neath & Brecon
NE	North Eastern
NL	North London
NS	North Staffordshire
PT	Port Talbot
R&SB	Rhondda & Swansea Bay
S&DJ	Somerset & Dorset Joint
SE	South Eastern
SEC	South Eastern & Chatham
SHT	Swansea Harbour Trust
SMJ	Stratford-on-Avon & Midland Junction
SR	Southern Railway
TV	Taff Vale
VS&P	Victoria Station and Pimlico
WC&E	Whitehaven, Cleator and Egremont
WELCP	West End of London and Crystal Palace
WM&CQ	Wrexham, Mold & Connah's Quay

Signalling Contractors:

EOD	Evans, O'Donnell
GWCo	Gloucester Wagon Company (do not confuse with GW = Great Western Railway)
McK&H	McKenzie, Clunes & Holland/McKenzie & Holland
McKH&WPSCo	McKenzie, Holland & Westinghouse Power Signal Co.
R&R	Ransomes & Rapier
RSCo	The Railway Signal Company
S&F	Saxby & Farmer

Form of Construction:

BTF	Brick to Floor
STF	Stone to Floor

Other Books (see Bibliography for full titles):

GWA	Vaughan, *GW Architecture*
GWS	Vaughan, *GW Signalling*
LMSA	Anderson & Fox, *LMS Architecture*
LNERS	Maclean, *LNER Constituent Signalling*
LNWRS	Foster, *LNWR Signalling*
SS	Pryer, *Southern Signals*

(2) Glossary

No Glossary is provided as such. Explanations of architectural terms are given in **Chapter 3** (the relevant page can be located via the Index). The architectural reader who is unfamiliar with basic signalling terms is referred to Kichenside & Williams (**see Bibliography**).

(3) Type Classifications

The 'Type' classifications of signal box designs used in this book are entirely our own invention, and in no case do they represent contemporary terminology. To the railway companies each successive design was simply the standard design.

A numerical system has been used (i.e. the first identifiable design is called **Type 1**, the second **Type 2**, etc.). In some cases sub-types have been designated by using letters. With the less standardised companies any attempt to classify boxes must necessarily be rather rough-and-ready, and in such cases there may be considerable differences between boxes classed as the same Type: in contrast, with the more standardised companies the difference between one Type and another may be quite small. Rather than try to make up artificial rules as to what constitutes a Type, we have simply divided each company's boxes into a manageable number of Types on whatever basis seemed most appropriate for that company.

One rule which has been used, however, is that 'material does not determine Type' (i.e. brick and timber versions of the same basic design are classified as the same Type). The only exception to this is the GW, where a Type-system based on material is already in recognised use. An 'illogical' Type numbering is also used for the LNW, where the three LNW box designs are already well-known as Types 3, 4, and 5, due to certain designs which are in fact S&F, being described originally as LNW Types 1 and 2.

Boxes of the post-grouping railway companies and British Railways have been given Type numbers from 11 upwards (except in the case of the GW, where the design history was unaffected by the Grouping) to avoid any possibility of confusion with pre-grouping companies' Types. The boxes of each post-grouping company and its successor BR Region have been numbered in the same continuous Type-series, as the design history was continuous. No attempt has been made to Type-classify the larger panel boxes, other than those built to the same design as contemporary mechanical boxes.

(4) Colour Schemes

The subject of signal box colour schemes is not dealt with here. Research on this subject has been carried out by members of the Historical Model Railway Society, and readers seeking information are invited to write (with s.a.e.) to the Secretary, Peter Ray, 44 West Street, Lilley, Luton, Beds. LV2 8LN, who will forward the query to the appropriate HMRS Company Steward. The HMRS's published books *Midland Style*, *Great Western Way*, *LSWR and SR Livery Register*, and *All about Midsomer Norton*, cover the colour schemes of Mid, GW, LSW, and S&DJ boxes respectively, and are available from specialist bookshops or from the Publications Sales Officer, 23 Whitestone Road, Berkeley Road, Frome, Somerset.

(5) Surviving Boxes

In some cases (normally where there are only a few left) we have listed all the surviving boxes of a particular Type. This refers to the state of affairs at mid-1985, and some of the boxes so listed will have been demolished by the time this book reaches the reader, but it was felt that the information would be useful on the whole.

Bibliography

General Works:
H. Raynar Wilson, *Mechanical Railway Signalling*, The Publishers of the Railway Engineer, 1900.
Westinghouse Brake & Signal Company, *A Century of Signalling*, 1956.
O. S. Nock, *Fifty Years of Railway Signalling*, I.R.S.E./Ian Allan, 1962.
G. M. Kichenside and Alan Williams, *British Railway Signalling*, Ian Allan, 1st Edition 1963, now 4th Edition.
O. S. Nock, *British Railway Signalling*, George Allan & Unwin, 1969.
Gordon Biddle, *Victorian Stations*, David & Charles, 1973.
M. A. King, *An Album of Pre-Grouping Signal Boxes*, Turntable Publications, 1976.

Works on Sepcific Companies:
L. G. Warburton, *A Pictorial Record of LMS Signals*, OPC, 1971.
A. Vaughan, *A Pictorial Record of Great Western Signalling*, OPC, 1973 (2nd Edition 1984).
A. Vaughan, *A Pictorial Record of Great Western Architecture*, OPC, 1977.
G. A. Pryer, *A Pictorial Record of Southern Signals*, OPC, 1977.
V. R. Anderson and G. K. Fox, *A Pictorial Record of LMS Architecture*, OPC, 1981.
R. D. Foster, *A Pictorial Record of LNWR Signalling*, OPC, 1982.
A. A. Maclean, *A Pictorial Record of LNER Constituent Signalling*, OPC, 1983.

Of the standard company histories, the following are particularly useful for information on signalling:

G. Dow, *Great Central*, Ian Allan, 3 vols.
J. T. Howard Turner, *The London, Brighton and South Coast Railway*, Batsford, 3 vols.
J. Wrottesley, *The Great Northern Railway*, Batsford, 3 vols.

Many of the histories of individual lines published during the last decade have detailed information on signalling.

Acknowledgements

We are particularly indebted to M. Christensen and F. Alexander for reading and commenting on the drafts.

We would also like to thank the following: M. J. Addison, M. Back, C. H. Betts, J. Bennett, A. Cartwright, R. J. Caston, D. A. Collins, M. J. Cruttenden, J. G. Dixon, D. W. Edwards, R. Farrant, T. L. Guest, M. Hale, M. Horne, J. T. Howard Turner, M. A. King, R. W. Miller, J. Minnis, M. Nicholson, E. S. Nicoll, O. S. Nock, C. J. L. Osment, D. J. Pollard, G. A. Pryer, A. Roberts, P. V. Starling, T. T. Sutcliffe, R. J. Talbot, D. J. Taylor, G. H. Tilt, A Vaughan, J. Wagstaff, C. J. Whitaker, D. Wilkinson, H. G. E. Wilson, C. J. Woolstenholmes, Gloucester Railway Carriage & Wagon Co. Ltd, Westinghouse Brake & Signal Co. Ltd, Public Record Office, Scottish Record Office, many County Record Offices and Public Libraries, National Railway Museum, and, most especially, a large number of British Rail offices.

We are also grateful to the various photographers whose work is individually credited.

Introduction

For over a hundred years, from the 1860s to the 1980s, the signal box at station, siding, and junction was one of the most common features of the British railway scene. In the heyday of mechanical signalling around the turn of the century, some 13,000 boxes were in current use, and the total number of boxes ever built was something like double this figure. Now, there are only 2,000 left, and they are disappearing at the rate of a hundred or more each year. This book, the first full study of its subject, comes just in time for the reader to be able to see a good selection of boxes still standing. The older remaining boxes now provide one of the least changed survivals from Victorian industry and, apart from station buildings, which are less fully 'characteristic' of their owning company, the last recognisable inheritance from the pre-grouping railway companies.

It is hoped that this book will be of interest to all students of railway signalling and all who are interested in railway and industrial architecture. Beyond the main subject of signal box design, there is much new information included on the signalling histories of the various railway companies, and the work of the signalling contractors.

The railway companies' Minute Books show that management regarded signalling as being of the same order of importance as motive power. But railway historians in the past were mostly so locomotive-orientated that it was not unusual, even in the 1960s, for histories of railway companies to be published with barely a mention of signalling at all. Since the late 1960s, however, interest in signalling has mushroomed, inspired no doubt by a realisation that mechanical signalling was disappearing rapidly without being properly recorded. The Signalling Record Society was founded in 1969 and has done much to co-ordinate research. Between 1971 and 1977 came the first published studies of the signalling of individual railways: L. G. Warburton's *A Pictorial Record of LMS Signals*, Adrian Vaughan's *A Pictorial Record of Great Western Signalling*, and George Pryer's *A Pictorial Record of Southern Signals*. However, at this period little research had been done on the specific question of signal box architecture. M. A. King's *An Album of Pre-Grouping Signal Boxes* (1976) was the first attempt at an overall illustration of box designs. Now, after some forty man-years' research, we are pleased to offer this book.

Other detailed studies of the signalling of individual companies are likely to follow over the next few years: R. D. Foster's *A Pictorial Record of LNWR Signalling* (1983) is already available, and covers LNW box design in full. But we would like to stress here the importance of also covering the history of signalling from a national viewpoint. Many of the most important developments in signalling were the work not of the railway companies but of the signalling contractors, and many boxes, particularly in the 1860s and 1870s, were built by the signalling contractors to their own architectural designs. More generally, the operational and Government requirements for signalling were much the same on one railway as on another, even if different techniques were used by different signal engineers to fulfil those requirements, and different preferences manifested themselves in signal box design.

A further reflection of the comparative lack of interest in signalling until recent years, is the fact that far fewer official or amateur records were made or preserved than in the case of locomotives and rolling stock. Few railway enthusiasts ever photographed a signal box (other than by accident!) prior to the 1960s, and only a small number of official photographs of boxes survive from the pre-grouping period. Nevertheless, many early station views also show the signal box and, all in all, it has been possible to examine photographs of nearly 10,000 boxes. Architectural drawings were prepared for many boxes, but not where designs were fully standardised, and some survive in the Public Record Offices at Kew and Edinburgh, and in BR and private hands. The railway companies' Minute Books, also now in the Public Record Offices, provide in some cases a large amount of information on dates and contracts, but in other cases are of little use. Also valuable are the Board of Trade Inspection Reports (MT6 and MT29 Classes at Kew), and the railway companies' signalling notices (where they survive). But for a minority of companies all efforts have so far failed to produce any large-scale source for the required information.

In the space available in this book, it is impossible to describe every signal box built for every railway company. In the case of those companies where design was very standardised, the box types described here cover virtually all the boxes built. However, a few companies had no real standardisation of design at many periods, and in such cases only a representative sample can be included, and the reader must be prepared to come across a proportion of boxes which bear little resemblance to those illustrated here. Other companies, such as the LSW, built many boxes to one-off designs, despite having standard designs in use concurrently.

It should be emphasised that this book is not a specialist study of signalling procedures and practices, nor of signalling equipment, although much reference is of course made to both these areas. Were it not for the fact that it would have more than doubled the length of the book, it would have been desirable to include a more detailed history and description of the different types of mechanical locking frame and the other major items of signal box equipment. The type of equipment provided obviously had an effect on the interior, and to a lesser extent the exterior, design and appearance of a signal box. We have given in **Chapter 3** some explanation of these effects, but it is admitted that this book gives less attention to the interior of the signal box than might be desirable in an ideal world.

The content of the book is restricted to England, Scotland, and Wales. In some ways this is an artificial restriction, although we hope the reader will understand the necessity for it. In particular, the whole of Ireland was of course a part of the United Kingdom until 1922. The Irish railways relied on the British signalling contractors, and many boxes in Ireland were built to the same contractors' designs as were used on the mainland, with Railway Signal Company boxes being particularly common. Further afield, the British contractors were responsible for the signalling of the railways of Australia, New Zealand, and India, and for much work elsewhere in the world (notably in South America). In the temperate zones, at least, box designs were not dissimilar to UK practice, but seldom or never were the identical designs used.

A work of this kind is bound to contain some errors, although we have tried to make it clear where there is doubt as to the accuracy of information.

Any corrections, comments, or further information are of course welcomed and should be sent to us c/o the publishers. The Signalling Study Group is an informal research group of Signalling Record Society members, and anyone engaged in signalling research who is not already a member of the Signalling Record Society is invited to write (with s.a.e.) to the Secretary at 178 Birmingham Road, Kidderminster, Worcs. DY10 2SJ, for details of membership.

R. D. Foster
J. Hinson
M. R. L. Instone
P. Kay
J. P. Morris
R. Newman
1986

CHAPTER ONE

The Evolution of the Signal Box

Since the 1860s, the term 'signal box' has meant a covered and glazed structure housing levers from which both signals and points are operated. Yet there can be no strict definition of what is, or is not, a 'signal box'. So, rather than trying to look for the 'first' signal box, this chapter describes the continuous process of development which turned the early policemen's and signalmen's huts, and junction 'platforms', into the signal box as we know it.

Constables, Time-Interval Working, and the Introduction of 'Fixed' Signals

The earliest tramways and railways, like the roads, had no signalling. Even when long-distance railways made their appearance in the 1830s, the practice of 'running on sight' continued in some cases. For example, the Eastern Counties Railway in 1840 had no signals, and its Rule Book provided that 'when an engine follows another on the same line of rails, the driver of the engine following shall keep at the distance of at least 500 yards from the first engine'. What with bends and other obstructions to the line of sight, not to mention regular interventions of darkness and fog, this form of operation was bound to result, from time to time, in serious collisions, as indeed happened on the Eastern Counties Railway on 14th September 1840.

It was, however, soon generally recognised that fast trunk railways required a better form of train control, and on most lines the 'constable' or 'policeman' appointed at each station to look after the company's property was also given the task of regulating the passage of trains. The constable decided whether to stop a train or allow it to proceed, not on any knowledge of how far in front the previous train was (prior to the installation of the electric telegraph on a line there was no technology capable of providing such information) but simply on the basis of how much time had elapsed since the previous train left. A common practice was to show a 'stop' signal for five minutes after a train left, and a 'caution' signal for a further five minutes after that. This was a definite improvement over pure 'running on sight', as it gave drivers, in most cases, some indication that they might be in danger of catching up with the previous train; but it had obvious potential for disaster whenever a train came to a halt, or proceeded unusually slowly, between stations. In theory, there was time for the guard to walk back and show a danger signal if his train made an out-of-course stop, but this was not always done. Nevertheless, 'time-interval' operation served the purposes of the 1840s quite well in practice, if only because trains on most lines were very infrequent and a train was therefore unlikely to catch up with the one in front in any case. More complicated forms of control were required to prevent collisions on single lines, but it would be beyond the scope of this book to seek to describe these. The 'time-interval' system remains in the BR Regulations today for use when all communications have failed.

At first, the constables conveyed their instructions to drivers by hand-signals, or flag-signals (which, again, remain in the Regulations for emergency use, and for local movements). But 'fixed' signals — that is, signals on a fixed post — had appeared in the 1830s on some lines, and soon became the norm. Of the many varieties of ball, bar, board, and arm that were used, the semaphore arm, first used for railway purposes by Gregory of the London & Croydon Railway in 1841, proved the most effective, and

Plate 1 This drawing on the headed letter paper of Messrs Stevens & Sons shows a pointsman/signalman at a location which could either be a junction, or the entrance to a station. He is holding over the points (which the artist has been unable to draw properly) for the approaching train, by means of a hand-lever. The handles for working the semaphore signals can be seen near the foot of the post. Note that there is only one semaphore for each direction, even though the approaching train has a choice of two lines. This particular letter was sent on 25th September 1853 to the Monmouthshire Railway & Canal Co., offering 'Double Semaphore Signals' to the design illustrated at £21.

Public Record Office

was generally supplanting the other types of signal by the 1860s. These early signals were worked by small handles on or near the signal post. At most stations there was only one signal for each direction, the two arms being mounted on opposite sides of the same post (**Plates 1 & 23**). The points were worked by individual hand-levers adjacent to each point, as the points in sidings still are today. There was nothing, other than the constable's memory, to ensure correlation between the signal and point settings.

Pointsmen and Signalmen

A Policeman on the Great Western Railway in 1841 was expected to:

'Preserve order in all the stations on the line of railway: give and receive signals: keep the line free from casual or wilful obstruction: assist in case of accident: caution strangers of danger on the railway: remove intruders of all descriptions: superintend and manage the crossings and switches: give notice of arrivals and departures: direct persons into the entrance to the stations or sheds: watch movements of the embankments or cuttings: inspect the rails and solidity of the timber: guard and watch the company's premises: and convey the earliest information on every subject to his appointed station or superior officer'.

With all this on his plate, it was not surprising that the constable might sometimes become confused in his train-signalling function. At the largest stations, it obviously took several men to fulfil the whole of this job description, and it was recognised that, rather than multiplying the number of general purpose constables, it was preferable to have one or more men specifically delegated to the management of points and signals. Thus the 'pointsman' (or 'switchman'), and the 'signalman', made their appearance. These were higher grades than that of constable. The same man normally operated both points and signals, but his title varied between one company and another. The term 'signalman', which was often spelt as two words in the 1840s, had been used previously in non-railway contexts.

In its first report on railways in 1841, the Board of Trade recommended that 'every station should have a fixed signal post and revolving lamp, and a signal man who has no distracting duties to perform'. But at the average wayside station it was to be another twenty years or more before this desirable state of affairs came to pass. The extra staff had to be begged on a station-by-station basis. For example, the GN's Managing Director, Seymour Clarke, applied to his Directors on 20th October 1853:

'From the frequency of trains, the formation of short (= local) trains, the removal of carriages from the down trains to the up sidings, there is such a constant use of the signals at Hatfield, and the station itself being so much hidden by the curve and the cutting, I think it desirable to put a policeman in charge of the signals there, whose sole business it shall be to work them'.

Gradually, the law and order and signalling functions became separated. But on some railways the signalmen were still under the Police Department in the 1860s and, to this day, signalmen are referred to as 'Bobbies' by other railway staff.

The Signalman's Hut

It seems that in the earliest years many constables, pointsmen and signalmen were not provided by their employers with any form of shelter from the elements. Indeed, at some locations this remained the case as late as the 1860s. In North Eastern Railway correspondence of 1865/6, we read that at Picton Junction:

'The signalman has to attend to the gates and the signals. The latter are separated from the station by the road. There is no shelter for the man except in the Second Class Waiting Room or in the shed on the up platform'.

TUNNEL SIGNAL—' ALL RIGHT.''

Plate 2 A Policeman on the London & Brighton Railway in 1844, stationed at the entrance to a tunnel. This engraving appeared in an *Illustrated London News* article, which commented cynically 'we rather incline to the belief that it is a sign of politeness on his part to welcome us into the tunnel, rather than any masonic understanding between the engineer, stoker, guards, and himself'. No fixed signal has been provided but, being remote from any station, the policeman has been given a tolerable hut, with a hearth. He also seems (like Bob at Wallingford Road) to have an interest in horticulture — something for which signalmen later became well-known.

Public Record Office

Plate 3 This circa 1870 view of Bromley (LCD) shows a station signalman's hut of the 1850s, probably typical in size and appearance of that decade. The 'watchman's hut/sentry box' connection is very evident. A hearth and brick chimney are provided. The line from Shortlands to Bickley was opened by the Mid Kent (Bromley to St. Mary Cray) Railway in July 1858, but was initially a single line worked on the 'one engine in steam' basis. The signal arrangements shown here would have been provided in 1859 when the line was doubled. The telegraph was installed by April 1859 when the SE (which worked the Mid Kent) sent a bill for £135 2s. to the company for this work. A telegraph pole (painted white) can be seen behind the left-hand end of the footbridge, and another shorter pole stands immediately to the right of the signalman's hut. On the wall of the hut, to the left of the signalman's head, is a white oval telegraph board, indicating that the instruments are in good order. The station signal to the left of the hut has a lattice iron post, which suggests that it may have been acquired from Stevens & Sons. To the right of the hut is a single lever for working the 'down' distant signal; this lever also has Stevens characteristics — presumably there is another such lever invisible on the other side of the box, for the 'up' distant signal. As the SE was responsible for working the line, it would almost certainly have been worked on the Absolute Block system from doubling. The hut itself is very similar to contemporary huts on the SE proper **(Plate 4)**. In 1862 the line passed into LCD control. Bromley Station was interlocked and a new signal box was built in 1873, when additional sidings were provided.

Authors' Collection

And at Harrogate, at 'the points of the parallel lines north of the station':

'The pointsman has to attend for every outgoing train in that direction, and as the points are 160 yards from the covered portion of the station, the man has no shelter during the whole of the day'.

However, it would have been against human nature if many men had not contrived some form of 'watchman's hut' on their own initiative if deprived of official accommodation, and, as time passed, the official structures also became more frequent in number and more generous in their dimensions.

Signalmen's huts were being described as 'signal boxes' from an early date. This term had been used in pre-railway days to describe the message stations of the various non-electric telegraph systems then in use for military and other purposes. 'Signalman's Box' and 'Pointsman's Box' were common variants in early railway usage, also 'Signal House', 'Signal Station', 'Signal Post', 'Signal Cabin', and, for the elevated junction installations described later in this chapter, 'Platform', 'Stage', and 'Tower'.

From the 1870s, 'Signal Box' and 'Signal Cabin' were the only terms in common use. In this book the term 'Signal Box' is gen-erally used when dealing with the later period, irrespective of the term used by the particular company under discussion.

A cynical view of life in a signalman's hut of the more primitive kind can be found in the *Memoirs of a Station Master*. The author was writing in 1879 about conditions at Wallingford Road Station (Great Western Railway) in 1861: some exaggeration must be expected as he demonstrates a considerable grudge against his former employers:

'That afternoon I had an hour's practice with Bob in his signal box. In his signal box I say, but half in and half out I ought to say, for there was only room for one person. In those days, there was no locking-gear system, and the men could not, as now, remain by their fireside in a glass-house and turn the signals and points, but they had to run, whatever the weather, to the mouth of the siding and open the points, by turning a lever on the spot'.

'As the safety of the trains depended on the vigilance of the signalmen . . . the Directors believed that the signal box should not be a source of comfort to the occupier. No door was provided, but the signalman was allowed to turn it round according to the direction of the wind . . . Bob had, however, taken a march on the regulations, for he had grown two huge bushes of the tea plant, which met at the top, and which, together with the signal box, a little brick paving, and a few odd pieces of rusty sheet iron interlaced in the top of the tea trees to make it watertight, formed quite a little Robinson Crusoe dwelling . . .'

'Bob assured me that the first winter he was at Wilderness Road station he was "well nigh frozed alive", and that the second winter, "it warn't much better": but his mother having given him the two little tea trees, and he having got it a bit dry underfoot, and built up a bit of a fireplace, kept going with coal he picked up on the line and which had shaken (sic) off the trucks when they were shunting, it was not so bad now. Bob had put a seat in his signal box, and planted primroses and violets outside'.

Given the conditions, it was perhaps not surprising that a Great Western Railway application form for posts of Policeman and Switchman in 1853 should specify that:

'The Candidate must be under thirty five years of age; he must stand five feet eight inches high, without his shoes; he must be able to read and write, and be generally intelligent; free from any bodily complaint, and of a strong constitution, according to the judgment of the Surgeon by whom he will be examined'.

The idea that uncomfortable conditions led to improved diligence and safety was slow to die in the minds of many railway Directors.

The Board of Trade Railway Department

The Board of Trade Railway Department had an important role in persuading the railway companies to adopt improved signalling methods, although, as is so often the case, it was set up primarily for other purposes. In the late 1830s, public concern about railways arose mainly from fear of monopoly in transport, and from the fact that lines were sometimes built in a different manner and alignment to that authorised by their Act. Safety of operation was a lesser issue. A Parliamentary Select Committee into the State of Communications by Railways sat in 1839 and, as a result of its report, the Railway Regulation Act 1840 established a new Railway Department in the Board of Trade to supervise the railway companies. It was provided that companies should notify the Board of their intention to open any new line, and of any serious accidents that occurred. The Board was to appoint officers to inspect new lines — originally the primary intention was that the Inspecting Officers would ensure that the line had been constructed exactly as authorised by its Act, but in practice they soon became more concerned with the general equipment of new lines and its adequacy for safe operation. The Board also made a practice of investigating in detail the causes of the accidents reported to it (although until 1871 it had no specific statutory authority to do this). By the Railway Regulation Act 1842, the Board was given specific authority to order the postponement of the opening of any line which its Inspectors considered inadequately equipped. It was these two functions of inspecting new lines and reporting on accidents that led the Board's officers to take an increasing interest in the need for improved signalling equipment.

The first full-time Inspector General was Lt. Col. Sir Frederic Smith, beginning a tradition, still maintained today, that Inspectors were appointed from the officers of the Royal Engineers. In 1841, Smith was replaced by Maj. Gen. C. W. Pasley, who stayed in office until 1846, building up useful experience for the Board. However, the Railway Department was then plagued with a plethora of reorganisations. In 1844 it was transformed into a 'Railway Board', in 1845 it reverted to being the Railway Department, in 1846 the railway powers of the Board of Trade were transferred to a new independent department called the 'Commissioners of Railways', and in 1851 the Board of Trade Railway Department was again re-established in its original form. The 1846 reorganisation was most damaging, as Pasley and the other more experienced members of the staff were displaced. As a result, it was not until the mid-1850s that the department really got into its stride again. The year 1853 saw the appointment as Inspector of Capt. Henry Tyler, and 1854 of Lt. Col. W. Yolland, who were to remain in office for 24 and 31 years respectively. From 1853, there were three, and from 1867 four, Inspectors. It was the vast wealth of knowledge which Tyler and Yolland were able to accumulate over these lengthy periods that gave the Department, by 1860, the persuasive influence which, in the face of the Board's limited statutory powers, it needed to push the railway companies into the adoption of safer operating practices.

The Department's role in relation to specific developments from the 1840s onwards is discussed in later sections of this chapter, and the procedures for the inspection of new lines are detailed in **Chapter 2**. For a fuller history of the Board of Trade Railway Department, 1840-70, the reader is referred to Henry Parris, *Government and The Railways in Nineteenth-Century Britain* (RKP, 1965).

The Electric Telegraph

The first practical application of the newly-invented electric telegraph was in 1837, in a trial installation set up by Messrs Cooke and Wheatstone for communication between Euston Station and the rope engine house at Camden, on the London & Birmingham Railway. Cooke hoped that the company would agree to extend the telegraph through to Birmingham, and use it for train signalling, but the company decided against this. When the first permanent telegraph line was provided along the GW route out of Paddington in 1839, it was used only for passing messages, and not for signalling trains (for two months the passing of every train at West Drayton and at Hanwell was telegraphed to Paddington, but only to test the reliability of the equipment).

In 1842, Cooke published a book *Telegraphic Railways, or The Single Way Recommended*, advocating the use of the telegraph for a 'space-interval' system of train signalling (that is, what is now known as 'Absolute Block' working). He described a notional installation on the Midland Counties line between Rugby and Derby as an example of how it could be done. Cooke's system was adopted for the single track Norwich & Yarmouth Railway in 1844, but it was not taken up for double lines. It took many more years to edge the railway companies away from their reliance on 'time-interval' working for double track routes.

The first permanent use of the telegraph for signalling was to protect the passage of trains through long tunnels, always a source of fear in the early railway traveller. Cooke visited Stephenson, the Engineer to the North Midland Railway, at the Clay Cross Tunnel during its construction in 1839, and persuaded him to use the telegraph through this tunnel from the opening of the line. A man with a telegraph instrument and a signal was positioned at each end of the tunnel. In 1841 this installation was improved by the provision of special instruments designed for signalling, with a brass pin to hold the needle to 'stop' or 'go on' positions — an early version of the modern 'block instruments'. (With the ordinary 'Post Office' type of instrument — then known as the 'speaking instrument' — on which each letter of a message had to be spelt out individually, there was no continuous record of the state of the line, so if a signalman failed to remember correctly what had been telegraphed, he might accidentally allow a train into the tunnel when it was still occupied by the previous train). During the 1840s, many other railway companies introduced 'space-interval' working by telegraph through their longer tunnels, or on other especially dangerous sections of line such as the Lickey Incline, but often using ordinary 'speaking instruments' only. A photograph of the elevated signalman's hut at Clayton Tunnel South, built by the LBSC for the introduction of telegraph working through the tunnel, can be seen in K. Marx's *LBSC Album* (Ian Allan).

The telegraph itself was installed over the full length of many companies' lines during the late 1840s and the 1850s, but in most cases it was used only for commercial and operating messages, with the instruments installed in the station offices, and not for signalling. The first company to use the telegraph for train signalling on a double track line on a full route basis (as distinct from short tunnel installations) was the South Eastern Railway. The SE

main line from Merstham to Dover was worked by telegraph from 16th February 1846, and the branches from around the same date. Absolute 'space-interval' working was enforced between adjacent stations. At first, the ordinary 'speaking instruments' were used for signalling as well as for other messages, plus an 'alarm' to call attention; but even on a comparatively sparsely-trafficked (outside London) line like the SE, this dual usage of the 'speaking instruments' soon began to cause problems, and between 1852 and 1860 the SE introduced a separate system of telegraph-worked bells for signalling purposes, the signalmen working by bell codes without any visual instrument.

Plate 4 Cuxton, South Eastern Railway. This station was opened in 1856, and the signalman's hut (with telegraph instruments inside) and double semaphore were, in all likelihood, original features. Two telegraph poles are visible. Because the SE branches were not interlocked until the 1890s, a large number of photographs of these 1840s/50s SE huts are known. In contrast, the 1850s' 'signal stations' on the LNW and GN main lines all disappeared in the 1860s and 1870s, virtually all escaping photographic record.

National Railway Museum

In the 1850s and early 1860s, other types of signalling instrument ('Block Instrument') were invented, notably by Tyer, Clark, Bartholomew, Preece, and Spagnoletti. These gave a continuous visual record of the state of the line, by needle or semaphore indication. In 1854, and again in 1861, the Board of Trade issued a circular 'drawing attention' to the desirability of 'Absolute Block' working by telegraph, but the response was very limited. There

were several reasons for this, foremost among which was the railway Directors' fears over the cost.

Given the SE's experience, there could be no doubt that additional circuits and separate instruments would be necessary. Moreover, traffic levels on the main lines north of London, where many slow freight trains were mixed in with the passenger trains, dictated a maximum distance of about two miles between adjacent 'signal stations' if Absolute Block working was to be practised, and this meant still further expense in the erection of intermediate 'signal stations' (i.e. signalmen's huts) between the more widely-spaced passenger stations, and in paying the wages of the additional men needed to work them. The SE had not needed intermediate 'signal stations' when it first introduced block working, due to its low traffic levels, although some subsequently proved necessary. The new huts for the valuable telegraph instruments would also have to be rather more substantial and better waterproofed than they had been previously when the signalman himself had been the only object of consideration.

However, it would be unfair to put all the blame on the Directors' parsimony, as the majority of railway engineers also held genuine (if partly misplaced) doubts about the desirability or practicability of telegraphic block working. The reliability of the early instruments caused concern as they were liable to derangement by lightning and, in some cases, could switch to the wrong indication without the signalmen being aware of it. Collisions still occurred on lines where Absolute Block working was in operation — most notably at Clayton Tunnel in 1861 — and this must have been 'grist to the mill' of those who opposed it, even though these accidents were generally due to lax operation rather than the system itself. There was also a strongly-held view that it would be impossible to work the traffic on the busier lines under the Absolute Block system, even with intermediate signal stations; although when companies did introduce Absolute Block working they often claimed that it increased the line capacity! All in all, the opinion of railway officers in the early 1860s was still that signalling by telegraph was a very good idea in certain limited situations, but that in general 'the vigilance of the enginemen' was still the key to safe operation.

The first companies to follow the SE's lead and introduce Absolute Block working over long sections of route were the NL, with its dense suburban traffic, in 1855, and the GN, between London and Hitchin, in 1854-6. In 1855, the LNW began signalling trains by telegraph on the London to Rugby line, but on a non-Absolute system under which trains were allowed to proceed, after being given a caution signal, when it was known that the previous train was still in the section. At much the same date, the LBSC introduced a similar method of working on the London end of its main line. The LNW and LBSC both deliberately rejected the Absolute Block concept on the grounds of delay to traffic.

In November 1860 the GN's General Manager reported to his Board:

'There is no doubt that our system is a very safe one but it causes very great delays',

and rather than spend money on additional signal stations, the GN Board decided to change to the less safe LNW system. This was a set-back for the Board of Trade, meaning as it did that only the SE and NL were now working on the Absolute Block system. A small consolation came from the fact that the LNW and GN were extending their systems of telegraphic signalling to cover other sections of their networks. By 1860, the LNW had 77 'signal stations' between Euston and Stafford, and by 1864 the GN had 57 between King's Cross and Doncaster. Most of these were 'intermediate' signal stations, but even at the passenger stations it is likely that the signalman was generally provided with a separate hut, rather than having the signalling instruments in the station offices.

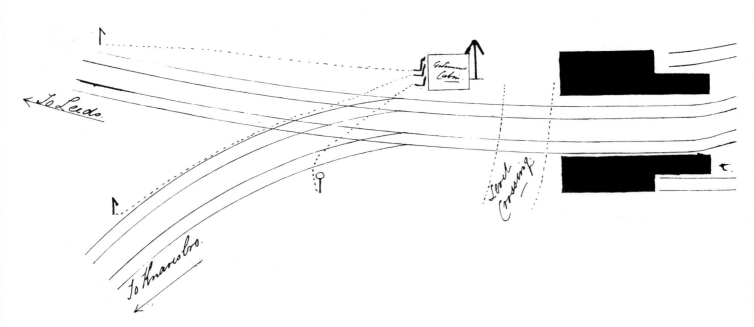

Plate 5   This sketch of Starbeck Station (North Eastern Railway) was made in 1858, when it was proposed to improve the arrangements (as described later in this chapter). The arrangement shown here probably dated from the opening of the line by the Leeds & Thirsk Railway in 1848, modified when the Knaresborough branch was added in 1851. To the right of the gateman's cabin is the normal double-armed station semaphore, worked by handles on the post. To the left of the cabin are three 'concentrated' ground levers working the semaphore distant signals from the Leeds and Knaresborough lines, and a disc signal. The distant from the Thirsk line was worked by a lever at the north end of the 'up' platform (just on the right-hand edge of the section of the drawing reproduced here). By day this was worked by the station porters, but at night there was only the gateman on duty. In June 1855, the gateman was reported for leaving this signal on all night. He replied that he 'did not consider it his duty' to attend to it, as the lever was 'some distance' from his cabin. His superiors were clearly not impressed by this as the words '40 yards' are written over! There is much evidence of vagueness and ill-discipline in signalling in the NE correspondence of the period.

Public Record Office

Concentration

In the mid-1840s, 'auxiliary', 'distance', or 'distant' signals began to appear. These were additional signals placed several hundred yards away from the station, in order to give train drivers an advance indication of whether they would be required to stop at the 'station signal'. Because of their distance from the station, it would have been impractical for the signalman to have to walk out to these signals to operate them, so they were instead worked by wire. Normally, the levers working the distant signals were placed on the ground near the foot of the post carrying the station signals, which itself would normally be adjacent to the signalman's hut (**Plates 3 & 5**). The new GN main line in 1850 was fully fitted with distant signals, and they soon became widespread. Before long, other signals at large stations were being worked by wire from a central point. For example, at the new King's Cross terminus, opened in October 1852, 'a small signal hut was provided west of the south portal of the tunnel, and the signals controlled from it by wires' (Wrottesley).

By this date, the further development could be found of the point levers, as well as the signal levers, being 'concentrated' outside the signalman's hut, so removing the need for him to be continually on the move. When the Board of Trade produced the first edition of the 'Requirements of the Inspecting Officers of Rail-ways' in 1858, it required that 'signals and distant signals in each direction' were to be erected at every station, and the 'lever handles of switches and signals placed in the most convenient position, and brought as close together as possible, so as to be under the hand of the person working them'. This made 'concentration' compulsory on new lines, but the levers were only placed close together, and were not connected in any way. In a very few cases, the levers may have been placed inside the signalman's hut, but if this did occur before the introduction of interlocking, it was very rare.

The Signalling of Junctions

The signalmen's huts, mostly ground-level structures and of timber or brick construction, which could be seen at many stations by the late 1850s, provide one of the strands in the development of the signal box. However, functionally and constructionally, they were little different from the 'watchman's hut' of time immemorial; and perhaps a rather more important influence were the 'platform' or 'stage' structures, with concentrated levers placed upon them, which appeared at junctions in the 1840s and 1850s. These were a new kind of structure evolved specifically for railway signalling purposes.

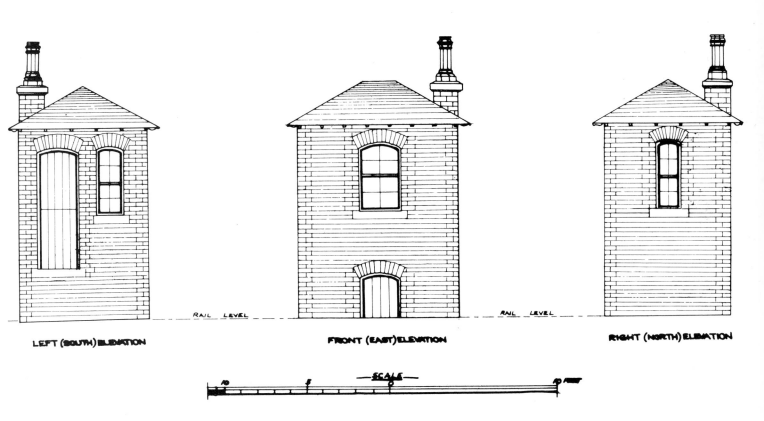

LEFT (SOUTH) ELEVATION   FRONT (EAST) ELEVATION   RIGHT (NORTH) ELEVATION

SCALE

Plate 6 By the late 1850s, signalmen at stations could be provided with quite substantial huts. This brick hut proposed for the Scottish Central Railway station at Shore Road, Stirling, in 1858, would probably have had the levers 'concentrated' outside.

J. Hinson, from an original drawing

Junctions were early recognised as a source of potential danger. At first junctions were mostly worked by the same simple methods as stations (i.e. a pointsman worked the points by hand-levers and the signals by handles on the post — **Plate 1**). However, where junctions were remote from a station and trains ran through at speed, an improved system was really needed if the risk of collision was to be minimised. It so happened that one of the first junctions of this type was on a line which had probably the most frequent train service in the country. This was Corbett's Lane Junction, where the London & Croydon Railway, opened in June 1839, joined the earlier London & Greenwich Railway, which had a regular 15 minute service rising to 5 minutes at certain peak times. Worried by this proposed junction, the 1839 Parliamentary Committee into the State of Communications by Railways took the opportunity to grill the Chairmen of the Croydon and Greenwich companies about it. On 30th April 1839, five weeks before the junction opened for passenger traffic, Moxon, the Croydon Chairman, defended his company:

'We are bound by the Agreement (i.e. with the Greenwich company) to go into a considerable expense, which we have already incurred, by building a lighthouse, and by keeping more than the usual proportion of persons at the point of junction . . . a person of rather superior pay to be the principal conductor of the lighthouse, and two switchmen'.

He went on to explain that the 'lighthouse' displayed three different coloured lights and was intended for use only at night or during fog. But it caught the public imagination, the reporter sent by *Herepath's Journal* to the opening of the Croydon line enthusing:

'At this junction is an octagonal light-house, with powerful parabolic reflectors, from which signals by coloured lights can be given a long way off to approaching trains, so as to prevent the chance of a collision'.

No illustration is known of this structure, but one should not envisage a tall lighthouse of the maritime sort. It is unlikely to have been more than an elaborate hut with a window through which the lamp signals were displayed. During the daytime, flag signals (or, according to some sources, disc signals) were displayed. Whatever the method, a red signal was given for Croydon trains, and a white signal for Greenwich trains. The points were worked by hand-levers on the ground, and not from the 'lighthouse'.

In retrospect, the Corbett's Lane lighthouse seemed a less wonderful thing than it had at the time. C. H. Gregory, who had been the Croydon company's Engineer from 1840 to 1845, recalled in 1874 only 'a signalman with two flags by day and hand-lamps by night'. The installation lasted only until 1842 when the line from London Bridge was quadrupled and the junction points removed. It appears that there was a similar installation outside London Bridge, where the two companies had separate stations. The Parliamentary Committee, incidentally, was not satisfied with the precautions proposed for Corbett's Lane, and recommended in August 1839 that railway junctions were unsafe and should not be allowed!

The first real raised 'platform' with levers upon it seems to have been that installed at Brighton Junction (the junction of the Croy-

Plate 7 A December 1844 engraving of the 1843/4 Bricklayers Arms installation. The signalman is operating one of the two point levers, which were placed either side of the signal frame. There are two signal arms in each direction, which soon became the norm at junctions, and here they are lettered 'BA' and 'LB' for the two routes. The view looks towards London, and the approaching train has just passed the site of the (by then removed) Corbett's Lane Junction.

Public Record Office

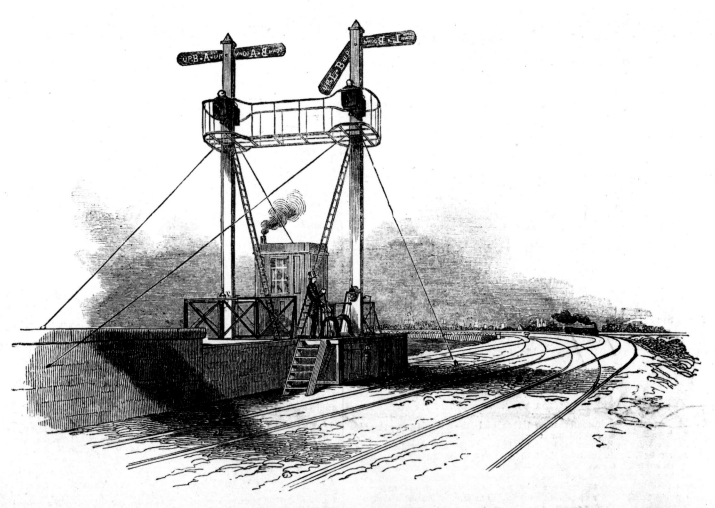

DOVER JUNCTION: DANGER: UP AND DOWN LINES, BRICKLAYER'S ARMS.   CAUTION, UP LINE; DANGER, DOWN LINE, LONDON BRIDGE.

don and Brighton lines, south of the present Norwood Junction Station), which opened in July 1841. Our knowledge of this installation comes from a special report written by Maj. Gen. Pasley in March 1843, after the North Union and Bolton & Preston Railways had asked the Board for advice following a difference of opinion on how to signal the junction between their lines.

'I beg to suggest', wrote Pasley, 'that there should be a small platform raised two or three feet higher than the level of the rails, in front of the switchman's cottage, as is the case at the junction of the Croydon and Brighton Railways, upon which platform he will be able to work the two levers (i.e. the point levers) that will be required, one for the up and the other for the down Bolton & Preston trains, to more advantage than by standing on the ground alongside of the junction'.

On 21st June 1843, Pasley inspected the North Union/Bolton & Preston Junction at Euxton, and duly found 'a small cottage, with a platform in front of it for a switchman'. The expressions used by Pasley suggest that the Brighton Junction and Euxton Junction 'platforms' did not have any huts upon them. The 'cottages' referred to might be either the signalmen's homes, or merely huts beside the line which they occupied when on duty. It is not clear either whether 'fixed' signals of any kind were provided.

However, by far the most revolutionary installation of the 1840s was that erected by Gregory in the winter of 1843/4 to control the new Bricklayers Arms Junction, where the line to the SE's Bricklayers Arms terminus left the Croydon line. Here, in addition to placing the point levers on the 'platform', Gregory placed the signal levers (in this case, in fact, foot-operated stirrups) together in a 'frame' with the mechanism arranged in such a way that conflicting signal aspects could not be displayed. The apparatus and signals were manufactured by Messrs Stevens & Sons of Southwark Bridge Road, London, who were responsible for many improvements to the original concept. This apparatus was an important step on the path to full 'interlocking', but at Bricklayers Arms Jn. the point levers were not connected in any way with the signal stirrups, so that signal aspects conflicting with the lie of the points could still be displayed. A second installation of Gregory/Stevens apparatus was made at Brighton Junction, Norwood, in 1844, when the construction of a flyover, to enable atmospheric working on the Croydon line, necessitated the replacement of the original 1841 'platform'. Both the Bricklayers Arms Jn. and the new Brighton Junction 'platforms' had huts on them for the signalmen, and semaphore signals.

After 1843, there was, for many years, no real advance in the available technology, but equipment of the Bricklayers Arms Jn. type passed into more widespread use. A number of firms of iron-founders and engineers branched out into the new field of railway signalling, supplying semaphore signals and posts and the hand-levers or stirrups for working them. In 1847, Stevens & Sons took out a patent for the 'stirrup' frame, and by the 1850s they were established as the country's leading signalling firm.

By the mid-1850s, 'platforms' with semaphore signals (but still with no connection between the signal and point levers) were to be found at most of the more important junctions, as the following accounts from contemporary inspection or accident reports show:

Warrington: Junction of LNW and Birkenhead, Lancashire & Cheshire Railways, 1855: 'Two double semaphores are erected at this junction, and with three auxiliary signals . . . together with the switches . . . are all worked from a box placed at this junction'. (A further junction was under construction 101yds. from the existing one: the Board of Trade required a new box to be built half-way between the two junctions, so that one man could operate both pairs of points from it).

Hitchin, 1859: 'At 350 yards to the north of this station is a junction box, provided with three double semaphores'. The junctions dated from 1850 and 1858.

As time passed, the huts provided for the signalmen became larger until, in some cases, the whole 'platform' area was enclosed (but not necessarily all glazed). **Plates 8-12** illustrate this development.

Plate 8   The first signal platform at Hastings Junction (later known as Montpelier Junction), Brighton. No written record of this structure is known, but it seems most likely that it was put up in 1846 when the junction was opened. Due to the sharp curve, the signal applying to trains from Lewes is set at 90 degrees from normal. The signal frame is not visible, but it was probably of the stirrup type. A plan dating from the 1850s shows this platform, and another at Lovers' Walk controlling the junction with the line to the Lower Yard.

Lens of Sutton

Plate 9   A view of the GN line north of Maiden Lane in November 1851. The signal platform (which must date from 1850) appears to control the entrance to the original Maiden Lane Station, rather than the junction (at right), with the new lines to King's Cross, not yet in full use at this date.

Public Record Office

Plate 10   Trent Valley Junction, Rugby (LNW) from the 1862 Edition of Measom's *The Official Illustrated Guide to the North Western Railway*. Note the telegraph poles and wires. Nothing is known about this box, which one would guess dated from the early 1850s. From 1855, it was one of the block posts in the LNW's 'two-mile telegraph' system. Although little detail is visible here, it seems quite likely that this was a two-storey brick box with a large timber balcony around it, similar to the Watford Tunnel North box illustrated in *British Railway Journal No. 8*. In the Watford Tunnel North photograph (the only other known illustration of these 1850s LNW boxes) the signal frame is visible on the balcony.

R. D. Foster

TRENT VALLEY JUNCTION (RUGBY).

STEVENS's JUNCTION SIGNALS, POINT LEVERS &c.

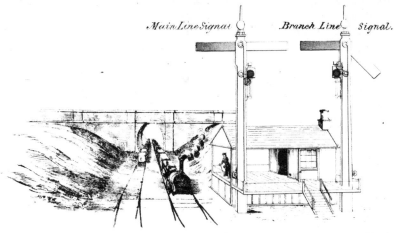

Main Line Signal.   *Branch Line   Signal.*

Every Junction is provided with TWO Semaphore Signal Posts, corresponding with the TWO meeting Railways; and the *Signals* for each Line are shown on the *Signal* Post appropriated to it.

The Signals for Caution and Danger, by Day and Night, are shown in the same way as on the **Station Signal Posts.**

The Semaphore Arms and the Lamps for DAY and NIGHT Signals at the Junctions are always set at **DANGER,** and no Engine Man is allowed to pass without the Arm is lowered to **CAUTION,** or the Green Light is shown, by the Signal Man.

At the Junctions there are no **ALL RIGHT** Signals, as it is necessary in passing them to go cautiously and slow.

THESE FORMS ON STOUT CARD BOARD FOR SIGNAL MEN, STATION MASTERS &c. MAY BE OBTAINED AT DARLINGTON WORKS LONDON

Plate 11 This advertisement was sent out by Stevens & Sons in 1859, and shows the then-current style of Stevens' junction platform, with full roof but with the levers still outside the glazed hut. Comparison with **Plate 1** shows that the box structure has been added (somewhat out of scale) to a version of the earlier drawing. This particular copy of the advertisement was included with Stevens' letter of tender of 23rd December 1859 to the Eden Valley Railway (the same day, interestingly, as Col. Yolland's penultimate inspection of Kentish Town Junction, where he refused to accept the Stevens' apparatus). Other tenderers for the Eden Valley's signalling were H. J. Morton of Basinghall Buildings, Leeds; James Tod & Son, Engineers, of Leith Walk, Edinburgh; Cowans Sheldon (later known as railway crane-makers); and John Ashbury of Openshaw, Manchester (better known as railway carriage builders), who offered a 'double junction signal with platform levers and stirrup frames complete' at £72 10s. 0d.

Public Record Office

Plate 12 Strood, South Eastern Railway. Despite the caption the photograph cannot have been taken in 1854, as it shows the second (the present) Strood Station, opened in 1856 for the Maidstone extension, and the signal box controlling the junction of the East Kent line opened in 1858. The newness of the earthworks suggests that the photograph itself must date from circa 1858. By the mid-1860s a road had been built along the near side of the railway. The surroundings were soon built-up, but the view (towards London) is still recognisable today, as the layout of the station has not altered. The box itself, also presumably dating from 1858, is a fully-developed structure, except for the absence of glazing. It is of timber, with a brick chimney. Comparison with **Plates 11 & 107** suggests that it may well have been built by Stevens. The junction signals and posts are just visible. They are separate from the main structure, and the post for the main (Maidstone) line signals is taller than that for the branch signals — an early example of what became normal practice.

Authors' Collection

STROOD. S.E.R. STATION. SEPT 1854

Plate 13 At a few locations various weird and wonderful structures were built in place of the normal ground-level hut or junction 'platform'. This signal turret, north of Dumfries, would have been built either in 1849, when the main line opened, or in 1859 when the branch opened. It survived in disuse into the 1970s.

R. D. Foster

The Junction 'Tower'

In addition to the increasing commodiousness of the signalman's accommodation, there was a strong trend in the 1850s for the 'platforms' themselves to be more elevated. Indeed, the word 'platform' faded from use, supplanted by the new term 'tower'. By 1860, an elevation of 20ft. or more above rail level was not unusual. With no block working in operation on most lines, the signalman had no idea of when a train might be approaching until he saw it coming, so at most locations, increased elevation meant safer working of the junction. But in some cases, of course, a low platform was more appropriate.

The internal correspondence of the North Eastern Railway at this period shows well the trend towards increased elevation. It also shows how often the incentive for the improvement of a particular junction came from an accident or near miss.

'Captain O'Brien (the Company Secretary) reported a narrow escape of a serious collision at the Holbeck Junction on 13th July . . . Directed that a proper semaphore with sufficient signals be provided at the junction, and that the signalman be placed in an elevated platform and provided with handles connected with the various points under his control' (*Traffic Committee, 31st July 1857*).

'The gateman's cabin (at Starbeck) is now upon the road level and it is very desirable that there should be a cabin erected somewhat similar to that at the Hessle Road Junction, with levers both of (sic) the semaphore, for signals and gates within its platform. The gates are now all connected together and perhaps could easily be adapted to work by lever' (*Traffic Committee, 12th July 1858*). (This, if carried out, was an extremely early case of working crossing gates mechanically from a signal box. The arrangements at

Hessle Road Junction, here put forward as an example to be followed, were, a few years later (1866), condemned as dangerous, and 'Saxby's system' was proposed instead).

'On 12th September we had a very narrow escape from a serious collision at Holgate Bridge . . . from this and many cases more I have come to the conclusion that the system on which our signals at places like Holgate Bridge are arranged is not so effective for safety as it might be . . . I think it desirable that the signals should be so arranged as to be visible from the greatest practicable distance . . . I recommend therefore that the signals at Holgate Bridge, at the North Points, and at the crossing of the Stockton and Darlington Railway should be very much raised'.

'I think it also essential that the Signalmen should be at such an elevation as to see the trains approaching at a considerable distance. In their present position at York the Signalmen are frequently not aware of trains till they are close upon them. At a similar junction at Doncaster the Great Northern Company have erected a high structure of brick, at the top of which the signalmen are placed, and from whence they can see the trains approach in all directions. Having examined both places I have no question in my own mind as to the superiority of the system provided by the Great Northern Company' (*Memorandum from O'Brien to the Directors, 24th October 1861*).

'Recommended that a signal cabin be put up on the south side of the bridge (at Thirsk) — the platform of the cabin to be of the same height as the top of the ladder of the present signal' (*Loco. Committee, 23rd April 1862*).

'Recommended that at Dairy Coates Junction a complete double semaphore be put up: that the signalman be placed in an elevated box, and the points connected and the handles placed in the box' (*Loco. Committee, 16th January 1863*).

'Signals at Hessle Junction — at this junction the signalmen are not elevated above the line as at other places . . . ' (*O'Brien to Loco. Committee, 11th January 1866*). (Note: This is a different place from the Hessle Road Junction referred to above).

The boxes referred to here were all non-interlocked installations. The invention of interlocking (for which see the next section) made no difference to the need for greatly-elevated junction boxes, but the introduction of block working gave the signalmen knowledge of when trains were approaching, and so removed the need for an early view of oncoming trains. Hence the very tall junction 'tower' as a regular feature was a phenomenon largely of the late 1850s and the 1860s, but many tall boxes continued to be built subsequently for other reasons, as described in **Chapter 3**.

Interlocking: Saxby's 'Simultaneous Motion', 1856

The first known case of interconnection between points and signals was the signal-post locking introduced by Atkinson of the MS&L at East Retford Junction in 1852. This did not interlock the levers, but consisted of a rod from the points that locked the rod operating the signal, thus ensuring that the main line signal could be lowered only if the points were set for the main line. This, however, and one or two similar devices, had little effect on the development of the signal box.

The first really major technical improvement after 1843 came with John Saxby's mechanism of 1856, patented by him on 24th June of that year. The patent described his invention as a 'Mode of Working Simultaneously the Points and Signals of Railways at Junctions, to Prevent Accidents', and the gist of Saxby's improvement was that he coupled the signal rods to the point levers, so that the signals automatically repeated the point settings. In its basic form, this would have meant that two of the four signals would always be lowered and, to prevent this, Saxby provided two extra levers by which the main line signals could be held to danger at any

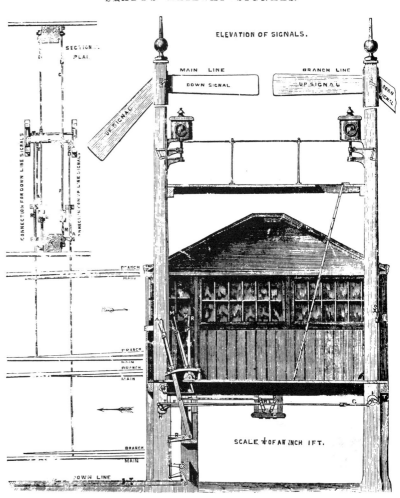

Plate 14 (right) This explanation of Saxby's 1856 apparatus appeared in *The Engineer* of September 24th 1858. The nearest lever (A) is the up point + signal lever, and the furthest away (R) the down point + signal lever. R is reversed, with the branch signal lowered. Between A and R are the two levers M and **И** (sic) for putting the main line signals to danger independently of the points (these are best seen in the sectional plan). On the right-hand post (O) are the set-screws for holding the branch signals at danger. Note how the placing of the signals on the structure necessitates the 15ft. width, to keep the arms from fouling each other. The cabin is of the form adopted generally by Saxby in the earliest years; vertical boarding, windows with one horizontal glazing bar, hipped roof, and no decorative features. The accompanying article noted: 'This invention, by Mr Saxby of the London & Brighton (sic) Railway Company's works, was favourably noted by us some months since . . . The object proposed by Mr Saxby is one which it is certainly marvellous was not proposed almost as soon as signals were used on railways, but one which, nevertheless, it seems to have taken a considerable amount of time to carry out in practice . . . A model of a junction . . . can be seen at Messrs George Spencer & Co.'s, 6 Cannon Street West, who, we understand, have been appointed agents for Mr Saxby'.

Brixton Library

Plate 15 (left) The Saxby box at Lewes Junction was built in connection with the 1857 rebuilding of Lewes Station. It was at the east end of the station where the lines from Keymer Junction and Brighton met. The contract for the rebuilding of the station was let on 30th April 1857, and the box was probably opened in or around November. In this later photograph, the box still has only the four signals with which it was originally provided. Where the signals were placed above the box in this way, drivers had to know where to stop their trains to avoid fouling other lines; in later practice, signals have always (save in very exceptional circumstances) been placed in rear of the 'fouling point'. About half the early Saxby boxes were tall 'towers'; others, such as Farlington Junction and Polegate Junction, were only a few feet above ground level.

E. J. Bedford

TABLE 1

The First Saxby Boxes

Box	Railway Co.	Date of Opening	Notes
Keymer Jn.	LBSC	Summer 1856	Experimental frame installed on existing 'platform'.
Bricklayers Arms Jn.	LBSC	July 1856	Second experimental frame, installed on 1843 Gregory 'platform'.
Norwood Jn.	LBSC	September 1857	Inspected 1st September 1857; junction opened 1st October 1857. Probably the first Saxby box. Controlled 4 points and 8 signals.
Lewes Jn.	LBSC	circa November 1857	Station opened November. Controlled 10 points and 4 signals **(Plate 15)**.
Bricklayers Arms Jn.	LBSC	10th January 1858	Opening date per LBSC notice. 'Erected December 1857' per LBSC signalling records. Replaced 1843 Gregory 'platform'. Controlled 6 points and 8 signals.
West Croydon	LBSC	1857/8	At north end of station. In use by September 1858. Controlled 2 points and 4 signals.
Battersea Jn.	LBSC (WELCP)	29th March 1858	Inspected 23rd March 1858. Controlled 7 points and 4 signals. At entrance to Pimlico terminus.
Bromley Jn.	LBSC (WELCP)	3rd May 1858	Controlled 3 points and 3 signals.
Uckfield Jn. (Lewes)	LBSC	October 1858	First box to have distant signals interlocked.
Havant Jn.	LBSC	December 1858	Inspected 24th November 1858. Junction not used in normal service until 1859 due to dispute between LBSC and LSW.
Cosham Jn.	LBSC	1859	Per LBSC records.
Farlington Jn.	LBSC	1859	Per LBSC records.
Portcreek Jn.	LBSC	1st January 1860	Per LBSC records.
Polegate Jn.	LBSC	1859/60	Station rebuilding scheme commenced September 1859.
Three Bridges Jn. (?)	LBSC	1859/60	Station rebuilding scheme in progress at October 1859. Not certain that a Saxby box was built here but likely given LBSC practice by this date.
Battersea Jn.	LBSC	1st October 1860	Complete at inspection on 28th August 1860.
Victoria	VS&P	1st October 1860.	'Hole-in-the-Wall' box. First installation of Saxby's 1860 patent frame. In use from opening of station, but not fully completed until several months later. 23 levers.
Beckenham Jn.	WELCP or SE	circa 1858-60	Junction opened in May 1858, but box possibly not built until 1860 when LCD main line trains commenced running.
Stratford Jn.	Eastern Counties	Summer 1861	In use by September 1861. 22 levers.
Shoreham Jn.	LBSC	July 1861	
Itchingfield Jn.	LBSC	September 1861	
Norwood Spur Jn.	LBSC	1861/2	1861 per LBSC records, but junction not opened to passengers until 1862.
Birmingham New Street North	LNW	Spring 1862	Ordered December 1861. North and South boxes, together, cost £850.
Birmingham New Street South	LNW	Spring 1862	
Clifton Jn.	Eden Valley	May 1862	Apparatus only **(vide Plate 34)**.
Battersea Jn.	LBSC	August 1862	Replaced 1860 box. Frame No. 24, 23 levers. **(Plate 16)**.
Brighton South (Brighton Yard)	LBSC	circa September 1862	'In course of erection', August 1862.
Brighton North (Montpelier Jn.)	LBSC	circa September 1862	'In course of erection', August 1862.
Lovers Walk	LBSC	circa September 1862	
-			Five sets of apparatus only ordered September 1862, for fitting to existing boxes (offered at £80 each, or £280 each for a complete box).
-	NE		
-			
Windmill Bridge Jn.	LBSC	1st December 1862	
Balham Jn.	LBSC	1st December 1862	
Selhurst Jn.	LBSC	circa 1st Dec. 1862	Boxes almost certainly built here, but no contemporary evidence yet found.
Norwood Fork Jn.	LBSC	circa 1st Dec. 1862	
Clayton Cutting	LBSC	1862/3	1862 per LBSC records. Introduction of Block System said to be imminent at 27th December 1862.
Keymer Jn.	LBSC	1862/3	
Folly Hill	LBSC	1862/3	
Ouse Viaduct	LBSC	1862/3	Introduction of Block System said to be imminent at 27th December 1862. **(Plate 17)**.
Tinsley Green	LBSC	1862/3	
Earlswood Common	LBSC	1862/3	

This Table lists all boxes known to have been built up to the end of 1862. Given that Battersea Jn. 1862 box had frame No. 24, the number of unknown boxes must be very small. Possible further boxes are:

Southerham Jn.	No knowledge of a box here but all other LBSC junctions of significance were interlocked by the end of 1862.
West Norwood	An S&F Type 1 box was built here, and the probability is that it was built prior to the end of 1862.
London Bridge	An 1861 Accident Report recommended that an interlocked box be provided in the 'Brighton Yard', but it is not known whether this was in fact done.
Balcombe Tunnel	It is possible that a box was built here for the introduction of the Block System in 1862/3.

time, and small pins (soon replaced by set-screws) on the signal posts by which the branch line signals could be held to danger at any time. A simple double line junction therefore required four levers. The levers were of what was to become the normal type, fitted with catch-handles and placed in a regular row. The mechanism could be adapted to work larger numbers of points and signals.

Born in 1821, Saxby had been apprenticed to a carpenter, and in 1840 joined the London & Brighton Railway. By 1856 he was a foreman in the LBSC's Brighton Works. He recalled in later life that his interest in signalling equipment had been prompted by his observing an error by the pointsman at Bricklayers Arms Junction in 1854. Experimental versions of the Saxby 'simultaneous motion' mechanism were installed at Keymer Junction, and then at Bricklayers Arms Junction, in the summer of 1856. The drawing on page 3 of *Southern Signals* shows the Saxby apparatus added on to the 1843 Bricklayers Arms Jn. 'platform', in place of the Gregory stirrup frame. The first full installations of the patented apparatus were authorised in April 1857 for Norwood Junction (North) and Lewes Junction, in both cases in new 'towers'. By 1859, a dozen of the LBSC's junctions, old and new, had been equipped. **Table 1** lists all the known early Saxby boxes. These boxes did not always control all the points and signals at the location concerned: the 1860 Victoria box, for example, worked only the main points at the station throat, and there were a further three pointsmen's huts at the platform ends.

Although the 1856 patent drawing and the drawing at **Plate 14** both show the levers in the open, outside of the signalman's hut on the 'platform', this was probably done only for clarity, as photographic evidence suggests that all these Saxby boxes were in fact built with a fully-covered 'platform', with the levers inside the hut. The signal posts were integral with the box structure, and emerged through the roof.

With a workable interlocking apparatus now available, the Board of Trade Inspectors soon began to try to cajole other railway companies into using it. In 1857, we find Col. Yolland, at the inspection of the new Welwyn Junction signals on the GN, laying 'great stress upon the necessity for connecting the signals and (point) levers' (but it is not at all certain that this was actually done). In 1858 the first published Board of Trade 'Requirements' demanded, in addition to 'concentration' at all stations as already referred to, that 'in the case of facing points at junctions, it is most desirable that the signals should be connected with the points so as to be worked in conjunction with them'.

Around 1857/8, Saxby began manufacture on his own account from a small works at Haywards Heath Station rented from the LBSC, with financial backing from William Hudson, Superintendent of the LBSC Goods Department. This put him in a position where he could supply to companies other than the LBSC (the earliest Saxby equipment had, one assumes, been made in the LBSC Brighton Works). However, in practice, Saxby did not succeed in making any 'outside' sales until 1860-62 and, with no other manufacturer offering interlocked frames prior to 1860, it must be concluded that there was in fact little or no interlocking outside of the LBSC until 1860. Saxby offered for sale both complete boxes or the apparatus on its own, for fitting to an existing box.

Saxby remained in the LBSC's service, as well as conducting his own business, until around April 1862, and his work kept the LBSC at the forefront of signalling progress. It is interesting to note Capt. Tyler's report on the 1861 Clayton Tunnel accident — in which, incidentally, Saxby would have been involved had he not missed his train — where, having giving the LBSC a sound thrashing for the lax operation of the tunnel telegraph, he concluded:

'In thus condemning the arrangements of the Brighton Company . . . I am happy to add . . . that I have frequently had occasion to hold forth the convenient huts and stages that they have erected for the accommodation of their men, and the precautions in connecting the points and signals together, according to their foreman's (Saxby's) patent . . . as an example to other companies'.

Interlocking: Chambers' 'Successive Motion', 1859

Great improvement as it was, Saxby's 1856 mechanism had been designed only for the operation of fairly simple junctions, and as a 'simultaneous motion' device was incapable of being expanded to interlock very complicated layouts. To achieve this 'successive motion' interlocking was required, whereby each point or signal is operated by a separate lever, and no lever movement can commence until the prior movements upon which it is dependent have been completed. The first interlocking frame of this type was evolved by Austin Chambers, an Engineer on the North London Railway, in 1859.

A frame (presumably to their 1847 patent) with stirrups for working the signals, and no interconnection between the signals and points, had been erected by Messrs Stevens & Sons 'on a stage over the line' at the NL's Kentish Town (now Camden Road) Junction, in preparation for the opening of the Hampstead Junction Railway. However, at the first inspection on 23rd September 1859, Col. Yolland made it clear that, as the traffic on the NL was so heavy, he would not approve the new line unless the junction was properly interlocked 'so that the signalman shall not have it in his power to give contradictory signals'. The officers of the railway companies accepted the need for this, Yolland explaining 'where such signals could be seen in full operation on the LB&SC Railway', and the Stevens' representative undertook to carry out the requirement. But the alterations made by Stevens still did not satisfy Yolland, who found on a subsequent inspection that he could still lower the 'up' main and 'up' branch signals simultaneously.

At this point, it would have been open to the NL to purchase a set of Saxby apparatus, but one suspects that Chambers saw the opportunity to make his own mark where Stevens had failed. By the end of December he had, by improvements to the Stevens frame, 'fitted up the Kentish Town Junction entirely to Col. Yolland's satisfaction. He did this by fitting 'stopping plates' actuated by the tails of the signal stirrups and point levers, which interlocked with each other in such a way as to prevent the movement of any one lever unless all the others were in the correct position. This was the basis of all subsequent interlocking frames. 'These arrangements', wrote Yolland in his fifth and final inspection report on 29th December 1859, 'carry out in an effective, and much more simple and inexpensive manner, the improvements in Junction Signals first introduced by Mr Saxby & Co.' Chambers was given a cheque for £50 by his General Manager to patent the locking arrangement, which he did on 5th January 1860.

Conceptually, Chambers was now ahead of Saxby, but within a matter of weeks both Saxby and Stevens had developed 'successive motion' frames of their own, with levers (placed in a regular row) for both signals and points. Chambers seems to have tried to set himself up in business, by manufacture or by licensing arrangements, but without any notable success.

As Saxby had never used stirrups, his new apparatus of 1860 did not, from the outside, look very different from his 1856 apparatus, but a larger number of levers was needed to do the same job. Saxby patented his new frame on 19th July 1860, and then took Stevens (who had not patented their new frame) to court for alleged breach of patent. However, Stevens' Counsel was able to demonstrate that a frame to their new design had been inspected at Yeovil Junction on 3rd March, four months before Saxby's patent. This was not to be the last time that Saxby's litigious nature got the better of him.

From 1860, the railway companies' demand for interlocking machinery began to take off. In the 1860s and 1870s many dozens of types of frame were invented and patented, but only a small proportion of the inventors succeeded in getting their ideas into commercial production. Fuller information on the various manufacturers is given in **Chapters 2 & 5**. Saxby himself obtained the promise of an extensive contract with the LNW and, with this and the LBSC work as a solid base, entered, on 7th May 1863, into partnership with John Stinson Farmer (Assistant Traffic Manager of the LBSC until his resignation to join Saxby). During 1863, Saxby and Farmer erected a large new signal works on land leased from the LNW beside the main line at Kilburn, to replace the original Haywards Heath establishment.

For the first few years after 1860, the Board of Trade restricted its demand for interlocking to junctions. By November 1863, Yolland could refer to junction interlocking as 'now almost universally adopted' (at new junctions, that is: the Board had no power to order the improvement of existing junctions at this date). However, some companies could not readily afford the new technology, and a minority were actively opposed to it on principle. Most notable amongst the latter was the Midland Railway, whose first clash with the Board on this subject came when Capt. Tyler inspected the Oakenshaw L&Y to Midland loop line in June 1861. 'At the L&Y junction', Tyler reported, 'a raised stage has been erected of a superior description, and the points and signals placed conveniently under the hand of the signalman'. But there was no interlocking, so he recommended that 'an apparatus shall be applied to them (the signals and points) such as is now coming into use'. 'Additional cover at the sides and front' was also required for the signalman (suggesting that the 'stage' as originally built was similar to that at **Plate 11**). The L&Y Engineer agreed to order a Stevens interlocking frame. The Midland junction, however, was 'very inferior'. The signalman was at ground level, and the 'handles' were 'neither of so good a description nor so conveniently arranged for working'. Permission to open was refused until the Midland Railway provided a 'raised stage with proper cover for the signalman', with interlocking. Allport, the Midland's General Manager, objected, arguing that 'the signalman being on the ground near the points is much more efficient than his being on a raised stage away from them'. Eventually, under pressure from the L&Y, the Midland agreed to install interlocking here so that the line could be opened. But this did not alter Allport's hostility to interlocking. He built up his argument with the claim that many accidents had been avoided by the last minute reversing of points when a driver was about to overrun a junction with the signals against him, which could not be done so quickly with interlocking. Yolland arranged a test which showed that it took only 1½ seconds to effect this operation with an interlocked frame, and the fact was, of course, that far more accidents had been caused by the lack of interlocking. Nevertheless, the Midland did not agree to any further installation of interlocking until 1866, and then only grudgingly.

The Board of Trade could only go so far in putting pressure on the railway companies, because of the uncertainty over its precise legal powers. It was empowered to refuse permission for the opening of a line because of 'incompleteness of works or permanent way', but there was no statutory definition of what constituted 'incompleteness', nor could there be given that the Inspectors were continually increasing their demands as improved technology became available. So when a dispute dragged on beyond a certain point, the Board would sometimes quietly back down, rather than risk a court case which might end with its powers being legally restricted to a more limited approach than that which it had tended to adopt. Hence there were a few cases as late as the mid-1860s

where new lines were allowed to open without even junction interlocking. Even the published 'Requirements', although in practice accepted as authoritative by railway companies, had no basis in law — indeed, the Board had no statutory authority to make regulations at all!

The 1860s Signal Box

During the early 1860s, the 'platform' and 'tower' were transformed into the signal box as we know it. In this development, Saxby had the greatest influence. His boxes of 1857 and subsequently were the first known to have had both full glazing and inside levers, and were the first built to a standard design in large numbers. The only further development of major import required after this was the adoption of an enclosed lower storey below the signalman's operating floor. This had not been deemed necessary on the earliest Saxby boxes as the 1856 frame had no locking in the modern sense, and the locking mechanism of the 1860 frame was fitted in at operating floor level, so that only the various shafts, rods, cranks, etc. were exposed below floor level. On the taller 'towers', an open platform of planks was built some 5-6ft. below the operating floor, to enable the fitters to get conveniently at the apparatus for maintenance (**Plates 15, 16 & 17**), and on the lower boxes this could be done from the ground. But it became recognised after a few years that it would be better to protect all this equipment from the weather by providing full boarding either right down to the ground or, in the case of tall boxes, down to the level of the fitters' platform. Subsidiary advantages of this were that the signalman's accommodation was made less draughty, and the whole structure was strengthened a little. The provision of a boarded lower storey in this way seems to have become normal Saxby practice during 1863. Itchingfield Junction of 1861 was fully-boarded in later years, but it is not certain that it was originally so. This lower storey of signal boxes is conventionally referred to as the 'locking room', as the locking mechanism of most later types of frame required a vertical space of several feet below the operating floor (**see Chapter 3**). The practice of placing the signals, or some of the signals, above the box roof was continued in some cases (notably at junctions) until circa 1869.

SAXBY & FARMER'S
PATENT RAILWAY SIGNALS.

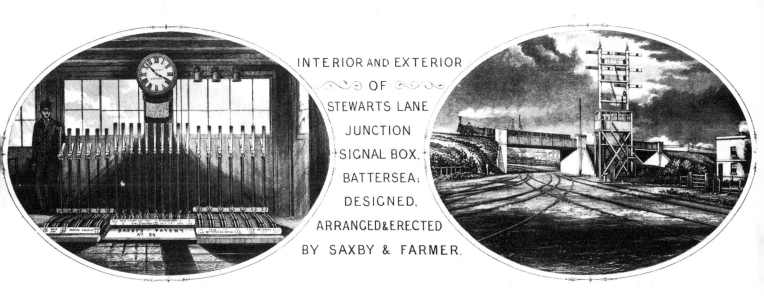

INTERIOR AND EXTERIOR
OF
STEWARTS LANE
JUNCTION
SIGNAL BOX,
BATTERSEA;
DESIGNED,
ARRANGED & ERECTED
BY SAXBY & FARMER.

A good Stage has been erected at Battersea Junction, and Signals have been provided for working in all directions in connection with the Points, under the excellent System of Mr. Saxby.— Vide Captain Tyler's Report to the Board of Trade, August, 1863.

Plate 16 A Saxby & Farmer advertisement of 1864, showing the box erected for the LBSC at Battersea Junction in August 1862 for the opening of the LCD line from Herne Hill. This was probably the third box at this location, now known as Stewarts Lane Junction. The view is towards Victoria. The LCD line is on the right, and the LBSC line (mixed-gauge in preparation for use by GW trains from the West London line) on the left. Off the picture to the right is the entrance to the LCD Yard, which accounts for the extra signals on the right-hand post. Beyond the bridge carrying the LSW main line is the junction between the Victoria and Battersea Wharf lines. The caption is erroneous as the box was actually inspected in August 1862, and not 1863. Although Capt. Tyler was indeed complimentary about the installation, he actually said 'in partial connection with the points', and he recommended that 'further facilities for working should be afforded to the signalman'. The box is of the earlier type without a boarded lower storey, and is probably accurately depicted. The low-pitched hipped roof is invisible. At some later date this box was considerably altered; it was abolished in 1886. In the interior view one might have expected to see the rods for working the signals passing up through the roof, but the artist may have omitted these for clarity. The frame has 23 levers. Maximum frame sizes increased rapidly in the 1860s; the 1866 Cannon Street box had no less than 67 levers. '24' is the frame number. All Saxby/S&F frames were numbered consecutively in order of manufacture; the extent to which business took off can be judged from the fact that it took Saxby five years to reach No. 24, but, only two years later, the London Bridge AB box **(Plate 20)** had frame No. 119. By the 1880s, numbers were in the 4000s. The exterior view of this box was adopted as the Saxby & Farmer trademark. It was retained as such until the end of the firm's existence, and was re-engraved many times, with steadily diminishing accuracy.

Public Record Office

Plate 17) (left) Folly Hill box (between Haywards Heath and Keymer Junction) was built as an intermediate block post for the introduction of Absolute Block working on the southern part of the LBSC main line in or about January 1863. It was one of the last Saxby boxes built without a boarded lower storey. The walkway in front of the front windows was a later addition.

Authors' Collection

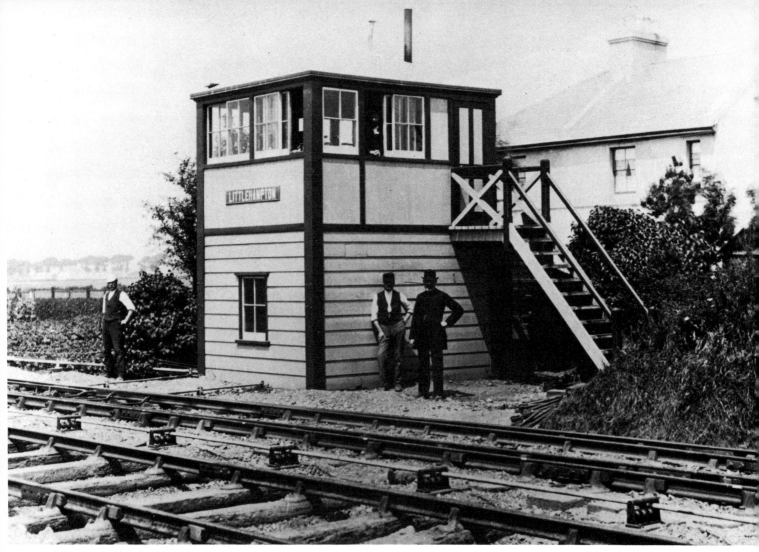

Plate 18   Built by Saxby in 1863 for the opening of the line, Littlehampton was one of the earliest examples of the fully-developed signal box, boarded down to the ground. The lower part has horizontal lapped boarding, and the upper part vertical boarding.

National Railway Museum

Plate 19   Hardham Junction was another 1863 Saxby box. The boarded lower storey was probably an original feature (although it is difficult to be wholly certain about such things) but here, because of the height of the box, the boarding does not extend down to the ground. The walkway is certainly a later addition. The considerable width of these early boxes is very evident here. This was one of only two pre-1867 boxes known to have survived into the 1960s and, when abolished on 21st March 1967, it was probably the oldest surviving box, most of its contemporaries having been replaced in the 1880s. Those 1860s Saxby boxes that did survive the 1880s had their roof signals removed at that period.

Pamlin Prints, Croydon

Plate 20 The approaches to London Bridge, circa 1866, looking towards the terminus. In the foreground are the two SE boxes, 'AB' and 'CD', built by Saxby & Farmer in 1864 in connection with the rearrangement of the station for the new high level line to Charing Cross. The eighteen signal arms above each of these boxes are the largest number known on any box. In the background two of the three boxes built for the new LBSC station in 1866 can just be made out. Prior to 1864/6, London Bridge Station, with six tracks on the approach from Corbetts Lane, had been worked by points-men located at many different boxes and with only verbal communication between them. Needless to say, accidents had not been infrequent! The

Southern termini provided S&F with a good deal of work in the mid-1860s. Apart from the five London Bridge boxes, there were boxes at Waterloo (SE) and Charing Cross in 1864, Cannon Street in 1866, and five new boxes at Victoria in 1866/7, to replace the 1860 'Hole-in-the-Wall' installation. The Charing Cross and Cannon Street boxes were placed across the tracks above the bridge girders and, perhaps because of their conspicuous positions above the river, were to a special decorative design with fancy ridge-tiles and curved window frames. The first interlocked box at Waterloo (LSW), however, was built in 1867 by Stevens & Sons.

Public Record Office

It is more difficult to establish in detail the contemporary design developments in non-Saxby boxes. The boxes built by the only other major contractor of the time, Stevens & Sons, seem to have remained comparatively crude in the early and mid-1860s. Otherwise, there is too little photographic evidence to comment. On some lines, huts of the smallest possible size remained the norm even after the introduction of interlocked frames. Nevertheless, it can be said that the fully-developed signal box, as pioneered by Saxby in 1863, was well-established nationally by 1870.

Although signalmen's huts at stations had often been built of brick, junction 'platforms' and 'towers' had generally been built of timber, being regarded not as permanent buildings but as temporary structures to be altered, moved, or replaced as the ever-expanding railway required. It was also probably easier and

cheaper for contractors such as Stevens and Saxby to erect a timber structure, the components of which could be fully prepared inside their own works. When interlocked boxes began to appear generally in the 1860s, timber construction remained the norm. This proved, in retrospect, a wise policy as most 1860s boxes were at important locations and so were soon rendered obsolete by expanding layouts, as well as by technical developments in frame design which made most pre-1870 frames unacceptable for continued use. However, from about 1868, interlocking began to spread to the less important intermediate stations, and it was realised that these boxes could expect a longer life. So by the 1870s, brick was becoming as common as timber for box construction. This too proved well-advised, for well over 100 boxes dating from the 1870s are still in use today.

19

Plate 21   A circa 1880 view of a station on the Lancashire & Yorkshire Railway, almost certainly identified as Crosby. Although there is no written record of this box, its appearance suggests that it was built by Stevens & Sons (who did much of the L&Y's work in the 1860s and 1870s) sometime in the mid-1860s. Note the lack of glazing on the front. Whereas all early Saxby boxes had hipped roofs, Stevens boxes always had gabled roofs, and in the 1860s were often built gable-to-track, a practice also found elsewhere at this period, but which became impossible in later years when the length of boxes increased.

L&Y Society Collection

Plate 22 On the LBSC, as on other lines, the first interlocked boxes at some locations were quite small huts. This view shows the signal hut at the Brighton end of the 1857 Lewes Station. The date of building of this hut is not known, but one would guess it to be the early 1860s. The 1857 'tower' was at the far end of the platforms and would not have controlled the points at this end. This photograph must date from circa 1887, as it shows work on the new alignment under way at the right.

Sometimes huts were built over existing lever frames. For example, the LSW Traffic Committee of 22nd September 1870 recommended 'the erection of a small signal box to cover the levers on the up platform at Porton Station, and that the levers at Grateley and Andover also be covered cheaply'.

Lens of Sutton

The Spread of Interlocking and Block Working, 1870-1895

We have so far concentrated primarily on events at the forefront of technical progress. Let us now sit back for a moment and survey the railway scene as a whole at the end of the 1860s.

Some 1,500 interlocked boxes existed by 1869, but the great majority were at junctions. Interlocking had been provided at most new junctions as a matter of course since the early 1860s, and the major companies were gradually fitting up earlier junctions. By 1869, the Board of Trade also expected interlocking at all stations on new lines, although this was not strictly enforced until the mid-1870s; and a very few companies, notably the LNW and LBSC, had begun the enormous task of interlocking all existing intermediate stations and sidings. However, the average station on secondary lines was still worked as it had been twenty years earlier, with local hand levers for the points and a 'station semaphore' worked by handles on the post (**Plate 23**).

The majority of double lines were still worked on the 'time-interval' system. Only two companies — the Metropolitan (from its opening in 1863), and the B&E (in 1866/7) — had followed the SE and NL and introduced Absolute Block working on a system-wide (or nearly so) basis. The LSW, LBSC, LCD, and a few lesser companies were slowly working towards this, but the LNW and GN were still using their 'hybrid' systems and most companies still had only a few tunnel installations and the like.

In fact, the prevailing picture was one of disorder. Many inter-locked boxes were not involved in any form of block working, whilst on the other hand most of the stations on those lines which were worked on the block system were not interlocked. In many cases, sections of Absolute Block working alternated with longer stretches of 'time-interval' working on the same route. Where the telegraph was used, it was not always operated in practice in the manner laid down in the Regulations, as many reports of accidents on the SE testify. The 'hybrid' systems were particularly subject to misinterpretation, the GN's being described as 'probably properly understood only by the Great Northern managers themselves'. On some railways, there were no signalmen on duty at night or on Sundays, such trains as were about at these times being left to fend for themselves. There were even cases of the locking mechanism in interlocked boxes being disconnected on busy days, 'to help work the traffic'.

In short, things were just not good enough. The dissatisfaction of the Board of Trade, and of the travelling public, increased as time went by. Public opinion had never been convinced that the railway companies maintained the correct balance between the interests of their shareholders and the safety of their customers, and was now well aware (for the railways were an endless source of interest to the Victorian public) that the equipment needed to ensure safety was available, but was not being used by most companies. The failure to adopt the block system attracted particular criticism. Passengers would often get out of trains that came to a stand between stations, anticipating that the train behind was as likely as not to run into it.

Plate 23 This 1875 view of St. Margarets Station, on the GE's Hertford branch, shows how primitive arrangements survived into the 1870s and 1880s on most secondary routes. The hand-lever for working the points can be seen, and the normal double-armed 'station semaphore'. St. Margarets was interlocked in 1887 and the signal box built by McK&H in that year is still in use. It is often forgotten that the mid-Victorian railway bore more resemblance to the 'Wild West' than to the neat and well-trimmed stations of the 1890s and later. Interlocking played a significant part in tidying-up the railway scene.

British Rail, Eastern Region

In May 1869, the Board of Trade attempted a further application of pressure in respect of block working, and sent each company, with the 1868 Accident Reports, a circular to the following effect:

'Although the Board of Trade have, with rare exceptions, refrained from interfering with railway companies, or even advising them, as to the regulation of their traffic and the management of their business, being unwilling to diminish the responsibility which rests upon directors to conduct their traffic in the safest and most efficient manner, yet, having regard to the experience of the last few years, to the great proportion of accidents which occur through collisions, and to the repeated expressions of opinion from the inspectors that such accidents, or many of them, might have been avoided by the adoption of the block system, they think it again their duty, in the interest of the public, to call the most serious attention of your directors to this subject. They are of the opinion that a grave responsibility will rest upon railway directors if, without sufficient reason, they refrain from adopting this system'.

The companies were required to state in reply what proportion of the network was worked on the block system.

In the early 1870s, the Board sought to get legislation passed to compel the railway companies to introduce block working and interlocking, but this was successfully resisted by the railway lobby. More limited extensions of the Board's powers came instead in the Regulation of Railways Act 1871, and the Railway Regulation Act (Returns of Signal Arrangements, Working, & c.) 1873. The 1871 Act extended the power of inspection to any alterations made to an existing (passenger) line, instead of just to new lines. Given the Board's expectations by this date, this effectively made it necessary for an interlocked box to be built at any location where alterations were carried out after 1871. The 1873 Act required each railway company to submit an annual return of the progress it had made with block working and interlocking, so putting some pressure on companies to carry out improvements everywhere on existing lines. These returns were made every year until 1895 and are summarised in **Tables 2 & 3**.

	DISTANCE APART. Miles. Chns.	Gradients.

4

A Cabin should be erected at Ferriby Station, on the south side of the lines, and just west of the Turnpike Level Crossing, the gates of which should be connected with, and worked from it. In order to admit of the interlocking being satisfactorily carried out, the through shunt between the Main lines should be removed further westward, so as to be between the sidings at each end of the station.

An advance Semaphore should be provided for the Up line.

Day and night attendance will be required at this Cabin.

10. FERRIBY STATION AND HESSLE STATION ... ... 2 51   Falling 1 in 610 for 1 m. 45 c. Rising 1 in 686 for 46 c. Falling 1 in 598 for 40 c.
N.B.—The distance, 2 miles 51 chains, between Ferriby and Hessle, may be found too great to admit of being worked in one section. If an intermediate Cabin is required, it should be erected on the north side of the line, about mid-way between the Ferriby and Hessle stations. There is no particular point which need be specified.

Advance Semaphores would not be required.

Day attendance would only be required, and a Switch would have to be provided.

Two houses would be required—one for the Signalman, and one for a platelayer.

A Cabin should be erected at the Hessle Station, on the platform, at a point where the Cattle Dock and the platform join : the length which will be taken from the platform by this to be added to the east end.

An advance Semaphore should be provided in each direction.

Day and night attendance will be required at this Cabin.

A long siding, leading from the Down Main line to the Chalk Quarry west of the station, put in for the purpose of ballasting, should be taken out.

11. HESSLE STATION AND HESSLE JUNCTION ... ... 1 62   Falling 1 in 598 for 32 c. Level for 1 m. 30 c.
A Cabin should be erected at Hessle Junction, at a point 400 yards west of the present site, on the north side of the lines.

An advance Semaphore should be provided towards Drypool Goods, and Hessle Road Junction.

There is day and night attendance here.

Houses are much wanted, and six should be erected for the Signalmen and platelayers.

12. HESSLE JUNCTION AND HESSLE ROAD JUNCTION... ... ... 1 18   Level.
There is a permanent and elevated Cabin at Hessle Road Junction, on the west side of the lines, having the signals and points connected with, and worked from it. Only the Block Instruments and their fittings are required.

An advance Semaphore should be provided for the Down line.

There is day and night attendance here.

13. HESSLE ROAD JUNCTION AND ANLABY ROAD ... ... 1 4   Level.
There is a permanent and elevated Cabin at Anlaby Road, on the west side of the lines, having the signals and points connected with, and worked from it. Only the Block Instruments and their fittings are required.

An advance Semaphore should be provided for the Up line.

There is day and night attendance here.

Plate 24 This extract, from one of a series of reports prepared by the North Eastern Railway prior to the installation of block working and interlocking on each line, shows the sort of work that had to be carried out on a typical main line, and the other improvements that were often effected at the same time as interlocking. This particular report is dated 1st January 1873. The Hessle Junction and Hessle Road Junction boxes have been mentioned earlier in this chapter.
Public Record Office

TABLE 2

Percentage of Double Lines Worked on 'Absolute Block' System

At end of year	1874	1876	1878	1880	1882	1884	1886	1888	1890	1892	1894
England & Wales	63	78	83	89	93	95	97	97	98.5	99.5	99.8
Scotland	33	51	61	71	85	95	97.5	99	100	100	100

TABLE 3

Extent of Interlocking (Percentage of Connections on Passenger Lines Interlocked)

End of Year	1875	76	77	78	79	80	81	82	83	84	85	86	87	88	89	90	91	92	93	94	95
B&M	31	31	31	31	34	38	39	41	42	57	68	70	70	70	73	73	73	83	100		
Cam	(early figures are unreliable ....)													47	45	53	68	82	89	93	97
CLC	78	84	89	91	92	93	93	93	94	94	96	96	96	100							
District	100																				
Furness	33	46	46	52	57	58	67	77	82	83	83	83	83	83	85	87	92	94	96	96	96
GE	39	41	42	44	50	57	64	70	75	78	80	83	86	89	91	92	95	98	99	99	99
GN	67	74	80	80	81	82	86	87	89	89	89	92	92	93	95	98	99	99	99	99	99
GW	57	66	70	73	75	78	80	83	85	87	89	89	90	91	92	92	94	96	97	99	99
L&Y	80	87	90	94	95	98	99	100													
LNW	69	73	78	82	83	85	87	89	91	93	94	96	97	97	99	100					
LSW	68	75	81	83	84	88	93	95	96	97	99	97	98	99	100						
LBSC	69	80	93	96	98	100															
LCD	50	57	62	83	99	99	99	99	99	100											
LT&S	16	22	34	35	35	49	84	84	84	85	88	88	88	88	89	91	91	100			
MS&L	29	39	48	50	56	58	60	64	65	73	79	94	94	94	95	99	100				
M&C	44	64	68	72	83	84	88	88	88	88	88	88	88	88	88	93	100				
Met	100																				
Midland	66	72	80	81	84	86	87	90	91	92	93	93	93	93	95	96	98	100			
NE	78	84	86	88	92	94	98	99	99	99	99	99	99	100							
NL	100																				
NS	88	95	97	98	98	100															
Rhymney	45	64	64	64	64	66	66	68	68	69	69	85	88	92	92	92	92	99	100		
SE	38	41	43	47	49	52	55	59	59	62	65	67	70	71	70	72	73	82	95	100	
TV	45	57	65	78	92	97	100														
England and Wales	63	69	73	77	80	82	85	87	88	90	91	92	93	94	94	95	97	98	99	99	99.7
Cal	67	-	78	82	86	88	89	90	90	90	92	93	93	94	94	95	96	99	100		
GSW	39	50	56	61	68	74	75	80	83	86	89	91	94	94	95	96	97	99	100		
GNoS	12	12	12	12	12	20	23	30	34	38	40	46	47	51	51	61	62	68	71	87	89
Highland	23	23	28	28	28	29	29	39	39	42	47	50	52	53	53	75	83	89	99	99	99
NB	26	29	33	36	44	46	50	53	58	65	69	70	71	76	78	81	82	88	97	100	
Scotland	35	49	52	56	61	64	67	69	71	75	77	79	79	82	83	87	88	93	97	99	99

The figures are given here as published (except that fractions have been rounded). The figures were calculated by the railway companies, and it is evident that they did not all calculate them in exactly the same way. Nevertheless, the table gives a reasonably fair idea of the relative progress of different companies. Note in particular the large amount of work already done by the largest companies by 1875 (almost all of which had been done since 1868). The Scottish companies were comparatively backward, and the Irish companies far more so. The smallest companies have been omitted from the table; most of them were well behind, but a few managed to claim high figures at an early date by building a very small number of boxes.

The Board of Trade's increased powers, the threat of compulsion if voluntary action was not taken, the large sums of money being paid by the railway companies in compensation to accident victims, the ever-improving equipment available, and the general attrition of the years, all combined to give the progressives the upper hand over the advocates of the status quo from around 1871. In a few years in the 1870s, over half the national rail network was converted to Absolute Block working; and slower, but steady, progress was made with interlocking. The rate of progress was determined more by the relative wealth of companies than by any remaining differences of opinion over the merits of interlocking and block working, which soon became a dead issue. On new lines, most companies provided block working, and interlocked boxes at every station, as a matter of course from the early 1870s; and, line by line, the immense task of introducing these improvements on the existing network was undertaken. On some lines, such as Lincoln to Barnetby, one can still see at station after station the original and identical signal boxes built for the introduction of interlocking on that route. During the 1870s and 1880s, it was often the case that a company's less important lines, being new-built, were interlocked, but some of its more important, older, lines still in unimproved condition.

Most large companies had a planned programme of improvements, but some smaller companies — the IoW was a classic case — only interlocked each station when it was forced upon them by the fact of alterations being carried out there.

Sometimes, block working (being cheaper and quicker to install than interlocking) was introduced by means of temporary huts prior to interlocking. The NE reports of the early 1870s refer to this:

'At those places where it is recommended that permanent cabins be erected, temporary cabins should be provided for block working, and so constructed as to admit of being removed to other lines for a similar purpose during the establishment of the block system'.

Similarly, the GE in 1883 spent £25 each for huts for the telegraph at Thurston, Elmswell, Buckenham, and Cantley, all of which were interlocked with new permanent boxes in 1887. There was also a wish to avoid the interlocking of stations which it was intended to improve in the near future. Conversely, the need for interlocking was often used to justify alterations to incommodious station facilities, and a general tidying-up of inconvenient or dangerous features.

By the late 1880s, the number of interlocked boxes was in excess of 10,000 and Absolute Block working was (except in Ireland) in near-universal use. However, a few of the more impoverished companies — notably the Cambrian, Highland, GNoS, and most of the Irish companies — were lagging a long way behind with interlocking. (As these companies' lines were largely single track, they had, in general, introduced telegraph working long before). Amongst other companies with less than 70 per cent interlocking in 1889 were the CV&H, Festiniog, Manchester & Milford, Neath & Brecon, Pembroke & Tenby, and Portpatrick & Wigtownshire. It seemed unlikely, in view of their financial situations, that these companies would ever introduce interlocking if left to their own devices; but the Board of Trade was able to seize the opportunity created by the public reaction to the 1889 Armagh accident to push through the Regulation of Railways Act 1889, which imposed on all railway companies a statutory obligation to complete block working and interlocking. (The Armagh accident was caused by 'time-interval' working and lack of continuous brakes, but was in no way connected with interlocking). In October 1889, the Board informed the companies that they intended to make Regulations under the Act setting a limit of twelve months for the full introduction of block working (except on single lines worked on the one-engine-in-steam principle, or by train staff without tickets), and eighteen months for the completion of interlocking of all connections with passenger lines. The railway companies were horrified by these timescales, particularly that for interlocking, and argued

that the manufacturing capacity of the signalling contractors was inadequate to complete the work in the time proposed, but the Board retained the original limits when the regulations were eventually made in October 1890. However, a face-saving arrangement was agreed whereby the Board would grant individual extensions of the limits for certain companies. In practice, most of the companies involved obtained these extensions, and much of the interlocking work was not done until 1893-5. Many companies had to raise additional loan stock to meet the cost (the Board of Trade was empowered under the 1889 Act to give companies a certificate authorising the issue of loan stock for this purpose, to relieve them of the need to obtain a special Act).

Even at the end of 1895, eighteen mainland, and many Irish companies were still not fully interlocked. The Waterford & Tramore and the Ravenglass & Eskdale, indeed, still had no interlocking at all, but perhaps the most significant offender was the GNoS, with only 89 per cent interlocking. Absolute Block working, on the other hand, was, for practical purposes, ubiquitous.

Despite these few recalcitrants, the fact was that over 99 per cent of stations in England, Scotland, and Wales had been interlocked by 1895, the vast majority of them with full-size signal boxes. After 1895, new signal boxes were built in somewhat lesser numbers, although a large number were of course still required for new lines, for the expansion of layouts, and for the renewal of worn out boxes and frames. In retrospect, the 1889 Act probably went a little too far in expecting the full interlocking with signal boxes of even the most lightly-used rural branches. The economic viability of such lines was threatened and, in 1896, a second Light Railways Act was passed to encourage the development of new rural lines free of some of the 1889 Act's more stringent requirements.

Developments in Signal Box Design, 1870-1930

We have already seen how the early 'platforms' were developed into the signal box as we know it in the space of a few years around 1860. So complete was this transformation that it was followed by a period of more than sixty years in which there were scarcely any

Plate 25 The Saxby & Farmer box at Daisyfield Station (L&Y) exemplifies the plain box designs of the early 1870s.

R. Newman

24

Plate 26 1880s decoration at Craigendoran Junction (NB).
F. Alexander

Plate 27 A 'typical' (in so far as one can speak of such a thing) box of later pre-grouping days. Dinting Station (GC) box was built in 1905.
R. D. Foster

developments of major significance in box design. The features of the signal box of this 'classic' pre-grouping period are described in detail in **Chapter 3**. There follows here only a resumé of such trends as can be seen over the period.

In the early 1870s, most boxes were small by later standards, as station layouts were still simple, and independent shunting signals were not usually provided. Windows were generally small, and comparatively few boxes displayed decorative elements. During the 1870s and 1880s, average box length tended to increase, windows grew larger, and decorative finials, bargeboards, fascia boards, eaves brackets, etc. became more common. However, from the early 1890s, many companies began to reduce the amount of decoration, partly for economy and partly as a reaction to mid-Victorian 'over-decoration'. Nevertheless, box designs in pre-grouping days generally contrived to maintain a smart appearance and only with World War I did standards of craftsmanship begin to slip. Many companies had a final standard box design in use by the turn of the century, which lasted in use until the Grouping or later.

In 1922/3 came the 'Grouping' of the railway companies, under which all the existing companies (save for a few minor concerns) were grouped by Act of Parliament into four large new companies, the LNER, LMS, SR, and an expanded GW. Once the new organisations had settled down, they introduced new standard box designs, so that from the late 1920s there was a great reduction of variety. Major changes in signal box architecture followed in the 1930s, when the 'modern architecture' style was adopted by some of the companies. This is dealt with in **Chapter 7**.

Power Frames and Track Circuiting: Signalling Developments, 1895-1930

Power working was an American and Continental, rather than a British, development. The world's first power frame was a pneumatic one, designed by George Westinghouse and installed on a US railroad in 1884. It was followed by a hydraulic system in Italy in 1886, and then by various electro-pneumatic and all-electric systems. Power working freed signalmen from heavy manual labour and enabled a reduction in the number and size of signal boxes. However, a power frame was of course more expensive to install than a mechanical frame, and had higher maintenance costs.

In Britain, where mechanical signalling had been brought to such a fine art, power signalling was looked upon with some suspicion by many, and it was not until 1899 that the first power frames were brought into use in this country. By 1914, some 120 power frames were in use **(Plate 310)**: details of the contractors

and railway companies involved are given in **Chapter 2**. In the 1920s and 1930s, the post-grouping companies brought many further power installations into use, mostly in connection with the resignalling of large stations. Nevertheless, the fact is that the power frame never really caught on in this country (other than on the London Underground railways) in the same way as it did in many other countries. Many of the larger British stations had been resignalled mechanically during enlargements of the 1880s-1900s, and could not justify further resignalling. The 1914-18 and 1939-45 wars, the Depression, and the comparative poverty of the post-grouping companies reduced the amount of work that could be undertaken and, having come late into the power frame era, the British railways were early out of it with the development of the 'panel' in the 1930s (**Chapter 7**).

The miniature levers or slides of a power frame could be placed much closer together than the levers of a mechanical frame, with the result that a power frame box needed to be only about half the length of a mechanical box controlling the same layout. Apart from this, the use of a power frame had little impact on the external appearance of boxes. The interlocking mechanism of power frames was normally placed above operating floor level, but a lower storey was still required for other equipment. Most power frame boxes in pre-grouping days were built to the same standard box designs as were used for mechanical boxes.

Another important development was the introduction of 'track circuiting', whereby electric circuits in insulated sections of track are used to automatically warn the signalman of the presence of a train on that particular section of the line, and prevent him from clearing signals for conflicting movements. Many accidents had previously been caused by signalmen forgetting the presence of a standing train, and it was the occurrence of another such accident at Hawes Junction in 1910 that provided the incentive for the introduction of track circuiting on large scale. Track circuiting had other benefits as well, as it eased the problems of box siting (**Chapter 3**) and facilitated, in connection with power operation, the development of automatic signals worked by the trains themselves, so removing the need for intermediate signal boxes on sections of plain track. Automatic signalling, based on track circuiting, was first used between Grateley and Andover Junction (LSW) in 1901, and then on a larger scale on the London Underground lines from 1903. However, it was not until the 1930s that stretches of automatic signalling became at all common on the main lines. By 1930 'colour light' signals were the norm for large resignalling schemes, instead of semaphores. Automatic signalling, and the development of the 'panel', gave the first indications of the fact that the 'signal box', as such, would eventually be rendered obsolete.

TABLE 4

Number of Signal Boxes on Each Railway at the Time of the Grouping

Railway Company	Number of Boxes	Actual date of count	Source of Information
GE	650	1922	(2)
CV&H	5	1923	(1)
GN	603	1922	(2)
M&GN	90	1913	(3)
GC	510	1922	(2)
H&B	71	1922	(3)
E&WYU	3	1923	(1)
NE	1,191	1922	(2)
Mid	1,203	1922	(2)
CLC	134	1907	(3)
LNW	1,254	1922	(2)
L&Y	752	1922	(2)
NS	146	1931	(3)
Wirral	15	1931	(3)
Mersey	8	1923	(1)
Furness	72	1905	(3)
M&C	29	1918	(3)
CK&P	12	1923	(1)
C&WJ	12	1923	(1)
Knott End	4	1923	(1)
SMJ	11	1923	(1)
GW (incl. PT and R&SB)	1,646	1922	(2)
Cam.	92	1922	(1)
A (N&SW) D&R	8	1922	(1)
B&M	42	1909	(3)
Rhymney	46	1915	(3)
TV	118	1922	(1)
Cardiff	11	1922	(1)
Barry	39	1921	(3)
N&B	13	1922	(1)
SHT	5	1922	(1)
L&MM	0	1922	(1)
BP&GV	6	1922	(1)
Corris	3	1922	(1)
MSWJ	21	1922	(1)
LSW	531	1922	(2)
S&DJ	41	1923	(1)
L&B	6	1923	(1)
LBSC	349	1922	(2) and (3)
IoW	7	1923	(1)
IoWC	10	1923	(1)
FY&N	5	1923	(1)
SEC (SE lines)	270	1922	(3)
SEC (LCD lines)	145	1922	(3)
NB	641	1922	(2)
GNoS	127	1923	(2)
Cal	666	1922	(2)
GSW	286	1922	(2)
Highland	154	1922	(2)
TOTAL	**12,063**		

Sources of Information:

(1) Miscellaneous

(2) Railway companies' returns to the 1922 Automatic Train Control Committee

(3) Railway companies' Sectional Appendix/Working Timetable lists of signal boxes.

Notes: Figures from sources (1) and (3) are of the number of block posts and exclude signal boxes that were not block posts. It is uncertain what definition of a signal box was used by the railway companies in calculating the figures in source (2).

Joint lines are included in the figures of the company responsible for signalling them (or that part of them), except that the M&GN and S&DJ are included separately.

The figures should not be taken as accurate to the nearest integer, but most are accurate to within a small percentage. The TV, A (N&SW) D&R, and Cardiff figures are of lesser accuracy; in the last two cases a meaningful figure is almost impossible as most of the boxes were both jointly owned and of uncertain status. The L&MM had a signal box, but it was not a block post. The GNoS and Highland figures are known to include 'minor' boxes/both boxes at one-block-post-but-two-box stations. The 1931 figures for the Furness and CLC (where the figures in the table are for an early date) are 69 and 128.

The total is not strictly statistically meaningful, but it gives a useful impression of the total number of boxes in existence around the time of the Grouping.

CHAPTER TWO

The Railway Companies and the Signalling Industry

The Signalling Industry

Well over half the signalling equipment required by the pre-grouping railway companies was not manufactured in-house by the railway companies themselves, but was purchased by them from firms of signalling contractors. Many signal box structures too were built by, and in some cases to the designs of, the signalling contractors. In this section, we outline the history of the British signalling industry. Later in this chapter we describe the various forms of contractual arrangement that existed between the signalling contractors and the railway companies, and in **Chapter 5** we examine the signal box designs of each contractor, list the railway companies to which each contractor supplied and, in many cases, give further details of the firms' histories.

It was noted in **Chapter 1** that a number of firms were supplying railway signalling equipment by the 1850s, of which Messrs Stevens & Sons were the leading firm. The apparatus in use at this period could be made without difficulty by any engineering works, but the coming of interlocked frames made railway signalling a more specialised business. John Saxby's entry into the market during 1857/8 was also noted in **Chapter 1**. Saxby (from 1863, Saxby & Farmer) and Stevens shared most of the market in the early 1860s; but another new firm, McKenzie, Clunes & Holland, founded in Worcester in 1861, soon began to get significant custom. In the 1860s and 1870s, the signalling business was very cut-throat, and the various firms made several attempts to drive their competitors out of business through the courts. The failure of Saxby's 1860 action against Stevens has already been noted, but much more important was his case against McKenzie, Clunes & Holland, which dragged on from 1869 to 1874. Here Saxby sought to argue that his 1856 patent covered the whole principle of interlocking, and that all subsequent patents such as McK&H's were therefore infringements of his, even though they were for quite different forms of mechanism. Had Saxby won this case, McK&H and (by implication) other manufacturers of interlocking frames could have been very seriously affected, and the history of the industry might have been very different. However, the House of Lords came down against Saxby, ruling (in effect) that principles could not be patented, but only methods of putting them into effect. Col. Yolland was called as a witness and helped McK&H's case by stating that an installation based on Saxby's 1856 patent would no longer be approved by the Board of Trade. The Lords' decision on 22nd June 1874 was greeted by public rejoicing in the streets of Worcester, where McKenzie & Holland (as the firm was by then known) had become a large employer.

At the same time, Saxby was involved in another case — over rival patents for catch-handle locking — with his ex-employee Walter Easterbrook, who had left S&F in 1867 to set up his own firm. Saxby won this case, which was complicated more by the general inadequacies of patent law than by the particular circumstances, in 1873. A further action was brought by Saxby against the Gloucester Wagon Co. during 1879-83, but this ended with the House of Lords finding against Saxby, which seems to have discouraged him from any further activities in the courts. When Easterbrook ruined his business in 1885 by losing a case he had brought against the GW, a general appreciation of the futility of all this legal activity seems to have sunk in.

During the 1870s, S&F and McK&H (both of which firms were to remain in the 'top league' of the industry) gradually captured many of Stevens' former customers. The expanding market also encouraged many other engineers to invent new types of interlocking mechanism, and try to break into the signalling business. But most had little or no success, and are known only as unsuccessful tenderers in the railway companies' Minute Books. In this category come such firms as R. Burn & Son of Epsom, Vickers & Sons of Sheffield, Shaw & Co., and the Thames Iron Works. Only six of the new entrants of the late 1860s and 1870s achieved a significant volume of sales. These were Easterbrook & Co., Ransomes & Rapier of Ipswich, E. S. Yardley & Co. of Castlefield, Manchester, I'Anson & Sons of Darlington, J. Tweedy & Co. of Carlisle, and the Gloucester Wagon Company Ltd., already then well-known as builders of railway vehicles. But even these six sold for the most part only to local railway companies, and of them only Tweedy lasted in the signalling business beyond the mid-1880s.

In the 1880s and early 1890s, the signalling market remained buoyant, and three further firms entered the business, all of them founded by former employees of the established signalling companies, and all enjoying a good deal of success. The first and most important was The Railway Signal Company Ltd., set up in 1881 by George Edwards, formerly the Gloucester Wagon Company's Signal Engineer. Edwards had some help from the L&Y in setting up the company, and an understanding that he would be given the L&Y signalling contract. With the L&Y work as a stable base, the RSCo rapidly moved into the top league. It gained much work by undercutting the now middle-aged S&F and McK&H concerns, and by displaying a greater willingness to adapt its products and installations to the customer's needs.

The other new companies were Dutton & Co. Ltd., set up in 1888 by Samuel Telford Dutton (formerly with McK&H), and operating from a works on McK&H's doorstep, and Evans, O'Donnell & Co. Ltd., founded in 1894/5. EOD was the last new mechanical signalling business of any importance to be founded in the UK.

The firms of S&F, Easterbrook, the RSCo, Dutton and EOD were wholly new establishments set up by signal engineers specifically for the purpose of manufacturing railway signalling equipment, although even these firms, with the apparent exceptions of Easterbrook (who had no manufactory of his own) and S&F, also undertook a certain amount of general engineering work. The other signalling firms had been in business as engineers/iron-founders prior to becoming involved in signalling or, in the cases of McK&H and R&R, were off-shoots of such existing firms; and of these other firms only Stevens and McK&H enjoyed a sufficient degree of success in the signalling market for signalling to become the major part of their business.

It should also be understood that, in addition to the main signalling firms mentioned so far in this chapter, who supplied a complete range of signalling equipment, there were other firms performing more specialist roles. Most notably there were the specialist manufacturers of electrical signalling instruments, of whom Tyer & Co. and the W. R. Sykes Interlocking Signal Co. Ltd. were the leading firms — although, as it happens, these two firms also engaged in some general mechanical signalling work in later years (**see Chapter 5**). Also, however, firms manufacturing points and crossings might supply point rodding, facing point locks, and other outdoor operating gear. Again, one of the main firms in this field, Henry Williams Ltd. did also supply a number of mechanical locking frames and parts in later years. The advances made in

Plate 28 Few photographs exist of the interiors of the signalling contractors' works. Here, however, we see the 220-lever double frame built for the LSW's new Waterloo 'A' box of 1892, under construction in a works which, although not named in the original caption, is almost certainly the older part (Nos. 237-243) of the Stevens works in Southwark Bridge Road, London. This photograph would have been taken specially to commemorate the manufacture of what was then one of the largest frames ever built. Unfortunately, the frame is so large that it obscures most of the works' equipment from view. The contractor's name — 'Stevens & Sons Patent, London & Glasgow' — is cast in the end of the frame, a common practice.

National Railway Museum

signalling technology after 1856 did not alter the fact that any railway or general engineering firm could make signals and signal posts, and any simple ironmongery (*cf. LNERS, Plate 25*).

The late 1890s brought changing conditions in the British market. The completion of the national interlocking programme, and the fact that a larger number of railway companies were now making their own signalling equipment, brought about reduced demand. Furthermore, it was becoming clear by 1900 that the long-term future lay not with mechanical frames but with power signalling. McK&H were the first British company into this field, entering in 1895 into an agreement with the Westinghouse Brake Co. Ltd. (the British company of George Westinghouse's USA-based empire) under which McK&H became licensees of the electro-pneumatic system of the Union Switch & Signal Co. (another Westinghouse company, in the USA). The first frame supplied under this agreement was for the GE's Granary Junction box at Bishopsgate, and was brought into use on 15th January 1899. (In the same month the LNW brought into use an all-electric power frame of their own design at Gresty Lane, Crewe). The Granary Junction frame was imported from the USA, but for the work which McK&H carried out on the NE and Caledonian in 1902-8, the electro-pneumatic frames were manufactured in England. The Westinghouse Brake Co. also undertook contracts itself, at Bolton West (L&Y) in 1903, and on the District and the new London tube railways in 1903-7.

Next into the power signalling business was J. P. O'Donnell, one of the founders of EOD, who set up in November 1900 a new company called the British Pneumatic Railway Signal Co. Ltd. to be the sole British licensee of the (American) Pneumatic Railway Signal Company's pneumatic system. The equipment was manufactured in the EOD works at Chippenham. The first contract gained was for Grateley (LSW) in 1901, and a fair amount of work on the LSW and GC followed. Other firms entering the British power signalling market in the 1900s were the RSCo, which took out a licence of the LNW system (but made only one sale — for Severus Junction (NE) in 1903); Siemens Bros. & Co. Ltd., the British firm of the German manufacturing empire, who supplied four of their all-electric frames to the GW in 1905-13, and one to the Midland in 1905; and the W. R. Sykes Interlocking Signal Co. Ltd., who sold their electro-mechanical system (under which the signals were power-worked, but the points mechanically worked) to the LBSC, SEC, and GSW. Only in a very few cases were the power contractors involved in the building of box structures, and the boxes concerned were all to railway company designs.

In contrast to the cut-throat rivalry of earlier years, relations between the various firms became quite friendly during the 1890s. Most of the pioneers were now dead, and businessmen rather than engineers were taking control of the companies. By 1898, all the remaining signalling firms, except Stevens and McK&H, had been converted from partnerships to Limited Companies. The problem of reduced demand was dealt with in 1901-03 by a co-ordinated restructuring of the industry. A series of agreements was entered into between the leading figures in the firms of S&F, McK&H, EOD, and J. F. Pease & Co. Ltd. (who had taken over the assets of Dutton & Co. in 1899), as a result of which a new holding company was formed in August 1901. This was originally called the Pneumatic Electric & General Engineering Co. Ltd., but in 1903 the name was changed to Consolidated Signal Company Ltd. The Chairman of the new company was Walter Holland (Junior), one of the partners of McK&H, and amongst the other Directors were O'Donnell, Evans, J. F. Pease, Charles Hodgson (Managing Director of S&F), and the other three partners of McK&H. During 1901/2, the whole of the shares in Saxby & Farmer Ltd. and Evans, O'Donnell & Co. Ltd. were acquired by various of the Directors of the new company; and in October 1901 the McK&H firm was formed into a Limited Company, with the four partners as the only shareholders. Also in October 1901, McK&H acquired the signalling assets of J. F. Pease & Co. Ltd., who thereupon withdrew entirely from the field. The net result of all this was that the directorate of the Consolidated Signal Co. Ltd. now owned all the shares in all three remaining companies, S&F, McK&H, and EOD.

In 1903 the S&F Kilburn works was closed down (although the

TABLE 5
The Mechanical Signalling Contractors

This table lists the contractors supplying mechanical locking frames to the British railway companies. The dates given are those at which the firm commenced and ceased the supply of mechanical locking frames, and are not necessarily the same as the dates at which the firm commenced and ceased its operations as a whole **(see this chapter and Chapter 5)**. Contractors who supplied power equipment only are not included in this table, but are all mentioned in the text of this chapter.

This table gives the exact legal name of each firm at every date. In the text of the book these names are generally given in abbreviated forms.

Firm	Supply commenced	Supply ceased	Notes
Stevens & Sons	1860	circa 1916	1
Scottish works became			
Stevens & Sons (Glasgow) Ltd.	1915	1923	
Saxby & Co.	1857		
became Saxby & Farmer	1863		
became Saxby & Farmer Ltd.	1893	1920	2
Chambers **(see text of Chapter 1)**			
McKenzie, Clunes & Holland	1861		
became McKenzie & Holland	1873		
became McKenzie & Holland Ltd.	1901	1920	2
Courtney & Stephens	circa 1864	1880s	
Easterbrook & Co.	circa 1867		
became Easterbrook, Hannaford & Co.	circa 1877	1885	
E. I'Anson & Sons, & Co.	1867	circa 1887	
E. S. Yardley & Co.	1867		
became William Smith	circa 1876	circa 1886	
Ransomes & Rapier	1869	circa 1881	
William Baines & Co.	circa 1870	circa 1872	
Crumlin Viaduct Works Co. Ltd.	circa 1871	circa 1878	
A. Poole	circa 1873	circa 1873	
J. Tweedy & Co.	1873		
taken over by			
Tyer & Co. Ltd.	1898		
mechanical work transferred to			
Tyer's Signals Ltd.	1927		
became B. P. & Tyer's Signals Ltd.	1934	1950s	
Gloucester Wagon Co. Ltd.	1876	1884	
The Railway Signal Co. Ltd.	1881	1974	
Dutton & Co.	1888		
became Dutton & Co. Ltd.	1889		
taken over by			
J. F. Pease & Co. Ltd.	1899	1901	3
Evans, O'Donnell & Co.	1894		
became Evans, O'Donnell & Co. Ltd.	1895	1903	4
W. R. Sykes Interlocking Signal Co. Ltd.	circa 1903	1907	
F. A. Atkinson & Co.	circa 1907	circa 1909	3
E. C. & J. Keay	circa 1900s		
work transferred to Tyer's Signals Ltd. in 1927.			
Westinghouse Brake & Saxby Signal Co. Ltd.	1920		
became Westinghouse Brake & Signal Co. Ltd.	1935	1978	5
Henry Williams Ltd.	circa 1920s	circa 1950s	
British Power Railway Signal Co. Ltd.	circa 1928		
work transferred to B. P. & Tyer's Signals Ltd. in 1934.			

Notes:
(1) Non-interlocked frames supplied since circa 1843/4
(2) Taken over by Westinghouse
(3) Taken over by McK&H
(4) Taken over by S&F
(5) Mechanical frames still produced for overseas sale

main building, in Canterbury Road, still stands) and production transferred to the newer EOD works. The EOD company ceased to trade, but it was kept in existence as landowner of the Chippenham site until 1922, and the EOD product range continued to be produced there under the S&F name. The Consolidated Signal Co. Ltd. Directors maintained financial control over the companies, but S&F and McK&H continued under separate management until 1917, and traded separately with their individual ranges of equipment right up to 1920. The country (indeed, the world) was divided into understood 'spheres of influence', to prevent S&F and McK&H from spending too much of their energies in competing with each other.

The Railway Signal Co. Ltd. had not been involved in the 1901 agreements, but during 1903/4 it too was taken over by the Consolidated Signal Co. Ltd. directorate, but again, it continued to trade separately. This left Stevens and Sons, and Tyer & Co. Ltd. as the only independent mechanical signalling contractors of any significance. Stevens showed no inclination to join the new empire, and, as they were still a partnership rather than a Limited Company, they were immune from unwished-for raids by the financiers. They were still a major company at the turn of the century, but their market share continued to decline, and they finally ceased trading around 1916 in England, and in 1923 in Scotland.

Tyer & Co, long-known as suppliers of electrical signalling instruments, had acquired a foothold in the mechanical market in 1898 when they took over Tweedy's signalling assets. A few other firms entered the mechanical market in the 1900s, but none made any great impact.

The final act in the reorganisation of the industry was the absorption of the Consolidated Signal Co. Ltd. companies into the Westinghouse group. The first direct connection between the two came in 1907 when the McKenzie, Holland and Westinghouse Power Signal Co. Ltd. was established as a joint concern to market the Westinghouse electro-pneumatic system, in place of McK&H's 1895 licence, and also the Taylor electric system for which McK&H had acquired a licence in 1904. The new company was to achieve sales on the L&Y, the GW, and the London underground lines. It was unusual in that when it was set up it recruited its staff mainly from the 'Underground' group, which had been the major user of power signalling up to that date. Previously it had tended to be engineers trained by the contractors who had gone to establish the railway companies' signal departments.

Major changes came during 1915-17 when separate executive control of the Consolidated Signal Co. Ltd.'s subsidiary companies was abolished, with the appointment of H. G. Brown as Managing Director of all four companies (the Consolidated Signal Co. Ltd., the McKH&WPSCo. Ltd., McK&H Ltd., and S&F Ltd.). Brown was an American signal engineer who had come to England in 1902 to supervise the Westinghouse Brake Company's work on the District Railway (see Chapter 9). In 1920, Brown was also made Chairman of the Consolidated Signal Co. Ltd. and oversaw the disposal of that company's holdings to the Westinghouse Brake Co. Ltd., which was transformed into the Westinghouse Brake & Saxby Signal Co. Ltd. (the 'Saxby' was dropped in 1935). Part of the rationale for the merger was that the brake business was regarded as a consistently expanding market which could help even out the ups and downs of the signalling market, but, in the event, the brake business was very poor in the 1920s. At first there was some American money in the new company, but by the 1940s this was no longer the case. The company's official headquarters was at the former Westinghouse Brake Co. works at 82 York Way (then called York Road), King's Cross, but mechanical manufacture continued at Chippenham. The Consolidated Signal Co. Ltd. was retained as an investment company and still exists as such.

In 1921, the McK&H Worcester works was closed and its work was transferred to Chippenham. The old S&F and McK&H companies were wound up in 1923 and 1925 respectively, but new purely nominal companies were formed at the same time to preserve the valuable names. (These new companies were both dissolved in 1976). Westinghouse soon standardised their product range, and from 1924 the only type of mechanical frame generally marketed was the new 'A2' design, based on later S&F practice. Although under Westinghouse financial control, the RSCo continued to manufacture at its Fazakerley works and to trade entirely separately.

The 1922/3 Grouping of the railway companies meant a further reduction in the signalling contractors' mechanical work, as a number of companies which had bought from the contractors were absorbed into the LMS and GW, which did their own work. Also, after 1923 the signalling contractors ceased (except for a very few cases in the 1920s and 1930s) to be involved in the building of signal box structures. Westinghouse and the RSCo had a very dominant position in the mechanical market in the post-grouping period. Westinghouse manufactured around 2,000 mechanical frames between 1923 and 1947, although most of these were for overseas customers. Other firms supplying small numbers of mechanical frames or parts to the British railways in this period were Tyer, E. C. & J. Keay, the British Power Railway Signal Co. Ltd. (as the British Pneumatic company had been renamed around 1918), and Henry Williams Ltd. (for further details of these firms' mechanical work see **Chapter 5**). In the power market, Westinghouse faced greater competition, from British Power, from Siemens (who in 1926 transferred their signalling work to a new subsidiary, the Siemens & General Electric Railway Signal Co. Ltd.), and from the General Railway Signal Co. Ltd., an American company whose British work was done in connection with the Metropolitan Vickers Electric Co. Ltd., trading as Metropolitan Vickers GRS Ltd. Between 1923 and 1947, Westinghouse supplied 45 electropneumatic frames (all to LT and constituents), and 35 electric frames (mostly to the SR and LMS). The other power contractors supplied comparatively few power frames. Both they and Westinghouse found that much of their work for the main line companies lay in the installation of colour-light signalling controlled from a reduced number of existing boxes. In the 1930s, the power contractors began the manufacture of 'panels' (see Chapter 7). The British Power Railway Signal Co. Ltd. ceased trading as such around 1934, but a new company, B. P. & Tyer's Signals Ltd., was set up to conduct the mechanical and power work previously carried out by Tyer and British Power, and continued this until the 1950s.

After nationalisation, there continued to be a reasonable demand for new mechanical frames from the contractors until the early 1960s, met by Westinghouse and the RSCo. The last mechanical frame supplied by Westinghouse to BR was that for Rotherham Central (ordered in 1961). The last RSCo frames followed a few years later and, having remained (since 1903) a supplier of mechanical equipment only, the RSCo went into liquidation in 1974. The last mechanical frames supplied by any contractor to any UK railway were those made by Westinghouse for the new Army boxes at Bicester in 1978. Westinghouse do still advertise other mechanical equipment (as do Henry Williams) and still produce some mechanical frames for overseas customers. The York Way building was abandoned in the 1970s, and all work is now done at Chippenham. In March 1979, the Westinghouse Brake & Signal Co. Ltd. became a subsidiary of Hawker Siddeley.

Recent developments in the power signalling industry (now, of course, effectively 'the signalling industry') are really outside the scope of this book. The main firms are now Westinghouse, GEC-General Signal Ltd. (a combination of Siemens and Metropolitan Vickers GRS), and ML Engineering (Plymouth) Ltd. Power frames faded from the picture at much the same time as mechanical frames, and all work is now with 'panels'.

From an early date, the British signalling contractors also carried out a large amount of overseas work. Separate overseas companies were founded in three cases; by Saxby in France in 1878, by S&F in India in 1905, and by Westinghouse in Australia in 1923 (taking over two works built by McK&H in the 1880s). Because the overseas railways were much later in their building, and in the provision of full signalling, they provided the British signalling contractors with a market that was still expanding after the home market had begun to decline. So far as is known, no foreign firm ever supplied mechanical signalling equipment to a British railway company.

Railway Company Responsibilities

In general, every railway company was of course responsible for arranging the provision of and bearing the cost of such signalling and signal boxes as were required on its lines, but in certain circumstances the position was more complicated:

(1) At junctions, where a new line built by one company joined an existing line owned by another, the generally accepted principle was that the cost of providing signalling fell upon the company building the new line. In some cases this company would do the work itself, and in others, the company owning the earlier line would claim the right to do the work and recharge the cost to the second company. An example of the latter course (Shaftholme Junction) can be seen in the GN Way & Works Committee minutes of 7th July 1869:-

'The NER are proceeding with their new line from Doncaster to York, and according to custom the (GN) Engineer has claimed the right to execute the works in connection with the junction, and to fix the locking apparatus and signals at the cost of the NER'.

Where all the lines at a junction between different companies' lines were new, or when such a junction dating from pre-interlocking days was being interlocked, the two or more companies involved had to come to agreement on the proportion of the costs to be borne by each. This was usually done on a standard 'leverage' basis — that is, by allotting the functions of each lever in the locking frame to one or the other company — but this still generated a lot of paperwork. As an example, when Dowlais Top was interlocked in 1887, the LNW paid 10/17ths of the costs and the B&M paid 7/17ths.

(2) Many different arrangements were made for joint lines. Three of the largest joint lines, the CLC, LNW/GW Jt (until 1885), and M&GN (from 1893), were for most purposes in charge of their own signalling; and in some other cases, particularly in earlier years, the signalling contracts were let by the 'Joint Committee' responsible for the line (as, for example, was done by the Dover & Deal Joint Committee). But the three most common options were:

(i)   The whole line was signalled by one of the owning companies (as, for example, the S&DJ by the LSW, the Dearne Valley by the L&Y, and the LNW/GW Joint by the LNW between 1885 and 1904).

(ii) The line was divided into two or more sections with each of the owning companies taking permanent responsibility for one section (e.g. the GC and H&B Joint, and the LNW/GW Joint after 1904).

(iii) Responsibility rotated between the owning companies for periods of so many years each (e.g. the Portpatrick & Wigtownshire Joint).

The arrangements for any one joint line were often changed, and the net result of all this was that some joint lines ended up with peculiar combinations of equipment. On the M&GN, there were Midland boxes with S&F frames, and GN boxes with Midland frames! It is regretted that, due to the large number of joint lines, it is impossible to describe fully in this book the arrangements adopted in each case.

(3) Many companies' lines were worked by other companies. Firstly, many branch lines were promoted by a nominally-independent company which was, in reality, the protégé of a neighbouring larger company, and were worked by that company from the day of opening. In some such cases, the signalling work was done by the working company or its contractors but, in other cases, the Board of the 'independent' company let the contracts. The exact position is sometimes not easy to establish. Secondly, some companies which had been fully-independent entered, in later life, into working agreements with larger companies, whereby they retained their independent existence but were worked by the larger company. The best-known examples of this were the LNW's working of the NL from 1909, and the GW's working of the R&SB from 1906, the Port Talbot from 1908, the South Wales Mineral from 1908 and the Liskeard & Looe from 1909. In these cases, the working company also assumed signalling responsibility.

(4) The ownership of many lines changed hands on more than one occasion in pre-grouping days, as a result of take-overs and amalgamations. Many of the main amalgamations took place before the days of interlocking, but any company taken over from the 1860s onwards might come to its new owner complete with interlocked signal boxes, and these sometimes remained for many decades as a reminder of the line's original independence. Even today there are still boxes of the Bristol & Exeter Railway in use.

(5) Only in a handful of cases did the peculiar situation arise of boxes being built by one company on the lines of another wholly-independent company. There were GN boxes on a GE line at Harston and Foxton — these were built by the GN because it operated the services on this line, but the cost was recharged to the GE — and there were two LNW boxes on the Cambrian at Welshpool, apparently built by the LNW as part of its contribution to the costs of enlarging the station, which was operated on a joint account basis but owned wholly by the Cambrian. These cases should not be confused with the more numerous examples of boxes appearing on the 'wrong' railway when reused second-hand after 1923. Two cases are also known of railway companies providing technical assistance in the signalling work of neighbouring smaller companies. The LSW did this for the MSWJ (indeed, in later years the MSWJ even built its boxes to the LSW design), and the Cambrian for the N&B, where there was no effect on box design as the two companies used the same contractors' designs.

The Choice Between Contractors and In-House Manufacture

The description of the procedures for building a signal box contained in the remainder of this chapter refers primarily to the situation between the commencement of mass interlocking around 1870 and the 1923 'Grouping', but reference is also made to post-grouping practices as appropriate.

The major choice facing a railway company in the signalling field was whether to let its signalling work to one of the firms of signalling contractors, or to manufacture its signalling equipment itself. In the early years of interlocking, the railway companies had few or no officers with signalling experience, and the majority of companies therefore preferred to leave the whole job to a contractor. In other words, the railway company said to the signalling contractor, 'interlock this station', and the contractor drew up all the plans and provided and installed the box structure, the locking frame and all other box fittings, the signals and signal posts, and

SIGNAL CABINS IN WOOD, BRICK, OR STONE

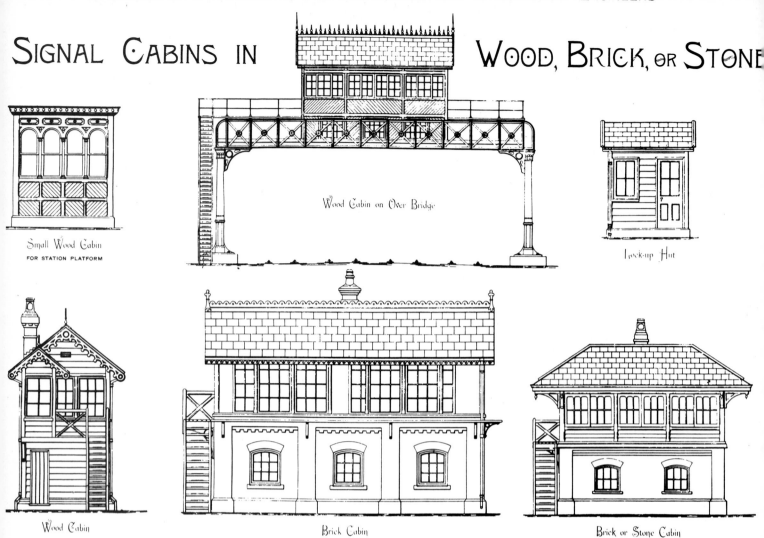

Small Wood Cabin
FOR STATION PLATFORM

Wood Cabin on Over Bridge

Lock-up Hut

Wood Cabin

Brick Cabin

Brick or Stone Cabin

Plate 29 Most of the signalling contractors regularly issued catalogues illustrating their equipment, and these usually included a page of 'signal cabins'. Sometimes the contractor's actual standard box designs were illustrated, but just as often the catalogue showed imaginary designs dreamt up by the artist, designs which were only used overseas, railway companies' designs, or even other contractors' designs — for example, the Tyer catalogues of the 1920s and 1930s showed an RSCo box, a GE box, and a Great Northern of Ireland box. This may have been intended to illustrate the point that the contractor would build boxes to any design desired, but all the same, one might have expected that the contractor's standard designs would always have been included as well. This page from a McK&H catalogue of 1895 shows, at the bottom, three designs to which McK&H had, in fact, built boxes on British railways; a McK&H Type 3/TV timber box at the left, a GE Type 4/McK&H brick box at the centre, and a Northern Counties Committee BTF box at the right. But the standard McK&H Type 3 design is not shown. At the top are two notional designs, for a platform box for underground lines at the left, and for an overhead box at the centre; a ground frame hut is shown at top right.

Public Record Office

all outside connections — all to the signalling contractor's own designs. (Some newly-incorporated railway companies, indeed, did not even arrange the letting of the signalling contract themselves, but left this to the civil engineering contractors who were building the line for them). Hence it was that so many early boxes were built to the signalling contractors' architectural designs. Many of the smaller railway companies continued to choose this option right up to the Grouping.

The majority of the larger railway companies also continued to rely on the contractors for all, or all except minor items of, their signalling equipment, right up to the Grouping; but they tended, as time went by, to take a more active role themselves, drawing up detailed specifications for the equipment and plans for each job. As part of this process most companies evolved standard box designs of their own, to be used instead of the signalling contractors' box designs. Some companies (e.g. the GC from 1905) also had locking frames made to their own design or, alternatively, specified that all frames were to be made to one contractor's design

irrespective of which contractor did the work (for example, the LSW, LBSC, and the LNER in Scotland had 'Stevens' frames made by several other contractors). The latter course was only possible if the patents had expired, or by agreement. Another development was that some companies began to use their own labour force for the installation of new frames and equipment, with the signalling contractor acting as manufacturer only.

Where railway companies had their own box designs, the boxes might still be built by the signalling contractor as part of an overall contract. This was normal practice, for example, on the GE and MS&L/GC in later decades. It meant, of course, that there might be several different signalling contractors building identical boxes on the same railway. Just as often, however, the building of the box structure was arranged separately from the signalling contract, either by direct labour (not very common in these circumstances) or by letting the work to a firm of builders. This was the general practice of, amongst others, the NE and most of the Scottish and Cumbrian railways. On a new line, the box structures were often

TABLE 6

Contractors or In-House Manufacture: The Practice of the Major Railway Companies

Company	Locking frames and other major items of signalling equipment bought from the signalling contractors:		Locking frames and other major items of signalling equipment manufactured in-house: boxes built (by direct labour or by building contractors) to the railway company's designs. A*** = assembly of frames from bought-in/reused components
	Boxes built by the signalling contractors to the signalling contractors' designs	Boxes built (by direct labour, building contractors, or signalling contractors) to the railway company's designs	
GE	Some until 1878	Some until 1878, all 1878-1919, some from 1919	Some from 1919 (A***)
GN	-	All (except a little circa 1870)	A little circa 1870 (A***?)
M&GN (from 1893)	-	All	-
MS&L/GC	Some until 1886	All from 1887	Some until 1886 (A***?)
H&B	All until 1897	All from 1897	-
NE	-	All (except a little circa 1870)	A little circa 1870 (A***?)
Midland			All
CLC	Some until 1885/6	Some until 1885/6	All from 1885/6
LNW	Most until 1873, some until 1876	A few until 1873, some 1874-6, a few until 1884	Some from 1874, most from 1876, all from 1884
L&Y	All until 1889/90	-	All from 1889/90
NS	All until 1876	All from 1876	-
Furness	A few (huts only)	Most	-
GW	Some until 1885	-	Some from 1863, all from 1885
Cambrian	All	-	-
B&M	All	-	-
Rhymney	All	-	-
TV	Most until circa 1895	A few in 1870s, all from circa 1895	-
Barry	-	All	-
MSWJ	All until 1900	All from 1900	-
LSW	Some in 1860s	All, except some in 1860s	-
S&DJ		All	-
LBSC	All until 1880, some until 1898	Some 1880-98, most/all from 1898	**(see Chapter 6)**
SE	Much until 1884, much 1892-(1903)	A very few	Some from 1867, all 1884-92, much from 1892
LCD	Much	-	**(see Chapter 6)**
SEC	**(see Chapter 6)**	**(see Chapter 6)**	**(see Chapter 6)**
NB	A few	Most	-
GNoS	A few in 1880s	Most	-
Cal.	-	All until 1890s, some until 1900s	Some from 1890s, all from 1900s
GSW	-	Early period	Later period (A***)
Highland	Until 1900s	From 1900s	-
Met.	Most until circa 1885	Most from circa 1887	Some circa 1889-96 (?)
LNER (Southern Area)	-	Some	Most (A***)
LNER (NE Area)	-	Until 1925	From 1925 (A***)
LNER (Scottish Area)	-	Most	Some (A***)
LMS (England & Wales)	-	Some	Most
LMS (Scottish Division)	-	A very few	Almost all
GW (from 1922)	-	Two cases only known (1933/5)	Almost all
SR	-	All	-
BR (ER)	-	Some	Most (A***)
BR (NER)	-	A very few	Almost all (A***)
BR (LMR)	-	-	All
BR (WR)	-	-	All
BR (SR)	-	All	-
BR (ScR)	-	-	All

NOTE: This table refers to mechanical frames and equipment. Power frames, and, in later years, 'panels', were generally acquired from the various power signalling contractors (except that the LNW made its own power equipment, and some small panels have been made up in BR workshops).

included in a general station building contract. As an example, McK&H's tender of £7,220 7s. 2d. for the GN's Skegness new line in 1913 was for 'signal work only, exclusive of buildings', and arrangements were 'to be made with Messrs Harold Arnold & Sons, the contractors for the railway buildings, for the erection of the signal cabins at a cost of £1,185'. Even in 1849 we find Peto's invoice for building the Eastern Counties Railway's station at Cambridge including, in its total of £55,649 4s. 3d., the sum of £129 10s. 6d. for 'building switchmen's boxes'. Where railway companies contracted out the building of boxes separately from the signal work, it was not unknown for the signalling contractors to put in tenders for building the box as well. S&F did this for the GN's Stanley box in 1884, but the builders W. Pickard & Son got the job. Conversely, it would also seem likely (although no reference to the practice has been found) that the signalling contractors might on occasion have sub-contracted the building of brick-built or stone-built boxes to local builders.

One cannot draw an absolute division between 'contractors' box designs' and 'railway companies' box designs', as there were some cases where railway companies had special versions of contractors' designs built (the Highland, for example, specifying vertical boarding and corrugated-iron roofs for all its McK&H and Dutton boxes), and other cases where contractors added a few of their own features to otherwise standard railway company designs (e.g. the covered landings on Dutton-built GE Type 7 boxes). These details are noted in **Chapters 5 & 6**, but the simple division will suffice for most purposes.

Where signalling contractors or building contractors built boxes to a railway company's designs, the railway company provided detailed architectural drawings and specifications for the structure. **Plate 286** shows an example of the contract drawing for a single box. In later years, standard drawings were more common. The GE's standard agreement with all the contractors in 1890 contained standard drawings of timber, brick, timber platform, and brick platform boxes (**Plate 153**) and nine pages of written specification (**Table 9**).

Only a dozen of the largest railway companies engaged in the in-house manufacture of signalling equipment, although the size of the companies concerned meant that nearly half the country's signalling equipment was produced in-house after 1890. The Midland was the only company to provide all its own frames right from the start, but the GW and the SE were also doing some of their own work in the 1860s, and other companies followed suit in the 1870s and 1880s. In some cases, purchasing from the contractors continued in parallel with in-house work for many years before the company had built up enough capacity to do all its own work. A railway company that wished to manufacture in-house had to design a locking frame and other equipment to new designs which did not infringe any of the contractors' patents or, alternatively, operate under licence. Most of the companies that manufactured signalling equipment in-house also built their signal box structures with their own labour force, the timber component parts being made up in the signal works. The LNW even made its own bricks! Building contractors were also used in a few cases.

The LNW was the only railway company (either pre-grouping or post-grouping) to make its own power signalling equipment, excepting that some small panels have been made up in BR workshops.

Fortunately for the signalling contractors, the possibility of railway companies manufacturing signalling equipment for sale to other railway companies was effectively ruled out in 1876 by a court ruling (in a case brought by the locomotive manufacturers against the LNW, which had manufactured some locomotives for sale to the L&Y) that such manufacture for sale was ultra vires of a railway company's powers. However, it it known that the Midland did supply signalling equipment to a number of industrial lines in its area.

Some railway companies which did not have the capacity for complete manufacture engaged in the assembly of their own locking frames, buying in the major components from one of the signalling contractors or from any ironfounder. The most notable case of this in the pre-grouping period was the GSW. Also, it became more common from the 1890s for railway companies to reuse in another box locking frames which had been displaced from their original box due to major signalling alterations, but which were of modern design and still in good condition. By about 1920, the majority of frames being displaced were to designs considered 'current', and this led the GE (from 1919) and then the LNER's Southern and North Eastern Areas (and their successive BR regions) to adopt the practice of making up the majority of the 'new' frames they required by reusing serviceable parts of old frames in combination with bought-in new parts. As time went by, other railway companies which manufactured their own frames began to make more use of serviceable parts from old frames.

Many companies which never manufactured their own locking frames or other major items of signalling equipment, nevertheless had their own small signal works, and made certain items for themselves. Every railway company needed a signal shop of some kind for maintenance purposes (except that, in the 1860s and 1870s, the signalling contractors sometimes undertook maintenance as well).

Irrespective of the company's policy for other items, the contract for certain electrical equipment, such as block instruments, might be given independently to a specialist supplier. It should also be realised that some of the features of signal box structures, particularly such things as iron and terracotta work, were often proprietary products bought in by whichever party was responsible for erecting the box.

The question of whether in-house manufacture is cheaper than purchasing from outside contractors is of course a perennial problem for businesses in all fields. H. Raynar Wilson concluded, after 25 years with the Midland and the L&Y, that there was 'no doubt in the end that those companies who employ contractors save money. If they specify all material to be to their own company's designs they will achieve that standardisation which is one of the arguments of those who do their own work'. But one also suspects that there were plenty of cases of railway companies being 'ripped off' by the signalling contractors, especially in the early period. The LNW got S&F to substantially reduce their prices on several occasions by dropping hints that they might terminate the contract. The sheer amount of money being paid to the contractors must also have attracted the larger companies to in-house manufacture. The LNW paid no less than £400,000 to S&F between 1864 and 1872.

The Choice Between Sole Contract and Competitive Tenders

Those railway companies which relied on the contractors for their signalling equipment varied considerably in their purchasing policies. At one extreme they might enter into a long-term fixed-price 'sole contract' arrangement with a single contractor, thereby increasing the danger of being 'ripped off'. At the other extreme they could invite tenders from a large number of contractors every time they wanted work done, running the risk of ending up with a very mixed bag of equipment, and making maintenance difficult in later years. Some companies did however manage a happy medium.

The best-known sole contract arrangements were those agreed between S&F and the LNW and LBSC in the 1860s. The LNW terminated its agreement at the end of 1873, but the LBSC remained tied to S&F until the 1890s. Other companies with de facto sole contract arrangements were the NS and (from around 1900) the NE Southern Division, both with McK&H, and the L&Y with the RSCo from 1881 to 1890. The contractors were keen to secure such arrangements and often made approaches to the railway companies to suggest them. In August 1871, for example, S&F wrote to the GE proposing a sole contract agreement at a 'special schedule' as with the LNW, but the GE's Engineer noted that, whilst it might be desirable to have only one system of interlocking mechanism, 'much depends on the prices', and no such agreement was ever made.

The GN became known above all others for the motley nature of its signalling equipment, resulting from a policy of accepting the cheapest tender each time. In the 1870s, the GN often had half a dozen tenderers for a job, and over the years it acquired frames from all the contractors of significance. When appointing a Signal Superintendent for the first time in 1902, responsibility having previously rested with the Engineer, the company noted, somewhat belatedly, that 'a change in dealing with signalling is desirable,

to ensure uniformity in the appliances used'. Other companies which acquired a good mix of equipment were the L&Y (pre-1881), the Furness, and the SE. There were of course more contractors to choose between in the 1870s and 1880s — and much more real competition between them — than there were after the 1901-3 mergers. However, the LNER was still getting competitive tenders for mechanical work in the 1930s.

Even the GN did not invite competitive tenders for every job. Much work was let on the basis of the same schedule of prices as had been agreed with the contractor concerned for another recent job. A more formalised version of this approach could be found on the GE, which negotiated one-year fixed-price agreements every year from 1876 to 1885, with McK&H in some years, and S&F in others, according to which offered the cheapest prices. These were not sole-contract arrangements, although it was understood that

Plate 30 Like any other business, the signalling contractors (in addition to their main catalogues) also produced smaller advertisements, for circulating to railway companies. This is one side of a single-sheet advertisement sent by Easterbrook to the North Eastern Railway on 10th May 1870. A number of sales followed (**see Chapter 5**).

Public Record Office

EASTERBROOK'S

PATENT RAILWAY SIGNAL APPARATUS,

LOCKING THE CATCH ROD PRINCIPLE.

The advantages gained by this principle over other systems at present introduced, are as follows:

By lifting the catch rod out of its notch cut in the quadrant, so as to free its main lever, but before the main lever itself is moved, all conflicting catch rods are instantly and firmly locked down in their respective notches, and so long as the conflicting rods are thus fixed, the levers to which they are attached are immoveable. Other Manufacturers accomplish the locking by the motion of the lever itself, at the same time as the signal is given or the points put right for a train to pass; but by this principle the Locking Action is effected before the lever is or can be moved.

SCHEDULE OF PRICES

For Railway Locking Apparatus upon this principle, with Signals and Connections, including labour, carriage, and superintendence, fixing, painting and completing to satisfaction of Engineer.

MATERIALS OF THE BEST QUALITY AND WORKMANSHIP.

JUNCTION SIGNAL BOXES.

Ordinary Signalman's Box elevated 6 feet above Rail level, 6½ feet from floor to eaves, glazed front and sides or all round as required, roof of slate, zinc, or painted canvas, lockers, steps, door, stove, fender, piping, frame for reception of Apparatus, painted and all complete,

10 ft. by 10 ft. £70.

14 ft. by 12 ft. £90.

Other sizes and heights in proportion.

Patent Apparatus and Machinery for working Points and Signals from inside of Signal Box, a separate lever with extended catch rods to each pair of Points, and to each Signal; painting and engraved plates, and all in complete working order to satisfaction of Engineer,

Not exceeding 12 Levers . . . . . £6. ~~£6 10~~ per Lever.

Exceeding 12 Levers . . . . . . £6 ~~£7 0~~ „

STATION AND JUNCTION SIGNALS.

Ordinary Wood Home Signal Posts, 25 feet above ground, with arms, lamps, spectacles, ladder and fittings complete £19 each.

35

GREAT NORTHERN RAILWAY.

TENDER

FOR

SIGNALLING WORKS AT *Welland Bridge.*
(Spalding & Sutton Br. Line)

To the Directors of the
Great Northern Railway Company.

Gentlemen,

Having examined the foregoing Specification, Quantities, Schedule, and Details, *&c* hereby agree to provide all the materials, plant, labour, &c., and to execute the whole of the works required to be done, according to the terms and conditions of this Specification, and to complete the same to the entire satisfaction of your Engineer, and to the satisfaction of the Board of Trade, within *1/2* calendar month*s* from *our* acceptance of the Contract, for the lump sum of *Four Hundred Ninety Nine* pounds *&c* shillings and *&c* pence (£ *499 „ 0 „ 10*); and in case the Engineer should determine to increase or diminish the quantity of work, or in case the quantity of the works should not equal that given in the Quantities *&c* hereby agree to accept an addition to, or deduction from, the above-mentioned sum (as the case may be), of an amount to be determined by measurement as specified.

Less 6 per | 499
Cent | 30
£ 469

see letter dated
Jan 13th 1883

Gentlemen,
Your obedient Servant,

Signature *McKenzie Holland & Co*
Address *Vulcan Works Worcester*
Date *31st May 1882*

Note.—This Tender is not to be detached from the Specification.

A.B.C. AND A.I. CODES USED.

TELEGRAPHIC ADDRESS.
SIGNALMEN, LONDON

GOLD MEDALS and HIGHEST AWARDS
FOR

TELEPHONE.
PADDINGTON 421.

RAILWAY SIGNALS & SAFETY APPLIANCES.

CHARLES HODGSON, M.I.M.E.
MANAGING DIRECTOR

PARIS, 1867, 1876, 1878, 1879, 1881 & 1885.
VIENNA, 1873, BRUSSELS, 1876 & 1886, PHILADELPHIA, 1876.
MELBOURNE, 1880, LONDON, 1882, 1885 & 1892.
ANTWERP, 1885, BARCELONA, 1888, EDINBURGH, 1890, NIJNI NOVGOROD, 1896. SOUTH AFRICA, 1899.

SAXBY & FARMER, LIMITED.

TRADE MARK

Patent Railway Signal Works,
Canterbury Road, Kilburn,
London, N.W. 24th. January 1900

J. Thomas Esq.,
10 Woodquest Avenue
HERNE HILL. S.E.

Dear Sir,

LISKEARD & LOO RAILWAY EXTENSION.
Coombe & Liskeard Junctions.

We have this morning received a letter from Mr. William H. Reele, Clerk to the Liskeard & Loo Railway Compy. in which he states that he is instructed by the Committee of Management to accept our tender as per our letter to you of the 11th. inst.

In reply we have informed him that our usual terms of payment are 50% of the Contract sum on delivery of material, 40% on completion of the work and the remaining 10% one month after completion

We notice that according to "Bradshaw's" Manual, the Liskeard & Loo Rly. is leased to the Liskeard and Caradon Compy. but we don't notice Mr. Reele's name as one of the Officers of either Company, so that we feel some doubt as to who will be Paymasters in this instance whether we shall look for our money to the Liskeard & Loo Railway Co. the Committee of Management, or the Liskeard & Caradon Compy.

It is necessary to have these points clearly specified, perhaps you will kindly let us hear from you.

Yours faithfully,
SAXBY & FARMER, Limited.

Plate 31 The tender returned by McK&H to the GN for signalling works at Welland Bridge, on the Spalding & Sutton Bridge line. A box was to be built here in connection with the introduction of block working. It will be seen that, in this case, the plans had been drawn up by the railway company; the 'specification' attached to the tender would have given the contractor's price for every item. The tender is signed by Walter Holland and dated 31st May 1882, but for some reason the tenders were not considered by the GN Way and Works Committee until 1st February 1883. The McK&H tender was successful. The box lasted only until 1893, when a new box called 'Welland Bank' replaced it.
Public Record Office

Plate 32 This 1900 letter from Saxby & Farmer shows how the contractors' headed paper, in later years, highlighted their exhibition awards. Note also the S&F Stewarts Lane trade mark. The letter is signed by Charles Hodgson, Managing Director. Note the concern, in the case of a small railway company like this, over where the money is to come from.
Public Record Office

---

the contractor concerned would get the larger part of the work. From 1886, the GE changed its system to one of long-term fixed-price agreements with all its signalling contractors, by means of which the company could calculate itself which contractor would be cheapest for any particular job. The various contractors' prices for box structures from the 1890 revision of these agreements are given in **Table 8**, but the agreements included prices for everything down to the smallest item of equipment.

The railway companies which did best were probably those which used one contractor for the majority of their work, but retained the freedom to use others if desired. The MS&L/GC, for example, used largely the RSCo after 1890, but also gave some work to McK&H.

There was a marked tendency for companies to purchase from the contractor whose works was geographically closest to them.

Authorisation and Completion

The exact procedures adopted for the authorisation of signalling work also naturally varied as between one company and another, but in outline they were usually as follows.

Before the start of each financial year the Signal Engineer (or whichever officer was responsible for signalling) would put in a bid for a certain level of expenditure for the year, and the Board would then decide what his budget was to be. Where the company did its own work, the subsequent proceedings would be left in the Signal Engineer's hands, except insofar as some schemes, notably large schemes involving station alterations and line improvements as well as resignalling, would have to have individual Board or Committee approval. Also, the Signal Department might be 'charged' for the services of other departments within the company. Where contractors were used, and competitive tendering was practised, the Signal Engineer would invite tenders and, when returned, they would be considered by the relevant committee, which would normally approve the lowest. However, in some companies the Signal Engineer might be empowered to let the contract to the lowest tenderer himself.

In the early period, generally, and with small companies at all times, the building of a signal box was regarded as a matter of some import. But with most companies it soon became a routine matter, and more and more responsibility was devolved from the Board and committees to the responsible officers. In later years, many companies permitted officers to authorise expenditure up to a certain level without advance approval. So, for example, we find the GN's Way & Works Committee, in November 1893, noting, with reference to the payment of £578 to the RSCo for work at Twenty, that 'as it was necessary to complete this work ready for the opening of the Saxby & Bourn line, and the men and plant of the Railway Signal Co. were on the ground' — they were resignalling Bourn(e) — 'instructions were given by the Engineer for proceeding with the work under the same schedule (of prices) as for Bourn'. Also, the procedures for authorising revenue expenditure were often simpler than those for capital expenditure and, as time passed, the proportion of new boxes which were replacements for existing boxes, and therefore classifiable as 'revenue', greatly increased.

Contractors were expected to complete the work in what seem nowadays to be very short periods of time. For the interlocking of the average station a period of about 8 or 9 weeks seems to have been the norm. **Plate 31** shows 1½ months given for a small box. For very complicated resignallings, where station or track works were usually involved too, longer periods of a year or more were obviously sometimes necessary. Contracts could be taken away from a firm which back-tracked over completion date. For example, the GN in 1904 transferred to McK&H a contract for work at Claypole which had initially been given to Sykes, when the latter asked for 13 weeks to do the work instead of the 6 weeks specified in the contract (despite a price difference of £85). Many contracts included penalty clauses.

Plate 33 There are very few photographs from the pre-grouping period showing signal boxes actually being built. In the few cases where official photographs were taken, the photographer would visit on completion. The post-grouping companies, however, were more prodigal in their photography, and here we see Grove Park box being built by the Southern Railway's workmen on or about 1st September 1938. This box was an emergency job, as the previous SE box had been burnt out on 23rd August. The brick base of the old box survived and the darker brickwork shows where it was partially incorporated into the new structure. The timber top for the new box was made up in the Angerstein Works, sent to the site by road (apparently in one piece) and erected by crane on the night of 31st August. After continuous day and night work the new box was brought into use on 4th September.

National Railway Museum

37

Board of Trade Inspection

The majority of new signal boxes had to be inspected by the Board of Trade Railway Department when completed. At no time did the legislation specify that new or altered signal boxes as such were subject to inspection, but they were regarded as an integral part of any new or altered works. Before 1871, only boxes on new or widened lines were inspected. Under the 1871 Act, inspection was extended to 'any additional line of railway, deviation line, station, junction (i.e. pointwork), or crossing on the level which forms a portion of or which is directly connected with a railway on which passengers are conveyed . . . '. As most new boxes were built in connection with such track alterations, their inspection was thereby made compulsory; but there were still some new boxes whose inspection was not compulsory, notably those built on freight-only lines, and those built in connection with signalling alterations or renewals only without any track alterations. However, some railway companies put all new boxes and major signalling alterations up for inspection in any case.

Companies had to give one month's notice of their 'intention to open' a new line, and ten days' notice of the date at which the works would be 'ready for inspection'. New lines could not lawfully be opened until inspected and approved, but alterations to existing lines could be brought into use under 'provisional sanction', and might not be inspected until some convenient later date, sometimes as much as a year or more later. The Inspectors were continuously travelling around the country, and tried to fit in minor jobs when they were in the area to deal with a major inspection. Their reports were usually written up immediately, and transmitted to the Board by post. The Board then wrote to the company to inform them officially of the results of the inspection. More often than not the Inspector would recommend that the use of the new works be sanctioned subject to certain minor alterations to which the company had already verbally agreed during the course of the inspection, but it was also quite common for permission for the opening of new lines to be refused, especially in the case of those built by small and impecunious companies. There was no appeal to the courts against refusal, although the President of the Board of Trade could be lobbied politically.

Inspectors' reports rarely made reference to signalling at all prior to 1860, and tended to make only discursive references for some years after that, but from the late 1870s it became normal for Inspectors to give in their reports a full list of all new and altered signal boxes, and the number of levers in each, which provides a valuable source for the historian.

Detailed plans of the works had to be sent to the Board prior to or with the ten days' notice, but many railway companies made a practice of sending plans of a scheme to the Board for preliminary approval prior to the commencement of the works. The companies knew from the published 'Requirements', first issued in 1858 and revised frequently thereafter, what sort of equipment and arrangements the Board expected to be provided in any given situation.

Not surprisingly, the railway companies sometimes failed to give notice to the Board of new works which should have been inspected. During April/May 1881, no less than 51 boxes were inspected on the southern part of the GN main line, some of them built as long ago as 1870. The inspector also found a whole new station at Ayot, which had been built in 1877 but not notified — 'it is not easy to explain why', he noted, before condemning it as unsatisfactory! Signalling contracts normally included a clause requiring the contractor to complete the works to the satisfaction of the Board of Trade, and to undertake at his own expense any alterations which the Board might require.

The President of the Board of Trade was answerable to Parliament for his Inspectors' actions, and this could, on occasion, result in signal boxes being discussed in that forum. For example, on 25th November 1909, Mr Winston Churchill was obliged to reassure the House, in response to a question, that the GSW's new signal box at New Cumnock had been brought into use in proper circumstances, and that the signalman did have a proper view from it!

Cost and Payment

The cost of signalling work decreased considerably over the period 1860 to 1900, and this, of course, helped to overcome the railway companies' initial hesitancy over interlocking. This decrease was due primarily to a very marked decrease in the cost of locking frames, as manufacturing technology improved and demand and competition increased. The cost of signal box structures remained stable over this period, at around £125-£200 for a box of average size. But with World War I, inflation began and prices started to rise. In most cases the only cost figure available for signalling contracts is that for the whole work, but **Table 8** lists a sample of cases where a specific cost for the box structure is known. The largest known mechanical signalling contract was that for the MS&L's London Extension, which was won by the RSCo at £37,360: 75 boxes were included. However, contracts of £5,000 + were not uncommon, and as early as 1875 McK&H had received a contract worth £16,000 for the GN's Derbyshire lines.

TABLE 7

The Cost of Locking Frames (Price per lever)

1864	S&F tender to NE	£10
1867	S&F contract with LNW, 'special schedule'	£7
1871	S&F tender to Monmouthshire R&C Co.	£6 10s.
1872	R&R offer to GN	£7
1872	Easterbrook offer to GN	£6 12s.
1874	Rapier's estimate of average price	£8
1881	Easterbrook invoice to Furness	£5
1882	RSCo invoice to Furness	£3
1890	RSCo standard contract with GE	£2 18s.
1900	Raynar Wilson's estimate of average price	'£2 upwards'

TABLE 8

Cost of Signal Box Structures

The examples here are all boxes built by signalling contractors or building contractors. For comparison, some costs of railway company built boxes can be seen at *GWS, pages 137-141 and LNWRS, page 267.*

1867	S&F contract with LNW: Brick box 10ft. x 10ft. x 6ft.	£80
	Brick box 14ft. x 14ft. x 6ft.	£100
1867	GN, tender for 'signal hut' at Hatfield	£109 10s.
1867	GN, tender for 'signal hut' at Werrington	£77 17s.
1868	GN, tender for 'signal hut' at Midland Crossing, Newark **(see Plate 159)**	£95
1868	Midland, tender for stone 'signal hut' at Water Lane Junction, Leeds	£67
1870	Easterbrook advertisement: Box 10ft. x 10ft.	£70
	Box 14ft. x 12ft.	£95
1872	GE, estimated cost for new intermediate boxes between Ingatestone and Witham, each	£50
1874	GN, Brick box, 16ft. x 12ft. internal: S&F tender	£139 10s.
	Easterbrook tender	£140
	McK&H tender	£170
1882	RSCo account to Furness for timber cabin, Barrow Central No. 1, 18ft. x 12ft. x 8ft.	£149
1882	RSCo account to Furness for timber cabin, St. Lukes Junction, 20ft. x 12ft. x 8ft.	£170
1882	RSCo account to Furness for stone cabin, Ormsgill Junction, 21ft. x 12ft. 3in. x 8ft.	£172 2s. 3d.
1884	GN, tender for Stanley	£169
1885	GN, tender for Wrenthorpe South Junction, brick box	£275 8s. 9d.
1890	GE standard contracts: Brick box 20ft. x 13ft. x 12ft.	
	McK&H	£196 15s.
	Dutton	£178
	RSCo	£201
	S&F	£195 10s.
	EOD (1897)	£175
	Timber box 20ft. x 11ft. 6in. x 12ft.	
	McK&H	£130
	Dutton	£135
	RSCo	£126
	S&F	£134
	EOD (1897)	£139
1896/7	RSCo accounts for MS&L London Extension	
	Brick box 17ft. x 12ft. x 8ft.	£148 5s.
	Brick box 28ft. x 12ft. x 8ft.	£194 15s.
	Timber box 37ft. x 12ft. x 8ft.	£244 5s.
1901	S&F contract with LBSC, Brick box 20ft. x 12ft.	£142
	Timber box 26ft. x 12ft.	£160
1914	GN, tender for Nutbrook Junction	£340 6s. 5d.

Where competitive tenders were sought, the different contractors' quotations were, in later years, normally within a close range. But in earlier times, and when firms were new in the business, there could be considerable variations, for example:

December 1867, locking apparatus for Wortley Junction (GN)
Stevens £236
E. S. Yardley & Co. £535 4s.
Saxby & Farmer £267

1871, signal arrangements at Lea Bridge (GE)
Stevens £50
Saxby & Farmer £80
Easterbrook £108 16s.
McKenzie & Holland £135

Contractors were paid in arrears in stages, either monthly or after completion of a specified percentage of the work, and in both cases on receipt of the railway company's Engineer's certificate that the work had been done satisfactorily to date. Final payment was not made until the expiry of a 'maintenance period' (usually in the 3-12 months range) calculated from the date of opening, during which the contractor had to carry out any maintenance and repair at his own expense. Where the contractor had tendered on an 'all-in' basis, he would normally be held to the contract price, but where the railway company had drawn up the scheme, and the contractor had tendered on a 'bill of quantities' basis at a specified price for each item, the payment to the contractor might exceed the tender sum due to larger quantities being required than had originally been envisaged. It was also common for railway companies to decide on alterations or additions to the work during the course of the contract. Therefore, final payments above the tender sum are often recorded. For example, S&F were paid £2,131 for work at Sleaford in 1882 as against a tender of £1,947, and £2,499 for Lincoln in 1884 against a £2,112 tender.

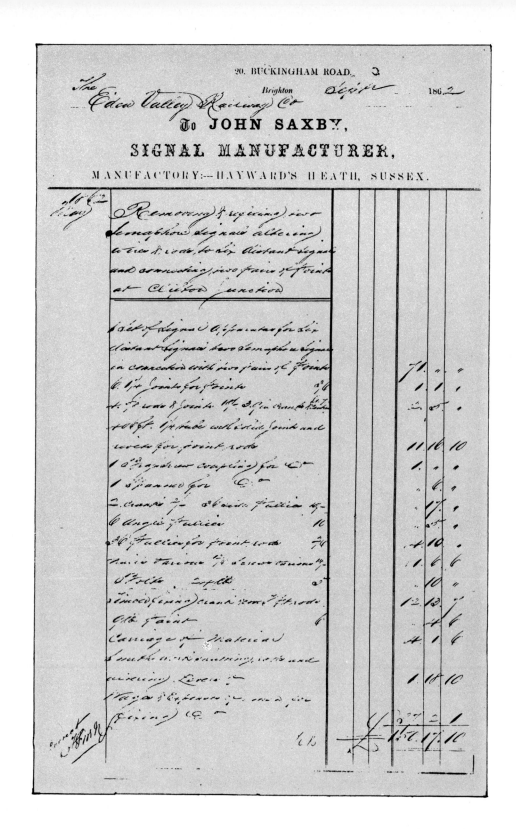

Plate 34 The invoice sent by Saxby from his home in Brighton to the Eden Valley Railway in September 1862 (prior to the move to Kilburn). The main heading (above the double lines) reads 'May 1862: Removing and refixing two semaphore signals altering wires and rods to six distant signals and connecting two pairs of points at Clifton Junction'. The first item on the bill, of £71, is for '1 set of signal apparatus for six distant signals two semaphore signals in connection with two pairs of points'. This apparatus was installed on an existing 'platform' or box. The junction was new at May 1862, and one suspects that the company had been told by the Inspecting Officer that the box was inadequate, and that interlocking apparatus must be installed. This junction was abandoned in the 1870s, and should not be confused with the 'Eden Valley Junction' to the north, where a box was built by Saxby in 1863.

Public Record Office

CHAPTER THREE

The Design and Construction of a Signal Box

This chapter refers primarily to the signal box of the 'classic' period, circa 1870 to circa 1930. The special features of 'modern architecture' boxes are discussed in **Chapter 7**.

The Signal Box as Architecture

Strictly speaking, the pre-grouping signal box was not 'architecture' at all, but rather an 'Engineer's vernacular' building. Architects were involved in only a few cases, notably when boxes were designed to match station buildings (**see Chapter 4**). In any case, the need for a large amount of continuous window space militated against any possibility of following contemporary architectural 'styles', which are distinguished to a large extent by variations in the treatment of individual window openings. However, the surface decorative features of signal boxes are, of course, in accord with contemporary tastes in domestic architecture.

Box structures were designed by Engineers working for the signalling contractor or in the railway company's Engineer's/Signal Engineer's Department, depending on the arrangements adopted. Some railway companies used a Consulting Engineer instead of employing a Staff Engineer, especially in the earlier period. The names of the individuals responsible for box designs are rarely known, as unlike new locomotive designs, nobody outside the Signal Department was likely to be interested in the introduction of a new signal box design. If at all, designs would be attributed to the Signal Engineer, but that does not necessarily mean that he did the design work himself. It was not generally necessary to design every signal box from scratch, as most companies had standard type drawings, and all that was then needed for an individual box was a specification of the dimensions, and drawings of the foundations and any other special features. In post-grouping days, mechanical boxes were in many cases still designed by the Signal Engineers, but the railway company architects began to assume an increasing role (**see Chapter 7**).

The 'classic' railway signal box was effectively a roofed and glazed elevated platform — a type of structure for which there was little demand in other fields. The most directly comparable buildings would be the few signal boxes built to control road traffic. There were tramway signal boxes at Old Haymarket Junction, Liverpool (installed by S&F), and at Colston, Bristol. There were also, in the late nineteenth century, one or two experimental mechanical signalling installations built to control general road traffic at busy junctions. The first 'colour-light' road signals, in Piccadilly, London, in 1926, were worked by levers (a nine-lever Westinghouse electric frame) by a policeman in a hut, but the perfection of automatic road traffic signals soon afterwards meant that the thousands of 'road' signal boxes, which rapidly increasing traffic would otherwise have required, never came into being! In other fields of transport too there were places functionally similar to the railway signal box — the control rooms of large canal locks, the control rooms of road swing-bridges or lift-bridges, and the airport control tower — but in most cases these were rooms in larger structures, bearing little external resemblance to the signal box. Sometimes, however, the equipment for bridges was supplied by the railway signalling contractors. The interlocking machinery supplied by S&F for Tower Bridge is still partially in situ. Also there were sometimes semaphore signals for shipping traffic, such as can still be seen at two bridges in the centre of Bristol.

One type of building that many signal boxes did resemble somewhat in external appearance (although not in function) was the horticultural greenhouse or 'glasshouse'. Although the large glazing area of signal boxes was not of course designed for the purpose of letting in the maximum amount of sunlight, there have always been plenty of signalmen willing to exploit the horticultural potential of their signal boxes, sometimes to the extent of blocking, with greenery, a good deal of the view for which the window space was originally provided!

Siting

The Board of Trade Requirements laid down conditions for the siting of boxes. Firstly, there was the question of the signalman's view. The Requirements stated (the exact words here are from the 1905 Edition):

'The signal box to be commodious . . . The point levers and signal levers to be so placed in the box that the signalman when working them shall have the best possible view of the railway, and the box itself to be so situated as to enable the signalman to see the arms and lights of signals and the working of the points'.

This imposed constraints on the siting of boxes wherever the line was not straight or the view was blocked by overbridges.

Secondly, there was the requirement that facing points could not be worked at more than a certain distance from a box. The permitted distance was increased in stages from 120yds. in 1874 to 350yds. in 1925 (with no limit from 1925 if the points were power-worked and full track circuiting was installed). In some cases, therefore, considerable thought had to be given to the track layout and the position of the box if a station was to be worked by one box only. Track alterations were sometimes made at the time of interlocking to facilitate this, and when station alterations were required in later years, the Signal Engineer would, on a well-organised railway, be consulted before plans were finalised. Nevertheless, when the 120yds. limit applied, two boxes were often necessary, even at quite small stations. Passing loops at stations on single lines were often more than 240yds. long. In many cases, the second box was abolished in later pre-grouping days after the limits had been raised, or on the installation of motor points.

Where the various constraints meant that boxes had to be built on difficult sites, one of the special forms of construction described in **Chapter 4** might be necessary.

Many signal boxes were built adjacent to level crossings, to enable the functions of signalman and crossing-keeper to be combined. However, the restrictions on the working of points meant that there were some stations where there was a level crossing but where the signal box could not be located at it. When the permitted distances were increased, the original box at such stations was sometimes replaced by a new one at the crossing — as at Magdalen Road (**Plate 86**) — or physically removed to a new location by the crossing, as was done at Gedney in 1926.

Equipment and Furniture

Although, as noted in the **Introduction**, this book is not intended to be a study of signalling equipment, it would be inappropriate to consider the dimensions and structural materials of the signal box without first noting its equipment and contents which, as in any other building, dictate the size and nature of the structure.

Mechanical signal boxes were generally of two storeys, the upper being known as the 'operating room' (or 'operating floor'), and the lower as the 'locking room'. The most important piece of equipment, occupying part of both storeys (**Plate 35**) was the locking frame, otherwise known as the lever frame (since, with most frame designs, only the levers were visible above operating floor level). At first, the frame was always placed in the front half of

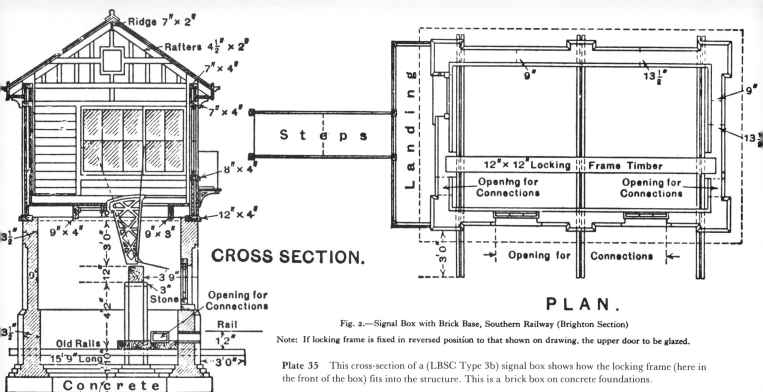

CROSS SECTION.

Ridge 7" × 2"
Rafters 4½" × 2"
7" × 4"
7" × 4"
8" × 4"
12" × 4"
9" × 4"
9" × 3"
3" 9"
3" 9"
Stone
3½"
9"
4½"
12"
Opening for Connections
Rail
1' 2"
Old Rails
15' 9" Long
3' 0"
Concrete
12"
3½"

Steps

Landing

PLAN.

9"
13½"
9"
13
12" × 12" Locking Frame Timber
Opening for Connections
Opening for Connections
3' 0"
Opening for Connections

Fig. 2.—Signal Box with Brick Base, Southern Railway (Brighton Section)

Note: If locking frame is fixed in reversed position to that shown on drawing, the upper door to be glazed.

Plate 35   This cross-section of a (LBSC Type 3b) signal box shows how the locking frame (here in the front of the box) fits into the structure. This is a brick box on concrete foundations.

Authors' Collection

Plate 36 A typical 19th century interior. This is Lydney Junction GW box, built by the Gloucester Wagon Co. in 1879 and photographed here when new. The photographer is standing by the operating room door. The instrument shelf is at the far end, and the train register desk is to the left of it. A notice board hangs above the open hearth. At the far end of the box front a gleam of light just shows through one of the 'upper lights', which are otherwise completely in shadow. Except for the plants, there are no comforts or clutter.

*Gloucester Railway Carriage &
Wagon Co. Ltd.*

the box, so that the signalman faced the track when operating the levers. The block instruments for signalling the trains from one box to the next were, at first, placed on a shelf at the end or rear of the operating room, as is still the practice in Ireland. But as traffic increased it became inconvenient to have the block instruments located separately and, during the 1880s, it became the practice instead to suspend the 'block shelf' from the roof timbers directly above the lever frame. Also suspended at this point was a diagram of the layout and signals worked by the box, in a glazed frame (some large boxes, worked by two men, had two diagrams). However, as layouts expanded, the number of block instruments needed increased and, with other types of instrument (signal and lamp repeaters, etc.) also appearing on the scene, the block shelf became more and more of an obstruction to the signalman's view. To remove this obstruction, whilst still retaining the block instruments within easy reach, many companies began, from around 1910, to place the frame and the block shelf in the rear of the box instead. Although the signalman was then facing away from the line when operating the levers and instruments, he could obtain a completely free view from the front of the box by turning around. By the 1930s, rear frames had become the norm for new boxes (except on the GW, which did not adopt the practice until circa 1955), and many old boxes have also been given a new frame in the rear.

Plate 37 This early 1970s view of Haven House (GN) shows the present-day appearance of the less-altered pre-grouping boxes. This box was built in 1899 but the frame, an S&F 'Rocker', was second-hand when installed here. As in many boxes nowadays, most of the levers are disused due to the removal of sidings, etc., and have been painted white accordingly. The block shelf and diagram are above the frame. In the foreground is the gate wheel. Note the second-hand domestic chairs and tables.

Authors' Collection

Locking frames were made up complete in the manufacturer's works, and tested before being part-dismantled for transport to the site. Sometimes, the frame was installed before the upper part of the box structure was built. Some frames were supported on independent timber, iron, or steel uprights fixed in the box foundations, and others were supported by beams fixed in the end walls of the box. The actual locking mechanism was in most cases below operating floor level (hence the term 'locking room'), but on some types of frame the locking was above operating floor level. The most notable examples in the latter category were the 1870s S&F 'rocker and gridiron' frame, the Ransomes & Rapier frame, and the Midland, LMS, and BR (LMR) standard frames. In these cases, the term 'locking room' for the lower storey is a misnomer, but it is convenient to use it all the same, as there is no visible external difference in the structure.

The other major items of equipment in the operating room were the gate wheel (only provided in some boxes working a level crossing) and the staff, token, or tablet instruments (only in boxes working a single line). The other furnishings required for signalling purposes were a desk for the train register, a clock, and a notice board. For the signalman's comfort there was usually a stove or hearth, a table and chair, and lockers for personal property. As time went by, telephones and other impedimenta appeared. In pre-grouping days boxes had what seems to modern eyes a somewhat spartan appearance, although it would not have seemed so to men who had started work in pre-interlocking days! In recent decades

Plate 38 The interior of a modern mechanical box, with a rear frame. This is the 1955-built BR (LMR) box at Long Meg Sidings on the Settle to Carlisle line. Modern boxes usually have a block shelf running the full length of the frame, due to the large number of instruments and indicators provided. The block instruments here are not modern ones but are old LNW instruments. The locking frame is to the LMR standard pattern, the final development of the Midland-style frame, with above-floor locking.

R. D. Foster

lino and cast-off carpets have replaced the bare boards, cookers and sinks have been fitted, and comfortable (if neither new nor elegant) armchairs, thrown out of the signalmen's homes, have been introduced by unofficial initiative. The operating floor of boxes was, and in many areas still is, kept by the signalmen in pristine domestic condition.

The locking room was the province of the Signal Department rather than the Operating Department. In addition to the locking apparatus itself, much of the space in the locking room was occupied by the lever tails at the bottom of the frame, and the rods and wires leading from them down to ground level cranks and wheels (**Plate 39**). The locking room was also the home of battery cupboards and other electrical equipment, and of any equipment which the signal and telegraph fitters wished to keep protected from the elements. In some cases this led to one end of the locking room becoming something of a junk heap.

Dimensions

The dimensions of signal boxes are conventionally given as length (external) by width (external) by height (from rail level to operating floor level), but some official records gave internal length and width measurements.

Length was determined primarily by the length of the lever frame. The number of levers provided to signal a given layout varied between one company and another. Some companies, for example, were very generous in the provision of shunting signals, and others very sparing. Frame designs also varied in the spacing between one lever and the next ('lever centres'): 4in. to 6in. was the normal range for mechanical frames. The choice of frame type could therefore have a considerable impact on box length. A space of 3ft. to 5ft. was normally left between the ends of the frame and the end walls of the box, to give the signalman easy access to the front windows, and some very large boxes had a gap in the centre of the frame for the same purpose. A percentage of spare levers, or 'spaces' for extra levers, was usually provided when a box was built, to enable minor signalling alterations to be effected subsequently without the expense of major extensions of the frame or the box. Where larger alterations were needed subsequently, it might be possible to extend the frame by cramming in extra levers up to the end walls, by converting levers to 'push-pull' operation (i.e. the same lever performing two separate functions), or by fitting a new frame with more levers but at smaller 'lever centres'. However, a very large number of boxes had to be extended in length, some on more than one occasion, in order to accommodate a larger frame needed for expansion of the layout. In many other cases boxes had to be replaced entirely on expansion of the layout, due to the original box being in the way of track alterations.

Where a gate wheel was provided as an original feature, an extra 3ft. or so of length would be required.

Some companies built all boxes to a small number of standard lengths, with component parts of standard sizes. The Midland, LNW, and L&Y were prime examples of this. Others simply built each box to the exact length demanded by the immediate requirements.

Over half the boxes existing at the 1923 Grouping were in the 15ft. to 25ft. range in length, although, as noted in **Chapter 1**, average length had tended to increase over the years. There were very few boxes more than 80ft. long. The very largest boxes were built in the 1890s and 1900s, when layouts were reaching their maximum complexity, but power frames were not yet in widespread use. The largest mechanical frame ever built was that of 295 levers for the NE's York Locomotive Yard box of 1909. The longest box now in use is the LNW's Shrewsbury Severn Bridge Junction of 1903, which is 96ft. 6in. long and has a 180-lever frame at 5½in. centres. The GW's Newton Abbot East box of 1926 has a larger number of levers (206), but, with the levers at 4in. centres, this box is only 79ft. 8in. long. Many early boxes were less than 15ft. long, but the most frequent cause of very small boxes being built in later years was the installation of extra 'break-

Plate 39 (left) A locking room interior. This is the GC box at Dinting, fitted with a GC-pattern frame made by the RSCo. The lever frame is supported on a horizontal steel girder (with the lever numbers painted on it) which is itself supported at its ends on posts adjacent to the box end walls. At 10-lever intervals are the main support frames for the cover plates (quadrants) which cover the spaces between the levers upstairs. The levers themselves (the below-floor portions of which can be seen at the top of the photograph) are pivoted independently on pedestals bolted to the top of the girder. On the right-hand side of the main support frames are bolted the large brackets supporting the locking trays, which on this type of frame are placed horizontally immediately below the operating floor (the most common arrangement, although many other arrangements are found). The floorboards above the locking trays can be removed when access to the locking is required. Mounted below the girder are a large number of electric switch boxes/circuit controllers, operated by rods attached to the right-hand ends of the lever tails. These would have been installed in connection with the modernisation of the signalling for electrification in the early 1950s. They confuse the view somewhat and should be disregarded when attempting to appreciate the basic functions. The operating rods and wires to work the points and signals are attached to the left-hand ends of the lever tails (by the box wall). The upper sections of the rods and wires are invisible here, as the girder and switch boxes obscure them, but the lower sections of several point rods can be seen in the foreground at the bottom, and several signal chains can be seen at the bottom centre. Chains are used instead of wire for any part of a signal run in which a change of direction via a wheel is required, as wire would wear on the wheel. At the bottom centre, also, several cranks and wheels can be seen; these convert the vertical motion created by pulling the levers into the horizontal motion required for moving the rods and wires running between the box and the points and signals. The rods and wires leave the box through a 'lead-off' space at ground level (normally in the centre of the front of the box — (**Plates 148, 182, 202, 248 & 268**). Where the object worked by a lever is a heavy pull (e.g. a distant signal a long way off), a balance weight is attached to the right-hand end of the lever tail to assist the signalman. A couple of these can be seen on the right, the nearest marked 'LNE 40' meaning that it is of 40lbs. weight. The pole supporting the operating floor beam at the right is probably not an original feature; in most boxes (except very long ones) the operating floor joists are supported on a single beam running between the box end walls without intermediate supports.

R. D. Foster

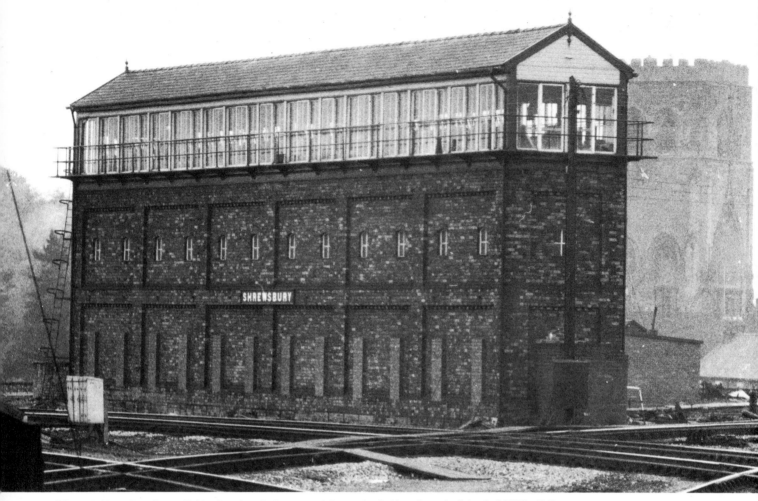

Plate 40 Shrewsbury Severn Bridge Junction, the largest surviving mechanical box. It was built by the LNW in 1903.

R. D. Foster

Plate 41 A small 'break-section' box. There were six such boxes on the LT&S line in the empty countryside between Upminster and Pitsea, built at various dates between 1905 and 1925. Warley was a Midland box of the minimum size that could be built from Midland standard parts, 10ft. by 10ft. It lasted until the 1961 resignalling. Most 'break-section' boxes had been abolished by the early 1960s; one which is still open is Weeton (L&Y) between Kirkham and Poulton.

C. H. Betts

section' boxes to split long block sections between stations. These dated mainly from the period 1895-1920, as traffic levels had not required such facilities previously. They normally controlled only one distant and one home signal for each direction, and so were rarely more than a minimal 8ft. to 12ft. or so in length. From around 1907, Intermediate Block Signals, relying on track circuits, were often installed instead of a break-section box.

Width varied comparatively little. Most companies had their own standard operating floor internal width, generally in the 10ft. to 12ft. range. The external width of a timber box would be some 12in. to 16in. greater than the internal width, whilst that of brick box would be some 18in. to 23in. greater. The internal width was dictated largely by the signalman's need to be able to operate the levers without coming into contact with any of the furnishings placed by the rear wall, or with the stove! The travel of the levers, and the distance that the frame had to be set back from the front wall in order to accommodate the locking mechanism, varied between one frame design and another. Very large boxes, with two or three men on duty at the same time and a larger amount of equipment, were often made a little wider than normal. In contrast, a lesser width than the standard might be enforced by site conditions (the presence of other buildings behind the box, or

the need to fit the box between two tracks). Beyond a certain point an oversailing operating floor would be necessary (**see Chapter 4**).

It was noted in **Chapter 1** that boxes of the 1850s and 1860s with signals above the roof had necessarily been some 14ft. to 15ft. wide, to keep the signal arms clear of each other. Some other early boxes were also built unusually wide by later standards, in many cases being built to a square plan, with the width dictated by the required length. There were good examples of this on the NE (Northern Division) and the LNW/GW Joint lines. Of the latter, Woofferton Junction is no less than 16ft. 8in. wide (*see LNWRS, Chapter 17*). The reasons for this practice are not fully understood: it may have been a residue from the days of signals above the roof.

Another special case was the small number of boxes built with two frames in parallel, and usually 20ft. to 25ft. wide. Most of these were at large termini where there would not have been room for a box of double the length, and others were built to control two separate sets of lines some distance apart on either side of the box. Some were made up of two standard box structures joined together with a double roof (for example, the LNW'S Euston No. 2 and the Midland's St. Pancras Passenger) — others had a single roof.

Height was very variable due to the need to provide a good view. The signalman had to be able to see all the signals under his control — unless an electrical 'repeater' was provided in the box to show the signal aspect — and any train standing at his signals. He also had to have a full view of any shunting operations, and of the tail lamps of all passing trains (even when other trains were standing or passing between the box and the train concerned) in order to check that trains had arrived complete, and had not become divided in section. These requirements meant that some boxes, notably those near to overbridges, had to be built to a height of 20ft. or more. The maximum height was around 30ft. No box was ever built taller than was absolutely necessary as, apart from the extra building costs, tall boxes were inconvenient and potentially dangerous in that the signalman could not communicate easily with trainmen, and could not see the tail lamps of passing trains in fog. An alternative approach, where bridges were a problem, was to set the box low so that the signalman could see under the bridge.

When track circuiting was introduced, the need to see by eye any train standing at a signal was reduced, and so from the 1910s there was no longer a need for very tall boxes because of overbridges, and siting became generally easier. However, taller than average boxes might still be required for one reason or another. In 1925, the wording of the Ministry of Transport Requirements was changed to 'the box to be so situated, elevated and constructed as to enable the signalman to get the best possible view of all the operations for which he is responsible'.

Plates 42a & 42b A 'double-framed' box. Tilbury South Junction was built in this way because the lines forked immediately to the north of the station platforms, passing on both sides of the box. Although the extra width of the box is quite evident, it was in fact (at around 16ft.) quite narrow for a 'double-framed' box. This box was built by the RSCo and opened at 07.00 on Sunday 29th July 1906. The frames were of 72 levers each. The photographs were taken in 1961 shortly before the box was abolished.

British Rail, Eastern Region

Plate 43 The Caledonian box at Straw-frank Junction (Carstairs) provides an example of a box built very tall to give the signalman a view over an adjacent bridge (from which this photograph was taken). This box dated from the opening of the new curve in October 1872. It is seen here surrounded by the paraphernalia of track realignment and resignalling, which was to lead to its abolition on 6th August 1972.

F. Alexander

Where the site did not cause special problems, most companies preferred a height of around 8ft. This was sufficient to see fully over a train on the adjacent track, but low enough to communicate easily with 'trainmen. Some types of locking frame required a height of up to 8ft. below the operating floor to accommodate the apparatus, but this was rarely a determining factor in the height of a box.

At small stations on secondary lines, where there were few trains to deal with and few buildings to block the view, it was common to find the signalbox on the station platform, with the operating floor at, or just above, platform level. Such boxes were not usually built on the platform itself. Rather, the platform was excavated away and the box built in the normal way, and the platform then restored with planks or flags in front of the box, over the rodding and wires.

Some boxes at intermediate level crossings and other less important locations were built at ground level. In any low box it might be necessary to locate the locking mechanism in a pit below ground level, unless the frame was one of those designs which had above-floor locking.

Not all boxes were constructed to a square or rectangular plan. Sometimes a between-tracks site, or a wall or building behind the box, necessitated a box of tapering width, as at Thornton Heath (LBSC), Rhondda Fach Junction North (TV), and Low Moor No. 2 West (L&Y). In other instances boxes were given 'splay corners' instead of 90 degree corners, as an architectural feature (**Plate 319**). In a further architectural variation, some Furness boxes had bases that tapered with height.

Plate 44 The low 'platform box' at Holmwood (LBSC). This S&F box was built in 1877.

R. Newman

Materials

Signal boxes were normally built of brick, or of timber, or of a combination of the two. In a few parts of the country stone was used as an alternative to brick. The choice of material was the railway company's, except in some cases when contractors' box designs were used. Different Signal Engineers and railway companies had different but usually fairly definite views on which form of construction was best.

In more detail, the forms of construction found were:

(1) Timber.
(2) Brick to Floor (BTF): that is, brick up to operating floor level, timber above. Some BTF boxes had the rear wall built wholly of brick.
(3) Brick: that is, brick up to the cills of the operating floor windows, but with timber mullions between the windows and timber above the windows. The rear wall was normally built wholly of brick.
(4) Brick-to-Roof: that is, with brick mullions between the operating floor windows and brick above the windows.
(5) Stone to Floor (STF): as with BTF.
(6) Stone: as with Brick.
(7) Stone-to-Roof: as with Brick-to-Roof.
(8) Concrete Blocks.

The terms BTF/Brick-to-Roof/STF/Stone-to-Roof are our own. Contemporary documents use only the terms, 'Brick', 'Stone', and 'Composite' for Classes 2-7 above, which are insufficiently descriptive for reference purposes.

Boxes of any material might have a full-height brick chimney.

Timber boxes were either supported on lengthy timber piles (**Plates 87 & 138**), or built on concrete foundations (**Plate 52**). The latter method provided greater resistance to timber rot, and also enabled, if desired, the provision of a few courses of brickwork at the base, as a further protection against rot. Many timber boxes not so built originally had to be 'bricked-up' in later years, in some cases right up to operating floor level. This should not be confused wth 'ARP' bricking-up (see **Chapter 7**).

It was noted in **Chapter 1** that most early boxes were of timber construction. Subsequently, timber had necessarily to be adopted where boxes were built on unstable ground — on an embankment or cutting side subject to slips, in a colliery subsidence area, or on any newly-made or boggy ground — and was the obvious choice for temporary boxes. Otherwise, the choice between timber and brick was finely balanced. Brick offered the prospect of less maintenance in the long term. Although some timber boxes have lasted over 100 years, many more have needed replacement because of structural decay. Timber offered greater scope for prefabrication of standard component parts. Some companies — notably the NE, LNW, LSW and NB — used brick or BTF construction in all cases other than those where the site prevented it. On the other side, companies such as the Midland and GSW used timber in virtually all cases. It was really a matter of personal preference. Some considered it was cheaper to use timber and, where most boxes were built of timber, with prefabricated parts, this might well be the case, but where only a few boxes were built of timber they could be more expensive than the brick boxes.

Stone was only used in those areas where it was locally available, and even in those areas was less common than brick. The largest numbers of stone-built boxes were to be found in the West Country (LSW and GW), Wales (notably on the Rhymney), Cumbria and the Borders (NE, NB, Furness and other Cumbrian companies), and parts of Scotland (primarily the GNoS). The L&Y had a few stone-built boxes in the West Riding, but stone was not used for boxes in the limestone belt. Stonework on signal boxes, as on other vernacular buildings, was usually roughwork rather than ashlar.

As a rough estimate, the construction of the boxes existing at the 1923 Grouping was:

Timber 45%
BTF 13%
Brick 36%
Brick-to-Roof 3%
Stone/STF/Stone-to-Roof 3%

Only a handful of boxes were built of concrete blocks in pre-grouping days. The GE experimented with concrete blocks in 1910, and built one or two boxes of this material, but did not adopt the idea on a large scale. Development of concrete generally was encouraged by the timber shortage during World War I. William Marriott of the M&GN was a leading exponent of concrete, producing concrete signal posts from 1916, and also concrete blocks for general building purposes. These were used for a number of M&GN boxes and crossing huts in the 1920s and 1930s. In August 1923, the GW also decided to experiment, and had a new box at Waltham Siding built with a steel frame and with concrete blocks as walling material. The cost was estimated at £650, against £870 for a brick box. The experiment was judged successful and, between 1927 and 1933, the GW built another 20 boxes in this way. However, after that, the use of concrete blocks was abandoned.

Brickwork

The arrangement of the bricks in a wall is known as the 'bond'. The two most common bonds on signal boxes (as on other vernacular buildings) were 'English Bond', with alternate courses of 'headers' (bricks set endways) and 'stretchers' (bricks set lengthways), and 'Flemish Bond', with alternate headers and stretchers in every course. Also common on signal boxes was 'English Garden Wall Bond', with three, four or five courses of stretchers between each course of headers (found particularly on the NE and the L&Y). Beyond these, a large number of other bonds are possible but rarely used. A peculiarity of the LNW was three courses of stretchers followed by one course of alternate headers and stretchers.

Until the recent introduction of a metric brick, all modern bricks measured approximately 9in. by 4½in. by 3in. The majority of pre-grouping boxes were built with walls 9in. (one brick) thick, but 13½in. (alias 14in.) walls were favoured by some companies (e.g. the GE, NCC, and Dutton). Some other companies, such as the GW, used 13½in. brickwork for large boxes only. Walls of 9in. and 13½in. are not externally distinguishable, and both English and Flemish Bond can be used for either. Many boxes otherwise of 9in. brickwork were built with a 13½in. 'plinth' for the first few courses from ground level, for extra strength. The plinth is topped by a course of splayed bricks known as 'plinth headers' or 'plinth stretchers'. Large boxes with mainly 9in. brickwork were sometimes further strengthened by the provision of pillars of 13½in. brickwork right up to operating floor level, giving the 9in. sections the appearance of a recessed panel (**Plate 40**). This is referred to in this book as 'panelled brickwork'.

Most boxes were built simply of the local brick, which varies in colour between one part of the country and another, but a few boxes were distinguished by the use of bricks of a different colour on parts of the structure for decorative effect. For example, the 1896 GW boxes at Reading had a few courses of yellow brick offsetting the general red brick (*GWA, Plate 524*), and GW Type 7 boxes had 'Staffordshire Blues' in the plinth, quoins, and door and window surrounds. These were hard engineering bricks chosen primarily for their extra strength, but they also gave a pleasing colour variation. A further distinction found on a few boxes was the use of 'bull-nose' (rounded) bricks for the quoins.

MATERIALS

Plate 45 Timber: Pontrilas.

J. P. Morris

Plate 46 (above) BTF (with brick chimney): Charing.

P. Kay

Plate 47 (above) Brick: Brent Knoll.

P. V. Starling

Plate 48 (right) Brick-to-roof: Kincardine Junction.

F. Alexander

Plate 49 Stone-to-roof: Weston-super-Mare.

P. V. Starling

Plate 50 Concrete Blocks: M&GN Crossing-keeper's hut at South Drove.

The Late E. L. Back,
copyright M. Back

Plate 51 The most common bonds.

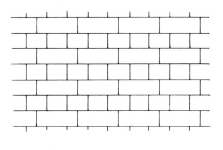

(i) English Bond.

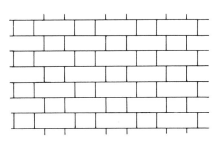

(ii) Flemish Bond.

(iii) English Garden Wall Bond.

(iv) Stretcher Bond.

On many old boxes, sections of the brickwork have had to be replaced, due to decay or accidents.

From the 1930s, many boxes were built with 'cavity walls' — either 4½in./cavity/4½in. or 4½in./cavity/9in. (the latter providing extra strength in the internal wall, to facilitate the hanging of heavy equipment inside the box). This requires 'Stretcher Bond' in the outer leaf of the wall (all stretchers in every course), which gives a rather lifeless appearance by comparison with the traditional bonds.

Timberwork

Plate 52 shows well the construction of a timber box, which is in essence the same as that of all English vernacular timber building. The basic members were the vertical corner posts and the broad horizontal beams at operating floor level. The corner posts were normally continuous from ground to eaves, and between 6in. and 12in. square in cross-section. Some were of the same cross-section all the way up, some tapered towards the top, and some reduced in size in steps. Between the corner posts, intermediate structural vertical posts of similar, or slightly lesser, dimensions were placed at intervals of about 5ft. to 8ft. and, between these, further minor verticals about 3in. square were placed at intervals of about 12in. to 24in., to assist in the fastening of the boarding.

The woods most commonly used for signal box construction were oak, deal, and pine. The upper part of a BTF or STF box was built in the same way as a timber box.

As was generally the case with nineteenth century transport and industrial buildings of timber construction, the weather protection of signal boxes was provided by timber boarding, instead of the 'wattle and daub' or brick infilling which had been used on most earlier domestic buildings. In most cases, the boarding was fastened to the outside of the framing, but some early boxes (**Plates 145, 232 & 253**) had it fastened on the inside of the framing. The latter practice, also found on many contemporary wagons, was found to cause maintenance problems, as the main structural members were fully exposed to the rain and therefore subject to rot. As a result, most of the boxes concerned were reboarded with outside boarding long before the Grouping.

51

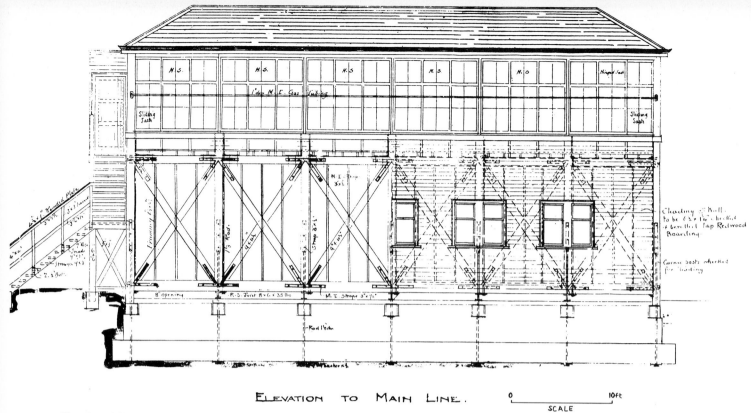

ELEVATION TO MAIN LINE.

SCALE 0 ___ 10ft

Plate 52 Official drawing of Thornton Junction box, North British Railway, showing the basic construction of a timber box.

Scottish Record Office

Plate 53 The various types of horizontal boarding (view from side).

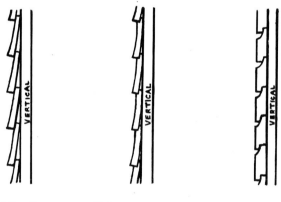

53(a) Simple weatherboarding.

53(b) Weatherboarding with rebate.

53(c) Lapped boarding.

Plate 54 Detail of weatherboarding at Whyteleafe South (SE), showing also walkway support bracket and underneath of walkway plank.

P. Kay

Many different types of boarding are found, with an almost infinite variety at the detailed level. Moreover, none of the terms used to describe the different types enjoy general acceptance. The primary types, and the terms used for them in this book, are:

Weatherboarding (alias 'clapboarding', or 'louvred boarding'). This was the most common type of boarding on industrial timber buildings generally, but on signal boxes, where a more 'finished' appearance was often sought, it was perhaps less common than lapped boarding. Weatherboarding is set horizontally, and the essential feature is that the boards are set at an angle to the side of the building in order to overlap each other. **Plate 53(a)** shows the simplest method of arranging this, but more often a rebate (a continuous notch) was used — **Plate 53(b)**. These variants are not externally distinguishable. Weatherboarding generally has an irregular appearance and looks best on a box of 'picturesque' design. The best comparison between weatherboarding and lapped boarding can be seen in the case of the early and late Midland boxes. The term 'weatherboarding' is sometimes used to describe all forms of timber boarding, but is not so used in this book.

Lapped Boarding (alias 'shiplap boarding', 'rustic boarding', or 'rusticated boarding'). This is also set horizontally, but the boards are set flush to the side of the building. The overlapping of the boards is obtained by cutting a rebate (usually curved or angled, so that the rain runs off) in the top of each board, and another rebate (usually right-angled) in the bottom of each board — **Plate 53(c)**. This creates an external appearance of strongly-defined horizontal grooves between one board and the next. In both weatherboarding and lapped boarding, the actual ('nominal') width of the boards is greater than the visible ('cover') width.

52

Vertical Boarding (alias 'matchboarding'). This is normally tongue(d) and groove(d), with the join between adjacent boards made by cutting a 'groove' into which is fitted the 'tongue' of the next board. The basic form — **Plate 56(a)** — is often improved upon by the addition of a v-joint — **Plate 56 (b)** — or beading at the exterior join. The v-joint or beading is not usually very large, and after a few coats of paint the different types are only distinguishable at close quarters. **Butt-edged Boarding**, with the vertical boards simply placed adjacent (without any tongue and groove), is also found.

Battened Boarding (alias 'board and batten'). This is vertical boarding given further weather protection by the addition of a batten (a thin narrow strip of wood) covering the joins between the boards — **Plate 56(c)**. It was not very common on signal boxes, but was favoured by the MS&L and the Highland (**Plates 175, 176 & 296-8**).

Boarding is very subject to decay, and the boarding seen today on the older surviving boxes is unlikely to be the original. In most cases, reboarding was carried out in the original style, but this was not always so, and one cannot always be sure what type of boarding a box originally had.

Internal lining (normally of closely-spaced vertical boards) was also provided in the upper (operating floor) storey of most signal boxes, to reduce draughts and heat loss; but many early boxes had only the one layer of boarding (either internal or external).

The descriptions of the various features of a signal box which follow are intended to highlight those aspects of the building that are particularly affected by the signalling function, rather than to repeat information on architecture and building techniques that can be found in any architectural dictionary. When it comes down to the details of building technique, a signal box is of course no different from any other building. **Table 9** will give the reader an idea of the labourer's and craftsman's view of signal box construction.

Plate 55   Detail of lapped boarding at Harlington (Mid).

P. Kay

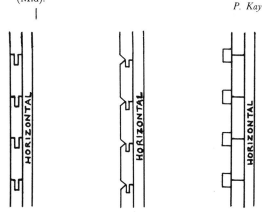

56(a) Basic tongue and groove boarding.

56(b) Tongue and groove boarding with v-joint.

56(c) Battened boarding.

Plate 56   The various types of vertical boarding (view from above).

Plate 57   Detail of battened boarding on an MS&L box.

R. Newman

TABLE 9

Specification for Signal Box Structures from GE Standard Contracts of 1890

Particulars of Signal Boxes

The general designs for Signal Boxes are shewn on Drawings Nos. 3159, 3165, 3166, 3274 and 3763, and the Contractor will be required to carry out each particular signal box in accordance with these general designs, and to the heights dimensions and description as marked on the Working Plans Nos. . . . .

Excavator & Bricklayer

The necessary excavations to be made for the foundations, areas, drains, and cesspools, to the several dimensions given on drawings, or as may be directed, to include all plumbing, strutting &c, and clearing away all surplus earth, beyond that required for filling in round walls, which said filling is to be thrown in and well rammed as the brickwork rises. No foundations shall be laid in, until the excavations shall have been inspected, and approved, by the Engineer or his representative. The Contractor will be held responsible for all settlements, fractures or other defects in the superstructure.

Throw in Concrete foundations to the several sizes given on drawings — those to brick boxes to be in blue lias lime and to timber boxes in Portland Cement; where the foundations to timber boxes are taken to a lower depth than shewn on drawing such extra depth is to be in blue lias lime concrete and of the width shewn on drawing in broken lines. Build in all bolts, washers &c.

Floors of brick boxes to be formed with a 6 inch layer of Cement Concrete, face of floor in these and timber boxes to be finished with ¾ inch of Portland Cement and sharp sand mixed in equal proportions and floated to a fine face.

The whole of the brickwork is to be laid with close points in old English bond; every course to be laid fair, well flushed with mortar, pointed flat joint on the outside, and interior of upper portions of boxes. Inside walls of lower portion to have the joints struck.

Lay in all walls under window cills, and over arches to lower windows two strands of hoop iron bond No. 16 gauge — 1½ inches wide — well tarred and sanded, and lapped at joints and angles — where this bond occurs the brickwork for three courses in height to be laid in cement, the joints being afterwards raked out and pointed in mortar.

All chimney shafts from top to one foot below eaves to be built in cement mortar, the joints afterwards being raked out and pointed flat joint in mortar.

In brick boxes the hearths are to be carried on ½ brick trimmer arches, flushed up solid with concrete and finished with inch cement face.

Arches to window and door openings to be in picked building bricks, fair axed and pointed.

The opening of point rods in brick boxes to be carried on old rails provided by Railway Company, and in timber boxes by fir cills as shewn these rails and cills to be temporarily supported until rods are in position and then to have permanent ½ brick in cement supports.

Build in all door and window frames, and point same with hair mortar. Parget and core flues. Build in all pipe flues, and neatly cut and point brickwork round same.

Build in all bolts, gratings, stoneware flues, ends of timbers and stone cills and point where necessary.

Lay in all walls at the levels shewn double course of Slates as damp course — all to break joint and bedded and floated in cement.

All internal brickwork, wood framing, and boarding to the lower portion of Signal Boxes to receive two coats of limewhite.

Splay course to plinths and internal window cills to be blue Staffordshire splay bricks set in cement. Bed and point ridging in cement.

Provide and build in to brick boxes 4 inch glazed Stoneware air flue in position shewn with 9" x 6" cast iron air grating at each end built in and pointed.

Build at foot of each rain water pipe on platforms half brick cesspool 9" x 9" x 9" internal size laid and rendered in cement and lead water from same through platform wall by 4 inch glazed stoneware drain pipe.

Mason

Provide and bed hard York Stone Steps to door openings of the scantlings and lengths given on drawing tooled and back-pointed with mortices for dowels of door frames. Provide 18" x 3" York cover stone over rails bridging opening for point rods well bedded in mortar. Provide tooled York templates under ends of rails.

Slabs for Stoves to Timber boxes to be York Stone 2½ inches thick rubbed on face and edges with quadrant corners.

Steps to areas to be 3 inches thick, tooled top and edges, and pinned into walls at end.

Provide 2 inch York Covers for Cesspools for rain water pipes on platforms with perforation for pipe in same.

Slater and Slate Mason

Roofs to be covered with Bangor Countess Slates, laid to a 3 inch lap and each slate secured with No. 2 compo nails put double courses to eaves. Between slates and boarding lay best asphalted roofing felt well lapped at joints.

Provide ¾ inch planed (one side and edges) slate slabs at back of stove and fix to woodwork with countersunk brass screws.

Carpenter & Joiner

Floors to be formed with timbers of the scantlings shewn on drawings well and securely framed together and secured with bolts and straps where necessary.

Long joists to be strutted with herringbone struts.

Trim for lever frame as shown — Trimming joists being supported (where ordered) from below by 7" x 3½" fir uprights fixed to fir cill to be provided and fixed at ground level. The uprights and cill will be paid for as an extra.

Cover with iron tongued battens and finish round walls with deal skirting for which in the case of brick boxes the walls must be plugged.

Construct roofs with timbers of the scantlings shewn and cover with inch rough boarding laid diagonally with close joints. Put tilter to eaves and form gutters at back of chimney shafts.

Finish gables with wrought deal beaded barge board with bed moulding under verge of slates.

Eaves to have wrought deal beaded facia and soffit with small deal bed moulding under gutter.

Framing to sides and ends to be of timbers of the several scantlings given on drawings, well and securely framed together, cills to be held down as shewn with iron bolts and running timbers secured at angles with wrought iron angle brackets bolted to timbers. All timbers exposed to view on outside, and on inside of upper portion of boxes to be wrought. Outside face of framing to be covered with wrot one side weather boarding of the thicknesses given. Interior and ceilings to be lined with ¾" wrought O.S. matched and beaded battens.

Provide and fix deal ovolo sashes in the positions shewn, those fixed to have wrought iron water bars for which form groove in sashes and cills. Provide all necessary deal beads and stops for above. Sliding sashes to have wrought iron check plates, cast iron rollers, with steel pins fixed at ends as shown on detail drawing with wrought iron running bar grooved into oak cill. Sashes to lower portion of brick boxes to be in fir solid rebated and beaded segment headed frames. Those to timber boxes to be secured with deal beads. Door frames to be solid fir rebated and beaded to brick boxes — those to timber boxes to be deal rebated and beaded linings.

Staircases and gallery to be framed together as shown, strings held together by bolts and treads to be secured at ends to fir cleats spiked to strings. Provide and fix with screws to each tread cast iron chequered nosing plate 24" long. Cill to be bolted down to concrete.

Gallery to be carried on Cast iron brackets details of which are given in Drawing No. 3166, and to be secured to framing by ¾ inch wrot iron screw bolts nuts and washers complete, gallery to be laid with 2 inch rough planking open joint with arris off edges. Gangway plank to timber boxes to be fixed with screws and bolts to wrought iron brackets and in the case of brick boxes to be spiked to fit wrought shaped bearers as shewn.

Bridging over opening for point rods in platform boxes to be covered with 3 inch rough planking laid close, and carried on old rails which will be provided by Railway Company.

The Contractor must find all labour etc, for fixing same including drilling holes for tie rods. Provide oak coping as shewn and bolt same to planking-heads of bolts on top side to be countersunk and covered. Each door to be hung with 1½ pairs of 3 inch wrought iron butts and secured with 7 inch strong iron japanned rim lock, with extra stout brass furniture — each lock to have two keys — doors in lower portion of boxes to have 7'' rim dead lock. Provide iron centres and plates for louvres in gable ventilators, these to have patent lines as described on Drawings and japanned iron cleats screwed to cill.

Flaps to lockers and desks to be hung with wrot iron butts and to be secured with iron box and desk locks respectively.

Provide 19 inch stove for Block Station huts, 24 inch stove for small signal boxes — and 30 inch stove for large boxes and fix with the necessary wrought iron pipe flues, collars caps etc: complete. To be approved by the Engineer and of the net p.c. value of 30/- 35/- and 40/- each respectively. Especial care must be taken in fixing these flue pipes in strict accordance with detail drawing. Air pipes to timber boxes to have perforated iron cap at lower end — and regulating valve inside box.

Provide and fix cast iron ogee guttering with all necessary outlets and stopped ends — also rain water pipes with swanneck bends, shoes &c complete.

Provide and fix to front of each box an enamelled iron name plate in 4 inch white block letters on blue ground, this plate is not to be framed,

and before manufacture, Contractor must make application in writing to the Engineer as to the exact name for each box. All doors to have blue enamel slips 15 ins. by 3½ ins. with the word ''Private'' in 1½ inch white letters on same.

All plates to be of approved manufacture, and to be fixed with brass screws.

Provide and fix wrought iron guard bars to sashes in the positions shown.

Provide all ironwork specified in other trades.

Plumber
Provide and lay 5lbs milled lead gutters, flashing etc, to chimney — raking out mortar joints where necessary, wedging with oak wedges and pointing in cement.

Painter and Glazier
All wrought woodwork to be knotted, stopped primed & painted 3 coats of the best oil colour (4 coat work) finishing coat to be in approved party tints. All ironwork to receive 4 coats of best oil colour, all rust being carefully cleaned off before painting. Eaves gutters to be painted inside and out.

Internal brickwork in upper part of boxes to have 4 coats of oil paint, with dado finished in dark tint as approved.

Sashes and upper door panels in lower portions of boxes to be glazed with ⅛ inch rough plate glass well puttied, back puttied and sprigged — sashes etc. to upper box to be glazed with best 26oz sheet glass perfectly free from all flaws and wavy surface, that in doors to be bedded in wash leather and secured with deal beads.

Leave all complete and perfect.

The Signalman's Access: Staircases, Landings, and Doors

The operating floor of most pre-grouping signal boxes was entered via an external timber staircase leading to a door at one end of the box. Wherever possible, the door was placed at the end where the signalman would be facing oncoming trains on the track nearest the box as he walked down the stairs, to minimise the chance of his stepping out in front of a train. Boxes with a front frame normally had the door placed towards the rear, and vice-versa. However, site conditions sometimes dictated that the door could not be in either end wall, in which case it would normally be placed in the rear wall, or even, in a very few cases, in the front. Doors were often moved (for example, from the rear part of the end wall to the front part of the end wall, when a rear frame replaced a front frame).

Most doors opened inwards, but some companies, such as the Midland and LNW, preferred outward-opening doors. The timber door itself was normally provided with a window, to avoid blocking the signalman's view. Most old boxes have had their original doors replaced, but this is not always easy to detect as styles have not varied much. A 'PRIVATE: NO ADMITTANCE' (or similar) sign graced most signal box doors. Sometimes a horseshoe was nailed above the door for good luck — often, unfortunately, with the shoe pointing downwards, in fact symbolic of bad luck! Another custom in some boxes, incidentally, was the keeping of a bible, signed by all the men who had worked the box since it opened: very few of these bibles survive.

The majority of staircases were of a single flight and parallel with the track, the length of the staircase depending upon its pitch and on the height of the box. Generally, a landing was provided at the top, about 3ft. wide (i.e. wide enough to open the door on to), with timber posts and rails on the outside, and supported on iron brackets or timber struts. In some cases the landing was no longer than the width of the door; in other cases, it was company policy to provide a landing some 6ft. long, to give a 'dog-leg' in the signalman's path; and in others still the landing extended across the

full width of the box. In the last case token exchange might be carried out from the landing. The greatest luxury was attained with the later Dutton boxes, which had a roofed full-width landing (**Plates 142 & 155**). Landings tended to be used as a home for water cans, mops, coal shovels, etc. Only a few boxes had no landing at all (although this was common on the GW)

Another common staircase position was parallel with the end wall of the box (usually directly attached to it). In this case the door had to be well to the rear (or front) of the box in order to fit in the staircase without resorting to excessive pitch, although a quarter-turn landing could be used, with the bottom part of the staircase parallel to the track, or a half-turn landing. A short landing by the door was generally necessary with this type of staircase, but a longer landing was impossible.

Brick staircases were rare in the pre-grouping period, the best example of their use being the later Furness boxes (**Plate 234**), but in 'modern style' designs (**Chapter 7**) brick or concrete staircases were widespread. Steel staircases have also been used on many new boxes since the 1920s, and as replacements for decayed timber staircases on older boxes. It was hoped that they would prove more durable than timber but, due to corrosion, this has not in fact been the case, and modern renewals are now often again in timber.

Porches of various kinds, with or without a second outer door, were found on a good number of pre-grouping boxes. Where the porch was an original fitting, it could be roofed with an independent gable (**Plates 127, 229, 241, 248 & 251**), a lean-to roof (**Plate 178**), or a partial continuation of the main box roof (**Plates 260, 296, & 299**). Many porches were later additions, knocked up in less than elegant fashion. Sometimes the porch was combined with a closet (**Plate 242**), but some structures which look like a porch at first glance are in fact simply closets. In the 1890s, the GW introduced the 'internal porch' — that is, draught protection by means of a second door inside the box, with a small lobby between it and the normal external door. Around the same time, the GW and the LNW also pioneered the 'internal staircase', entered through a door at ground level. This became a common feature of 'modern style' boxes.

Operating Floor Windows

It was noted in **Chapter 1** that a few early boxes had operating floors, but this occasional practice died out in the 1860s. The operating floor windows were in many ways the most important feature of the architecture of a signal box. The operating floor was normally glazed continuously for the whole length of the front, and for the whole or the greater part of both ends. In addition, boxes at level crossings often had a short glazed area at the rear to give the signalman a better view of approaching road traffic, and boxes which had running lines behind, as well as in front, might have the whole of the rear glazed (or all except the chimney space). A few large boxes had an oriel window (colloquially known as a 'bay window') in the centre of the box front, to provide a better view of passing trains. On one LMS box design (**Plate 329**) an oriel window was a standard feature.

The height ('depth') of operating floor windows was normally in the range 3ft. to 7ft., and tended to increase with the passing of time. A few boxes (including some GN boxes as early as the 1870s) were glazed right down to floor level. In most boxes the top ('head') of the windows was about 12in. below eaves level, with boarding between windows and eaves; but a good number of boxes were glazed right up to the eaves. The large window area of signal boxes naturally made them rather hot in summer and rather cold and draughty in winter, and many signalmen tried to improve on this by painting out or stuffing with newspapers the top-most and lowest panes. This was especially the case with those boxes where the operating floor glazing was divided into a main section where opening sashes were provided, plus fixed 'upper lights' above and/or fixed 'lower windows' below (**see Plates 119, 120, 136 & 137**). In 1900, Raynar Wilson — who would have been thinking of the RSCo/L&Y box design — was already lamenting that 'many signalmen do not appreciate the importance' of lower windows (in providing a view of the line immediately beneath). Sometimes also the upper lights were painted over because it was found that the box lighting was unduly visible from outside — Board of Trade requirements demanded that box lights should not be directly visible from outside, lest drivers mistake them for signal lights — or as part of more extreme black-out precautions in 1940. In recent times, too, the upper lights and lower windows in many boxes have been boarded over to save the expense of a proper renewal of the woodwork and glazing.

Pane sizes tended to increase with the passing of time, as better manufacturing techniques became available. Specification varied between 15oz. sheet glass for the smallest panes and 32oz. sheet glass for the largest. Only a very few pre-grouping boxes had undivided plate glass windows. Panes were divided by timber (not lead) bars. The number of panes in a window or sash is notated as, for example, '4 up, 3 across'.

The great majority of pre-grouping boxes had sliding sash windows — that is, sashes which slide in the horizontal direction. These move on iron or brass rollers running on a metal strip (**Plate 60**). The proportion of fixed and sliding windows varied greatly between designs. In many boxes, each bay (a bay is the space between one vertical post ('mullion') and the next) contained one fixed window and one sliding, overlapping by about 2in. when shut to form a weatherproof join. In other cases, such as the LNW (*see LNWRS, pages 125/6*) and RSCo/L&Y standard designs, each bay contained 3 or 4 sections, of which two or more were sliding. The Midland, and in later years the GW, preferred all sliding sashes in every bay. At the other extreme, some companies, such as the MS&L, provided sliding sashes only at the front corners of the box, the central bays having all fixed glazing on the grounds that the signalman had no easy access to them in any case (**Plates 179 & 180**).

Plate 58 An inside view of the 'upper lights' in an S&F box. Both the 'upper lights' and the heads of the main windows have curved framing.

P. Kay

Plate 59 A view along the walkway at Earlswood Junction (LBSC). This is a single-plank walkway with outside railings. The box has sliding sash windows with three sections in each bay, the central one fixed and the other two sliding behind it. Note the small solid eaves brackets.

P. Kay

Plate 60 Detail of sliding-sash window at Earlswood Junction. The window is nearly fully-opened here. Note the metal strip in the cill, and the handle on the inside of the sash.

P. Kay

Plate 61 A vertical sash window at Whyteleafe South.

P. Kay

Comparatively few signal boxes had the vertical sash windows which were ubiquitous in nineteenth century domestic architecture. Such an arrangement does not lend itself so conveniently to leaning out of the windows to display hand signals or speak to trainmen. The SE and the NB, however, did prefer vertical sashes for their boxes. On some modern boxes, casement windows are found (**see Chapter 7**).

Some boxes with sliding sash windows had dowels (small wooden pegs) fixed in the cills against the windows, for extra stability (**Plates 258 & 344**).

The proportion of fixed and movable windows in a box was influenced by the preferred method of cleaning. Obviously it was very important that the operating floor windows should be kept clean but, in most cases, the outside of the windows could not be reached by a man standing on the ground. Ladders and/or long-handled mops could be used, but this was not very desirable when the box was adjacent to a busy running line. In later pre-grouping days, the preferred solutions to this problem were either to have a large proportion of sliding sections so that all the windows could be reached from inside the box, or to build a walkway or gallery at operating floor level, around the outside of the glazed sections of the box, on which the signalman could stand to clean the outside of the windows. These walkways consisted of a plank supported on iron brackets (**Plates 54 & 59**). When standing on the walkway the signalman might have a grabrail on the windows to hang on to, or alternatively a railing on the outside of the walkway. Some companies were safety-conscious enough to provide an outer railing as a matter of policy; others did so only on very tall boxes. Railings were normally about 3ft. high. The access to the walkway was in some cases from the landing at the door end of the box, in others by climbing through the windows. On boxes where the staircase was attached to the end wall of the box, a plank might be provided for

access to the walkway, hitched up when not in use so that the signalman did not hit his head on it when using the stairs (**Plate 186**).

Where overhead electrification has been installed, boxes are normally provided with a large 'safety screen' of netting in front of the operating floor windows, to prevent any contact with the wires, or arcing.

Windows, like other timberwork, often need replacement due to decay. As with boarding, this may or may not be done to the original design. Many boxes have one or two replacement sashes to a different design, which are easily spotted (**Plate 157**), but sometimes there is a complete rewindowing, which can cause confusion if the replacement windows are of a type normally associated with a different box design. In recent years some boxes which are infrequently used, or in particularly vandal-prone areas, have had their windows partly or wholly boarded up, or fitted with wire netting to deflect missiles.

Roofs

The great majority of pre-grouping boxes had either a hipped or a gabled roof. Hipped roofs were more common up to the 1880s, and gabled roofs, considered easier to build by some, were more popular later. Of the major contractors and companies, the NE (Northern Division), Midland, Furness, Caledonian, LSW, NB, and GSW built their boxes with hipped roofs throughout. S&F, McK&H, and the GE, MS&L/GC, CLC, LNW, and LBSC began with hipped and changed over to gabled at various dates between the mid-1870s and mid-1890s; and Stevens, the GWCo, the RSCo, Dutton, EOD, the GN, and the NE (Southern Division) preferred gabled throughout. The GW was the only major company that never came to a firm view.

Other types of roof found on a few boxes were:

half-hip (top part hipped, bottom part gabled): found at Penruddock, CK&P.

lean-to: mainly on small ground-level boxes.

flat: on a few boxes in large stations, protected from rain by the station canopy, and in tunnels; and generally in a few cases from circa 1905. In post-grouping days, flat roofs became much more common (**Chapter 7**).

Most signal box roofs were, in accordance with normal building practice, strengthened by tie-beams across the width of the box at eaves level at intervals of 10ft. or so. Some roofs also had 'king posts' and/or diagonal struts. False ceilings at eaves level were rare in pre-grouping days, but have been put in subsequently in some old boxes as a heat conservation measure.

Slates were generally the most popular roofing material, and 'Bangor Countess' (20in. by 10in.) was the preferred size. The normal pitch of a slated roof is around 30 degrees. but, on signal boxes, hipped roofs tended to be pitched at 20 to 30 degrees, and gabled roofs at 30 to 45 degrees. Other roofing materials used for signal boxes were:

Zinc: Very popular up to the mid-1870s. It had the advantage of initial cheapness but tended to need replacing within 15 years. By the turn of the century only a few of the boxes concerned retained their original zinc roofs. Zinc roofs have a pitch of only 15 to 20 degrees, and so are often invisible in photographs taken from ground level.

Tiles: Rare in pre-grouping days, but more common on post-grouping hipped boxes. Tiles require a pitch of 45 to 50 degrees.

Corrugated Iron: Standard on the Highland Railway.

Asbestos Sheets and Asbestos Tiles: Used on a few boxes from circa 1915.

Roofing Felt: Used on some post-grouping boxes.

Slated roofs required additional weather protection on the top ridge, and on the four hips of a hipped roof. This was provided by lead flashings or ridge tiles. Ridge tiles could be plain or (on the top ridge only) decorative 'cockscomb' tiles (**Plates 151 & 248**). The tiles on the hips were sometimes held more firmly in place by an iron hip-hook at the bottom of the hip (**Plate 246**). The Midland used neither lead flashings nor ridge tiles, but mastic joints (tarring beneath the slates).

The two ends of the top ridge were often finished off with a finial. Signal box finials were normally of timber; most were thin and elongated to a 'ball and spike' design, but there were also some very fat 'balls' (**Plate 175**). Terracotta finials were sometimes used in connection with decorative ridge tiles; cast-iron finials are also known. On the Midland, and on a few McK&H boxes, the signal box finials were similar in design to those on the same company's signal posts.

Bargeboards — A selection of some of the more decorative bargeboard and finial designs

Plate 62 (above) Williton (B&E), 1875.

J. P. Morris

Plate 63 (right) Honington Junction (GN), circa 1880.

R. Newman

58

Plate 64 (above)   Grand Sluice (GN).

R. Newman

Plate 66 (below)   Ipswich (GE), circa 1883.

P. Kay

Plate 65 (above)   Wellowgate (MS&L), 1880.

R. Newman

Plate 67 (below)   Elmswell (GE) — McK&H-built, 1887.

P. Kay

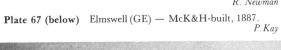

Plate 69 (right)   Bourton-on-the-Water, Gloucester Wagon Co., 1880.

M. Christensen

Plate 68 (below)   Mill Road (GE) — S&F-built, 1889.

P. Kay

The end rafters of gabled boxes were generally covered with bargeboards, for improved weather protection and a more finished appearance. From the 1870s to the 1890s, the bargeboards on signal boxes (as on other contemporary buildings) were usually carved in decorative designs, but in later years plain bargeboards became more common. From 1915, the quality of both finials and bargeboards deteriorated markedly. Normally the roof overhung the end wall of the box a good way, but in a few cases the bargeboards were placed directly over the boarding of the end wall, with the finials partly inset (**Plates 121 & 218**).

On most box roofs the feet of the rafters were covered with fascia boards (on the front and rear of a gabled box, and all four facades of a hipped box). Sometimes the fascia boards were decoratively carved, usually in a style corresponding to that of the bargeboards (**Plates 151 & 152**). On a few boxes, notably on the LSW and LBSC, decorative valancing — more familiar on station canopies — was provided, extending down in front of the upper panes of the windows (**Plates 253, 255, 259 & 263**). Although this did provide some protection from driving rain, it was probably intended just as much for decorative purposes.

Behind the fascia board was a horizontal board(s), the eaves plate, the width of which varied according to the overhang of the roof. Timber eaves brackets were provided on many boxes, particularly those with a large overhang, to stiffen the structure, and for decoration (not to support the roof). The back of the eaves bracket was attached to the box wall, above or between the operating floor windows, and the top was attached to the bottom of the eaves plate.

Some boxes, however, had the feet of the rafters left uncovered, with no fascia board and no eaves plate (and no brackets). This was a particularly common practice on the Furness and GSW (**Plates 237 & 295**).

Guttering was usually attached to the fascia board. Downpipes at the rear or the end of the box led to a drain or water butt.

Bargeboards and finials have often disappeared due to decay, and roofing materials have often been renewed in a different form. More drastically, a few boxes (such as York Yard North) have had their whole roof removed to make room for a new bridge built over the top of the box. Otherwise, the full reconstruction of a box roof is very rare, but has sometimes occurred after fire damage, or in connection with extensions.

Heating and Lighting

Heating facilities were provided in signal boxes from the very earliest days — even in some cases where there was no glazing (**Plate 12**). At first, boxes (even those of timber construction) were generally fitted with an open hearth, placed in most cases either in the centre of the rear wall or in one of the rear corners. A brick chimney was constructed, either built up from ground level (**Plate 48**), or stepped out at operating floor level (**Plate 82**). In a minority of boxes the chimney was built within the main box outline, rather than outside it.

By the turn of the century, however, stoves had become more popular than open hearths, especially for timber boxes. Above the stove a stovepipe chimney emerged through the roof. The stovepipe was jacketed up to roof level to protect the roof timbers from its heat, and the opening through the slates had lead flashing for weather protection. The inside wall of the box behind the stove was protected by metal or asbestos sheets.

When rear frames were introduced, the hearth or stove had to be placed in the front of the box. **Plate 277** shows a box with a brick chimney in the front. Boxes with a stove in the front were sometimes continuously glazed but, in other cases, a boarded section was provided by the stove (**Plate 295**).

Some large boxes had several hearths or stoves. In a few large boxes central heating was provided, even in pre-grouping days, and modern power boxes are always provided with central heating and a full environmental control system, for the benefit of the electronic equipment. The only boxes where no heating was provided at all were those at stations where the instruments were in the station buildings, and the signalman spent only brief periods in the box.

Plate 71 (below) It is rare to find a photograph of alterations in progress. Here, however, is Fleet (M&GN), during the demolition of the hearth and brick chimney, prior to the installation of a replacement stove and stovepipe.

The Late E. L. Back, copyright M. Back

Plate 70 (below) An S&F type large eaves bracket at West Malling (LCD). Here the eaves plate consists of three boards, due to the large overhang of the roof.

P. Kay

Many boxes which originally had open hearths had them replaced by stoves in pre-grouping days, and in recent decades modern oil, gas, or electric heaters have been introduced into older boxes on a wide scale. The open hearth is now virtually extinct. In many cases the whole chimney has been removed, but in other boxes, the chimney still acts as a flue to the replacement heating system.

In pre-grouping days most boxes were lit by oil or gas lamps, and ventilation had to be provided to deal with the fumes produced by these (and by the fire). In the case of hipped boxes, an iron vent on the top ridge was the most common form of ventilation device. Like other ironwork, these vents were proprietary products, and sometimes the same type could be seen on different companies' boxes. The 'torpedo' (**Plate 246**) was a common type. Also easily recognisable was the S&F type, used by that firm throughout its life (**Plate 44**). A particularly splendid type appeared on some LBSC boxes (**Plate 263**).

Some LSW boxes had a large timber vent structure on the ridge. Another form, sometimes adopted on hipped boxes, was a triangular slatted ('louvre') vent on the side of the roof, as on some Midland boxes in the Derby area (*LMSA, Plate 562*), or at the apex of the hips, as on some NE (Central Division) boxes (**Plate 194**). Most Midland boxes, however, simply had a number of holes in the wall near eaves level, with a movable iron grille behind to open up or shut off the airflow.

Gabled boxes too sometimes had iron ridge vents, but more often had a louvre vent in the gable end (**Plates 190 & 243**), or an opening gable window pivoted at the top or centrally (**Plates 69, 136 & 176**). Such gable windows, which were standard on many box designs, should not be confused with the larger windows provided as a special feature in the gable ends of a few boxes, for the purpose of improving the signalman's view of some particular signal or other object near the box (**Plate 152**).

Electric lighting has, of course, been normal in new boxes of recent decades, and has been fitted also in many (but by no means all) older boxes.

Plate 72 (below) Ventilation holes, fascia board, stovepipe, and finial on the Midland's Alston Junction box.

M. Christensen

Lavatories

Signal boxes, like railway carriages, were not at first provided with any lavatory facilities. At stations, the signalman could use the station lavatories. However, suitable earth closets were available on the market, and when increasing traffic began to make it more difficult for the signalman to leave his box, some companies began to install them in signal boxes. Water closets were also available, but few signal boxes had the mains water supply needed for their operation. The GN, for example, was providing earth closets in new boxes by the late 1870s, the L&Y had water closets in all 'town cabins' by 1900, and the LNW and NL had closets in most boxes by the Grouping. The majority of boxes, however, still had no facility at the time of the Grouping.

The favoured positions for a closet, whether provided from new or added to an existing box, were:

(i)   In a partitioned area inside the box, sometimes in the operating floor and sometimes in the locking room.

(ii) In a hut on the landing, sometimes combined with a porch. The signalman could hear the block bells from here. This position was normal on the GN, LNW, and others (**Plates 157, 166, 171, & 219**).

(iii) On the ground, in a separate timber, corrugated-iron, or concrete hut. Normal on the GE, Midland, and others; and the easiest course when providing facilities for an existing box.

In the 1970s, the 'Portaloo' spread across the country, and virtually all boxes now have some kind of lavatory facility.

Locking Room Doors and Windows

The locking room was entered by a door (usually unglazed) of normal height, located in most boxes at the same end as the operating room door, and often directly beneath it.

In the days before electric lighting was installed in signal boxes, there was not normally any artificial lighting in the locking room; there is still none in some boxes. It was therefore necessary to provide windows so that the locking fitters and telegraph linemen could work by natural light, assisted if necessary by handlamps. In the case of a timber box, locking room windows could be provided very easily and without weakening the structure, simply by glazing instead of boarding the space between two vertical posts. As a result, the window area could be made quite large (**Plate 78**). Cills and lintels were, of course, of timber.

In the case of brick boxes, however, an arch of some form had to be made for each locking room window, which limited their size and number. The brick arches of locking room windows were usually 'rough arches' (i.e., ordinary bricks were used, and the arch was formed by the mortar joints), but some boxes had the 'axed arches' normal in better quality architecture (i.e. specially-made wedge-shaped bricks). The 'segmental arch' was the most common shape of arch used, formed usually of one course of stretchers or two courses of headers. The 'semicircular arch' was less common, and the 'pointed arch' rare. Many companies used a stone lintel or (later) a concrete lintel, instead of a brick arch. Cills were of stone, brick (using plinth bricks), cast iron, or (later) concrete. On stone boxes, lintels and cills were normally of stone.

The windows themselves were mostly timber-framed, either fixed or with sliding sashes (**Plate 78**), or with vertical sashes (**Plate 76**), but fixed cast-iron window frames were used as an alternative on many brick boxes.

Boxes on station platforms often had an iron grille over the locking room windows to prevent damage by barrows and vandals. Many boxes had their locking room windows bricked up around 1940 (**see Chapter 7**), and others have been bricked up subsequently. In some cases also the original locking room windows have been replaced by new ones of a different design (**Plate 132**). Many new boxes since the 1930s have been built without any locking room windows, due to their being provided with electric lighting from new.

A few boxes had opening trap doors in the front of the locking room, to give outside access to parts of the locking mechanism that would otherwise have been difficult to reach. This was particularly so in the case of very low boxes, but was also found on some SE boxes of normal height (**Plate 269**). The same end was achieved by the very large removable locking room windows on some later NL boxes (**Plate 225**).

Plate 73   A fairly 'typical' locking room window in a brick box, with segmental arch formed of stretchers (some of them axed in part) and a fixed timber window frame. Below the cill the top of the plinth of the box can be seen (LBSC Type 3 box).

P. Kay

Plate 74   The well-known Saxby & Farmer type of locking room window. This type of fixed cast-iron frame and cill in one piece was first used by S&F in the 1860s, and was later adopted by the LNW, GWCo, RSCo, L&Y, and LMS. All were the same size, 2ft. across and 2ft. 6in. from top to bottom in the centre. Here the segmental arch is formed of one course of headers plus one of stretchers (S&F Type 10 box).

P. Kay

Plate 75   A finely-executed semicircular-arch locking room window at Oban (Caledonian Railway). The arch is of axed bricks, except for the brick at the head, which is uncut. The window cill is formed of splay bricks. Below the cill is the opening for the 'lead-offs' of the rods and wires, formed (as was the most common arrangement) of old rails supported on brick pillars. Here the rods and wires have been removed, as the photograph was taken after closure of the box.

P. Kay

Plate 76   The pointed-arch locking room window at Heckington (GN) with opening vertical-sash window. The arch uses bricks of different colours for decorative effect. Above the arch a course of angled bricks marks the transition from 9in. brickwork (below) to 13½ in. (above).

R. Newman

Names and Nameboards

The earliest boxes carried no name, there being no need for such identification when boxes were few and far between, but by 1870, a nameboard of some kind was usual.

The methods used were:

(i) Name painted directly on to the timberwork. Done in a few cases in the early years.

(ii) Cast-iron letters screwed directly on to the timberwork. Standard with several companies, most notably the LNW.

(iii) Cast-iron letters screwed on to a timber board. The most common practice.

(iv) Cast-iron nameplate with letters and plate cast in one piece. Standard on the GW between the 1890s and the 1940s.

(v) Enamel nameplate (actually an enamelled iron or steel plate). Used by a few pre-grouping companies, notably the GN (**Plate 63**), Rhymney, and SE. Adopted as standard by the Southern Railway and then by all BR regions, at first in six different regional colours, then from the late 1960s in 'Corporate Image' lower case black letters on a white background.

(vi) Large letters cast in a concrete block. Used on some 'modern style' boxes (**Plate 300**).

(vii) Freestanding letters. Used on some 'modern style' boxes (**Plate 339**).

In pre-grouping days, nameboards were generally placed on the front of the box, below the operating floor windows. The GN, however, adopted a policy of placing a nameboard at each end of the box at eaves level instead, which gave better visibility. By the Grouping, the GE was doing the same, and the LNER (and in 1935 the LMS) also adopted the practice, making new nameboards for most older boxes. The Southern and GW, however, stuck with the old system, and practice remains different on the respective BR regions today.

A very large number of boxes have received new nameboards in BR days, and few pre-grouping nameboards now survive.

The actual name given to a box was an obvious enough choice in most cases, being simply the name of the station, siding, junction, or road crossing controlled. However, in the vicinity of large stations, and in complicated industrial areas, some further notation was often required to distinguish boxes close to each other. The available options were:

(i) Lettering — i.e. calling the various boxes A, B, C, etc. This system was used by the GW in the 1870s, and by BR Southern Region (who 'converted' the boxes at many stations from other systems). The highest letter known was the GW's Swindon K.

(ii) Numbering — i.e. calling the boxes 1, 2, 3, etc. This was used by the LNW at many locations, and in some cases by the GN, MS&L, NL, and others. The highest numbers known were the LNW's Edge Hill No. 20, Carlisle No. 13, and Willesden No. 11, and the MS&L's Sheffield No. 11. The NL called the two pairs of lines on its quadruple track section the 'No. 1 lines' and 'No. 2 lines', and there were two signal boxes at each station numbered accordingly. Some of the GN boxes carried the number only without the station name. When additional boxes were built at a station with numbered boxes, they might be given a suffixed number to avoid having to renumber all the others, as, for example, the LNW's Preston No. 1A and No. 2A.

(iii) Compass points or geographical — i.e. North/South/East/West, or, where that did not suffice, 'Middle', 'Central', etc. This system was favoured by the GW in later years, and by the LBSC and LSW. The LSW equated 'West' with 'furthest from Waterloo', and so called the boxes at the east and west ends of Fareham Station 'West' and 'East' respectively.

(iv) By lines controlled. Boxes in complicated areas often controlled only some of the lines passing by them, and so were distinguished as 'Up', 'Down', 'Goods', 'Passenger', 'Yard', 'Shunting', etc.

(v) Naming each box by some immediate local feature — e.g. the boxes at Inverness were called 'Millburn', 'Welsh's Bridge', 'Loco Box', and 'Rose Street'. The NE also favoured this system, which produced the most interesting names. Some boxes on the LNW, at Carlisle and elsewhere, had names as well as numbers, but generally only carried the number on the outside of the box.

The name was often abbreviated on the nameboard for the sake of economy. All Junction boxes on the GE were JUNC, and on the GC Jc. The GSW offered multiple variations including JCT, JCN, JNCT, JCTN, and JUNCT. The GC sometimes indulged in abbreviations of very marginal benefit, such as PENISTONE WST and GUIDE BRIDGE EST. In contrast, some companies felt obliged to include the word CABIN, BOX, SIGNAL BOX, or (on the SE) SIGNALS on every box nameboard. The GW had a fondness for excessively long names, extending to such as QUAKERS YARD WEST TUNNEL JUNCTION SIGNAL BOX. Some companies, notably the Midland, gave the JUNCTION suffix even to boxes which controlled only a running crossover between different pairs of lines. Others, such as the NE, hardly used it even for boxes which controlled route junctions.

Many companies in the USA did not name boxes, but gave them a code letter in sequence from one end of the line to the other. After the American C. T. Yerkes took over the District Railway, the boxes were all code-lettered on this system. The box at the east end of Earl's Court Station became EA, with subsequent boxes in that direction EB, EC, ED, etc., and the box at the west end of Earl's Court became WA, thence WB, WC, etc. The new tube lines of 1906/7, controlled by Yerkes, had their boxes sequentially lettered from the start, and the system was subsequently adopted for the whole LT network, where it is still used. The Mersey and Liverpool Overhead Railways also adopted a sequential lettering system. The Southern Railway adopted it for signal numbering, but retained the box names.

Some peculiar names were to be found in the case of those boxes which were named after adjacent features. Several, such as BO PEEP JUNCTION, DOLPHIN JUNCTION, and NORTH POLE JUNCTION, were named after public houses. MAUD FOSTER and TWENTY FEET RIVER were named after drains in the fens (the former drain being itself named after a landowner).

The NE offered DEAF HILL, DRAGON, HELL BECK, and CHARITY — the last referring to adjacent land held by a local charity — and even turned to Latin for ERIMUS at Middlesbrough (after the town's motto) and SEVERUS at York (after the Roman Emperor). In contrast, the GN seems to have found little inspiration in the local features of rural Hertfordshire, and was reduced to NINETEENTH MILE for an additional box of the 1860s. In later years there was a TWENTIETH MILE UP and a TWENTIETH MILE DOWN.

The precise names of boxes in complicated areas often changed, as companies did not always stick to the same system, and the building of an additional box might require the renaming of existing boxes or the addition of suffixes not previously necessary. Also, the renaming of a station generally resulted in the renaming of the box(es) as well. As an extreme case, the box which started life as STOATS NEST CENTRAL ended up as COULSDON NORTH No. 1. In recent years the most common change has been the abolition of suffixes when box closures have left only one box in use at a location. In some cases the obsolete suffix is taken off the nameboard or painted out; in other cases it remains in practice.

Another feature of some boxes was a contractor's maker's plate. These were small iron plates screwed on to the front of the box. They appeared only where the box structure was built by one of the signalling contractors, but even then only certain contractors provided them; S&F, RSCo, and EOD examples survive. Also, in the days before telephones, boxes were supplied with movable 'S' and 'T' boards hung on the front of the box. In the normal position these indicated 'All well', but, when reversed, (usually with a different colour displayed) they indicated a defect in the signal or telegraph apparatus respectively. Passing train crews were expected to notice when the boards were reversed, and report the matter at their next stopping place so that the fitters could be sent to the box. No doubt all concerned were very pleased when the introduction of telephones (used in signal boxes from as early as the 1880s) rendered this cumbrous system obsolete.

Plate 77 A Saxby & Farmer maker's plate.

R. D. Foster

Accessory Structures

A collection of accessory structures was clustered around every signal box to service it. Mention has already been made of the fact that the closet was often located in a hut on the ground near the foot of the box stairs. Also normally placed near the stairs were a coal bunker and ashes bunker, made up of brick, old sleepers, or concrete, and now obsolete in those boxes where coal is no longer used for heating. The meagre official allowance of coal was traditionally topped up by persuading coal to fall off wagons and locomotives! A lamp hut and oil store were necessary to service the signal lamps. A telegraph pole stood adjacent to most boxes, with wires leading from it into the box, but nowadays the telegraph poles on many lines have been replaced by buried cables or ground-level troughing. Timber walkways were constructed over the rodding and wires in front of the box (and elsewhere, if necessary) to provide a safe path. A timber token exchange platform was sometimes erected on the ground, at those boxes controlling single lines where the exchange could not be carried out from the operating floor or landing. The token exchange point, wherever it was, was illuminated by a lamp for the benefit of trainmen at night. Where there was no mains water supply, a large water butt was placed against the rear or end walls of the box, and collected the rainwater from the gutters to provide the box's primary water supply for washing and cleaning. Drinking water was delivered in cans, either by freight train or by a nearby farmer. Fire buckets (water and sand) were hung on the box walls, usually underneath the stairs.

In recent years further collections of steel location cabinets, etc., have appeared. The photographs elsewhere in this book show, at random, all the above features.

Structural Alterations

It was noted in earlier sections of this chapter that the exposed timberwork of boxes (doors, window sashes, staircases, boarding, bargeboards, etc.), and certain other minor parts of boxes, often require renewal, due to decay. However, a good many boxes have also undergone more fundamental structural alterations during the course of their lives.

The most common such alteration was the extension of a box (lengthways) to accommodate an extension to the frame; or sometimes, in the case of small boxes, other additional equipment such as a gate wheel or single line instruments. If possible, the extension was made at the non-door end, where less work was involved. The materials of the original end wall were normally re-erected to form the new end wall. Some boxes (e.g. Paignton South) were extended on more than one occasion. Extensions of timber boxes are normally quite easy to spot, even where the job was well done (**Plate 78**), as the original corner posts generally remain. Where the extension was done on the cheap, with lean-to roofs to avoid the expense of having to alter the original roof, it is even more obvious (**Plate 79**). The extension of a brick box, however, can sometimes be missed at first glance. The division between old and new brickwork, and old and new slates on the roof, is clear enough when new (*GWS Fig. F1*) but can blur after a few decades. The best clue from the front often lies in the arrangement of the window sashes, which is frequently non-symmetrical on an extended box (but rarely so otherwise). Locking room windows may also be non-symmetrically located after extension. The rear of a brick box often gives away an extension much more obviously than the front, as the break between old and new brickwork can usually be seen on the full height of the box at the rear, and the chimney is likely to be non-symmetrically placed.

The extension of boxes was, in most cases, done to the original design, an extreme example being Coldham Lane Junction at Cambridge, which was built circa 1880 and extended to the same

Plate 78 (above) Croesnewydd North Fork (GW) displays a typical extension to a timber box. This box was 33ft. 6in. long when opened in 1905, and was extended to 41ft. 10in. in 1940.

J. P. Morris

Plate 79 (right) An extension on the cheap; West India Dock Junction, a S&F Type 2a box built for the East & West India Dock Co., circa 1871, and extended at a date unknown. Note the S&F maker's plate. This box survived (in PLA ownership) until the 1960s.

C. H. Betts

Plate 80 (left) This Dutton Type 2 box was built for the Cambrian, circa 1894. It was then Portmadoc East and had a 14-lever frame. In 1932, the GW abolished the West box, and extended this box to accommodate a new 36-lever frame. As usual, the extension was done at the non-door end, and the original timber-work from the end wall re-used. The different tone of the new bricks and slates is still clear, and the non-symmetrical window-pattern of the front is fairly obvious. The extension has settled a little due to poor foundations.

J. P. Morris

Plates 81 & 82 (below) Henwick was a McK&H Type 1 box of the 1870s, extended in 1897 from 14ft. 4in. to 23ft. 8in. Here a new roof was added at the time of extension, to the GW Type 7a pattern, and new locking room windows provided. Otherwise (apart from some refacing of the brickwork) the original section of the structure was unaltered up to eaves level. At the rear, the extension can be spotted a mile off!

P. V. Starling

design in 1955. A few boxes, however, were partially or wholly 'converted' on extension to the then-current design (**Plate 81**). There was virtually no limit to the strange things that might happen to boxes on extension. The GC's Wath Junction had an extension of a different width to the main part of the box, and the same company's West Silkstone Junction acquired a roof which was hipped (as originally) at one end, but gabled at the other!

A very few boxes have been shortened after rationalisation (for example, Pontypridd), but this is rarely worth the effort. Frames, however, are often shortened on rationalisation, and in some boxes a short section of the original operating floor has been divided off

by a partition wall to form the new operating room, the remainder of the box being left empty and unheated. Examples of this are Llandaff Loop and Princes Risborough North, where part of the mechanical frame remains in use and the rest has been removed, and Altofts Junction, where the frame has been wholly removed and a panel installed.

A few boxes are known to have been increased in height. The brick box at March East Junction (GE), built in 1885, was 'raised' in 1897 in connection with signalling improvements following an accident in the previous year; the alteration in the brickwork is still noticeable. Similarly, Midland notices in 1913 refer to the 'renewal

Plate 83 The scene at Muchalls (Caledonian Railway) after a derailment in pre-grouping days. The train has made a clean job of the front of the box, and two temporary posts have been inserted to prevent the roof collapsing. However, the frame seems to have survived unscathed. Behind the box are the remains of a footbridge.

Authors' Collection

of timber and raising' of Millbrook box and three others.

Conversely, a few boxes were reduced in height. This sometimes happened when rotting sections of corner posts were simply cut out rather than replaced, as at Grafton and Collingbourne on the MSWJ. The only brick box known to have been reduced in height was the NS's Alsager.

From time to time, signal boxes were hit by derailed trains and seriously damaged, sometimes with fatal injuries to the signalman. More often, boxes have been burnt down, either by vandals or by fires caused by stoves left burning overnight. When brick or BTF boxes were burnt down, the brick portion of the structure sometimes survived in a good enough state for a new timber superstructure to be erected upon it, as was done at Rufford and Smithy Bridge by the L&Y.

A number of timber boxes were moved in their entirety, either to a new position at the same station as a result of track alterations, or to a completely different place after becoming surplus to requirements at their original location. In the former case, the box would normally be moved in one piece (**Plate 84**); in the latter case a partial dismantling would be necessary, in order to fit within the loading gauge during the rail-borne removal operation. The fact that a box is second-hand is not generally noticeable on the ground, and one suspects that rather more boxes were reused in this way than those for which documentary evidence of removal is available. Instantly identifiable as second-hand, however, are those boxes which were moved after 1923 to a new location on the 'wrong' pre-grouping company's lines. Examples of this can be seen at **Plates 85 & 86**.

Plate 84 (left) The South Eastern box at Lewisham Junction is pictured in 1928, in the process of being moved 20ft. on rollers to accommodate track alterations (the new line from Nunhead). In other cases, boxes, or box superstructures, are known to have been moved on trolleys by manpower, or suspended from the jib of a rail crane!

Authors' Collection

Plate 85 (right) This North Staffordshire box found its way from an unknown original location to Ruthwell, on the GSW main line, where it opened on 1st November 1942 to control new loops provided for increased war traffic. The reuse of a BTF rather than a timber box is unusual. The new brick base was built in proper NS fashion.

R. Newman

Plate 86 (left) Another wanderer was this GC Type 5 box which was moved to Magdalen Road (GE) in 1927, again from an unknown original location. It replaced a box situated at the junction points south of the station and so enabled the separate post of crossing-keeper to be abolished. The scheme was approved by the LNER Works Committee on 2nd December 1926, at an estimated cost of £1,869.

P. Kay

CHAPTER FOUR

Special Types of Signal Box

Difficult Sites: Oversailing and Overhead Boxes

The operational requirements for the siting of a signal box necessitated the use, in some cases, of difficult sites. Sometimes these difficulties were minor. For example, a 'normal' signal box could be built on the side of an embankment simply by supporting the rear on timber columns (**Plate 87**), or, more expensively, by supporting the whole structure on brick arches (*GWS Plate 94*). Conversely, where the railway was in a deep cutting, an elevated operating floor might be achieved by building a box of average height at the top of the cutting, or part-way up it, rather than a very tall box built from rail level. This, however, brought problems in carrying the rods and wires down to rail level (**Plates 88 & 89**). In some cases where there was a cramped site, the box was built to the normal plan, and the other requirements accommodated to it, rather vice-versa. At Broughty Ferry, for example, the steps of the station footbridge passed through the locking room of the signal box, and at Bramley & Wonersh the footpath to the platform passed underneath the rear of the box, which was supported on columns.

Plate 87   The exposed columns at the rear of Ollerton Colliery (GC) box. Although only some 3ft. of them is visible above ground, they actually extend to 15ft. below rail level.

M. A. King

Plate 88 (left)   At the NB's Winchburgh Junction, the box was built near the top of the cutting slope, and the rodding and wires were run down at an angle. It was, of course, only possible to build boxes on the cutting slope like this if the ground was very stable.

R. D. Foster

Plate 89 (right)   Ystrad Mynach South, on the Rhymney Railway, shows an alternative approach, using a timber platform in front of the box and two extra sets of cranks, to give all 90 degree turns in the rods (the wires run separately). This is a stone-built McK&H Type 3 box; the roofing material and 'torpedo' vents are GW replacements.

R. D. Foster

There were many more cases, however, where the signal box itself had to be of a special form of construction in order to fit within a restricted site. The most common such special construction was the oversailing ('jettied') operating floor, adopted when some ground space was available but not enough to build a box base of the normal width. An oversailing box had normally to be of timber or BTF construction. The oversailing timber upper storey was stiffened by timber struts or iron support brackets. In most cases, the oversail was at the front of the box, as obstructions to the rear of the site were the usual reason for the restricted width of the site.

A front-oversailing box had generally to be somewhat taller than the standard 8ft., in order that the oversailing upper storey should not be foul of the structure gauge. There were often problems in fitting the frame and locking mechanism into the front of an oversailing box. These problems varied according to the frame design, but always imposed some limit on the amount of oversail possible. With a rear frame there were no problems, and sometimes a company which never installed frames in the rear in normal circumstances would do so in an oversailing box.

Plate 90 The GSW box at Kirkconnel provides a fairly typical example of an oversailing box. Rear frames were standard on the GSW by 1911, when this box was built. By the time this photograph was taken the siding immediately in front of the box, the existence of which had made an oversailing box necessary, had been lifted. Curiously, this siding was not in fact put in until 1916; it must have been anticipated in 1911.

R. Newman

Plate 91 The Midland box at Kilby Bridge, oversailing at both front and rear.
R. Newman

A few boxes had an oversail at the rear instead, or on both sides. Where a very tall box was required, a full two storey timber box could be built on top of a narrower brick base, as at Crewe North Junction (*LNWRS, Plate 2.1*) and Maidstone West.

A slight oversail could be achieved in brickwork, by stepping out each course of bricks a little further than the course below it. Other methods used in a few cases were curved steel girders (as at Dawlish), two rows of iron columns (as at Canterbury LCD — *SS, Plates 147/8*), or a single row of columns (*GWR, Plate 120*).

Oversailing boxes were, in fact, fairly common, more so than the photographs in this book (which illustrate, wherever possible, boxes with wholly standard features) would suggest.

At some sites, no ground space at all was available, in which case an overhead box had to be built above the lines. In the early years, overhead boxes were normally supported on timber gantries (**Plate 20**), or, in a few cases, on brick arches. However, iron gantries became more usual from circa 1880, and steel gantries from circa 1900; this parallels the development of signal gantries. Gantry boxes were most common in the 1890s and 1900s when a large number of line widening schemes were carried out. Normally, an overhead box was supported on two rows of columns, one either side of the tracks spanned; but in some cases the rear of the box was supported instead on an adjacent building (*LNWRS, Plate 10.18*) or a cutting wall. The timber box structure on the gantry and the locking frame were, in most cases, orientated parallel to the track in the normal way, with the gantry (unless it spanned only one track) being wider than the box structure (**Plate 92**); but sometimes the box structure and frame were placed at right-angles to the tracks (**Plate 93**). A full two storey box structure was generally built on the gantry, but some companies — notably the LNW (*LNWRS Plate 10.16 ff*) — preferred to build a single-storey structure with special above-floor locking mechanism. On LT lines, there were even some brick overhead boxes (on steel gantries) — **Plate 353**.

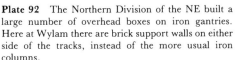

Plate 92 The Northern Division of the NE built a large number of overhead boxes on iron gantries. Here at Wylam there are brick support walls on either side of the tracks, instead of the more usual iron columns.

H. G. E. Wilson

Plate 93 An overhead box on a steel gantry, at Canterbury (SE), with the frame at right-angles to the tracks.

M. Christensen

Some overhead boxes were built, not above the tracks, but above station canopies. Examples of this were at Bath on the GW, and Bournemouth, built by the Southern in 1928.

Overhead boxes were naturally more expensive to build and maintain than a conventional box, and few were built after the introduction of track circuiting and the extension of the limits for mechanical working widened the choice of box sites. A notorious demonstration of the undesirability of overhead boxes was the collapse, in May 1965, of the LSW's Clapham Junction A box, due to corrosion of the supports.

Boxes Designed to Match Station Buildings

In a few cases, signal boxes on new lines were built to special designs prepared by the architect responsible for the station buildings, in order to produce a harmonious ensemble. The most notable cases of this were the GE's Seven Sisters to Lower Edmonton line of 1872, where the boxes were linked to the main station buildings by a curtain wall (**Plate 94**), various LBSC lines of 1880-83 in Sussex (**Plate 95**), and the NB's West Highland line of 1894 (**Plate 275**). In other cases, a matching signal box was designed when an individual station was built or rebuilt. Very striking examples of this were the SE's 'Domestic Revival' box for the new station at Nutfield in 1883, and the Furness' original Carnforth Station Junction box (long disused but still standing) in 'Tudor' style. Others, less striking, were the CK&P's Threlkeld of 1894 (contiguous with the main buildings), and the LNER boxes for the York to Northallerton widenings of 1933, of which Beningbrough and Otterington still stand.

A further possibility, when it was desired to match a new box with existing station buildings, was to build the box to the standard outline but to add special decorative features. A notable case of this was Wolferton on the GE, built during 1883/4 and designed to match the original carstone station rather than the grand mock-Tudor extensions of the late 1890s. The Furness Railway, prior to 1900, made considerable efforts to match the materials and details of signal boxes to those of station buildings on a widespread basis. The LNW box at Kenilworth, (*LNWRS, Page vii*) had a special 'gothic' panelled base to match the other station buildings, but above that was a perfectly standard box; even the brickwork changed to the cheaper standard Crewe bricks halfway up!

The SE was unique in that almost all its home-built boxes were constructed to a design that was also used for (some) station buildings. This, however, was done for cheapness rather than out of concern for architectural harmony. There were only a few stations where both station buildings *and* signal box were built to this design!

In general, the railway companies did not of course wish to incur the expense of special box designs, and with no 'planning permission' being required in pre-grouping days, they were able to erect boxes to standard designs even in prominent locations where they were by no means in harmony with other buildings nearby. However, in a few cases, special designs were forced on the railway companies for environmental reasons. Most notably, plans for new signal boxes in the City of Edinburgh had to be submitted to the 'Dean of Guild Court' for approval. This produced a number of special NB designs (**see Chapter 6**). Other cases were the M&GN box at Roughton Road Junction, which had to be given a fancy decorative roof at the insistence of a local landowner; and the NE box at Knaresborough which, whether by concern or compulsion, was built in a style such as to minimise its impact on the adjacent Georgian houses. Similarly, the new box built at East Gate Junction, Colchester, in 1924, was designed in what was described as 'the Old English style', in order to 'harmonise to some extent with the old-fashioned houses in the vicinity'.

Plate 94 Pointed arches everywhere at the GE's Bruce Grove Station, one of the most extreme examples of integration of signal box and station buildings. The signal box has vertical-sash windows, one of them open in this view.

Lens of Sutton

Plate 95 (right) The 1881 LBSC station at Midhurst. On these Sussex lines, the boxes were designed to harmonise with the station buildings, rather than being identical as at Bruce Grove. The upper part of most of the station buildings on these lines had to be tile-hung in later years, as the original finish was insufficiently weatherproof. Midhurst North box is just visible at the extreme left. Midhurst South box, in the foreground, closed on 4th April 1925 and was converted into an office for the stationmaster.

Lens of Sutton

Plate 96 The GE's splendid (and, as this photograph shows, still beautifully-preserved) box at Wolferton. The proposed interlocking of Wolferton Station was referred to in a letter of 2nd November 1883 from James Bond, Assistant Secretary of the Hunstanton and West Norfolk Railway (which owned the line until 1890), to the GE (which worked it), as follows: ' . . . with regard to the signalling, this Company (the Hunstanton) will obtain tenders and undertake the cost of carrying out the same in the usual manner, but if the GE Coy. are desirous of making the signal box at Wolferton of an ornamental character, that expense must be borne by them as the (Hunstanton) Coy. decline to bear any portion of such extra cost'. The end-product shows that the GE did desire that the box be of 'an ornamental character', in order to impress the Royal travellers to and from Sandringham House, which the Prince of Wales had acquired in 1862. Wolferton is basically a GE Type 5 box **(cf. Plate 151)** but with several additional decorative features, notably the tile-hanging in the gable ends, the finials, and the elaborate carving of the landing timberwork. The roof pitch is also steeper than normal. The front of the box is faced with the local brown carstone, but the plinth, quoins, and four courses below the windows are of brick. The measurements are 23ft. 1in. by 12ft. 7½in. by 8ft. Wolferton box was abolished on 21st September 1967 but is preserved along with the station buildings as a 'Royal station' museum site.

R. Newman

Subsidiary Boxes at Large Stations

At some large through stations, subsidiary boxes were built to control central crossovers which were out of sight of the main boxes at either end of the station. These subsidiary boxes were usually block posts, although many of the signals they controlled were slotted with the main boxes. Often there was one subsidiary box on the 'down' side of the station, and one on the 'up' side. The type of structure varied a great deal. Some were built as independent structures to the standard designs (but with a flat roof if under the shelter of the station canopy), either on the platforms (Sheffield Midland A and B) or off the platform (Crewe Station A). Others were independent platform structures of special decorative design (York Platform, and the original Derby A). Where subsidiary boxes were planned in connection with the complete rebuilding of a station, they could be located within the island platform buildings, with a bay window looking out on to the platform on either side (Nottingham Victoria East and West, Nottingham Midland A and B, Leicester London Road East and West). Carlisle No. 4A and Perth Down Centre were also within the island platform buildings, but at first floor level, with oriel windows. Edinburgh Waverley North and South were bracketed out from the curtain walls; Perth Up Centre was gantried over the tracks.

Another type of subsidiary box was found at some large termini. This was the 'buffer stops' box provided where the signal-men in the main box did not have a clear view of all the platforms as far as the buffer stops. The main function of the man in the buffer stops box was to indicate to the main box, by means of electrical or mechanical instruments, whether the lines were clear through to the stops, or whether there were standing vehicles. Track circuiting rendered this function obsolete. Some buffer stops boxes also controlled the locomotive release crossovers, which would usually be beyond the limit of the main box, but which were and are more frequently worked from an open ground frame. Most buffer stops boxes were gantried above the tracks adjacent to the stops. Examples were Euston No. 1, Tattenham Corner B, Bexhill (SE), and Norwich Thorpe.

Boxes Combined with Station Offices

At some small and unremunerative stations, staff economies were effected by making the booking office serve also as the 'signal box'. The frame and signalling instruments were placed in most cases in a bay window on the platform side, to give a view of the line. This economy was rare in pre-grouping days (examples were the LNW's Claydon and Marsh Gibbon & Poundon) but further such installations were made by the post-grouping companies to enable the closure of conventional boxes, notably by the SR in the 1930s (**Plate 100**).

An alternative method was to have the instruments only in the station office, and an independent signal box structure with the frame in it, to which the person responsible for signalling resorted only when it was necessary to work the points and signals. On some Highland lines, there were two boxes at each station, one at each end of the loop, and the instruments, together with two levers with slots on the starting signals, were in the booking office. This saved one signalman's post, but at the cost of extra delay in crossing trains. On many LNW branches, such as the Amlwch line, there were simply open frames on the station platforms (*LNWRS, Plate 11.22*), and a couple of the Southern's 1930s installations were also so done (*SS, Plate 138*).

The converse economy was also effected at some stations, by closing the booking office and transferring the ticket-issuing equipment to the signal box. This has been more common in BR days, as, for example, at Cooksbridge, Beddington Lane, and Milborne Port on the Southern Region.

The railway companies had to build a large number of houses for signalmen in rural areas, and in a very few cases, at remote crossing loops, the 'signal box' was built within the signalman's house. There were several such boxes on the Callander & Oban line.

Boxes in Converted Buildings

A few signal boxes were conversions of earlier structures originally used for other purposes. Dunbridge (*SS, Plate 114*) was a standard LSW box top of the 1870s, placed on top of a single storey crossing keeper's cottage; and the new Totton box of 1925 was also a rebuild of a crossing keeper's cottage. Peculiar things were to be found on some industrial lines (**Plate 359**). At the GN's Manchester Road Station in Bradford, a new box was opened in 1916 in what had previously been the ladies' waiting-room. The GW's Quakers Yard High Level box of 1902 was similarly located in an ex-waiting-room. In recent years a number of 'panels' have been installed in station buildings, rather than in new structures, for example, Birmingham Snow Hill (1960), St. Germans (1973), and Salisbury (1981).

Temporary Boxes

Temporary signal boxes were often required:

(i) For controlling temporary single line working in connection with bridge, tunnel, or viaduct reconstruction.

(ii) For 'stageworks' during track widenings.

(iii) As emergency replacements after a box had been destroyed, whilst a new permanent box was being built, or other new permanent arrangements were made.

(iv) As additional 'break section' boxes, when traffic was expected to increase for a brief period due to some special event.

Temporary boxes were always of timber construction for rapid erection. Some companies, such as the GW, kept a small 'stock' of timber boxes especially for use as temporary installations. In recent years, the Eastern Region has used 'Portakabins', with panels, as temporary signal boxes.

Tunnel Boxes

There were very few signal boxes inside tunnels on the main line railways. In steam days, it was difficult to see signals in a tunnel because of swirling smoke, and the conditions for a signalman were correspondingly unpleasant. A box once existed in the MS&L's Woodhead Tunnel, but it had to be abandoned because of these problems. Better known was the Midland's St. Pancras Tunnel box, in use between 1889 and 1958 (**Plate 101**). The Mersey had two intermediate tunnel boxes, River and Adelphi Street, the former of which was underneath the river (the only known case of an underwater signal box!). All these boxes were built by excavating a hole in the tunnel wall.

There were many more underground boxes on the urban 'tube' lines, but they were mostly at the stations, usually as independent flat-roofed structures at the end of the station platforms (**Plate 230**). Some LT-built boxes on tube lines were in rooms in the cross-passages between the platforms, invisible to the passenger except for a door.

Plate 101   The grimy exterior of St. Pancras Tunnel box. The building of an intermediate box here was recommended in Major Marindin's Board of Trade Report on an 1888 collision, caused by a train overrunning signals at the Metropolitan's Midland Junction box. The frame for the Tunnel box left Derby stores on 6th December 1889, and the box opened very shortly after this. It was reached from ground level via a spiral staircase.

C. H. Betts

Swing Bridge Boxes

Several dozen swing (or lift) bridges were to be found on the British railway network, and these presented especial problems for the Signal Engineer. The engine and control mechanism for working the bridge were in most cases placed in a cabin on the bridge, either slung on to the side (as at Trowse, GE), or gantried between the bridge girders above the line (as at Goole, NE, and Sutton Bridge, M&GN). The control mechanism in the bridge cabin was interlocked with the adjacent signal boxes, so that the bridge could not be opened until all relevant signals were at danger. Alternatively, there might be a combined signal box-plus-bridge cabin, as at the GE's Somerleyton and Reedham swing bridges, both replacements of 1904.

Before a bridge could be swung, any point rodding or signal wires passing over it had to be disconnected. But telegraph wires could be carried on high masts above the bridge, or by underwater cables. Some bridge cabins controlled semaphore signals for river traffic (still used at Selby). The company's Act of Parliament often dictated that river traffic should have precedence over rail. When the railway line was (temporarily) closed, the bridge had to be left open to river traffic, and the bridge operator had to leave by rowing boat. The rowing boat was useful also when (as all too frequently happened) the bridge was rammed by a ship, or stuck in the open position due to expansion of the metal in hot weather.

Huts and Ground Frames

In addition to 'full-size' signal boxes, there were, at the time of the Grouping, many thousands of ground level huts, a good number of which are still in use. It was noted in **Chapter 1** that most signalmen had been housed in ground level huts in the days before interlocking, but from the 1860s it was normal practice to build a full-size two storey signal box at any location which was a 'block post' (i.e. where the box was equipped with block telegraph instruments for controlling the passage of trains). From the 1860s, therefore, ground level huts were found mainly in inferior roles, the most common of which were the control of non-block post level crossings between stations, and the control of points and shunting signals in a yard.

Some railway companies had a large number of huts at level crossings, but on others most crossings were worked by a keeper living in an adjacent cottage, and no hut accommodation was necessary. The levers might be inside the hut (**Plate 103**), or outside in the open (**Plate 104**). Signals were not always provided and, where they were, there might be 'distants' only (the targets on the gates acting as home signals). A stove was normally provided in crossing huts, as they had to be continuously manned when the line was open for traffic. Nevertheless, most crossing huts were very cramped and not a comfortable place in which to spend a 12 hour shift! In the last twenty years, many level crossings have been automated, and manned crossings are now fairly rare, except on the Eastern Region. Some of the remaining manned crossings are controlled from full-size boxes which were formerly block posts, but which lost that role, either through power resignalling schemes, or as an economy measure whereby a signalman could be replaced by a crossing keeper at a lower rate of pay (but at the cost of lengthening the block sections). A classic scheme of the latter kind was carried out by the LNER on the York to Scarborough line.

Many medium-sized yards had one or two huts, with a frame inside, or immediately outside, for the shunters to work the points and shunting signals. These huts were, in many cases, only used intermittently, and so had no stove; the shunters would have mess accommodation elsewhere in the yard. The largest yards, however, might be worked from several continuously-manned full-size boxes, as is still the case at Willesden and Washwood Heath; these

Plate 102 Goole Swing Bridge (NE) is the original structure opened in August 1869. Originally there was a signal box at either end of the bridge as well as the bridge control cabin shown here, but in 1933 a small signalling panel — the world's first — was installed in the bridge cabin, and the other two boxes were closed. This is now the oldest signal box structure in BR use.

R. Newman

boxes were still not necessarily 'block posts', as 'yard working', rather than 'block working', was normally used. Conversely, the smallest yards could be satisfactorily worked by individual hand levers for each point and signal (if, indeed, signals were provided), or by a concentrated (but not always interlocked) open ground frame. Large numbers of new open ground frames were provided in the power box schemes of the 1960s and 1970s, to control the connections between sidings and running lines, at less cost than working the points direct from the panel box. The term 'ground frame', incidentally, is now often used to describe any signalling installation which is not a block post (even full-size boxes) but in this book the term is used to refer to small open-air frames only.

Ground-level huts were mostly built of timber, but some level crossing huts were of brick. It is likely that some crossing huts used into recent years dated from the opening of lines back in pre-interlocking days. A few of the larger railway companies, notably the LNW (**Plate 106**), Midland (**Plate 213**), and GW (**Plate 103**), had special designs of standard signal hut; McK&H and Dutton also advertised special design of small hut. Other companies, such as the RSCo (**Plate 105**), L&Y, and LBSC, built their huts from

the same standard components as were used for full-size boxes. But most companies exercised no central control over the 'design' of huts, so that all sorts of ad hoc erections could be seen on the same line (*SS, Plates 159, 160 & 162*). In the case of those companies where there was no standardisation of hut design, no attempt has been made to describe hut designs in **Chapters 5, 6 and 8** of this book, but it should be borne in mind that many huts did exist on every company's lines.

Locking frames in ground-level huts frequently had above-floor locking mechanism. Special 'knee frames' with above-floor locking were made by several of the contractors, specifically for use in ground-level boxes.

Some companies built huts for non-signalling purposes to the same design as signal huts; the LNW was the most notable example of this. Others, such as the Midland and GC, built general purpose huts from the same components as were used for full-size signal boxes. The tops of abolished signal boxes were also sometimes given a second life as huts for other purposes, especially as store huts for the Signal Department.

Plate 104 (above)   The crossing hut with outside frame at Lincoln Road, Enfield.

P. Kay

Plate 103 (above left)   A GW standard (Type 29) small ground frame hut, measuring 5ft. by 7ft., at Crundale Crossing (north of Haverfordwest). It opened in 1916, replacing a block post signal box, the top of which still resides in a nearby garden.

J. P. Morris

Plate 105 (below left)   Rochdale Down Platform box, a hut built from standard RSCo box components (but with plain bargeboards by the date of this photograph).

R. D. Foster

Plate 106 (below)   An LNW standard hut at Crewe Carriage Siding. Only the points connecting with the running lines are worked from the interlocked frame in the hut; the points in the sidings to the left are worked by individual hand levers.

P. Kay

CHAPTER FIVE

The Signalling Contractors and their Box Designs

The contractors are listed in the order in which they commenced signalling work, as set out also in **Table 5**. This Chapter contains a section on every firm known to have supplied mechanical locking frames to the British railway companies, although (as explained) a few of these firms were not in fact involved in the design or erection of signal box structures.

Stevens

The firm of Stevens & Co. (which in due course became Stevens & Son, and then Stevens & Sons) was founded in the 1820s by John Stevens, as gas and general engineers. After operating from various addresses in Southwark, the firm settled by the early 1840s in Darlington Place off the east side of Southwark Bridge Road, from which the name 'Darlington Works' was taken. Subsequent expansion took place on the same site (which, however, was renumbered as 16-19 Southwark Bridge Road in the 1840s, and then as 237/9/41/43 Southwark Bridge Road in 1869), and in a further building on the other side of the road acquired during the 1850s (then 178 Southwark Bridge Road, but renumbered as 104 Lancaster Street in 1869). In addition, there was by the late 1860s a Scottish works at 640 New City Road, Glasgow.

Stevens' first known involvement in the new field of railway signalling was in 1841, when they manufactured the first semaphore signals for Gregory of the London & Croydon Railway. Soon they were supplying similar signals to the London & Brighton and South Eastern Railways, and establishing themselves as the country's leading signalling firm. As described in **Chapter 1**, 'stirrup' frames were supplied from around 1843/4, and interlocked frames from 1860. In 1870, Stevens patented the 'tappet' frame, essentially the first 'modern' type of mechanical interlocking, and this helped them to hold on to a good portion of the market for a while. However, by the mid-1870s, S&F and McK&H had driven Stevens out of the top place; and Stevens did not help their own cause by failing to pay the first renewal fee on the 1870 patent when it became due in 1873, with the result that any manufacturer could now adopt tappet locking (albeit that few in fact did so until after 1884, when the patent would have expired anyway). By 1890, Stevens were supplying in quantity only the NE, LSW, NB, GNoS, and Caledonian. The decline of the firm may have been due to a falling-off of interest in later generations, as is commonly seen in family firms, and perhaps also to an inability to effect the same cost reductions as the more recently-founded firms. The Stevens frame design itself was a very marketable product, as is demonstrated by the fact that several railway companies had frames built by other contractors to the Stevens design, and by the near-universal adoption of tappet locking on later frame designs.

During World War I, the London works was shut down (the buildings were demolished in the 1960s). But there was still a good volume of work from the Scottish customers, and to retain this the Glasgow works was incorporated as a separate Limited Company, Stevens & Sons (Glasgow) Ltd., in January 1915. This company continued to trade until 1923, whereupon the Glasgow assets passed to the Balbardie Steel Works, Bathgate.

Early, pre-interlocking, Stevens boxes are illustrated at **Plates 11 & 12**. **Plate 21** shows a gable-to-track box of the 1860s, and other boxes built in this way were Summit Tunnel East (L&Y), and Dryclough Junction (L&Y). The design of these early Stevens boxes was not standardised in detail, but they generally had vertical boarding (if timber), and window sashes with small panes (2 or 3 panes up, 2 panes across).

By 1871, however, a standard **Stevens** box design had also been evolved. Most examples were of timber construction, with vertical boarding, but those on the L&Y were of brick or stone, as was normal on that railway, and there were a few brick examples elsewhere. In all cases, there was vertical boarding in the gable ends, usually extending down to form a very shallow 'valancing', with a v-notch at the foot of the boards. This shallow valancing was found also on the front and rear. Bargeboards were usually plain and without finials, but decorative bargeboards were provided on some L&Y and some Whitehaven, Cleator & Egremont boxes. Operating floor windows had very large panes for the period; sashes had no vertical glazing bars and generally three horizontal bars, the lowest being thicker than the others. However, the smallest boxes, and some others, had only two horizontal bars (*LNWRS, Plate 17.21*). The last boxes known to have been built to this Stevens design were in the mid-1880s, and after this, all Stevens' customers had the boxes built to their own designs. Only two standard Stevens boxes now exist; Grain Crossing (SE), and Woolley Coal Siding (L&Y).

Plate 107 Buckland Junction shows the standard **Stevens** box design. Built circa 1880/1, this box would have been ordered either by the LCD or by the Dover & Deal Joint Committee (which is known to have given Stevens the contracts for Martin Mill and Walmer). It closed on 7th December 1980. The brick base is probably a later addition, and extra outer frames have been added to the windows nearest the door.
M. Christensen

A number of CLC boxes were built to what appear to be special Stevens designs. Cheadle, Baguley, and Northenden Jn. were brick boxes of the 1870s with decorative bargeboards, Stevens-type vertical boarding and 'valancing' in the gables, and 3-panes-up, 2-across operating floor window sashes, with curved framing at the head. Hunts Cross East Jn. (circa 1882) and Knutsford East (1866) were timber boxes with horizontal boarding, plain 3-panes-deep operating floor windows, and 'flowing' decorative bargeboards. Identical in outline to the latter two boxes was the **Stevens/MS&L** Type of circa 1882-6, which, however, had vertical battened boarding (as was standard on the MS&L at this period), and bargeboards that were plain except for a small roundel near the foot. A few boxes to other special Stevens designs are known on the CLC and the L&Y.

Notes applicable to Tables 10, 11, 13, 15, 16, 17, 18, 20, 21, 22 and 23

(i) Further information on the work done by each contractor for individual railway companies is in many cases given in **Chapters 6, 8, 9 and 10**.

(ii) The work listed in these tables does not pretend to represent a complete list of the work done by each contractor, but all important contracts should be included (overseas contracts excluded).

(iii) Where uncertainty is expressed in the right-hand column, further explanation may be available in the text of **this chapter**, or in **Chapters 6, 9 or 10**.

(iv) These tables list the railway companies to which the contractor concerned supplied mechanical locking frames. Normally, of course, the contractor would also have supplied other signalling equipment to these railway companies at the same periods. The tables do not include companies to which the contractor supplied other items but not locking frames. Also excluded from the tables are the power frames supplied by McK&H, the RSCo, and Westinghouse.

TABLE 10

Railway Companies Supplied with Stevens' Frames
(Excludes pre-1860 work)

Railway Company	Work done by Stevens	Whether Stevens box designs used
GE	Some 1870-84	No (in most cases: but possibly some in early 1870s)
GN	A little 1866-88	No
MS&L	A little circa 1882-6	Yes (Non-standard design)
NE	S. Divn: some in 1870s	No
	C. Divn: most in 1880s/90s	No
	N. Divn: most 1867-circa 1916	No
LT&S	Some in 1870s	Not known (likely)
CLC	Much, until 1886	Some (Non-standard designs)
LNW/GW Joint	A little in 1870s	Not known
WC&E	Most, until 1877	Yes
NL	Some, until 1878	No
L&Y	Some 1861-83	Yes
M&C	Most	No
C&WJ	Some	No
Northampton & Banbury Jn.	One contract, 1897	Not known
Cornwall Minerals	Some circa 1875	Not known
LSW	Most 1860-1890s, some subsequently	No
S&DJ	Most	No (but see **Chapter 6**)
LBSC	One contract, 1866	Not known
IoW	Most (work done 1875-82)	Some
SE	Some, until circa 1884	Yes
LCD	Some, until circa 1881	Yes
NB	Most	No
GNoS	Most	No
Cal.	Much, until 1900s	No
GSW	All (but see **Chapter 6**)	No
Portpatrick	One contract, 1877	No
Manx Northern	All (four frames, 1879-86)	No

Saxby/Saxby & Farmer

The story of John Saxby's patents, and of the foundation and subsequent history of the firm of Saxby & Farmer, has already been largely told in **Chapters 1 & 2**. The partnership between Saxby and Farmer was terminated in 1888 (although the name of the firm was not altered), when Saxby went to France to manage a French offshoot. Farmer died in 1892, and in 1893 the firm was made a Limited Company. Saxby returned from France in 1900, at the age of 79, to retirement in Sussex. He died in 1913, leaving an estate of over £80,000. S&F was always one of the top three British signalling firms, although its heyday came perhaps in the 1870s.

The early Saxby boxes were also described and illustrated in **Chapter 1**. As noted there, design was fairly standardised right from 1857: timber construction with vertical boarding, low-pitched hipped roof, windows some 3ft. deep with one horizontal glazing bar and each sash 2 or 3 panes across, and no decorative features. The boxes built up to mid-1863, without a boarded lower storey (**Plates 14, 15, 16 & 17**), have been classified **Type 1a**. These boxes (other than those built after December 1862) are all listed in **Table 1**. Post-1863 boxes, with a boarded locking room, are classified **Type 1b**. Until circa 1867, vertical boarding remained the norm (**Plate 19**), although some boxes of circa 1863 had horizontal lapped boarding in the lower part, and vertical boarding above operating floor level only (**Plate 18**). From circa 1867 horizontal lapped boarding was normal, and this remained the case on all subsequent S&F box designs, except for the aberrant Type 3. Brick boxes also appeared from circa 1867. Some boxes continued to be built to the plain Type 1b design into the 1870s, but most boxes from circa 1868/9 were to the more sophisticated designs described below. Special variations on Type 1b were the LNW/GW Joint Type 1 boxes (**Plate 221**), and the **Chester & Holyhead** and **Lancaster & Carlisle** designs on the LNW (*LNWRS, Plates 9.2 & 9.3*), which may well have been built by the railway company and not by S&F.

The developments in S&F box design from 1868 can be divided into two strands, the boxes for the 'northern' lines (primarily the LNW, L&Y, and MS&L) following one course, and those for the 'southern' lines another. Dealing first with the 'southern' strand, the first change came with the provision of upper lights to enlarge the glazing area (**Type 2a**). Type 2a boxes were particularly widespread on the southern part of the LNW (in BTF construction) and on the LBSC and GW (in timber construction), but the only examples remaining today are the much-altered Banbury Lane (*LNWRS, Plate 9.9*) and the top of one of the Cornwall Railway's Truro boxes of 1874, now used as a shed. **Type 2b** (from 1874) differed only in the addition of small decorative eaves brackets. Type 3, however, was very much an aberration, having vertical boarding with broad battens (otherwise unknown on S&F boxes). The earlier **Type 3a** boxes (Cooksbridge, Southerham Junction, Partridge Green, Southwater, and the Crystal Palace boxes) had no upper lights and no eaves brackets, but differed from Type 1 in that there was boarding between the windows and eaves. The later **Type 3b** boxes (from 1875) had small eaves brackets as on Type 2b, but again did not have glazed upper lights. Instead they had panelled boarding above the windows (Slinfold, Cranleigh, Baynards), or a very broad fascia board (Bramley & Wonersh). The boxes for the GW at Westbourne Bridge (circa 1877) and Westbourne Park were also virtually to this design.

Type 4, used only on the B&E and the South Devon from 1874-6 (but quite numerous, as most of the stations on those lines were interlocked in this period) introduced the curved framing for the upper lights, which was to be used also on Type 5. Small eaves brackets were provided and, uniquely, were placed above the upper lights rather than on the posts between them. With one bracket above each vertical glazing bar, they were also more closely spaced than the eaves brackets on other S&F designs. Almost all Type 4 boxes were of brick construction.

The culmination of the 'southern' designs was the **Type 5**, introduced in 1876. This had a much greater overhang to the roof with much larger eaves brackets, and curved framing at the head of the main window sashes to complement the curved framing of the upper lights (**Plates 58, 70, 114 & 115**). Overall, it was one of the most stylish signal box designs ever built. Several hundred Type 5 boxes were built, on more than a dozen different railways, including some in Ireland, but most notably on the LBSC. Only a few (all on the LBSC) were built after 1890. Timber, BTF, and brick examples are known. The only significant variation within the type

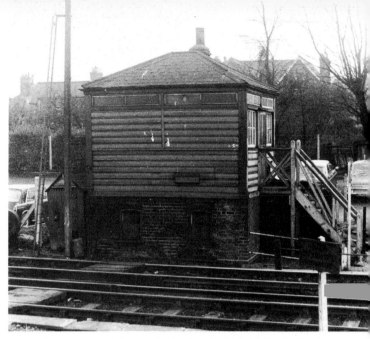

Plate 109 Billingshurst is the last **S&F Type 1b** box in use. According to LBSC records, it was built as late as 1876. It certainly has a S&F 'rocker' frame (No. 2273) of that year, but it is just possible that the box was actually built earlier than this. Another (disused) Type 1b box still stands at Kemp Town Junction (1869). Billingshurst measures 13ft. 7in. x 10ft. x 10ft. The operating floor windows are 3ft. 1in. deep. The locking room window is 3ft. 3in. across and 3ft. 7in. deep. Most S&F timber boxes had locking room windows of this style, although few were 2 panes across rather than 3. The horizontal lapped boarding on this box is of 6½in. cover width.

R. D. Foster

Plate 110 This box, at the north end of Wimbledon Station, was one of the few examples of a BTF **S&F Type 2a** box outside of the LNW. Built during 1868/9 in connection with the expansion of the station, it is uncertain whether it was ordered by the LSW or the LBSC. The contemporary LBSC Peckham Rye to Sutton, LBSC/LSW Joint Streatham to Wimbledon, and LSW Wimbledon to Kingston and Kensington to Richmond lines also seem to have had S&F Type 2a boxes. This box stood until comparatively recent years, but had long been disused (hence the boarded windows). A timber Type 2a box can be seen at **Plate 79**.

L. Crosier

Plate 111 The timber **S&F Type 2b** box at Purley (LBSC) was built in 1874, and replaced when the line was quadrupled in 1897. The photograph dates from circa 1890.

Croydon Public Libraries

TABLE 11

Railway Companies Supplied with Saxby/Saxby & Farmer Frames

Railway Company	Work done by Saxby/S&F	Whether S&F box designs used (and types known)
GE	Most 1861-circa 1875, some later	Some, until 1878: 1, 2a, 5
CV&H	Most (work done 1888-94)	No
GN	Most 1867-90s, some later	No
M&GN and Constituents	Most	No
MS&L/GC	A little	Some, 1874-7: 6, 8
LDEC	Half of route, 1893-7	No
H&B	All 1885-97, 1903-20	Yes, 1885-97: 10, 12b
NE	S. Divn: some in 1860s and 1870s	No
	N. Divn: some in 1870s	No
CLC	Some, until 1886	Not usually, but one case known: 8
LNW	All 1861-73, some until 1884	Most until 1873, some until 1876: 1, 2a, 2b, 6, 8
LNW/GW Joint	Most, 1860s-84	No (but see **Chapter 6**)
NL	Some, until 1878	No
MSJ&A	All 1877-82	Yes: 9
L&Y	Most 1860s-1879, some until 1881	Yes: 1, 6, 7, 8, 9
CK&P	Most in 1870s	Yes: 6
GW	Much until 1876, some until 1885	Yes: 2a, 3b, 5
B&E	Virtually all (work done 1870-76)	Most: 2a, 4
South Devon	All (work done 1873-76)	Yes: 2a, 4
Cornwall	Some 1875-6	Yes: 2a
Liskeard & Looe	1901 boxes	Yes: 12b
DN&S	Southern Section, 1885	Yes: 11
Golden Valley	1889 work (no boxes)	
Monmouthshire	Some	Not known
Manchester & Milford	Most (work done 1895)	Yes: 12b
B&M	Some	Yes: 12b
Barry	All 1888-95, 1903-20	No
LSW	Some throughout	Some in 1860s: 2a
Somerset & Dorset	Bath Extension, 1874	Not known
LBSC	Virtually all 1857-98, much 1898-1901, all 1901-04	All until 1880, some until 1898: 1a, 1b, 2a, 2b, 3a, 3b, 5
IoW	Some work circa 1892	Yes: 12b
IoWC and Constituents	Some	Not known
SE	Some until circa 1884, some 1892-5	Yes: 1, 5, 12a
LCD	Much	Yes: 1, 5, 10, 12a
SEC	Some	No
NB	Some	No
Cal.	Some until 1900s	No
Wigtownshire	Work for opening, 1875-7	Not known
Girvan & Portpatrick Jn.	Most work for opening, 1877	Not known (likely)
Met.	Most until circa 1886	Some: 5
District	Most until circa 1901	Yes: 2a, 5
Bideford, Westward Ho! & Appledore	All (work done 1901-5)	No
East & West India Docks Co.	Some, circa 1870	Yes: 2a
London & St. Katharine Dock Co.	Some, 1880s	No
Beckton Gas Works	Some	Not known

lay in the locking room windows of some BTF and brick boxes. Whilst the majority had the standard S&F locking room window (**Plate 74**) found on all S&F designs, most LCD examples had a slightly larger segmental-arched window 3 panes up and 2 across, and many of the taller LBSC boxes had much larger semi-circular-arched windows (**Plate 116**). Further variants of locking room window found on a few large LBSC boxes were pointed arches (Eastbourne, Polegate Crossing, Windmill Bridge Junction) and very large segmental arches (Newhaven Harbour North, Sutton Junction, Streatham). Many of the larger boxes also had 'panelled' brickwork.

(continued on page 87)

Plate 112 Slinfold box; **S&F Type 3b** design. LBSC records state that this box was built in 1875; it was put up for inspection, along with the other boxes on the line, in 1878. It was originally 'Slinfold North', as the Board of Trade requirements demanded two boxes at this tiny station. Note the unusually small locking room window.

Authors' Collection

Plate 113 A typical **S&F Type 4** box at Cheddar (B&E). This box was inspected in September 1876 but had been brought into use sometime previously. The standard S&F roof vent can be seen here. The photograph was taken on 16th April 1965, two weeks before the box was abolished. Stoke Canon is now the only surviving Type 4 box.

C. L. Cadd

TABLE 12

Summary of Saxby/Saxby & Farmer Box Designs

Type	Period	Roof	Eaves Brackets	Operating Floor Windows	Boarding of Timber Boxes or Sections	Remarks
1a	1857-1863	Hipped	None	2 panes deep	Vertical	No boarding below operating floor
1b	1863-1870s	Hipped	None	2 panes deep	Vertical, or Horizontal lapped	Have boarded locking room storey
2a	1868-1874	Hipped	None	2 panes deep plus upper lights	Horizontal lapped	
2b	1874-1876	Hipped	Small	2 panes deep plus upper lights	Horizontal lapped	
3a	1872-1875	Hipped	None	2 panes deep (boarding above)	Vertical battened	
3b	1875-1878	Hipped	Small	2 panes deep (boarding above)	Vertical battened	
4	1874-1876	Hipped	Small	2 panes deep plus curved upper lights	(Uncertain)	
5	1876-1898	Hipped	Large	2 panes deep (curved frames) plus curved upper lights	Horizontal lapped	
6	1869-1876	Hipped	Small	2 panes deep	(Uncertain)	
7	1874-1876	Hipped	Small	2 panes deep plus lower windows	(Brick only)	
8	1874-1878	Hipped	Small	2 panes deep plus lower windows plus upper lights	Horizontal lapped	
9	1876-1883	Hipped	Large	2 panes deep plus lower windows plus upper lights	Horizontal lapped	
10	1884-1885	Gabled	None	2 panes deep	Horizontal lapped	
11	1885	Hipped	None	2 panes deep	Horizontal lapped	
12a	circa 1890-1894	Gabled	None	2 panes deep	Horizontal lapped	Deeper windows and larger roof overhang than Type 12b
12b	circa 1884-1901	Gabled	None	2 panes deep	Horizontal lapped	

Plate 114 A splendid view, taken in 1910, of the timber **S&F Type 5** box at West Drayton & Yiewsley Loop. This box opened with the new Staines & West Drayton Railway (a child of the GW) on 9th August 1884, and closed on 29th May 1927. The GW main line is visible in the background. Note the S&F roof vent, the 'T' (telegraph) board above the (not original) GW cast-iron nameplate, and the ladder and lamp for exchanging the single line staff. Brick coal and ashes bunkers are also prominent. There is no locking room window in the front; as the box faced north, there was probably a window at the rear instead.

British Rail

Plate 115 A brick **S&F Type 5** box at Lingfield (LBSC). This box opened with the line on 10th March 1884. The right-hand one third of the box is an extension of 1894, very nicely done but with brickwork of a slightly different colour. Lingfield is still in use, as are some 40 other Type 5 boxes (see **Plate 44** for another box of this type).

R. D. Foster

Plate 116 A page from the January 1880 S&F Catalogue. At the centre is a large BTF Type 5 box with panelled brickwork, and large semicircular-arched locking room windows; at the right is a timber Type 5 box. Note that both these boxes are shown with operating floor window sashes 3 panes across, as found on a minority of S&F boxes of all types, in place of the more common 2 panes across sashes. At the left, where one might have expected a small brick Type 5 box, is a figment of the artists's imagination — but cf. the later LDEC boxes **(Plate 182)**.

Public Record Office

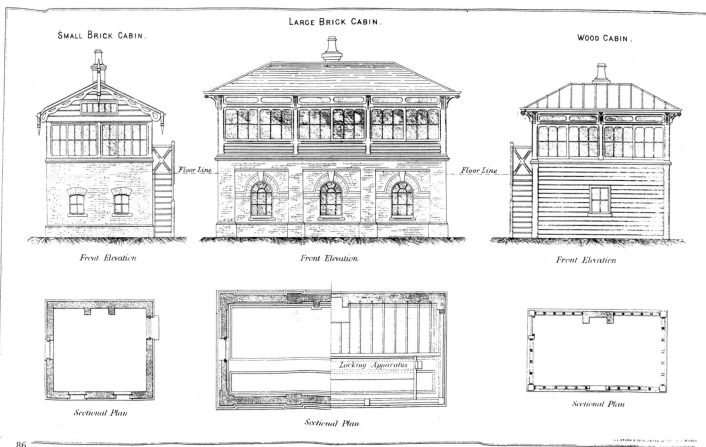

21.

SAXBY & FARMER'S RAILWAY SAFETY APPLIANCES.

SMALL BRICK CABIN.

LARGE BRICK CABIN.

WOOD CABIN.

Floor Line

Floor Line

Locking Apparatus

Front Elevation

Front Elevation

Front Elevation

Sectional Plan

Sectional Plan

Sectional Plan

86

Turning now to the 'northern' course of development, **Type 6** introduced in 1869 differed from Type 1b only in the addition of small eaves brackets. Type 6 boxes were widespread on the L&Y and the northern part of the LNW, mostly in brick construction. **Type 7** saw the addition of lower windows, with sliding sashes — a feature never provided on the 'southern' designs, but retained on the later 'northern' Types 8 and 9. Only a dozen L&Y boxes are known to this design, which was supplanted immediately by the **Type 8** design with the further addition of upper lights. By this date (1874) upper lights had of course already been used for six years on the 'southern' designs. But the upper lights on the 'northern' Types 8 and 9 boxes were never given curved framing, nor was curved framing ever used in the main sashes on the 'northern' designs. From 1874, the L&Y was the only company on which the S&F 'northern' designs appeared in significant numbers. A handful of aberrant boxes of 1874/5 were given double-height lower windows almost as deep as the main windows (Penistone L&Y, Lytham Station, Crewe North Junction).

As in the south, developments culminated in 1876 with the introduction of large eaves brackets (identical to those on Type 5 boxes) and a greater overhang to the roof (**Type 9**). Otherwise, Type 9 was identical to Type 8. BTF construction was normal for Types 8 and 9, with some STF and timber examples. The last Type 9 boxes were built in 1883, as there were no customers left using S&F box designs in the 'northern' area after the L&Y turned away from S&F in that year.

Stylish though they were, the Types 5 and 9 boxes cannot have been particularly cheap to construct, so it is perhaps not surprising that simpler designs should have been developed in the mid-1880s, when RSCo competition began to bite. The first ever S&F gabled design (**Type 10**) appeared in 1884 on the LCD's Maidstone to Ashford line, and in the following year on the H&B. The BTF construction of these boxes, and the bargeboards placed directly over the boarding, made them very reminiscent of the LNW Type 4 design. Also dating from 1885 were the plain hipped timber boxes (**Type 11**) on the southern half of the Didcot, Newbury & Southampton Railway. Another gabled design, Type 12, was evolved at the same time as Type 10 but proved longer-lasting. Again of very plain appearance, Type 12 boxes were built in BTF or timber form. The SE and LCD examples of this design (**Type 12a**) had deeper windows, and a greater overhang to the roof at front and back, than did the boxes built for other companies (**Type 12b**). The last known type 12 boxes were those for the Liskeard & Looe Railway in 1901; after this S&F were supplying only to railways with their own box designs.

Other boxes for which S&F seem to have had a partial rather than complete design responsibility were several GE designs and the S&F-built LDEC boxes (**see Chapter 6**).

Plate 117 (left) Fish Dock Road (Grimsby) was one of a handful of **S&F Type 6** boxes on the MS&L. The line here was doubled in 1874 and the box was most likely built then. It is set at an angle to the lines for better sighting round the extremely sharp curve. The small brackets on the 'Northern' types tended to be flatter than those on the 'Southern' types, although as hand-turned items, both were subject to some variation (**vide Plate 119**). Fish Dock Road was abolished and demolished in 1985: Type 6 boxes still in use are Lambrigg Crossing (LNW, 1872), Daisyfield Station (L&Y, 1873 — **Plate 25**), and Horrocksford Junction (L&Y, 1873).

R. Newman

Plate 118 (right) Several of the **S&F Type 7** boxes were on the Liverpool to Preston line, as exemplified by Maghull (1875). The locking room windows have been bricked up. Maghull and Streethouse West are the only surviving Type 7 boxes.

T. T. Sutcliffe

Plate 119 The **S&F Type 8** box at Moss Side Station (L&Y) built in 1876. Although much painting-out of window panes is evident, this box was better-preserved in later years than most of the type, many having the upper lights and lower windows boarded over. The bricks in the locking room window arches of this box were arranged in an unusual way. Moss Side was abolished on 30th March 1983. Surviving Type 8 boxes are Brierfield Station (L&Y, 1876), Chaffers Siding (L&Y, 1876), Hall Road (L&Y, 1878), Hale (CLC), and Shireoaks Station (MS&L, circa 1874).

R. D. Foster

Plate 120 Also well-maintained until the end was the 1878-built **S&F Type 9** box at Clayton West Station, which retained its L&Y nameboard. The base of this STF box was built with very regular coursing. It was abolished on 22nd January 1983. Ten Type 9 boxes remain in use.

R. Newman

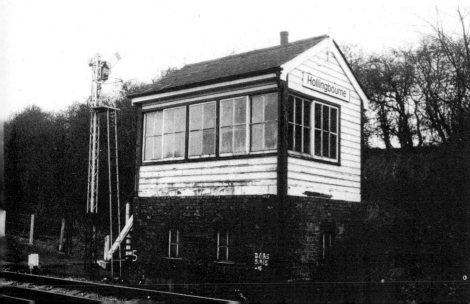

Plate 121 Opened on 1st July 1884, the **S&F Type 10** boxes at Bearsted, Hollingbourne, and Charing were all abolished on 14th April 1984, leaving Hothfield as the last Type 10 box in use until it too was abolished on 16th February 1985. Hollingbourne is shown here three days before the end; a rear view of Charing is in **Plate 46**.

P. Kay

Plate 122 A good number of **S&F Type 12a** boxes were built on the SE in the early 1890s. Stonegate (originally Ticehurst Road) was inspected, along with the identical boxes at Frant and Etchingham, on 6th May 1893. Stonegate measured 12ft. by 10ft., with 5ft. 1½ in. deep windows. It closed on 30th May 1984, leaving nine surviving examples of the type.

P. Kay

Plate 123 The largest number of **S&F Type 12b** boxes was on the Manchester & Milford Railway, interlocked in 1895. Here is Llanilar, one of the timber examples, photographed, two years after closure, in 1966. Note the gap in the paintwork above the locking room window where the S&F maker's plate has been removed. Like most of the M&M boxes, Llanilar measured 9ft. by 9ft., and it was 9ft. high. The Type 12b boxes on the B&M and the Liskeard & Looe differed in having finials. Only two Type 12b boxes survive, Sandown (IoW) and the preserved Rhiwderin (B&M).

M. Christensen

McKenzie & Holland

The partnership between the engineers John McKenzie and Thomas Clunes, and the financier Walter Holland, was formed on 25th June 1861. The new company, McKenzie, Clunes & Holland, took over the business operated by Clunes at the Vulcan Ironworks, Shrub Hill, Worcester, and began to branch out into the field of railway signalling. It is said (but cannot now be checked, as the Patent Office licensing records have been destroyed) that the company operated at first by taking out a licence of Chambers' patent. The first of McK&H's own frame designs was patented in 1866, and it was this 1866 patent that was challenged by Saxby in the courts (**see Chapter 2**). McK&H's business seems to have built up more slowly than S&F's, and little is known of their work in the 1860s: but by the mid-1870s they were one of the 'top three' signalling firms, and they retained that position until 1920. Clunes left the partnership at the end of 1873, and the firm was renamed McKenzie & Holland, although McKenzie was in fact dead by this date. Several subsequent changes were made in the partners, with Holland's son (also Walter) as the leading figure in later years. The events leading to the formation of a Limited Company in 1901, and subsequently to the take-over by Westinghouse in 1920 and the closure of the Worcester works in 1921, were described in **Chapter 2**. McK&H's major customers in later years were the GE, GN, NE, NS, and the South Wales companies. Offices were opened in London, Cardiff, Malton, and Stoke-on-Trent to deal with customers in those areas. McK&H were also very active in

Australia, opening a works in Melbourne circa 1884, and another in Brisbane in 1886.

The story of McK&H box designs is a very simple one, as only two designs were used in quantity, and there were no changes at all after 1876. No photographs are known of McK&H boxes of the 1860s; the **Type 1** design may have been in use prior to 1870, but the known examples all date from 1870-75. Type 1 was a hipped design, appearing in brick or timber construction, but with a brick chimney in all cases. Distinctive features were the curving of the boarding under the eaves, and the use of vertical sashes in combination with sliding sashes in the operating floor windows. The locking windows of some (perhaps all) of the earlier brick boxes had stone lintels, but by 1873 the large nearly-semicircular arched locking room windows, used also on subsequent McK&H designs, had been introduced. Type 1 boxes were built to standard sizes as shown in **Table 14**. The only Type 1 boxes now existing in recognisable form are the NS examples at Tutbury Crossing and Leek Brook Junction.

The **Type 2** design, which appeared in 1875, was identical to Type 1, except for having deeper (3 panes deep) operating floor windows. Very few were built, the only ones known being Canonbury Junction (GN or NL), Bath Road (NL), Hartlebury Station (GW), and Hartlebury Junction (GW). Rather similar (but not proved to be McK&H-built) was the 1875 Met. box at Liverpool Street (still standing), which has curved eaves brackets similar to those on contemporary McK&H-built GE boxes.

(continued on page 92)

Plate 124 A 19ft. 3in. long **McK&H Type 1** box, with stone-lintel locking room windows, at Pinfold Crossing (NS). This box had additional glazing down to operating floor level at the centre front. It closed on 28th January 1981.

R. D. Foster

Plate 125 Blythe Bridge (NS) was a 12ft. 3in. long **McK&H Type 1** box with arched locking room windows (two, due to the height of the box). These McK&H arched locking room windows were 36in. across, mostly 4 panes across, but in a few cases 3 panes across with wider panes. They were often very tall, the tallest known being those at Bollington, which were 10 panes up. As at Pinfold, Blythe Bridge has additional operating floor glazing, here at the level crossing end. The hipped porch, with valancing, is most likely original. Blythe Bridge was abolished on 16th March 1980.

R. D. Foster

Plate 126 Hartlebury Station (GW) is the last surviving **McK&H Type 2** box. It was originally known as Hartlebury Centre and was inspected, together with Hartlebury Junction, on 24th June 1876.
R. Newman

Plate 127 (left) A BTF **McK&H Type 3** box at Baschurch (GW), built circa 1880. Gabled porches with a window like this were common on Type 3 boxes, but not all had valancing. A timber Type 3 box is illustrated in **Plate 45**, and a stone example in **Plate 89**. Baschurch is one of twenty Type 3 boxes still standing.

J. P. Morris

91

TABLE 13

Railway Companies Supplied with McK&H Frames

Railway Company	Work done by McK&H	Whether McK&H box designs used (and types known)
GE	Much throughout	Some, until 1878: 1, 3
East Norfolk	Most (work done 1870s)	Yes: 3
Felixstowe R&P Co.	Work for opening, 1877	Yes: 3
CV&H	One contract, 1882	Yes: 3
GN	Much throughout	No
Stafford & Uttoxeter	All (work done 1881/2)	Yes: 3
MS&L/GC	Some, 1905-20	No
WM&CQ	Some, 1885	Not known (likely)
NE	S. Divn: some from 1870s, all from circa 1900	No
	N. Divn: A little from 1890s	No
Severn & Wye	Some	Not known
Clifton Extension	All original boxes (1874-7)	Yes: 1
CLC	Some, until 1886	Not known
LNW/GW Joint	A little, until 1884	No (see Chapter 6)
NL	Some, until 1878	Some: 2
West Lancashire	All work for opening, 1882-4	Yes: 3
NS	All known work	Until 1876: 1
GW	Much until 1885	Yes: 1, 2, 3
Bristol & North Somerset	Work for opening, 1873	Yes: 1
Newent	Work for opening, 1885	Not known (likely)
Monmouthshire	Some	Not known
Manchester & Milford	One contract, 1893	Yes: 3
Pembroke & Tenby	All boxes (1893-4)	Yes: 3
Maenclochog	All original boxes (1876)	Yes: 3
R&SB	All work (1885-1906)	Yes: 3 variant
PT	A little, circa 1897	Yes: 3
Cambrian	All until 1890, some later	Yes: 1, 3
A (N&SW) D&R	All known work	Yes: 3
Pontypridd, Caerphilly & Newport	All known work (1884)	Yes: 3
B&M	Most	Yes: 1, 3
Rhymney	All	Yes: 3
TV	Most	Yes, 1876-95: 3 variant
Cardiff	All known work	Yes: 3
N&B	Most	Yes: 1, 3
SHT	All known work	Yes: 3 variant
Corris	All known work (1883)	No
LSW	Some from 1890s	No
LBSC	A little circa 1900	No
SE	Some 1893-5	Yes: 3
Highland	Most	Yes, until 1900s: 3 variant
Met.	A little in 1870s	(See text)
Festiniog	Three boxes	Yes: 3
North Wales N.G.	Most (1877-8)	Yes: 3
Tyne Commissioners	Most	Not known
Ashington Collieries	Some	No
Lambton Collieries	Some	No
Oxfordshire Ironstone	All	No

TABLE 14

Standard Dimensions of McK&H Type 1 Boxes

Standard Width:	12ft. 3in.	
		Window pattern on front
Standard Lengths:	12ft. 3in.	2s-2/2/2-2s
	14ft. 4in.	2s-2/2/2v/2-2s
	16ft. 8in.	2s-2/2/2v/2/2-2s
	19ft. 3in.	2s-2/2v/2/2/2v/2-2s

(s = sliding sash, v = vertical sash)

Also during 1875/6 came the change to gabled roofs, producing the **Type 3** design (otherwise similar to Type 2). Used until 1921, this was one of the longest-lasting of all box designs. It is known on the lines of twenty or more railways, including some in Ireland, in timber, BTF, brick and stone construction. The timber boxes were weatherboarded. Some Type 3 boxes had a small 2-panes-across gable window/vent. Bargeboards were usually plain, except for a rounding at the foot, but a few boxes (e.g. Ruabon Middle) had 'flowing' decorative bargeboards similar to those in **Plate 166**, and all Type 3 boxes on the TV and R&SB had a special form of bargeboard as shown in **Plate 248**. Type 3 boxes on the Highland were built with vertical battened boarding and corrugated-iron roofs (**Plate 296**).

Also worthy of mention is the McK&H design of ground frame hut, with lean-to roof. This was in use by the 1880s or earlier.

Other box designs showing McK&H influence were several GE designs (**see Chapter 6**), the NS boxes of 1876-85 (**see Chapter 6**), and Chester No. 5 box on the LNW/GW Joint line (**see Chapter 6**). The first and last of these had the McK&H 'parachute' finials as used on McK&H signal posts.

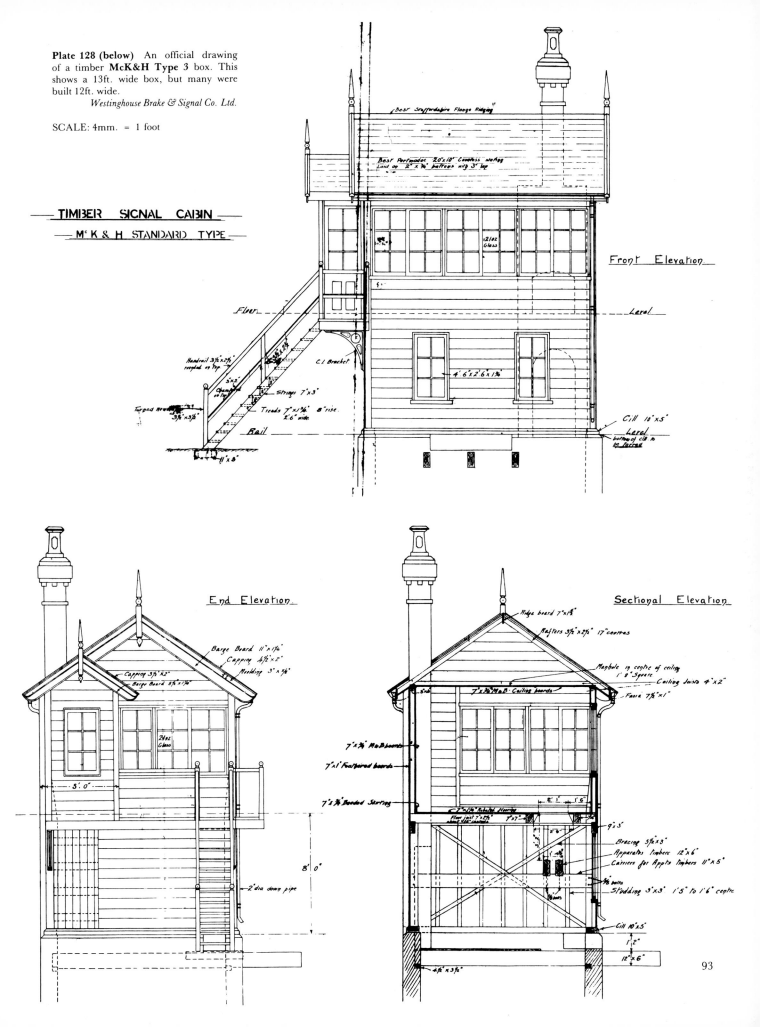

Plate 128 (below) An official drawing of a timber **McK&H Type 3** box. This shows a 13ft. wide box, but many were built 12ft. wide.

Westinghouse Brake & Signal Co. Ltd.

SCALE: 4mm. = 1 foot

TIMBER   SIGNAL   CABIN

Mᶜ K & H   STANDARD   TYPE

Front Elevation

End Elevation

Sectional Elevation

93

Courtney & Stephens

The Dublin firm of Courtney, Stephens & Co. (alias Courtney, Stephens & Bailey) was active in the signalling market by the mid-1860s. Locking frames were manufactured to W. Anderson's patent of 1864. Sales were primarily to the Irish railways, but in 1868 the firm claimed that Anderson's apparatus was being 'fast adopted' on 'the Lancashire lines'. This seems most likely to be a reference to the L&Y, but nothing is known of Anderson frames in Lancashire from any other source, and one suspects that sales in England were in fact very few.

Another frame was patented by Bailey in 1874, and the firm was certainly still supplying to the Irish railways in the 1875-7 period. From 1877 to 1882, they acted as Irish agents of the Gloucester Wagon Co.

Courtney & Stephens do seem to have built signal box structures to their own design in Ireland, but there is no information as to whether they did so in the case of their English contracts.

As far as is presently known, Courtney & Stephens were the only Irish firm to manufacture locking frames.

Easterbrook

Walter John Easterbrook, born in or near Newton Abbot in 1841, spent several years in the service of Saxby & Farmer prior to 1867/8, when he took out three patents for locking frames, and left S&F to commence business on his own account. His financial backing came from George Henry Hannaford. The company was originally known as Easterbrook & Co., but around 1877 the name was changed to Easterbrook, Hannaford & Co. It operated from a London office (originally at 3a Finsbury Place South, then at 122 London Wall, and finally at 4 Queen Anne's Gate) but never owned any manufactory. The equipment was made instead by other firms, initially by Hennett & Co., Ironfounders and Engineers, of Bridgwater, Somerset, who in 1873 incorporated themselves as The Bridgwater Engineering Co. Ltd.

By 1873 Easterbrook's business was beginning to build up, but in that year Saxby emerged victorious from the court case which he had brought over his and Easterbrook's rival 1867 patents for catch-handle locking. This must have damaged Easterbrook, but he kept going. In 1878 he had to seek new manufacturers, as The Bridgwater Engineering Co. ceased to trade. By 1885 he was using the Bristol Wagon Works Co. Ltd. as his manufacturers, but it is possible that he used other firms as well.

Although he continued to achieve a reasonable turnover, Easterbrook finally destroyed himself by the failure of an attempt to get his own back on Saxby. Around 1883 he served writs on several leading railway companies which had used S&F frames, alleging infringement of one of his 1867 patents (a different one from that with which the 1873 case was concerned). As it happened, Easterbrook had never manufactured any frames to this particular patent, except for an installation at Leigh-on-Sea Sidings in 1881. The test case against the GW was decided in the railway company's favour in July 1885, with heavy damages awarded against Easterbrook, and a condemnation of his equipment as dangerous. Although the equipment which Easterbrook sold was in fact perfectly safe, being based on later patents, this judgment and the damages ruined his company. He moved to Bristol late in 1885 and attempted to trade under the name of the Bristol Wagon Works, but this did not last long, and he was soon out of the business altogether. In 1887 we find him as the proprietor of a fruiterers and pie shop in Bristol. He died in January 1914.

The Furness and the LT&S were Easterbrook's best customers. The last Easterbrook frame, at Green Road, was taken out of use on 31st July 1981, and is now at the National Railway Museum.

Any signalling contractor supplying generally at this period would necessarily have had a signal box design of his own, and box structures are indeed included in the Easterbrook advertisement in **Plate 30**. However, due to a lack of photographs of the relevant boxes, it has not been possible to identify beyond all doubt the Easterbrook box design, although it is very likely that the early LT&S boxes (**Plate 129**) were Easterbrook-designed and Easterbrook-built.

RAINHAM. STATION

Plate 129 Rainham box (LT&S) was built in 1881. Although there is no information as to the contract for this particular box, other contemporary LT&S boxes to the same design are known to have been Easterbrook contracts. A brick example can be seen on page 81 of George Dow's *LT&S Album* (Ian Allan). Rainham was replaced by a Midland box at the level crossing in 1924.

Lens of Sutton

TABLE 15

Railway Companies Supplied with Easterbrook Frames

Railway Company	Work done by Easterbrook	Whether Easterbrook box design used
GN	A little circa 1872	No
NE	N. Divn: a little in 1870s	No
LT&S	Most circa 1880-85	Probably (see text)
NL	Some circa 1869	Not known
Furness	Some circa 1880	No
Minehead	Work for opening, 1874	Not known

I'Anson

An interlocking frame was provisionally patented in 1867 by Charles I'Anson and Alfred Kitching of Darlington, the latter a Director of the NE and previously of the Stockton & Darlington Railway. In 1869 a second and more modern frame was patented by James I'Anson (Junior). Between 1867 and the mid-1880s, the firm of E. I'Anson & Sons, & Co. manufactured a good number of frames for the Darlington (Central) and Northern divisions of the NE. They are not known to have supplied elsewhere. Several I'Anson frames survived into recent years, but none now remain. As all NE boxes were built by building contractors to the railway company's designs, I'Anson would not have been involved in the provision of box structures.

Yardley/Smith

The Manchester ironmongers E. S. Yardley & Co., owned by Emily Yardley, appear to have entered the signalling field in 1867. The firm's signalling expert was William Smith, who patented a locking frame in 1870. The factory, called the Patent Railway Signal Works, was at Canal Street, Castlefield. Smith seems to have taken over the business himself around 1876, as the firm traded as William Smith from that date.

The great majority of the firm's work was for the L&Y and, in accordance with normal L&Y practice, the contractor's work included the design and building of the signal box structures. Three Yardley/Smith box designs are known. **Type 1** of 1872-78, found in brick or stone construction, had a hipped roof, 2-panes-by-2 sashes in the main operating floor windows plus upper lights, and a standardised type of segmental-arched locking room window (2 panes up, 3 across). **Type 2** of 1878-82 differed in omitting the upper lights and having curved framing at the head of the main sashes; only five boxes are known of this design. An entirely different design (**Type 3**) was used for the few known timber boxes.

Smith's business was badly affected by the start of the L&Y's sole contract arrangement with the RSCo. There are no known Smith signalling contracts after 1882, and the firm's name disappears from the Manchester directories altogether after 1886.

Plate 130 The **Yardley/Smith Type 1** box at Whitley Bridge (L&Y), built in 1875. The curious window arrangement at the near end is due to the door having originally been here; it is now at the other end. The stovepipe is a replacement for a brick chimney. Otherwise, the box is in original condition. It is still in use, as are other Type 1 boxes at Hensall Station and Bromley Cross.

R. Newman

TABLE 16

Railway Companies Supplied with Yardley/Smith Frames

Railway Company	Work done by Yardley/Smith	Whether Yardley/Smith box designs used (and types known)
GN	One contract, 1867 (fittings only)	
NE	N. Divn: a little in 1870s	No
L&Y	Some 1870-82	Yes: 1, 2, 3
Girvan & Portpatrick Jn.	One contract, 1876	Yes: 1

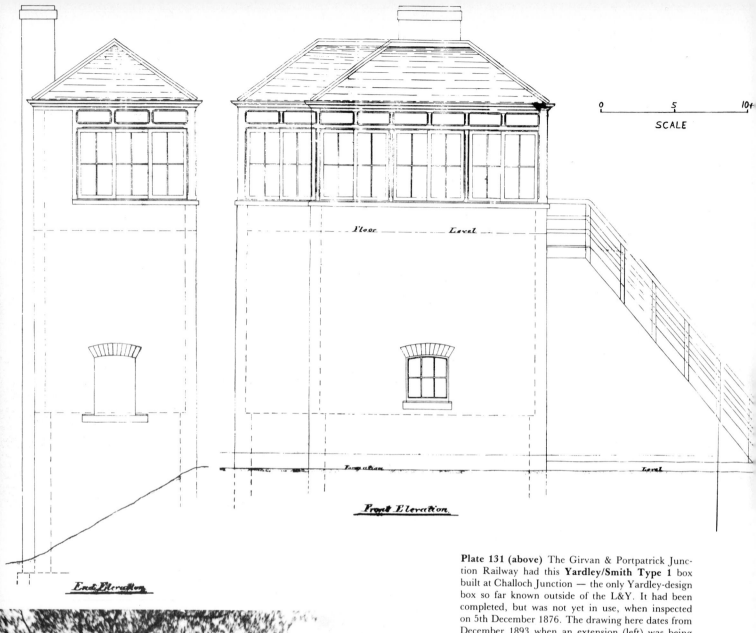

SCALE

Floor Level

Front Elevation.

End Elevation.

Plate 131 (above) The Girvan & Portpatrick Junction Railway had this **Yardley/Smith Type 1** box built at Challoch Junction — the only Yardley-design box so far known outside of the L&Y. It had been completed, but was not yet in use, when inspected on 5th December 1876. The drawing here dates from December 1893 when an extension (left) was being planned. The box closed on 15th January 1939.

Scottish Record Office

SCALE: 4mm = 1 foot

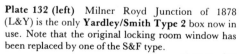

Plate 132 (left) Milner Royd Junction of 1878 (L&Y) is the only **Yardley/Smith Type 2** box now in use. Note that the original locking room window has been replaced by one of the S&F type.

T. T. Sutcliffe

Plate 133 The **Yardley/Smith Type 3** box at Clifton Junction (L&Y). This box was built in 1875 and is proved to be a Yardley contract by the presence of the company's stamp on the plan submitted to the Board of Trade. It was replaced by an L&Y-type box in 1901. A similar box existed at Robin Hood (L&Y). Note the two-piece door.

National Railway Museum

Ransomes & Rapier

The firm of Ransomes & Rapier was formed in 1869 to carry out the manufacture of railway equipment, as an offshoot of the well-established firm of Ransomes, Sims & Jefferies, the agricultural machinery specialists. Richard C. Rapier was in charge of the signalling side, and it was he who patented the 'horse-rake' frame in 1870. This was perhaps the most unusual locking frame ever produced in this country. It was specially designed for simplicity, with a minimal number of moving parts, so that it could be maintained by non-specialist labour. Rapier's patent also claimed that 'the circumstance that all the apparatus can be arranged entirely above the floor of the signal house . . . will greatly add to the warmth of the signal box and the comfort of the signalman'. Rapier became something of a leading light in the signalling profession for a brief period in the 1870s and, in March 1874, delivered a lengthy paper on signalling history and practices to the Institution of Civil Engineers.

The first known R&R contracts were (perhaps not surprisingly, given that the firm was based in Ipswich) for the GE, in 1871. R&R also carried out the signalling work for the Bury St. Edmunds & Thetford Railway in 1875. But the major sales were to the Great Northern Railway. R&R wrote to the GN in October 1872 'suggesting that one or two sets of their locking apparatus recently invented should be bought to give them a trial'. The GN's

Engineer reacted favourably to the simplicity of the design and the price which, at £7 per lever, was the cheapest he had come across. Over the next decade, the GN bought several dozen R&R frames, most notably for the Boston District. However, the simplicity of the Rapier frame also proved its downfall, as it was difficult to adapt the design to the increasingly complex layouts of the 1880s. No contracts are known after 1881, although the firm's 1888 catalogue still included signalling items. The company remains active in other fields of engineering. In railway circles it became better known for turntables and steam cranes than for its signalling equipment.

It is probable (but unproven) that the box structures on the Bury St. Edmunds & Thetford Railway were designed and built by R&R (see photograph of Barnham in Plate 102a of C. J. Gammell's *LNER Branch Lines 1945-65* published by OPC). Nothing is known of the design of the GE boxes. On the GN, the box structures would not have been an R&R responsibility.

The last R&R frame in use on the GN was that at Rauceby, removed on 4th May 1975, but another, at Vickers Gun Range Sidings on the Furness, lasted until 16th April 1983, and is now at the National Railway Museum. The origin of this frame is unknown; it must have been second-hand due to the date of the box (1897), and it may indicate that R&R carried out some work for the Furness in the 1870s.

William Baines & Co

William Baines of The Railway Plant Works, Smethwick, took out various patents for locking frames from 1868-73. The firm is known to have supplied frames for Dalton Junction (1870) and Lindal Cote Junction (1872) on the Furness Railway, and may have gained a few other contracts.

Crumlin Viaduct Co.

The Crumlin Viaduct Works Co. Ltd. was formed in 1871, taking over the works of Messrs Kennard Bros. It advertised itself as a supplier of signalling equipment (including locking frames). The only contract known to date was for part of the Severn & Wye Railway in 1875. The company was wound up in 1878.

Poole

A. Poole patented a locking frame in 1873 and, on 1st October of that year, the B&E authorised the installation of a Poole frame at Langport. No further installations are known.

Tweedy/Tyer

Joseph Tweedy of J. Tweedy & Co., Engineers, of Carlisle, patented a locking frame in 1873 and subsequently obtained a fair amount of work, mostly from railways in the immediate vicinity. Tweedy & Co. lasted in the signalling business for longer than any other of the new entrants of the late 1860s and 1870s, and in 1898 they were taken over by Tyer & Co.

Edward Tyer had established himself in the manufacture of railway signalling instruments in 1851. His company, originally Tyer & Norman but renamed as Tyer & Co. in the 1870s, was the leading company in its field, but had no interest in mechanical work prior to the take-over of Tweedy & Co. Edward Tyer retired in 1897, although he continued to take an active interest in the business until his death in 1912. Tyer & Co. was made a Limited Company in March 1898, and took over Tweedy in May. The manufacture of mechanical equipment continued to take place at Carlisle, as there was no possibility of extending the Tyer works in Dalston. Mechanical sales continued at a satisfactory level even after the 1923 Grouping.

In 1927 the Carlisle works was closed and mechanical manufacture was transferred to the works of E. C. & J. Keay at James Bridge, Darlaston (Keay's earlier work is described in a later section of this Chapter). In connection with this change a new company, Tyer's Signals Ltd., was formed: but the Tyer & Co. Ltd. company continued to exist (dealing with the electrical instruments side), as did the Keay company, whose main interests were outside of signalling. Further changes came in 1934 when Tyer's mechanical manufacture was moved again, this time to the 'Windsor Works' of G. D. Peters & Co. Ltd. at Slough. Peters had become involved in the signalling field around 1920, when they bought up a large shareholding in the British Power Railway Signal Co. Ltd. (for the foundation of which, as the British Pneumatic Railway Signal Co. Ltd., see Chapter 2), and had its manufacture transferred from Chippenham to Slough. From around 1928, British Power, perhaps finding the times lean, had undertaken some mechanical contracts in addition to its main power signalling interests, including the manufacture of a few mechanical locking frames for the LNER. When Tyer's mechanical work too was moved to Slough, a new company, B. P. & Tyer's Signals Ltd., was formed to succeed both the British Power and the Tyer's Signals companies. B. P. & Tyer's Signals Ltd. and Tyer & Co. Ltd. retained close links and indeed advertised jointly until the 1950s, when mechanical work seems to have finally petered out, although few if any complete locking frames can have been produced in later years.

There is some difficulty in identifying a Tweedy/Tyer box design, but it seems very likely that the few boxes involved in the Cambrian contracts were Tyer-designed and Tyer-built (**Plate 134**).

Plate 134 Llandre box on the Cambrian was built in 1911 (the station was known as Llanfihangel until 1916). The resignalling work at Llandre was a Tyer contract. It seems likely that this box was Tyer-designed, given that the near-contemporary Pwllheli West box (1907) was built to the contractor's design (McK&H). Other Tyer boxes on the Cambrian were Porthywaen Junction, Blodwell Junction, and Nantmawr Junction on the Tanat Valley line in 1903/4, and Castle Caereinion on the Welshpool & Llanfair in 1907 (the last still stands). These were similar to Llandre in being fairly plain gabled structures, but differed in detail. The photograph was taken in July 1965, a few months before closure.

C. L. Caddy

TABLE 17

Railway Companies Supplied with Tweedy/Tyer Frames

Railway Company	Work done by Tweedy/Tyer	Whether Tweedy/Tyer box design used
GE	A little circa 1920	No
GN	Some from circa 1918	No
NE	N. Divn: much in 1870s/80s	No
M&C	Some from circa 1915	No
CK&P	All known work after 1880	No
C&WJ	All work for original line (1879) and some later	No
Cam	Much from 1901	Yes (see text)
BP&GV	Some 1909-13	No
NB	Some in Borders area	No
Wigtownshire	One contract, 1877	Not known
LNER	A little in 1920s and 1930s	No
SR	A little in 1920s and 1930s	No

Gloucester Wagon Company

The Gloucester Wagon Co. Ltd., founded in 1860, decided to diversify into signalling in 1876 due to a slump in the wagon market. To manage this new side of the business the company secured the services of George Edwards, then Signal Superintendent of the LNW. The GWCo was tendering for signalling work by the end of 1876, although Edwards' patent for the new GWCo frame was not taken out until March 1877. Edwards was paid £500 per annum plus a percentage of the signalling profits. Sales did not really take off until the signing on 19th October 1878 of a five year contract with the L&Y, under which the GWCo carried out the majority of the L&Y's work in the years 1879-81. Several other sizeable contracts were gained from 1880 onwards. As part of their diversification, the GWCo also began to build station buildings (e.g. for the Golden Valley Railway and (in part at least) the Severn Bridge Railway), and other railway structures.

A standard gabled signal box was designed, and supplied in timber or BTF form (**Plates 36 & 135**). Most of the GWCo's customers did in fact have their boxes built to the **GWCo** design. There were many GWCo boxes in Ireland in addition to those on the English railways listed in **Table 18**. Lapped boarding was used for the timber portions. The main operating floor windows were 3ft. 9½in. deep, in 2-panes-by-2 sliding sashes with (from 1879) curved framing at the head. On the front of the box only there were small 'upper lights', which served virtually no useful purpose, as

TABLE 18

Railway Companies Supplied with GWCo Frames

Railway Company	Work done by GWCo	Whether GWCo box design used
GN	Small amount 1877-82	No
Severn Bridge	Work for opening, 1879	Yes
LNW/GW Joint	Six boxes, 1877-9	Not known (unlikely)
L&Y	Some from 1877, most 1879-81, some until 1882	Yes
Bury & Tottington	Boxes for opening, 1882	Yes
Evesham, Redditch, & Stratford-on-Avon Jn.	Work for opening, 1878-9	Yes
Northampton & Banbury Jn.	One contract (probably no box), 1880	-
GW	One contract of significance, 1877-8	Yes
Bridport	One contract, 1883-4	No
Banbury & Cheltenham Direct	Work for original section, 1878-81	Yes
DN&S	Work for original section, 1882	Yes
Golden Valley	Work for opening, 1879-81 (no boxes)	-
Leominster & Bromyard	One contract, 1881	Not known (likely)
B&M	Small amount 1880-3	Yes
Swindon, Marlborough & Andover	All work for opening, 1881-2	Yes
Swindon & Cheltenham Extn.	All work for opening, 1883	Yes
North Wales Narrow Gauge	Some work, 1881	Not known

Plate 135 Wakefield Goole Junction cabin, a BTF **GWCo** box, photographed late in 1882 shortly after its completion. Wakefield (Kirkgate) was the last L&Y station to be interlocked; the work was noted to be 'ordered and proceeding' in February 1881. The curved framing at the head of the windows is just visible, but the 'upper lights' are completely obscured by the shadow from the fascia board. A GWCo maker's plate can be seen below the name-board. The walkway, of an unusually generous type for the period, has timber posts, the ends of which are shaped in the same way as the bottom of the roof finials. The large timber framework at the left carries the signal wires above the lines, as was done at some complicated locations at this period instead of taking them beneath the rails. This box was replaced by a much larger box called Wakefield East in 1901.

Gloucester RC&W Co. Ltd.

the presence of the fascia board prevented them letting in any light (**Plate 36**). Additionally, fixed 'lower windows' were generally provided (not, however, on the Didcot, Newbury & Southampton boxes). Timber boxes had 2-panes-by-2 locking room windows; BTF boxes had the S&F/LNW type locking room window (predictably, in view of Edwards' former employment with those two companies). A pivoted window was placed in the gable ends for ventilation, and decorative bargeboards were provided to a distinctive design (**Plate 69**). This GWCo box design was subsequently adopted by the RSCo and the L&Y, remaining current into the 1920s.

The only significant variant to the standard GWCo design was the use of hipped roofs on most of the Askern branch boxes of 1880.

From 1879 to 1883, the GWCo was haunted by a court case brought by S&F for infringement of patent. S&F lost this case at every hearing, but insisted on taking it to the House of Lords, where they again lost. Despite the payment of costs by S&F, the GWCo was still left £3,400 out of pocket. Further trouble for the company came in September 1880 when the L&Y gave notice (as it was entitled to) of its intention to terminate the GWCo's contract early, on 19th April 1881. Edwards was instructed to make every effort to negotiate a new contract, but instead used his L&Y contacts to stab his employers in the back by setting himself up in business on his own account, and taking the L&Y's work himself (*see under* **The Railway Signal Company,** *below*). The GWCo appointed a new Signal Superintendent and continued in the signalling business until 1884, but they never really recovered from the loss of the L&Y contract.

Only five GWCo boxes now remain; Blackrod Junction, Chorley No. 3, Crumpsall, and Waterloo on the L&Y (none of which have their original frames), and Bourton-on-the-Water (Banbury & Cheltenham Direct), used as a garage. The only extant GWCo frame is that at Barkston East Junction on the GN.

The Railway Signal Company

Early in 1881, George Edwards made approaches to the L&Y to see if he could gain the L&Y signalling work, if he set up a new company for that purpose. By 8th March, he felt sufficiently confident of success to write a letter of resignation to the GWCo Board. On 23rd April he bought land adjacent to the L&Y main line at Fazakerley, and on 3rd June the new company, The Railway Signal Co. Ltd., was registered. It was the only signalling firm to be a Limited Company from the very start. Edwards was to be Managing Director as long as he continued with the company. Formal approval of the contract for the L&Y's work came from that company's Board on 6th July, and the new RSCo works became operational during that same month. The likelihood is that the L&Y gave Edwards some assistance in setting up the company, but the exact form of this has not yet been established.

The RSCo enjoyed the whole of the L&Y's work until 1889/90, and this formed the backbone of its production at first. However, the company was already obtaining contracts elsewhere by the end of 1881, and soon had a very substantial business. By the mid-1890s, when the huge MS&L London Extension contract was won, the RSCo was taking a large share of the national market.

Initially, the RSCo produced equipment to the same designs as had been used at Gloucester (the patents were in Edwards' name). This included the adoption of the GWCo box design, with the minor differences that the RSCo boxes soon began to omit the (anyway invisible) 'upper lights', and the curved framing at the head of the main sashes. The RSCo retained this box design throughout its life, and it appeared on the lines of over thirty railway companies, including many in Ireland. Timber, BTF, brick, STF, and stone examples are known. The boxes were built without the 'lower windows' if so desired; this version of the design was preferred by the Wirral, LT&S, SMJ, and many smaller companies, which suggests that it was cheaper.

The standard sizes of RSCo and L&Y Horwich-built boxes (see Chapter 6) are given in Table 19. Each size was one 2-panes-by-2 window sash greater in length than the previous size. However, some boxes are known to have been shorter (3, 4, or 5 sashes) or longer (up to 36 sashes) than the normal size range tabulated. The standard width was 12ft.

Variations to the standard RSCo box design, specified by some railway companies, included larger locking room windows on many LT&S and MSJ&A boxes, and hipped roofs of different types on some NB and GNoS boxes (Plates 139 & 140).

The RSCo also built a few timber station buildings, out of the standard box components. Notable cases were on the E&WYU, and at Nethertown on the Furness Railway (although the latter may have been built from second-hand signal hut parts).

Edwards retired in 1900 and died in 1914. As noted in Chapter 2, the RSCo came under Consolidated Signal Co. Ltd. financial control from 1903/4, but continued to trade separately both then and after the 1920 mergers. Large quantities of mechanical equipment were supplied by the RSCo to the LNER and LMS, and to BR (ER) into the 1970s, but no RSCo-design boxes would have been built in the UK after 1923. In later decades, the RSCo was completely under Westinghouse control, and when it was eventually wound up in May 1974 the assets passed to Westinghouse CVB Ltd. The RSCo had the distinction of being the longest-lived firm of mechanical signalling contractors in the UK. The Fazakerley works has now been demolished, but the road past the site is still called 'Signal Works Road'.

Plate 137 (above) BTF Size 9 **RSCo** box at Kirkham Station, L&Y, opened 1889 and closed 1975. The closet, with its RSCo bargeboards, is most likely original.

R. D. Foster

Plate 136 (left) The timber Size 4 **RSCo** box at Barrow Road Crossing (MS&L), built in 1885.

R. Newman

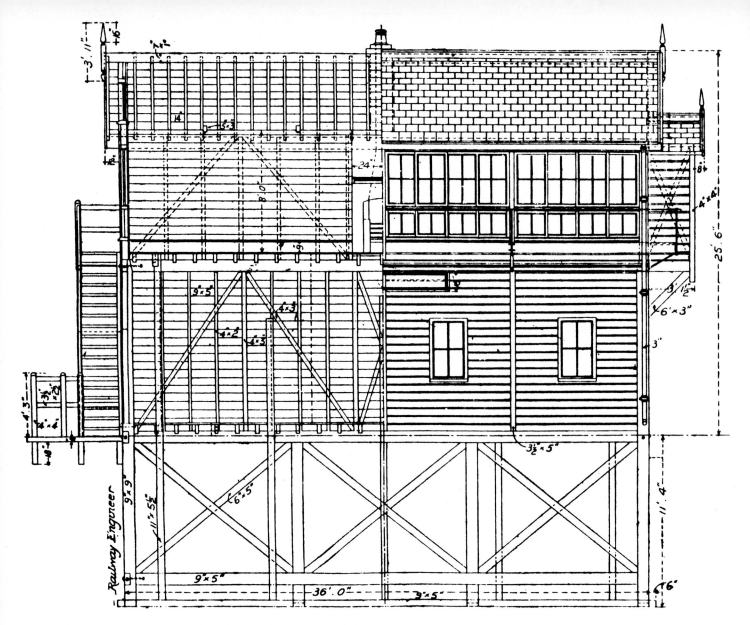

Plate 138   An official drawing of a timber **RSCo** box (Size 11) on timber piles.

Authors' Collection

SCALE: 4mm = 1 foot

TABLE 19

Standard Lengths of RSCo and L&Y Boxes

Size No.	Length	Number of Window Sashes	Nominal Number of Levers
1	14ft. 1⅜in.	6	10
2	16ft. 7in.	7	15
3	18ft. 2⅞in.	8	20
	(L&Y — 18ft. 7¾in.)		
4	20ft. 8½in.	9	25
5	22ft. 9¼in.	10	30
6	25ft. 0¼in.	11	35
7	27ft. 1in.	12	40
8	30ft. 1¾in.	13	45
9	31ft. 8½in.	14	50
10	34ft. 3¼in.	15	55
11	35ft. 10in.	16	60
12	38ft. 4¾in.	17	65
13	40ft. 5½in.	18	70
14	43ft. 6¼in.	19	75
15	44ft. 7in.	20	80
16	47ft. 1¾in.	21	85
17	49ft. 2½in.	22	90
18	51ft. 3¼in.	23	95

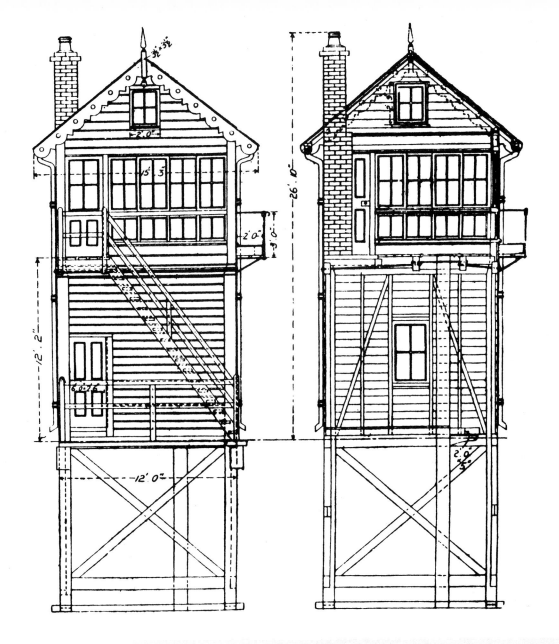

Plate 139 (right) One of the two known **RSCo hipped** boxes, standard apart from the roof. This is Craigellachie (Speyside) box (GNoS), which opened, along with two other new boxes at Craigellachie, at 11.30am. on 10th December 1900. All three closed together on 16th December 1968. The other known box of this type is Kennethmont West (GNoS), opened on 30th July 1888 and still in use. It is possible that Craigellachie Speyside was second-hand from Kennethmont East, where a box had opened on the same day as the West box but closed on 9th August 1896. The GNoS was fond of reusing box structures, and it is most unlikely that the RSCo had been asked to interlock half a station. One assumes that the GNoS asked the RSCo to build these boxes with hipped roofs, but why they should have done so remains a mystery, as the standard GNoS box design of the time had a gabled roof!

D. Collins

TABLE 20

Railway Companies Supplied with Railway Signal Co. Frames

Railway Company	Work done by RSCo	Whether RSCo box design used
GE	Some from 1886	No
GN	Some from 1881, much from 1890	No
MS&L/GC	Almost all 1885/6-1905, most 1905-23	Until 1886
LDEC	Half of route, 1893-6	No
WM&CQ	Some, 1885	Yes
E&WYU	All (work done 1902/3)	Yes
NE	Some circa 1890	No
LT&S	All circa 1889-1912	Yes
Southport & Cheshire Lines Extn.	All (work done 1884)	Yes
LNW	One contract only (for WC&E), 1882	No
LNW/GW Joint	One contract, 1884	No
MSJ&A	All 1886-1903	Yes
L&Y	Much from 1881/all from 1883, until 1889/90	Yes
West Lancashire	All 1887-97	Yes
Liverpool, Southport & Preston Jn.	All (work done 1887-93)	Yes
Seacombe, Hoylake & Deeside/ Wirral	All known work	Yes
Mersey	All (work done 1886-92)	Some
Furness	Most from 1882	Some
C&WJ	Some in later years	No
Knott End	Some	Yes
East & West Junction	All (1880s-1890s)	Yes
Stratford-on-Avon, Towcester & Midland Jn.	All (1891)	Yes
SMJ	All (1910-23)	Yes
Banbury & Cheltenham Direct	Part of line (1884-7)	Yes
Abbotsbury	All (1885)	Yes
PT	Most (1897-1900)	Yes
TV	A little	No
BP&GV	Some 1909-14	No
LSW	Much from 1880s	No
LBSC	Some, circa 1899 and from 1905	No
IoWC	Most	Yes
Newport, Godshill & St. Lawrence	All (1897-1900)	Yes
FY&N	One contract, 1913	Yes
SE	Some, circa 1892-5	Yes
LCD	One contract known, 1886	Yes
NB	Fair amount from circa 1890	A few
NB (West Highland Extension)	All (1901)	All (variant)
Invergarry & Fort Augustus	All (1901-3)	All (variant)
GNoS	A little	Some (variant)
Cal.	Some	No
LNER	Some in England, most in Scotland	No
LMS	A little in both England and Scotland	No
BR (ER)	Fair amount (until circa 1965)	No
Met.	Some	No
Great Northern & City	All (1902-4)	No
Liverpool Overhead	All (1893-1905)	No
Snowdon Mountain	Work for opening (1896)	No
East & West India Docks Co.	Tilbury Docks (1886)	No
Mersey D&HB	Some	Yes
South Shields, M&W	All (1888)	No

Plate 140 The **RSCo/West Highland Extension** type of 1901 is exemplified here by Mallaig. These boxes were built by the RSCo but with Stevens-pattern frames. The design is basically a standard RSCo box without lower windows, but with a hipped roof and large eaves brackets, possibly specified to cope with local weather conditions. The operating floor windows also have curved framing at the head, as on GWCo boxes.

R. D. Foster

Dutton/Pease

Samuel Telford Dutton, who had long worked as an engineer with McK&H (latterly as manager of the Worcester works), left the service of that company in 1888 to set up business on his own account, in partnership with the accountant Sutton George Corkran. Dutton took over part of the West Central Wagon Works, adjacent to the McK&H works in Shrub Hill, Worcester. He was able to use the many patents taken out in his own name in the years 1885-8. In June 1889, the business was incorporated as Dutton & Co. Ltd. A large amount of work was gained on the Cambrian, Highland, GE, and GN, all of which had previously been McK&H customers in whole or part. But once the interlocking of the Cambrian and Highland was completed, Dutton fell upon leaner times. Despite a reconstitution in November 1898, the company had to be wound up in November 1899. The assets were sold to J. F. Pease & Co. Ltd. of Middlesbrough, owned by the Pease family which had close connections with the North Eastern Railway, but manufacture continued at Worcester, to the same designs as before. Pease were involved in the negotiations leading to the setting up of the Consolidated Signal Co. Ltd., and were at first represented on the Board: but in October 1901 Pease sold their signalling assets to McK&H and withdrew from the field. Some equipment to the Dutton patterns continued to be produced by McK&H after 1901. S. T. Dutton himself went to the East India Railway after selling out to Pease.

The Dutton box designs, which were adopted by a large proportion of Dutton's customers, were very much modelled on the McK&H Type 3 design. The only significant differences between the latter and the Dutton **Type 1** design of 1888-92 were that the Dutton boxes had 6¼ in. lapped boarding, and bargeboards with decoration and a fuller rounding at the foot. The Dutton **Type 2** design (1892-5) introduced the 'roofed landing' also incorporating the porch. (Portmadoc East box of this type is illustrated at **Plate 80**). Finally, **Type 3** of 1894-1901 had a new design of operating floor window, with the lower of the two horizontal glazing bars omitted, but was otherwise similar to Type 2.

TABLE 21

Railway Companies Supplied with Dutton/Pease Frames

Railway Company	Work done by Dutton/Pease	Whether Dutton box designs used (and types known)
GE	Some 1891-1901	No (but see **Chapter 6**)
GN	Some 1892-1901	No
WM&CQ	Some 1890-5	Yes: 1, 3
North Pembs. & Fishguard	1895 work for reopening	Yes: 3
Cambrian	Almost all 1890-1901	Yes: 1, 2, 3, 4
TV	A little from 1888	No
N&B	Much circa 1895	Yes: 2
MSWJ	Most 1891-1901	Yes: 1
LSW	A little from 1889	No
LBSC	A little circa 1899	No
SE	A little circa 1893	Yes (see text)
Highland	Much 1890-97	Yes: 1, 3, 4 variants
City & South London	All work for opening, 1890	No
Isle of Man	Douglas, 1890	**(See Chapter 10)**

Plate 141 The **Dutton Type 1** box at Criccieth (Cambrian) opened on 11th July 1892 and closed on 16th October 1977. Like many platform boxes it had locking room windows of lesser depth and with a flatter arch than normal. There are now only two Dutton Type 1 boxes left in use; Barmouth South (brick), and the small box at Caersws (BTF).

C. L. Caddy

Plate 142 Forden (Cambrian) was a **Dutton Type 3** box of 1897, built to replace a box dating only from 1890. It closed in 1966 but, as this 1982 photograph shows, it still stands in good condition. Newton (South) is the only Type 3 box now in use. The bargeboard decoration should be compared with the McK&H/GE version shown in **Plates 29 & 67** and the EOD version in **Plate 144**. It will be seen that the McK&H/GE and EOD versions are curved throughout, whereas the Dutton version has a straight section underneath each hole. As in many Dutton boxes, the locking room window arches at Forden are of blue bricks, forming part of a 2-course band of blue bricks running around the whole box.

R. D. Foster

Plate 143 The **Dutton Type 4** box at Talsarnau (Cambrian), opened on 18th May 1891 and now closed, but surviving in good condition as shown. This box was never a 'Block Post'. Corrugated-iron roofs, and simplified 'hole-less' bargeboards, were normal on boxes of this type.

R. D. Foster

For the interlocking of some of the smaller Cambrian stations in 1890-4, a special design (**Type 4**) was used. These small boxes (nearly all of them 10ft. x 8ft.) were built on the station platforms, of BTF construction. The operating floor windows were only two panes deep and, in some cases, there was only partial glazing on the box front. For even smaller stations a ground frame hut with lean-to roof was produced, similar to the McK&H version.

The few Dutton boxes on the SE — Wadhurst (1893) and Blackwater are the only known examples — were to the Type 1 outline, but had pendant eaves brackets and plain bargeboards. It is uncertain why this should have been the case but one theory is that these boxes had been intended for overseas sales.

Dutton boxes on the Highland, like their McK&H counterparts, were built with vertical battened boarding and corrugated-iron roofs. Highland versions of Types 1, 3, and 4 are known (**Plate 298**).

Dutton/Pease boxes of 1898-1901 on the GE were built to the normal GE Type 7 outline, but were provided with 'Dutton' roofed landings, and the same type of operating floor windows were used as on the Dutton Type 3 design (**Plate 155**).

Evans, O'Donnell

Arthur George Evans and John Patrick O'Donnell, then Dutton's London agent, both took out a number of signalling patents from 1890. In 1894, they acquired a works by the GW main line at Chippenham and entered into partnership as signalling contractors. In December 1895, the firm was made a Limited Company, Evans, O'Donnell & Co. Ltd. The new company soon obtained all the work on the H&B and Barry railways, and a good deal of work elsewhere. By 1900, O'Donnell had come to realise that mechanical work would decline, and set up (as described in Chapter 2) the British Pneumatic Railway Signal Co. Ltd. In connection with this, the Evans, O'Donnell firm was reconstituted. O'Donnell was a leading figure in the establishing of the Consolidated Signal Co. Ltd. This, and the 1903 conversion of Evans, O'Donnell & Co. Ltd. to a landowning company only following the transfer of S&F manufacture to Chippenham, were also fully described in **Chapter 2**. O'Donnell remained actively involved as a Joint Managing Director of S&F for some years after 1903, and EOD-pattern equipment continued to be made at Chippenham. Evans too was made a Joint Managing Director of S&F, but had other active interests in South America.

The **EOD** box design, of which some forty examples seem to have been built in total, had several features in common with the McK&H and Dutton designs. The operating floor windows were similar to those of the Dutton Type 3 design, in having only one horizontal glazing bar near the head, but in the EOD boxes it was much closer to the head. The bargeboards were nearly fully-rounded at the foot, as on Dutton boxes, but the bargeboard decoration was of the McK&H/GE type, rather than the Dutton type. Small gable window/vents with one vertical glazing bar were provided. These had appeared on a few McK&H Type 3 boxes, but not on Dutton boxes. Most EOD boxes were built of timber, with weatherboarding. The EOD box design was not used after 1903.

TABLE 22

Railway Companies Supplied with Evans O'Donnell Frames

Railway Company	Work done by EOD	Whether EOD box design used
GE	Some 1897-1901	No
GN	Some 1895-1900	No
H&B	All 1897-1903 *	No
Furness	Some	No
Easton & Church Hope Joint	Easton, 1902	Yes
Barry	All 1895-1903 *	No
MSWJ	Some 1901-2	No
Lynton & Barnstaple	All (work done 1897-8)	One
LBSC	A little circa 1899	No
SE	Most circa 1897-1903 *	Yes
Ealing & South Harrow	All (work done 1899)	Yes
City & South London	Work for 1900 Extensions	No
Central London	Work for opening, 1900	No

* Indicates EOD pattern frames supplied by S&F subsequently

Plate 144 The standard **EOD** box at North Kent West Junction (SE). This photograph shows the enamel SE nameplate, which lasted until the box's abolition on 29th August 1981. Only two EOD boxes now remain; Maidstone (SE, 1899) and Ryde St. John's Road (second-hand from Waterloo SE).

Lens of Sutton

Sykes

The W. R. Sykes Interlocking Signal Co. Ltd. of Voltaire Road, Clapham was, like Tyer & Co., primarily concerned with electrical signalling instruments. But the firm also had a number of patents for mechanical frames and equipment, and tendered successfully for a few mechanical contracts in the mid-1900s, notably on the GN, MSWJ, and Met. It is unlikely that any of these contracts included the building of the box structures. Other contracts were gained for the Sykes 'electro-mechanical' system, under which signals were power-operated by Sykes' equipment, but points mechanically worked by a conventional frame. The major installations were at Victoria, LBSC (6 boxes), and Glasgow St. Enoch, GSW (6 boxes). Sykes did supply the mechanical frames for the Victoria contract. They were also required to build three of the box structures (Grosvenor Road, Battersea Pier, and Battersea Park), but in the event this building, and much other, work was subcontracted to McK&H after Sykes got into difficulties with the contract. Due to these problems, Sykes did not undertake any further mechanical work after 1907.

Atkinson

F. A. Atkinson patented a frame (a forerunner of the standard EOD frame) in 1891. In the late 1900s, he traded on his own account as F. A. Atkinson & Co. Known contracts were for Barrow-in-Furness North (Furness) in 1907 — this frame is still in use — and for the GN's Enfield to Cuffley line in 1908. These contracts are unlikely to have included the box structures, which were in any case to the railway companies' designs. Little is known of Atkinson's operations; he is said to have sold out to McK&H in 1909.

Keay

The Darlaston firm of E. C. & J. Keay was primarily concerned with the fabrication and erection of steelwork for bridges and buildings. At some date around the 1900s, however, they branched out into the railway signalling business. Locking frames to the S&F 'Duplex' pattern were advertised. Keay's advertisements claimed sales of frames to 'leading British and Foreign railway companies', but it would appear that the majority of their sales were in fact overseas, as no other record is known of Keay frames on a British railway. In 1927, Keay's signalling work was amalgamated with the mechanical work of Tyer & Co. Ltd., as described earlier in this chapter.

Westinghouse

The history of the Westinghouse Brake & (Saxby) Signal Co. Ltd., the major British signalling firm after 1920, was fully told in **Chapter 2**. The known sales of mechanical frames are listed in **Table 23**. Only in a few cases in the 1920s were Westinghouse involved in the building of signal box structures; a few McK&H Type 3 boxes were provided for the South Wales companies from 1920-22, and a few GC Type 5 boxes for the LNER (**see Plate 181 and Chapter 8**).

Henry Williams

Henry Williams, formerly a Signal Inspector on the LNW/GW Joint line, took out, from 1884, a number of patents for signal and point operating mechanisms, and established himself in business, as Henry Williams Ltd., at Cathcart. Later, the firm moved its operations to the 'Railway Appliance Works', Darlington. A locking frame was patented in 1921, but the firm's primary interests

TABLE 23

Railway Companies Supplied with Westinghouse Frames

Railway Company	Work done by Westinghouse
H&B	All 1920-2
NE	All 1920-3
Rhymney	All 1920-2
Cardiff	All 1920-2
Barry	All 1920-2
Highland	All 1920-3
LNER	Some
BR (ER)	Some
GW	Two frames only (1933/5)
SR	Most from circa 1929
BR (SR)	Most
Met.	Some circa 1925
LT	Ground frames only
Lambton Collieries	Most, 1920s and 1930s
Ashington Collieries	Most, 1920s-1940s
Beckton Gas Works	Two frames in 1920s
Southend Pier Railway	Two frames, 1929
Military Railways	Most, 1920s-1978
Port of London Authority	One frame, 1936

Note: Other pre-grouping companies which had purchased from S&F or McK&H up to 1920 would no doubt have purchased from Westinghouse in 1920-2/3, if they required any new frames in this period.

continued to be in outdoor signalling gear and permanent way work. In the 1940s, however, they did supply a large quantity of parts for McK&H-pattern locking frames, plus some complete ground frames, to the LNER North Eastern Area. Subsequently they widened their signalling interests by acting as British agents for the Swiss 'Integra' signalling panels used in Western Region panel boxes in the 1960s. The company still exists, and still advertises some mechanical signalling items.

British Power

The British Power Railway Signal Co. Ltd. undertook some mechanical work in later years, as described in the Tyer section of this chapter.

Signal Boxes of the Pre-Grouping Railway Companies

Great Eastern

The first interlocked signal box on the GE (then still the Eastern Counties) was a Saxby box, built at the main junction at Stratford in 1861. This was the first Saxby installation north of the Thames, and was visited on completion by the officers of several other railway companies. Another early GE box, probably of 1865, was that at the junction with the CV&H line at Haverhill (an S&F Type 1b box with signals above the roof). Although progress must have been affected by financial problems — the GE was in receivership in 1867 — the Board decided in 1868, after an accident at Broxbourne Junction, that 'new signals and an elevated box were required for all similar junctions'. By 1873 there were several dozen interlocked boxes, but almost all were at junctions, and most were in the London area. During the same period, the 'train telegraph' was extended along the main line, reaching Ingatestone in 1872 and through to Ipswich in 1875. Subsequent progress with block and interlocking was solid rather than rapid; 69 stations still awaited interlocking in 1889. The bulk of this last work was done

in 1891, contracts for no less than 51 stations being let between January and April of that year.

The GE always relied on the contractors for locking frames, with the exception that the GE's signal shops did make up small ground frames, and, after the opening of a new frame shop at Leyton in 1919, large 'new' frames from reused parts. In the 1860s, S&F seem to have been the main supplier, although a payment to Chambers is also recorded in 1863. Stevens wrote 'seeking orders' in February 1870, and were given a fair amount of work between then and 1884. R&R received a couple of contracts in 1871. McK&H had their first known contract in 1872 and within a few years were enjoying the majority of the GE's work, which they continued to do until the Grouping. The practice of obtaining competitive tenders for each job was partially abandoned in 1876, when annual agreements on a schedule basis were initiated, under which most (but not all) of the work for the next year went to the contractor who submitted the cheapest schedule prices. These annual contracts went to McK&H over the period 1876-8 and from 1882, and to S&F from 1879-81. From 1886, there was a further

Plate 145 The **GE Type 1/S&F** box at Fulbourne. The contracts for interlocking Fulbourne and Six Mile Bottom were awarded to S&F in June 1875 for £579 and £722 respectively; both boxes remained in use until May 1983. The original boarding shown here was, however, replaced many years ago by horizontal lapped boarding. The station house behind is in typical Newmarket Railway style.

Lens of Sutton

Plate 146 The interlocking and resignalling of the Norwich Thorpe and Trowse area was entrusted to McK&H in November 1872 for a total of £4,265, but the work was not completed ready for inspection until August 1874. Several **GE Type 1/McK&H** boxes were built in connection with this contract, of which Trowse Swing Bridge box is seen here. The signal post in the foreground demonstrates how the finials used on these boxes were identical to those on McK&H signal posts.

Lens of Sutton

change to long-term 'call-off' contract agreements with all the suppliers (S&F, McK&H, Stevens, and the RSCo). When these were renegotiated in 1890, Stevens were rejected and Dutton added; and in November 1897 EOD were added to the list. A further renegotiation of the contracts occurred in 1901.

The GE's practice was to include the signal box structure in the signalling contract. Contractors' box designs were used for most boxes until circa 1873, and for some until 1878. Examples were the McK&H Type 1 boxes at Hackney Downs Junction (1872), Edmonton Junction (1872) and Highams Park (1873); S&F Type 2a boxes at Bishop's Stortford North (1869) and St. Olaves Swing Bridge Junction (1872 — and mysteriously reported as having been 'robbed' by one R. Pope in October of that year); and S&F

Plate 147 (above) Halesworth, a **GE Type 2** box with plain barge-boards and windows with a horizontal glazing bar. The locking room windows here are 1½ times the normal depth. The walkway with high rails, seen in this 1983 photograph, was a recent BR addition. The contract for interlocking Halesworth was given to S&F on 19th April 1881.

P. Kay

Plate 148 (right) Downham was also interlocked in 1881, but here the **GE Type 2** box was given notched bargeboards, and windows without a horizontal glazing bar. The painting of this box shows well how the 4in. intermediate posts in the upper part of Type 2 boxes were always immediately above those in the lower part (contrast the arrangement in Type 7 boxes).

D. J. Taylor

Type 5 boxes at Noel Park (1878) and on the Sutton to Needing-worth line (1878). However, the GE's own **Type 1** box design was also in use by the late 1860s, and was used for most boxes of 1873-6. There is no obvious reason why the contractors' box designs should have been used in some cases, and this GE design in others, at the same period. Type 1 boxes were hipped, and all were of timber construction. The original boarding seems to have been vertical below operating floor level, and diagonal interspersed with vertical (or with horizontal) above. The S&F-built boxes at least originally had inside boarding below operating floor level, with exposed struts. Other details of Type 1 boxes varied according to the signalling contractor responsible — an unusual practice; but one found also on the later GE Types 3 to 7. **Type 1/S&F** boxes were of plain design, with 2-panes-by-2 window sashes and S&F-type roof vents (**Plate 145**). Of the dozen or more **Type 1/Stevens** boxes only very poor photographs are known, but they too seem to have been of plain design. In contrast, the **Type 1/McK&H** boxes had 'parachute' finials, small eaves brackets, and operating floor windows with no horizontal glazing bars (**Plate 146**).

In 1876, the GE changed to gabled roofs. At first a few gabled boxes were built which were otherwise to the Type 1 outline — for example, Hatfield Peverel and Halifax Junction — but during 1877/8 the new standard **Type 2** design was introduced. This had deeper (5ft.) operating floor windows, with one horizontal glazing bar on some boxes (**Plate 147**) and none on others (**Plate 148**). The roof overhung considerably on all facades. Bargeboards were either plain or 'notched', and there were no finials. Locking room windows normally followed the pattern of the operating floor windows. Type 2 boxes were mostly of timber construction, with weatherboarding of approximately 6⅓ in. cover. The varieties of window and bargeboard design within the type cannot be related to date, location, or contractor. The Type 2 design was used until

Plate 149 (left) The **GE Type 3/McK&H** box at Ipswich Station was built in connection with the station alterations of 1883. It was abolished on 8th April 1984. BTF construction was very rare on the Great Eastern.

P. Kay

Plate 151 Bealings was a **GE Type 5/S&F** box; the contract was let in April 1884 for £403 17s. 1d. Unusually, this box had standard S&F-type locking room windows, instead of the larger segmental-arched windows normal on GE Types 3 to 6. The walkway railings were a BR addition. Bealings was closed in 1984, and March East Junc. and March West Junc. are now the only surviving Type 5 boxes.

P. Kay

Plate 150 The **GE Type 4/McK&H** box at Stonea. The contract for this box was let on 6th March 1883. Notice that the door is set in brickwork, a normal feature of Type 4 boxes. Like most buildings in the peat fens, this box suffered from subsidence, and it had to be shored up at the rear. Also, as a result of the brick and timber portions of the structure getting out of line, the top five courses of the brickwork had to be rebuilt, and part of the sash frame at the near end shaved off. Eventually, in November 1984, structural problems reached the point where the box had to be demolished and replaced by a Portakabin. For a drawing of this type see **Plate 29**.

R. Newman

1882, during which period a very large number of boxes were built.

A few of the later Type 2 boxes were built of brick, with plain brickwork and segmental-arched locking room windows. From 1882, there then followed a brief period in which brick construction became the norm on the GE — indeed, all known boxes of Types 4, 5, 6, and 8 were of brick, with 'panelled' brickwork. At the same time, there were very rapid design developments, making the mid-1880s the most interesting period in GE box design.

Types 3, 4, and 5 all retained the overhanging gabled roofs of Type 2, but now with decorative bargeboards of various designs, terracotta finials, and cockscomb ridge tiles. **Type 3** boxes (1882-3) had a unique '7-light' window design. Most were built by McK&H and had bargeboards similar (not identical) to those of the McK&H boxes on the TV, and boarding arranged, most unusually, in 'rusticated' rectangles (**Plate 66**). Type 3 boxes are known in brick, BTF, and timber form, but always with brick chimneys. **Type 4** boxes (1883-5) had 4-panes-deep operating floor windows, mostly in sashes three panes across. Most were built by McK&H and had a new form of decoration on the bargeboards and fascia boards, which was to be used on all McK&H-built GE boxes until 1890 (*see* **Plate 67** *for details*). The fewer S&F-built examples of Type 4 had plain bargeboards but McK&H-type decoration on the fascia boards, except Yarmouth Vauxhall of 1884, which had 'Type 5' fascia board decoration. The two known Stevens-built Type 4 boxes had plain bargeboards and fascia boards.

Type 5(1884-9) introduced the 3-panes-deep operating floor windows which were to be used on all subsequent GE boxes but, in

the case of Type 5, these had the upper panes divided into four as a decorative feature. Most Type 5 boxes were S&F-built, with very splendid bargeboard and fascia board decoration of a unique type. The boarding in the gable ends was arranged in 'rusticated' fashion, but not in the same way as on Type 3 boxes (**Plate 68**). The only known McK&H-built Type 5 box, Shelford Junction, had plain bargeboards and fascia boards.

Type 6 boxes (1885-6, plus two examples in 1891) were all McK&H-built, and had the McK&H/GE-type decoration (as on Type 4) on bargeboards and fascia boards. The operating floor windows were in 3-panes-by-3 sashes. The roofs were of slightly steeper pitch than on most GE boxes, and there were no cockscomb ridge tiles but, uniquely amongst GE boxes, there were timber finials.

The end of these rapid developments in GE box design was heralded by the arrival during 1885/6 of a new and plainer design, **Type 7**, which was to remain in use into the 1920s. **Plate 153** is the official drawing of the standard brick and timber versions of this design. Over 90 per cent of Type 7 boxes were, in fact, built of timber. The majority of the timber examples of 1886-8 had brick chimneys; from 1888 they had stovepipes. The few brick Type 7 boxes had plain brickwork. McK&H-built Type 7 boxes of 1886-90 had McK&H/GE-type decoration on the bargeboards, but plain fascia boards. **Plate 67** shows an 1887 McK&H-built Type 7 box with brick chimney. Post-1890 McK&H-built boxes, and all S&F,

Plate 152 (right) The **GE Type 6** box at Norwich Thorpe Junction. McK&H's tender of £5,040 15s. 2d. for signalling the new Norwich Thorpe Station and its approaches was accepted in 1885, and the three new boxes involved were inspected on 27th April 1886. The large gable window in this box was a special feature for sighting purposes. This box is to be abolished under the current Norwich resignalling, which will leave Lowestoft as the last Type 6 box.

P. Kay

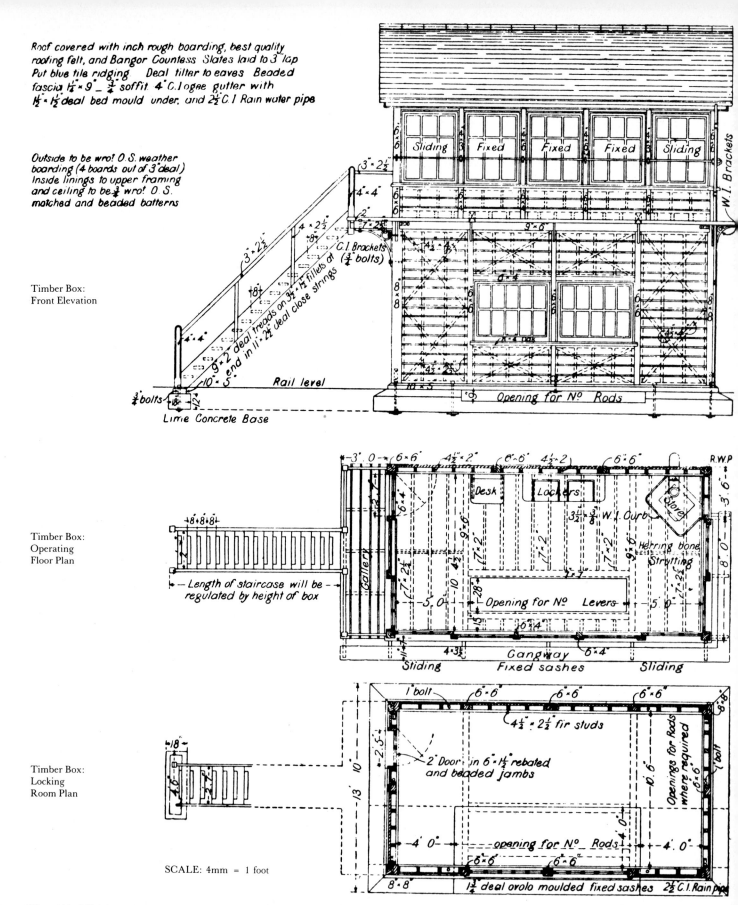

Timber Box:
Front Elevation

Roof covered with inch rough boarding, best quality roofing felt, and Bangor Countess Slates laid to 3" lap Put blue tile ridging   Deal tilter to eaves Beaded fascia 1¼" × 9" − ¾" soffit 4" C.I ogee gutter with 1½" × 1½" deal bed mould under, and 2½" C.I Rain water pipe

Outside to be wro.! O.S. weather boarding (4 boards out of 3" deal) Inside linings to upper framing and ceiling to be ¾" wro.! O.S. matched and beaded battens

Timber Box:
Operating
Floor Plan

Timber Box:
Locking
Room Plan

SCALE: 4mm = 1 foot

Plate 153 Official drawings of the timber (in full) and brick (end elevation and cross-section only shown) versions of the GE Type 7 box. These are the drawings used in the GE's contracts after 1890. **Table 9** gives the full specification for these boxes, and **Table 8** gives the prices quoted by the various contractors for building them.

Authors' Collection

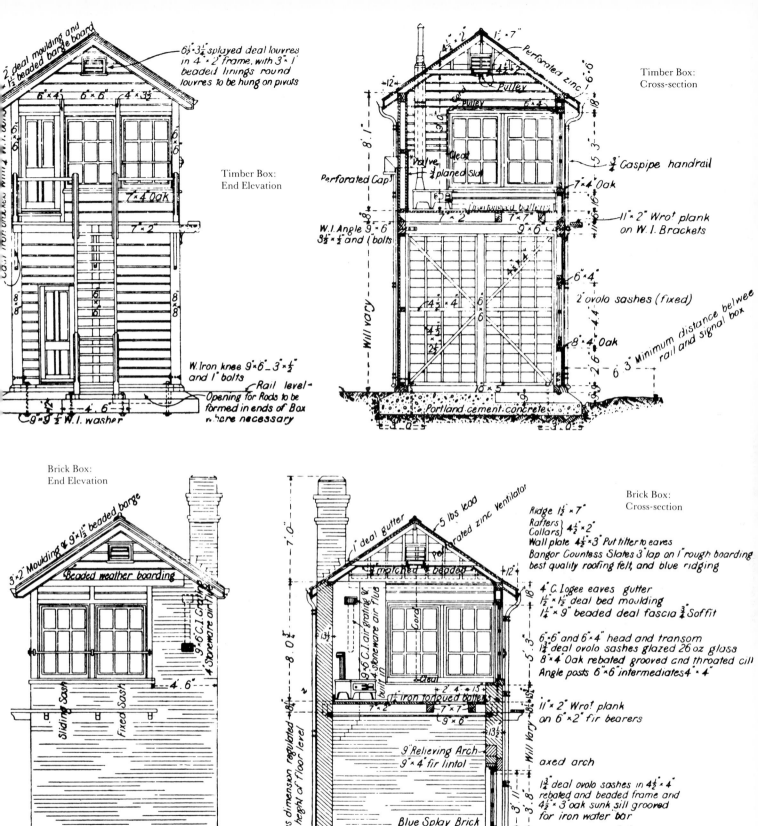

Timber Box:
End Elevation

6½·3¼ splayed deal louvres in 4"× 2" frame, with 3"·1" beaded linings round louvres to be hung on pivots

2" deal moulding and 1½" beaded barge board

6"× 4"   6"× 6"   4"× 3½"

6"× 6"

6"× 6"

7"× 4" Oak

7"× 2"

Cast iron brackets with ¼"·2"·¼"

6"× 6"

8"× 8"

8"× 8"

W. Iron knee 9"× 6"· 3"· ½" and 1" bolts

Rail level

Opening for Rods to be formed in ends of Box where necessary

9·9½" W.I. washer

4·6"

Timber Box:
Cross-section

4½·3"   1"· 7"

Perforated zinc   6"× 6"

12"

Cord   Pulley

Pulley

¾" Gaspipe handrail

Perforated Cap

Valve ½ planed Slat

8·1"

5·3"

7"× 4" Oak

Unstoweyd battens

7"× 2"   7"× 7"

W.I. Angle 9"× 6" 3½"·½" and 1 bolts

9"× 6"

11"× 2" Wro't plank on W.I. Brackets

1·6"

14½·4"   6"× 4"

6"× 4"

2" ovolo sashes (fixed)

Will vary

4½·3"   4·4"

2½"

8"× 4" Oak   6"× 4"

6"· 3" Minimum distance between rail and signal box

Portland cement concrete

10·5"   1·0·5"   1·0·5"

Brick Box:
End Elevation

3"·2" Moulding & 9"× 1½" beaded barge

Beaded weather boarding

9"× 6" C.I. Grating & 4" Stoneware air pipe

Sliding Sash   Fixed Sash

4·6"

Openings for Rods to be formed at ends where required

G.E.R

Brick Box:
Cross-section

1" deal gutter   5 lbs lead   Perforated zinc Ventilator

Ridge 1½"× 7"
Rafters 4½"× 2"
Collars 4½"× 2"
Wall plate 4½"× 3" Put tilter to eaves
Bangor Countess Slates 3" lap on 1" rough boarding best quality roofing felt, and blue ridging

matched + beaded   12"

4" C. Logee eaves gutter
1½"× 1½" deal bed moulding
1¼"× 9" beaded deal fascia ¾" Soffit

6"× 6" and 6"× 4" head and transom
1¾" deal ovolo sashes glazed 26 oz glass
8"× 4" Oak rebated grooved and throated cill
Angle posts 6"× 6" intermediates 4"· 4"

9"× 6" C.I. airgrating & 4" Stoneware air Flue built in

13½"

Cord

5·3"

Cleat

7"× 2"   7"× 7"
9"× 6"

11"× 2" Wro't plank on 6"× 2" fir bearers

2·4·15"

8·0"

7·0"

This dimension regulated by height of floor level

8·4"

13½"

9" Relieving Arch
9"× 4" fir lintol

axed arch

1¾" deal ovolo sashes in 4½"× 4" rebated and beaded frame and 4½"· 3" oak sunk sill grooved for iron water bar

York Stone Cill 9"× 4"

Blue Splay Brick in cement

Will vary

3·11"   3·8"

Damp Course
Cement Concrete with floated face

18"   18"

24"

G.E.R   2·0"   3·6"   18"

6·0"

Minimum distance

2·2"   2·2"   3"

Rail level

Blue lias Concrete

113

RSCo, Dutton, and EOD-built Type 7 boxes, had plain bargeboards and plain fascia boards. However, the later Dutton/Pease-built boxes of 1898-1901 differed from the standard Type 7 design, in having operating floor windows with the lower of the two horizontal glazing bars omitted, and a roofed landing, as with the contemporary Dutton Type 3 design.

A few Type 7 boxes were given roofs of a steeper than normal pitch, notably those on the new Fairlop Loop and Lowestoft to Yarmouth lines of 1903. A further example of special treatment for new lines was the **Type 8** design used on the 'New Essex Lines' of 1888-9. These boxes had steeply-pitched roofs with decorative ridge tiles and terracotta finials, and McK&H/GE-type decoration on the bargeboards and fascia boards (all were McK&H-built).

Similar boxes, but without the bargeboard and fascia board decoration, were built (again by McK&H) on the new Cheshunt Loop line of 1891, and there was a stray example at Wivenhoe.

In 1910, the GE experimented with concrete blocks for the station buildings at Gidea Park, and the signal box at Ponders End South. Following this experiment, the Engineer was instructed in October 1912 to arrange with McK&H a schedule price for building boxes of this material, the blocks to be supplied by the GE at cost price. However, in the event, nothing seems to have come of this.

The normal widths of GE boxes were: Type 1 — 10ft., Type 2 (timber) — 11ft., Type 3 — 11ft., Type 4 — 12ft., Types 5, 6, and 8 — 13ft., Type 7 (timber) — 11ft. 6in.

Plate 154 GE Type 7 timber box at Oulton Broad North Station, built in 1901. This box has been extended at the right-hand end by one bay, and the stairs and door moved from the near end.

P. Kay

Plate 155 Pingle was an 1899-built **GE Type 7/Dutton** box. It closed on 14th March 1976, and was photographed here in July 1977. Horsemoor and Kings Dyke are surviving boxes of this type.

M. Christensen

Plate 156 The **GE Type 8** box at Fambridge. McK&H were given the signalling contract for the Southminster line in December 1888, and the line opened for passenger traffic on 1st July 1889.

P. Kay

The **GN and GE Joint line** had a complicated history which had some effect on box design. The Joint Committee came into being in 1882, taking over the new section of joint construction from Spalding to Lincoln, and other lines which had previously belonged to the GE (south of March) or the GN (north of March). The contracts for the new Spalding to Lincoln line had been divided into two sections. S&F had the signalling contract for the northern section (including the Lincoln loop), which was supervised by the GN Engineer, and Stevens that for the southern section (Ruskington and south thereof), which was supervised by the GE Engineer. All the boxes were built to the GE Type 2 design, but those on the GN-supervised section were given earth closets and gable window/vents, which were standard features elsewhere on the GN, but unheard-of luxuries on the GE. When the Spalding to Lincoln section opened, the GN took responsibility for the signalling of all the joint lines north of the point where the Sleaford to Boston line was crossed, and the GE took responsibility for all the joint lines south thereof.

The lines south of March were therefore always under GE control, but the March to Spalding line was interlocked by the GN during 1881/2 prior to its handover to the Joint Committee, with boxes to the GN Type 1/'Bessacarr' design. None of the original boxes on the March to Sleaford section were replaced during the period (1882-1923) of the GE's responsibility for it. But the GN's responsibility for the line north of Sleaford was marked as early as November 1882, when the original GE Type 2 box at Potterhanworth was destroyed by a freak wind, and replaced by a GN Type 1/'Bessacarr' design box. The Pyewipe Junction to Black Carr Junction section had been interlocked by the GN some years prior to its becoming part of the joint line. Although it subsequently remained a GN responsibility, the new boxes at Sykes Junction in 1885 and Kesteven Siding in 1891 were, perversely, close copies of the GE Types 2 and 7 designs; but so were some contemporary GN boxes elsewhere.

Three GE constituents are known to have been interlocked prior to take-over. These were the **Felixstowe Railway and Pier Co.** (worked by the GE from 1879), whose line of 1877 had McK&H type 3 boxes, in one case with special valancing for environmental reasons (*LNERS, Plate 257*); the **Bury St. Edmunds & Thetford Railway** (taken over 1878), whose signalling work (including, probably, the box structures) was carried out in 1875 by R&R; and the **East Norfolk Railway** (taken over 1881). The last had McK&H Type 3 boxes at Coltishall, Buxton Lamas, and Aylsham on the branch of 1879/80, and probably also at Gunton (1876) and Cromer (1877), but the design of the original boxes on the Whitlingham to North Walsham section is unknown, as all were replaced in GE days.

Plate 157 The **GE Type 2/GN** box at Branston, with the earth closet prominent. The GN could not resist the chance of providing a decorative bargeboard, even on something as small as the closet gables of these boxes! This box closed on 15th February 1976.

M. A. King

Colne Valley & Halstead

This small company had the distinction of owning five signal boxes all of different designs. There was no interlocking until the opening of an additional station at Ford Gate (later known as Earls Colne) in 1882, where a McK&H Type 3 box was provided. The original stations were not interlocked until 1888-94, the work being carried out by S&F. These later boxes were to local designs. Sible & Castle Hedingham, Halstead, and Yeldham were similar in so far as they were all gabled brick boxes with segmental-arched locking room windows, but they were far from identical. Birdbrook was a hipped box of entirely different design.

Plate 158 A May 1947 view of the CV&H station at Sible & Castle Hedingham. The signal box (built circa 1893) and goods shed somewhat dwarf the earlier station buildings! The brick chimney in the end wall was unique to this box. Yeldham and (particularly) Halstead boxes were rather more like the GE Type 7 design in appearance. One guesses that these boxes were put up by local builders.

British Rail, Eastern Region

Great Northern

Early block working on the GN was described in **Chapter 1**. By the end of 1864 the GN had a total of 75 'Signal Stations', a few of which were listed as 'Towers', the remainder no doubt being mostly ground-level huts. However, there was no interlocking until April 1866, when a most remarkable box was erected over the junctions at the south end of Spalding Station. The *Stamford Mercury* described it thus:

'A wooden stage 90ft. by 16ft., supported by eight massive iron pillars 30ft. in height . . . The stage is surrounded by a trellis work fencing of iron 5ft. in height . . . In the middle of the stage, immediately over the centre opening, is a handsome look-out constructed of wood and glass with a leaden roof exhibiting great taste. Under the stage are three 30ft. openings . . . through which the various trains pass. Midway between each couplet of pillars is a lofty iron patent signal by Stevens & Son . . . The whole is very tastily constructed and reflects great credit on the contractors'.

Plate 159 The contract for building this box at Newark Crossing was let by the GN to Mr J. G. MacKenzie, a building contractor, in November 1868. There is no record of the GN buying the locking apparatus for this box, which may therefore have been supplied by the Midland. In later years the box did have a Midland frame (although this was not of course the 1868 frame). The lines controlled were straight with good views in all directions, so very little elevation was required. The box was of BTF construction and built gable-to-track. It was in use until 17th May 1981, and was probably the oldest working box in the country at the time of its abolition.

J. Hinson

By March 1867, a similar structure had been built at Pelham St. Junction, Lincoln. This had a 'hut' on the gantry 25ft. long by 17ft. wide, with a 33-lever frame.

In November 1867, the GN Board ordered that 'locking apparatus be provided at the principal junctions'. Following this order, authorisation was given in 1867 for 'signal huts' at Hitchin, Barkston Junction, Werrington Junction, Hatfield, Wortley Junction, and Welwyn Junction, and in 1868 for Grantham Junction, Newark Lincoln Road, and Newark Midland Crossing. These were more conventional brick boxes, and Newark Midland Crossing (**Plate 159**), the only one to survive into recent times, was probably typical of them.

Between 1867 and 1873, the main line was converted to full Absolute Block working, and by later stages of this operation new interlocked boxes were being built at every station, typified in design by those in **Plates 160 & 161**. By 1880, 188 stations out of the GN's total of 255 had been interlocked — not a bad record considering that a large part of the network consisted of rural branches. Interlocking was completed in 1892. After that comparatively few new boxes were built, except for the main line widenings of the 1890s and the few new lines. The GN had a particular fondness for extending existing boxes wherever possible rather than building new boxes, and much reframing was undertaken up to 1914.

Around 1870, the GN made a number of locking frames itself, including those for Balderton in 1871 — this survived until closure in 1977, and is now at the NRM — and Westborough in 1872. However, this in-house manufacture did not last long. Although the Engineer was asked in 1881, and again in 1887, to investigate the possibility of establishing a full signal works, this was never done. Instead (as noted in **Chapter 2**) the GN became known for its very varied collection of locking frames, resulting from letting much of its work on a 'cheapest tender for each job' basis. Eleven contractors' frames are known, but some 90 per cent of the work was shared between S&F, McK&H, and the RSCo.

No boxes were ever built to contractors' designs on the GN proper. Indeed, the box structures were often built under separate contract by building contractors. All known GN boxes (except for the peculiar octagonal structure at Boston Dock Swing Bridge, and a very few other hipped boxes in Yorkshire) had gabled roofs. The boxes of the 1870s and 1880s, most of which were built of brick, and the brick boxes of the 1890s, defy all attempts at categorisation, and have all been classified simply as **Type 1**. Few were identical, but all had in common steeply-pitched roofs with large finials and decorative bargeboards, and a common 'atmosphere' varying, according to site and condition, between the picturesque and the shabby. The most common bargeboard designs are illustrated here (**see also Plates 63 & 64**), but there were others found on one or

Plate 160 The **GN Type 1/Arksey** design was used on the northern part of the main line in the 1870s. Arksey itself was inspected on 24th August 1878; others were Ranskill (now the only survivor), Rossington, Carlton, and Claypole. The **Type 1/Decoy** design used in the same area in the 1880s and 1890s was similar but had 4-panes-deep windows extending up to the eaves; examples were Black Carr Jn., Balby Jn., Bridge Jn., Decoy Nos. 1 and 2, and Carr.

R. Newman

Plate 161 Woodside Park, a **GN Type 1/Balderton** design box. This was a small version of the 'Arksey' type, with a different style of bargeboard, and with no locking room windows. It was used for the smaller block posts built on the northern part of the main line in the early 1870s (Balderton, Egmanton, Barnby Moor, Crow Park), for the High Barnet branch of 1872, and for Muswell Hill box in 1873. Note here, and in **Plate 160**, the unusual feature that the sliding sash is the central sash of each bay. Known as Torrington Park until 1882, Woodside Park box would have opened with the line on 1st April 1872. It was replaced by a new box in 1906, and the new box was itself abolished by LT, but both are still standing in good condition. The 1872 box of this design at High Barnet also still stands, although it was abolished as long ago as 1888, and the GN box at East Finchley can also still be seen.

P. Kay

Plate 162 East Holmes was one of the few timber boxes built to the **Type 1** outline. It probably dates from the diversion of the passenger lines in 1873. Another box glazed in this fashion was Grantham Yard of 1875.

R. Newman

Plate 163 The **GN Type 1/Arlesey** design. Arlesey box seems to have been built in 1874, but it was not put up for inspection until 1881. Other boxes to this design, with its distinctive curved sash-frames, were Biggleswade, Sandy South and North, St. Neots South, Huntingdon North No. 2, and Baldock. Some had 3 instead of 4 panes deep windows. All are now demolished. Arlesey itself closed on 13th June 1976, seven weeks after this photograph was taken.

P. Kay

Plate 164 The **GN Type 1/Bessacarr** design box at Haxey. The contract for interlocking and resignalling the Stow Park-Gainsborough-Bessacarr line was given to S&F in July 1876 for £7,022. The boxes were all to this design. Surviving boxes from this contract are Finningley, Beckingham, Walkeringham and Stow Park. Unusually for the GN at this period, other boxes were built subsequently to the same design, at such widely-scattered locations as Kirton (1877), Linby Colliery (1881), Postland/Murrow/Cowbit/French Drove/Sleaford East (1882), Willoughby Station (1887), and Gainsborough Lea Road South (an additional box of 1895). Most of these boxes had 'panelled' brickwork, otherwise unusual on the GN. Some other boxes were identical to the Bessacarr type except for having bargeboards to various different designs. Notable among these were the M&GN boxes with RSCo bargeboards (**Plate 171**).

J. Hinson

two boxes only. Vertical boarding was normal in the gable ends, with large gable window/vents 3-5 panes across. As for the main operating floor windows, in the 1870s 3-panes-deep windows (about 5ft. deep), with vertical boarding above, were quite common (**Plate 160**); and in a few cases such windows were combined with additional glazing right down to operating floor level (**Plate 162**). In a few boxes the main sashes themselves extended down to floor level, as at Bingham West (5 panes deep), the **Plate 165** drawing (6 panes deep), and Arlesey (**Plate 163**). Most common of all, however, especially in the 1880s and 1890s, were windows 3 or 4 panes deep extending from about 12-18in. above floor level right up to the eaves (**Plates 164, 166 & 167**). In most cases,

individual sashes were two or three panes across, with one fixed and one sliding sash in each bay. Locking room windows often had segmental arches (**Plate 160**), but stone lintels (**Plate 164**), pointed arches (on a few 1877 boxes — **Plate 76**), and semicircular arches (Hitchin Yard) are also known. In all types of locking room window there might be fixed glazing or vertical sashes.

Whilst many Type 1 boxes were unique in their combination of the various features, it is possible to identify several groups of boxes built with similar features, usually in the same area and built around the same time. These groups have been identified under the name of a typical example, as noted in the photograph captions.

119

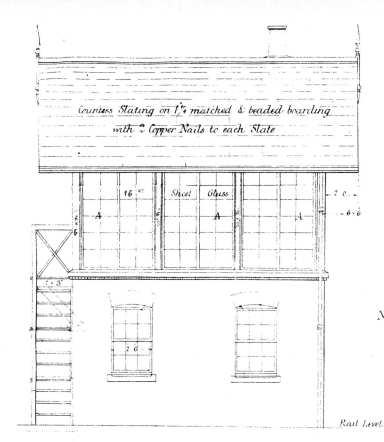

Countess Slating on 1¼ matched & beaded boarding
with 2 Copper Nails to each Slate

16 0"   Sheet Glass
A   A   A

2 6

ELEVATION TOWARDS RAILS

Plate 165 This official drawing was made by the GN to accompany standard contract agreements signed with S&F and McK&H in February 1874. The prices quoted by them (and by Easterbrook, the agreement with whom was not signed) for building boxes to this specification are given in **Table 8**. However, whilst many contemporary Type 1 boxes share some of the features of this drawing, no box is actually known to the precise design of the drawing! The normal internal width of GN boxes was 12ft. Note the location of the block shelf at the rear of the box.

Public Record Office

SCALE: 4mm = 1 foot

G.N.R. SIGNAL BOX.

NOTE Sashes marked A to slide, all others to be fixed
The figured dimensions are to be taken

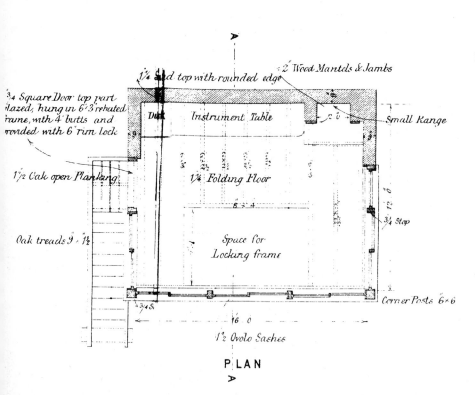

2" Wood Mantels & Jambs
1¼ and top with rounded edge
¾ Square Door top part
glazed, hung in 6'3 rebated
frame, with 4" butts and
rounded with 6" rim lock

Desk   Instrument Table   Small Range

2 0

1½ Oak open Planking

1¼ Folding Floor

¾ Stop

Oak treads 9 . 1½

Space for
Locking frame

Corner Posts 6×6

16 0

1½ Ovolo Sashes

PLAN

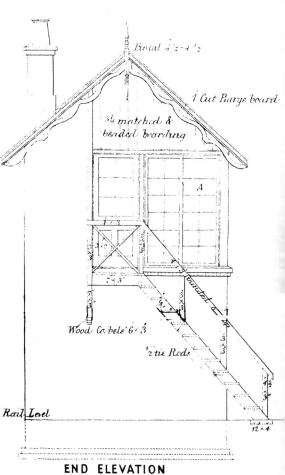

Finial

1 Cut Barge board

¾ matched &
beaded boarding

A

Wood Corbels 6.3

½ tie Rods

Rail Level

END ELEVATION

120

Plate 166 Netherfield Lane, a **GN Type 1/Yorks & Notts** design box. GN boxes of the 1870s-1890s in Yorkshire and the Nottinghamshire coalfield generally had 'flowing' bargeboards like these (but with many detail variations) and 4-panes-deep windows. Netherfield Lane was built in 1876. It is seen here shortly after closure, which occurred on 14th June 1981. Note the use of Flemish bond here — most GN boxes were in English bond.

P. V. Starling

Plate 167 (left) Eastville illustrates the **GN Type 1/ East Lincs** design. These boxes dated from the interlocking of the Boston to Grimsby line during 1887-90. Eastville was inspected on 22nd November 1890 along with all the other boxes on this section, but could well have been built a year or two earlier. The gable window vent pattern was unique to this design. Signs of subsidence are visible here on the fen soil.

R. Newman

Plate 168 (below) Wood Green No. 4 was a **GN Type 2** box, opened in June 1883. In mechanical days it controlled only the 'up' lines — separate 'Up' and 'Down' boxes were common on the GN south of Welwyn — but it is seen here in June 1975 after a panel had been installed to work the whole area. It finally succumbed on 8th August 1976, by which time it was the only GN box left south of New Barnet.

P. Kay

Although a few timber boxes of the 1870s and 1880s were built to the Type 1 outline, other contemporary timber boxes were built to much plainer designs. These have been classified **Type 2**, but there was no standardisation at all. Many were weatherboarded and superficially similar to the GE Type 2 design.

Some standardisation was at last achieved in 1888 with the **Type 3** design (used until circa 1905), but only timber boxes were built to this design, brick boxes continuing to be built to Type 1 variants until the turn of the century. The proportion of boxes built of timber increased during the 1890s, as the Type 3 design was used for most of the new boxes for the main line quadruplings south of Huntingdon. Type 3 boxes had a low-pitched roof, narrow plain bargeboards with no finial, 4-panes-deep operating floor windows (with fixed glazing in the central bays on the front), and 2-panes-deep locking room windows. They had vertical boarding, usually with battens. The plainness of the design was very marked by comparison with the exuberant carving of many Type 1 boxes.

Full standardisation arrived around 1905 (shortly after the company appointed a Signal Superintendent for the first time) with the Type 4 designs, used for all the (few) new boxes built after that date.

These boxes were similar in outline to Type 3, but had a new broader bargeboard design, decorative on **Type 4a** (up to circa 1915) — **Plate 170**, plain on **Type 4b** (from circa 1915, when skilled labour became scarce due to the war). Brick examples had segmental-arched locking room windows. Timberwork was covered with horizontal boarding, except that the 1906-built Woodside Park retained the vertical battened boarding of Type 3. The Type 4b design was developed by the LNER into its new Southern Area standard type (**Chapter 8**), but some boxes also continued to be built to the pure GN Type 4b design until as late as 1931.

The GN inherited five McK&H Type 3 boxes from the **Stafford & Uttoxeter Railway**, apparently built as part of the take-over agreement in 1882.

The resignalling of the main line in the 1970s took a heavy toll of GN boxes, nor are there now any GN boxes left in Yorkshire or on the Notts. & Derbys. lines. However, the remaining GN boxes in Lincolnshire retain an unusually good selection of old frames and equipment.

Plate 169 (above) A typical **GN Type 3** box at Woolmer Green, built in 1891 to control the connections from double to newly-quadrupled track north of Welwyn. Since the King's Cross resignalling, no Type 3 boxes remain; Woolmer Green closed on 10th October 1973.

M. A. King

Plate 170 (below) The **GN Type 4a** box at Bellwater Junction. The 1913 Skegness new line had a string of these boxes, all built of brick and all with the closet at the rear, under a continuation of the main roof. As noted in **Chapter 2**, they were built by Messrs Harold Arnold & Sons, builders. In contrast, the Type 4a boxes on the Enfield to Cuffley line of 1909/10 were all of timber construction.

R. Newman

Midland & Great Northern Joint (and constituents)

The history of the M&GN's constituent companies was a very complicated one. As far as the lines west of Lynn are concerned, however, there is no need to detail here the various changes in ownership and organisation prior to 1893, as the responsibilities for signalling remained unaltered throughout the period 1866-93. The Midland was in charge from Peterborough to Lynn, and the GN from Bourne to a point immediately west of Sutton Bridge Junction. The first known box on the Midland section was Sutton Bridge Junction, a Midland Type 1 box of 1880 which remained in use until 1961. By 1889, however, the Midland had built boxes, to the Midland Type 2a design, at virtually all locations on the Peterborough to Sutton Bridge section; and in 1891 boxes were built (again of Midland Type 2a) on the Sutton Bridge to South Lynn section. Doubling work on the Peterborough to Sutton Bridge section during 1890-2 meant the replacement of many of the original boxes by further new Midland Type 2a boxes. On the GN section, the earliest box was Sutton Bridge Dock Junction of 1879, built to the GN Type 1/'Bessacarr' design. In 1883 block working was introduced between Spalding and Sutton Bridge, but only one box was built in connection with this, at Welland Bridge (**Plate 31**). The general interlocking of the GN section was carried out in 1891. It was an RSCo contract, let for £5,809 2s. 1d. The price suggests that the box structures were included, and thus helps explain the fact that the boxes were built with RSCo bargeboards. Except for the bargeboards, this **GN Type 1/RSCo** design was identical to the 'Bessacarr' type. Most were of timber construction, with brick chimneys, but Holbeach East and West were of brick. The small hut at Weston level crossing was not built to this design, but of standard RSCo components — the only known 'contractor's box' on the M&GN. New boxes in 1893 at Bourne East and West and Welland Bank were also to the GN Type 1/RSCo design.

Turning now to the Eastern section, the **Lynn & Fakenham Railway** of 1879-80, and its Norwich extension of 1882, had interlocked boxes from the start, built to its own gabled design (**Plate 172**). It seems that a similar box design was used on the **Yarmouth & North Norfolk Railway**, but photographs of the original boxes here are few and poor. When the two companies merged in 1883 to form the **Eastern & Midlands Railway**, the L&F box design continued in use, on the new lines from Melton Constable to North Walsham (1883), Holt (1884), and Cromer (1887). The lines east of Lynn were fully (97 per cent) interlocked at 1889. Such little evidence as is available (as the companies' Minute Books have mostly been lost, and most of the boxes concerned had disappeared by 1910) suggests that the L&F, Y&NN, and E&M bought S&F frames.

In 1893, the Midland and the GN jointly acquired the whole of the E&M, and the Midland & Great Northern Joint Committee was set up in its final form. Henceforth the M&GN had a largely independent responsibility for its own signalling, working from the signal shops at Melton Constable, which were enlarged in 1896 to cope with the increased workload. A new M&GN box design was evolved without delay (**see next paragraph**), but several new Midland boxes were also built in the first few years after 1893. There were Midland Type 2b boxes at Sutton Bridge Station and East (1897), and at Clenchwarton and Walpole (1899), and a Midland Type 3a box at Stalham. The last GN box was that at Clay Lake (1896), another GN Type 1 box, but with bargeboards similar to some other contemporary GN boxes (e.g. Wainfleet) rather than of the RSCo type.

Plate 172 (below) The oversailing **L&F** Type box at Sheringham. This 14-lever box was inspected on 4th June 1887, and the line opened on the 16th. An oddity is that there is no nameboard (although a board in the normal place would certainly not be very easy to see). This box closed in 1906 when the station was enlarged and two new boxes built.
Authors' Collection

Plate 171 (below) Bourne (then Bourn) Station was resignalled in 1893, in connection with the opening of the new line to Saxby. The contract was let by the GN Engineer to the RSCo for £3,216 in April 1893, the cost to be recharged to the M&GN. Here is the **GN Type 1/RSCo** design box at Bourne East which, like so many M&GN boxes, closed on 28th February 1959. Another box of this type can be seen at **Plate 71**.

The Late E. L. Back, copyright M. Back

Plate 173 A new crossing loop was opened at Honing on 23rd June 1901, with two new signal boxes (East and West) to the **M&GN Type 1a** design. The East box, shown here, is now preserved at the Barton House Museum, Wroxham. The locking room windows of Type 1a boxes were normally in the front.

M. Marshall

Plate 174 Murrow illustrates the **M&GN Type 1b** design. A replacement for the original Midland box, it opened at 12 noon on 24th January 1912, and was abolished on 31st October 1965. In 1968 it was pulled down and sold for firewood!

The Late E. L. Back, copyright M. Back

The new M&GN box design clearly owed more to GN than to Midland practice, and can be compared with the contemporary GN Type 3 design. All boxes were of timber construction, with gabled roofs, and decorative bargeboards executed in a very standardised fashion. The sashes of the operating floor windows were all 4 panes up x 3 across. **M&GN Type 1a** boxes (1894 — circa 1903) had vertical boarding with the main beams and posts exposed, and gable window/vents 4 panes across. **Type 1b** (circa 1903-circa 1916) saw a change to horizontal lapped boarding of approx. 6in. cover, and gable window/vents 3 panes across. More than two dozen boxes were built to the Type 1a design, as a result of the large amount of doubling work carried out in the late 1890s. After this, fewer new boxes were needed. Most new boxes after 1893, including some Midland-type boxes, had S&F frames: but some, including some M&GN-type boxes, had Midland tumbler frames.

It was noted in **Chapter 3** that the M&GN's Engineer, William Marriott, had a special interest in the use of concrete, and that concrete building blocks had been produced at Melton Constable Works from circa 1916. The last Type 1b box, East Rudham of 1916, was built of these blocks up to operating floor level. Cromer Yard box was built of concrete blocks up to eaves level, and was to a new design, with a hipped roof without fascia board and 3-panes-deep windows. A number of gate huts were also built of concrete blocks up to the 1930s — for example, North Drove, South Drove (**Plate 50**), and Counter Drain — and the earlier Midland-type boxes at Sutton Bridge Junction and Massingham were given new bases of concrete blocks.

There was a very large number of gate huts throughout the M&GN system, but no standardisation of design is evident.

The M&GN's independent existence came to an end in 1936, when the LNER assumed signalling responsibility, although no new boxes were built after this. As a result of the mass closure of the network, only one M&GN box (Cromer Yard) survives in use, but several disused M&GN Type 1 boxes still exist — Raynham Park, Langor Bridge, Guestwick, Sheringham East, Weybourne (second-hand from Holt), and Honing East (**Plate 173**).

Manchester, Sheffield & Lincolnshire/ Great Central

The MS&L in earlier years was not very progressive in signalling matters. There was no block working until 1869 and no known interlocking until 1873. The first block working, between Darnall and Orgreaves, was effectively only a tunnel installation. However, a general extension of the block began in 1870, and from 1874 interlocked signal boxes were built in connection with new block installations. When the Sheffield to Penistone section was dealt with in 1878, it completed the installation of the block through from Manchester to Retford, but in Lincolnshire nothing was done until 1880. The last lines to be dealt with were Wrawby Junction to Lincoln and Woodhouse to Beighton, both in 1890. Many of the original 1880s boxes in Lincolnshire are still in use.

In the present century, the GC signal department, under A. F. Bound, turned around the company's earlier reputation and became one of the most progressive in the country. The most notable work was the pneumatic signalling installed between Ardwick and Newton during the period 1903-6 (**Plate 310**), and at Keadby (where 3-position signals were used) in 1912-16.

Prior to 1886/7 about one-third of MS&L boxes were built by the signalling contractors and to the contractors' designs. A small number of S&F boxes are known in the 1870s (S&F Types 6 — **Plate 117** — and 8); and rather more Stevens boxes (to the special **Stevens/MS&L** design described in **Chapter 5**) in circa 1882-6, notably on the Stairfoot to Nostell line in 1882. In 1885, the MS&L bought its first RSCo frames, and a large number of RSCo boxes were built during the period 1885-6, notably on the Wrawby to Gainsborough, Wrawby to Thorne, and New Holland lines (**Plate 136**). All the RSCo boxes were of timber construction, and had the lower windows.

The remaining two-thirds of pre-1886/7 boxes were to MS&L designs and had frames of a design unique to the MS&L. The place of manufacture of these frames is not known, but it seems likely that they were made up by the MS&L themselves, using parts supplied by ironfounders (the MS&L had opened new signal shops at Godley in 1875). In the latter part of 1886, however, the MS&L gained a new Engineer and a new Telegraph & Signal Superintendent, and this resulted in a changed policy. From 1886/7 until 1905, all frames were bought from the RSCo. Finally, from 1905, the GC had frames made to a standard design of its own, mostly by the RSCo but also by McK&H and, in one case, S&F. All boxes from 1887 were to MS&L/GC designs, but they were built by the signalling contractors as part of inclusive contracts.

The **MS&L Type 1** box design of the period 1873-80 was one of the most distinctive of all signal box designs. Particularly memorable were the large ball and spike finials (unfortunately the only Type 1 box left in use, Worksop West, has lost these). All Type 1 boxes were built of timber, with 5in. vertical battened boarding. The operating floor windows, which had no horizontal glazing bars, were only 2ft. 10in. deep, although many boxes in fact had double-height windows at the centre front to improve the view. A curious feature was that the window cills at the ends were set at two different heights. The locking room windows were placed in the ends, and not in the front.

With the **Type 2** design of 1880-87, the MS&L made a permanent change to gabled roofs. At first glance, the Type 2 might seem merely a gabled version of the Type 1, but in fact the dimensions were rather different. The operating floor windows were 3ft. 6in. deep, with one horizontal glazing bar. Only one box, Cleethorpes of 1880/1, had any double-height windows. The battened boarding — all boxes were of timber construction — was of 4½in. width, and was set diagonally in the gables. A large opening gable window/vent, 2 panes x 2, was provided; this remained a standard feature of all later MS&L/GC designs. The locking room windows were again placed in the ends. Type 2 boxes were a standardised 12ft. in width (Type 1 had been 13ft.), and this width was adopted for all later designs. A late Type 2 box, Barnsley Junction of 1887/8, was given a porch. Porches became common on GC boxes from the mid-1890s, but closets were not generally provided.

Vertical boarding was abandoned in 1887/8 with the introduction of the weatherboarded **Type 3** design. This also had much deeper operating floor windows (3 panes deep). Unlike all other MS&L/GC box designs, which had sliding sashes adjacent to the front corner posts and fixed glazing elsewhere, the operating floor windows of Type 3 boxes were arranged with two sliding sashes (and a central fixed portion) in each bay. The locking room windows were in the front, one per bay. The bargeboards differed from those on Type 2 boxes in that the protruding spikelets in the corners of the roundels were very much smaller. The brick Type 3 box at Brookhouse Colliery, and the BTF examples at Fallowfield and Levenshulme (1891), were the first MS&L boxes (other than the S&F boxes of the 1870s) to be built of other than timber construction. They were RSCo-built and had the S&F/RSCo type of locking room window.

A new design, **Type 4**, was used for the London Extension. The contract for the 75 boxes was let to the RSCo in November 1894, and the boxes were completed at various dates between 1896 and 1898. The majority were built of brick, with brick chimneys and stone lintels to the locking room windows. The timber boxes, and the gable ends of the brick boxes, had lapped boarding; and the gable window/vents were square, rather than rectangular as on the weatherboarded Types 3 and 5 boxes. The bargeboards were the same as on Type 3, but the roof pitch of boxes on the London Extension was somewhat less than the MS&L/GC norm. The London Extension boxes were built to standard sizes — the majority in fact were of exactly the same size, 28ft. x 12ft. x 8ft. — and had plenty of spare room for the expanded layouts which never came. Only one London Extension box (Loughborough North) is

Plate 175 (above) Built circa 1875, Grange Lane was the finest of those **MS&L Type 1** boxes which lasted into recent years, but it did not long survive closure on 2nd February 1980. It was 20ft. long by 13ft. wide.

R. D. Foster

Plate 176 (right) The **MS&L Type 2** box at Worksop East. The BR nameplate was clearly very new at the date of this photograph, as the woodwork behind the removed LNER nameboard has not yet been painted over. The boxes in **Plates 175 & 177-180** still display their LNER nameboards.

R. Newman

Plate 177 (left) The **M&SL Type 3** box at Retford Thrumpton was inspected on 15th March 1889. The fourth bay at the far end is an extension of 1927, hence its odd window pattern. Note the presence of a full stop in the middle of the box name! This box is still in use (now with a panel) as are many on the Wrawby to Lincoln line.

R. Newman

Plate 178 (below) The **MS&L Type 4** brick box at Ashby Magna, photographed in August 1966. The boxes on the Leicester to Woodford section were built in 1897. Ashby Magna was of the most common size, 28ft. x 12ft. x 8ft., and the box structure cost the standard £194 15s. for this size.

M. Christensen

standing today. The Type 4 design was also used generally on the MS&L/GC in the years 1895-1905, although comparatively few boxes were built outside of the London Extension in this period. Orgreaves Colliery and Darnall West are surviving examples. All Type 4 boxes had lean-to porches.

Special boxes with panelled brick bases, plate-glass windows, and hipped roofs with very overhanging eaves, were built on the London Extension at Marylebone Station and Goods and Nottingham (Victoria) North and South (**see also Plate 98**).

The first examples of the final GC design, **Type 5**, appeared in the late 1890s, but it was only with the Ardwick to Newton resignalling that Type 5 boxes began to appear in large numbers. In the 1900s, the GC also built several boxes with non-standard detail features, or non-standard combinations of features. Over 100 boxes were built to the Type 5 design, which was used until circa

Plate 179 (below) The timber version of the **MS&L Type 4** design is seen at East Leake. This section of the line was signalled in 1896. East Leake was another 28ft. x 12ft. x 8ft. box. It was one of the last Extension boxes in BR use, closing on 4th January 1970.

R. D. Foster

Plate 180 (below) Wath Staithe Crossing, a standard timber **GC Type 5 box. Plate 27** shows the brick version.

R. D. Foster

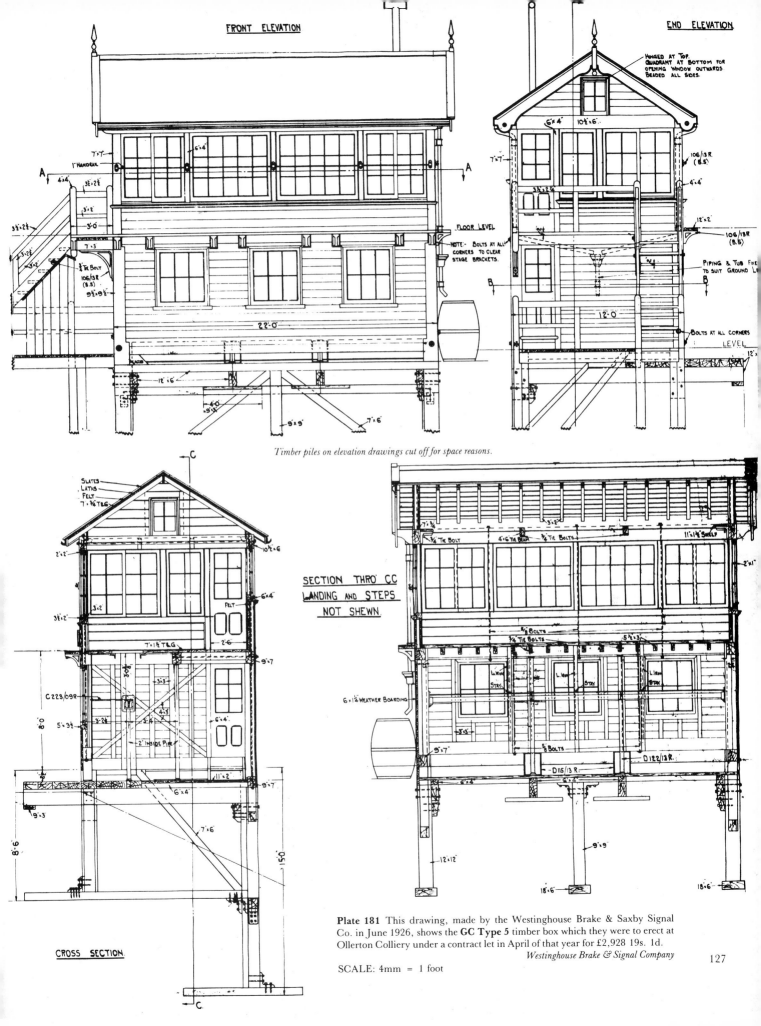

FRONT ELEVATION

END ELEVATION

HINGED AT TOP. QUADRANT AT BOTTOM FOR OPENING WINDOW OUTWARDS BEADED ALL SIDES.

FLOOR LEVEL

NOTE:- BOLTS AT ALL CORNERS TO CLEAR STAGE BRACKETS.

PIPING & TUB FIXED TO SUIT GROUND LEVEL

BOLTS AT ALL CORNERS

LEVEL

22'-0

12'-0

Timber piles on elevation drawings cut off for space reasons.

SLATES
LATHS
FELT
7 × ¾ T&G

SECTION THRO' CC
LANDING and STEPS
NOT SHEWN.

6 × 1¼ WEATHER BOARDING

CROSS SECTION.

Plate 181 This drawing, made by the Westinghouse Brake & Saxby Signal Co. in June 1926, shows the **GC Type 5** timber box which they were to erect at Ollerton Colliery under a contract let in April of that year for £2,928 19s. 1d.

Westinghouse Brake & Signal Company

127

SCALE: 4mm = 1 foot

1930. Three-quarters were built of timber, now with weather-boarding again. Locking room windows in the timber boxes were much larger than before — most often 2 panes up, 3 across, but there were many variations. Brick boxes had stone lintels to the locking room windows, as Type 4. All Type 5 boxes had stove-pipes. Bargeboards were to a new design, with the central roundel omitted, and usually broader than on previous types. The fixed windows in the central bays of the box front were variously 3, 4, 5, or 6 panes across (in Type 4 they had invariably been 4). The sliding sashes adjacent to the corner posts were usually 2 panes across, sliding behind a 2-panes or 3-panes across fixed section (in Type 4 always 2 behind 2). Dawes Lane and Crosby Mines (both 1913) were peculiar in having the sliding sashes in the centre of the box front instead of at the corners.

The **Wrexham, Mold & Connah's Quay Railway** was inter-locked, and block working introduced, in 1885. The Wrexham Exchange to Buckley section was done by the RSCo and the Brymbo branch by McK&H. The subsequent extensions (Hawarden line in 1890, Wrexham Central North in 1895) were signalled by Dutton. Contractors' box designs were used in all cases. The WM&CQ was taken over by the GC in 1904. The last WM&CQ box, Caergwrle Castle (RSCo), was abolished in 1982.

The **Lancashire, Derbyshire & East Coast Railway** was pro-vided with some 30 boxes for its opening during the period 1896-8. Those on the section from Chesterfield to Tuxford were built by S&F, and the remainder by the RSCo. All were similar in outline, but the S&F-built boxes had 3-panes-deep operating floor windows, decorative bargeboards, and gable window/vents 2 panes across; whereas the RSCo-built boxes had 4-panes-deep operating floor windows, plain bargeboards, and gable window/vents 4 panes across. The brick boxes had the standard S&F/RSCo locking room windows. The design as a whole was very reminiscent of the GN. The GC took over the LDEC in 1907 and several GC Type 5 boxes appeared subsequently.

Hull & Barnsley

On its opening in July 1885, the H&B was equipped with some 40 boxes built by S&F to their Type 10 design. Save for a few tim-ber boxes on embankments, they were of BTF construction. In later years most of them had conventionally-overhanging barge-boards, but some had the bargeboards directly over the boarding (as on the LCD examples of this type), and it is possible that all did originally.

The H&B remained loyal to S&F for a time, and the Denaby branch of 1894 had timber boxes to the S&F Type 12b design. However, in 1897, the company turned to EOD instead, and from then until the Grouping bought only EOD frames, although from 1903 these 'EOD' frames were of course supplied by S&F.

The EOD box design was not used; instead an H&B standard design was evolved. This **H&B Type 1** design, which appeared in timber and BTF form, was very much based on the S&F Type 10, but had curly eaves brackets, and a different style of segmental-arched locking room window on the BTF boxes. Some 30 boxes were built to this design between 1897 and 1915, as replacements for 1885 boxes, additional break-section boxes, for new lines such as the Wath branch of 1902, and for expansion in Hull.

Plate 182 (above) The **LDEC/S&F** Type box at Tuxford Central (originally Tuxford Town), opened in 1896. This was the last LDEC box in use, closing in 1984.

R. Newman

Plate 183 (below) A standard **H&B Type 1** box, Holderness Drain — the 'South' was added after amalgamation to avoid confusion with an NE box of the same name — opened on 26th June 1914 and closed in December 1973.

L. Carr

HULL & BARNSLEY RAILWAY
— SIGNAL CABINS —

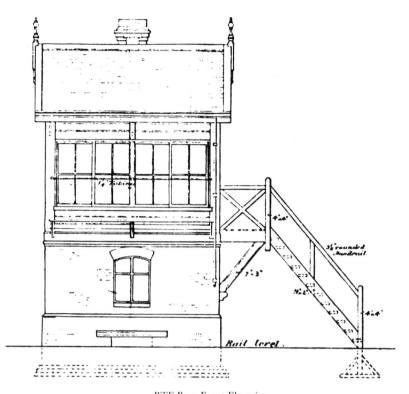

BTF Box: Front Elevation

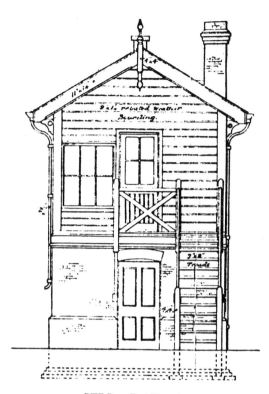

BTF Box: End Elevation

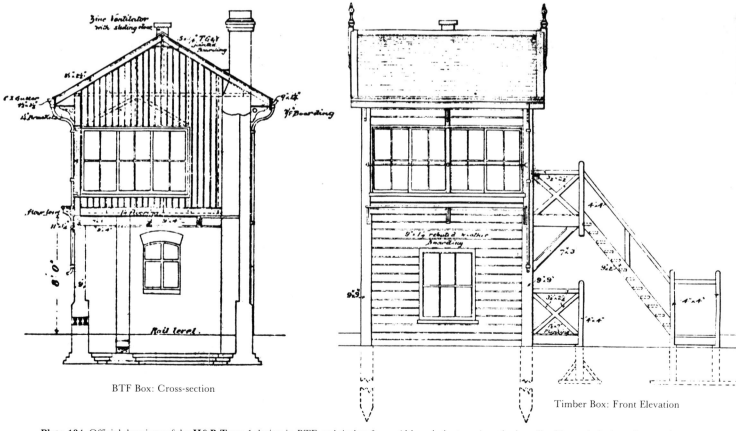

BTF Box: Cross-section

Timber Box: Front Elevation

Plate 184 Official drawings of the **H&B Type 1** design in BTF and timber form. Although the term 'weatherboarding' is used, the boarding on these boxes was what is known in this book as 'lapped boarding'.

SCALE: 4mm = 1 foot

Public Record Office

For the H&B/GC Joint line of 1916, which the H&B signalled as far south as Bullcroft Junction, and for replacement boxes on the main line at North Cave and West Bank Hall in the same year, a revised design (**Type 2**) was used, with deeper operating floor windows (3 panes deep) and long continuous locking room windows.

After 1916, the H&B built only one further box, at Spring Bank West, which opened in February 1923. This was a plain brick box with 2-panes-deep windows, not dissimilar to the old Type 1 design but with no eaves brackets. The H&B had amalgamated with the NE in 1922, and the next box built, Spring Bank North opened in June 1924, was to the NE Type S4 design.

Plate 185 The **H&B Type 2** box at Bullcroft Junction, opened on 1st May 1916 and closed on 6th September 1970.

A. P. Hinchcliffe

East & West Yorkshire Union Railways

This ramshackle railway had signal boxes at Stourton, Rothwell, and Robin Hood. They were ordered from the RSCo in September 1902, in preparation for the introduction of passenger services. Robin Hood survived into the 1960s and was an RSCo type box as, presumably, were the others. The station buildings at Robin Hood were also built of standard RSCo components.

North Eastern

Reference was made in **Chapter 1** to some of the early junction 'towers' on the NE, and (**Table 1**) to the NE's purchase of its first interlocked frames from Saxby in September 1862. Large scale interlocking began around 1867; the Northern Division had 30 locations interlocked by the end of 1870, and the Southern Division 87 by the end of 1872, but almost all of these were junction boxes.

Moreover, until 1871, there was no Absolute Block working on the NE apart from a few tunnel installations. Improvement was called for, and it came very rapidly. The 37 per cent of locations interlocked at 1873 had increased to 84 per cent by 1876; and by the end of the 1870s block working was in use over virtually the whole network, with interlocked signal boxes at almost all stations. Because so much was done in these years, few new boxes were required in the 1880s and 1890s, particularly in the largely rural Southern Division.

Except for a few home-made frames around 1870, the NE purchased all signalling equipment from the contractors. It was the largest railway company to do so. The three divisions into which the NE was divided — Southern, Central, and Northern — had independent responsibility for their signalling and other works; they used different signalling contractors and had their boxes built to different designs. The Southern and Northern divisions existed throughout, but the Central Division (which consisted of the ex-Stockton & Darlington lines, and had been known as the Darlington Section prior to 1876) was abolished in 1899, and its lines split between the other two divisions. Signalling contracts were arranged on a schedule basis from an early date (**Table 24**), but there was a considerable variety of frames in the 1870s, particularly on the Northern Division. From the 1880s, McK&H acquired a dominant position in the Southern Division, and Stevens in the Northern, but at least one major Southern Division contract, for the resignalling of the York & Beverley line in 1890, was given to the RSCo. The Central Division used I'Anson in earlier years, and then Stevens. NE boxes were generally built separately by building contractors (vide **Table 24**), not by the signalling contractors. Full-size NE boxes were always built of brick or stone except where site conditions enforced timber construction.

Turning now to the box designs, the **Southern Division** will be considered first. The **Type S1** gabled design of brick-to-roof construction was in use by 1873 and continued as the standard design until 1903. So many were built that over 50 are still standing. The majority (**Type S1a**) had stepped bricks in the gable end, and 'buttresses' at the corners on the upper part of the box with stepped-out bricks at their commencement. The operating floor windows were always three panes deep but varied in depth between 43in. and 50in. Normally the glazing was in short sections divided by brick pillars, most commonly with one sliding and one fixed sash, each three panes across, in each section; but a few boxes such as Kildale had continuous glazing on the front. The locking room windows had semicircular arches and measured a standard 24in. across by 48in. high (to top of arch). Most boxes were 11ft. 6in. to 12ft. wide. A few, for example Heslerton and Weaverthorpe, were built gable-to-track.

Type S1b boxes omitted the stepped bricks in the gable and the corner buttresses. Most were small low or ground-level boxes, either without locking room windows or with a long segmental-arched opening. However, a few boxes of normal height were also built to the Type S1b design, with the standard semicircular-arched locking room windows. A few Type S1b boxes also had continuous glazing on the front (e.g. Bootham and Whitby).

A few Type S1 boxes were built of stone or timber; the latter were weatherboarded.

With so many Type S1 boxes built, it is not surprising that a number should have displayed variations from the standard. Some had hipped roofs, and in several cases this was probably due to a rerooffing on extension (Sherburn North, Selby West and Castleford Gates), but in others it seems to have been an original feature (Deviation). The hipped boxes had full-height buttresses, as did a few gabled boxes (Sutton). Moss and Heck (1873) had decorative bargeboards and fascia boards, and several boxes of 1874/5 on the Hull to Scarborough line had valancing (the disused box at Burton Agnes is the best surviving example). Operating floor windows of double the normal depth were to be found at Deviation and

TABLE 24

Contractors approved by NE Way & Works Committee on 17th April 1874

	Contractor	Description of Work
Southern Division:	Saxby & Farmer	Interlocking Apparatus
	Stevens & Son	Interlocking Apparatus
	McKenzie, Clunes & Holland	Interlocking Apparatus
	T. H. Aspinall	Building Signal Cabins
	J. Keswick	Building Signal Cabins
Northern Division:	Saxby & Farmer	Interlocking Apparatus
	Easterbrook & Co.	Interlocking Apparatus
	E. I'Anson & Sons & Co.	Interlocking Apparatus
	J. Tweedy	Interlocking Apparatus
	Stevens & Son	Interlocking Apparatus
	Thos. Nelson	Building Signal Cabins
	Jos. Lawton	Building Signal Cabins
	J. Hirst & Sons	Building Signal Cabins
	Thos. Bulman	Building Signal Cabins
	J. W. Lowry	Building Signal Cabins

Contractors' names are quoted as given

Plate 186 (above) Wressle, a standard **NE Type S1a** box. It was built circa 1873 when block working and interlocking were introduced on this line. Only the different colour of the bricks gives away the fact that the near end of the box is an extension, probably of 1905, when the present frame was installed. NE boxes were built in English Garden Wall bond with three courses of stretchers for every course of headers. The arch of the nearer locking room window is formed of stretchers (the most common arrangement on these boxes); that of the other is of two courses of headers. This form of stairway was found on most Southern Division boxes. Note the plank provided for access to the walkway, swung back against the wall.

H. G. E. Wilson

Knaresborough. Many boxes located at level crossings had extra large windows at the crossing end, but most of these seem to have been later insertions. Several boxes had stone lintels to the locking room windows.

During the 1870s and 1880s, several completely non-standard boxes were built, with hipped roofs and 'splay' corners, at special locations, notably Holgate Junction and Waterworks at York, and Anlaby Road at Hull (*LNERS, Plate 362*).

In the early 1900s, Southern Division box designs developed rapidly. Two designs were used in parallel in the years 1903-5. **Type S2**, used on the Staddlethorpe to Hull quadrupling, was of brick instead of brick-to-roof construction. The gable ends were weatherboarded, with a 3-slat gable vent (found also on Types S3 and S4). There were no bargeboards, the ends of the purlins being left exposed. The operating floor windows were three panes deep. The only sliding sashes were those by the front corner posts (another feature repeated on Types S3 and S4). The brickwork of the base was relieved by two two-course bands of blue stretchers. The old semi-circular-arched locking room windows were retained. Rather more striking was the **Type S3** design found mainly on the York to Burton Salmon quadrupling. This introduced a new style of locking room window, 4 panes up and 3 across, with concrete cills and lintels. The operating floor windows also had concrete cills, and there was an additional concrete band at operating floor level. Bargeboards were provided, shaped into a concave curve at the head and a convex curve at the foot, but most memorable was the very large area of glazing provided by adding fixed 2-panes-deep upper lights above the 3-panes-deep main windows.

This period of development came to an end in 1905 with the adoption of the **Type S4** design, which remained standard into the 1930s, with very large numbers built. The new-style concrete cills and lintels of Type S3 were retained, but the concrete band at

Plate 187 (below) The **NE Type S1b** box at Howsham, an intermediate level crossing on the York to Scarborough line. It will be seen that this box originally had small locking room windows with stone lintels.

R. D. Foster

Plate 190 (above) Beverley Station box of 1911 illustrates the **Type S4** design.

M. Nicholson

Plate 188 (left) Welton, an **NE Type S2** box of 1904. The bands of blue bricks do not show up very well here; the lower one cuts across the locking room windows, the upper one is just below the walkway. Other surviving Type S2 boxes are Broomfleet, Brough East, Gilberdyke Junction and Saltmarshe.

R. Newman

Plate 191 (right) This NE drawing was made on 2nd May 1910 for a new box of **Type S4** at Northallerton High Junction. Note the provision of doors and stairs at both ends, and the door leading on to the walkway at the centre front. Very detailed drawings of all the component parts of the Type S4 design can be seen in the Public Record Office (File RAIL 527/609) but are too large to reproduce here.

SCALE: 2mm = 1 foot

Public Record Office

Plate 189 (below) Bolton Percy was built to the **NE Type S3** design in 1904. It was glazed on all four sides, and closed on 13th March 1983. Church Fenton North and York Yard North are now the only surviving examples of the type.

R. Newman

NORTH EASTERN RAILWAY
ALTERATIONS AT NORTHALLERTON
NEW SIGNAL CABIN FOR HIGH JUNCTION

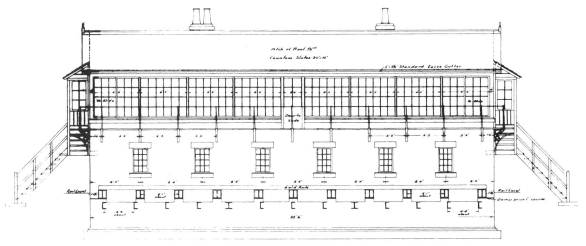

ELEVATION

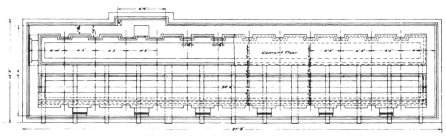

PLAN OF GROUND FLOOR

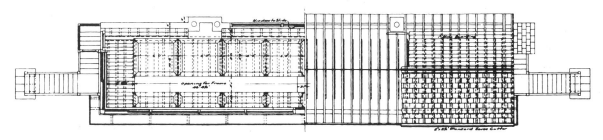

HALF PLAN OF FIRST FLOOR   HALF PLAN OF ROOF

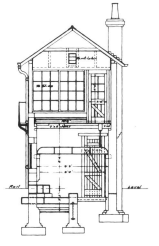

CROSS SECTION

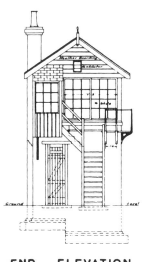

END ELEVATION

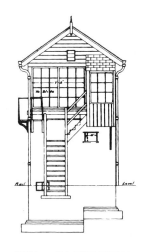

END ELEVATION

operating floor level was not. The operating floor windows were four panes deep. Bargeboards were plain except for a notch near the foot.

In later years, the Southern Division favoured timber construction for small low or ground-level boxes at minor stations and crossings. These small boxes were not standardised, but were generally weatherboarded, with 3-panes-deep windows. For convenience, the classification **Type S5** has been adopted.

Central Division boxes of the 1870s and 1880s (**Type C1**) were, like contemporary Southern Division boxes, gabled and of brick-to-roof construction. The most memorable feature of this design was the bargeboards, with intersecting cross-timbers, and finials over 6ft. long! Unlike Type S1, Type C1 boxes had continuous glazing. The windows were three panes deep and arranged with sliding sashes in every bay. The brickwork of the base was 'panelled'.

Central Division 1890s boxes (**Type C2**) had hipped roofs and were of brick rather than brick-to-roof construction. The operating floor windows were three panes deep as previously, but now there were sliding sashes by the front corner posts only. There was diagonal boarding between the head of the windows and the eaves. **Type C2b** boxes built from circa 1899 were distinguished from the earlier **Type C2a** by the addition of a large triangular slatted vent at the apex of the gable, plus, in most cases, a hipped porch. The Type C2b design continued in use until about 1905, and some of the last examples were built on lines which had not actually formed part of the Central Division.

Northern Division boxes are not easily categorisable. Most boxes throughout from the 1870s to the Grouping were of brick, hipped, and of generally plain appearance. Most had 2-panes-deep operating floor windows, with sliding sashes in each bay, each sash 2 panes across. However, there were also some boxes, particularly in earlier years, with 3-panes-deep windows. The only feature to show changes which correlate with date was the locking room windows, and the categorisation has accordingly been based primarily on these. **Type N1** boxes (1870s-1890s) had comparatively small locking room windows with stone lintels. **Type N2** (1890s and early 1900s) had easily recognisable 'triple' locking room windows, and **Type N3** (from circa 1905) had a very large segmental-arched version.

Plate 192 (above) The small **NE Type S5** box at Cattal.

M. Marshall

Plate 194 (below) Battersby, built in 1902 to the **NE Type C2b** design.

R. D. Foster

Plate 193 (above) The **NE Type C1** box at Appleby East. The opening date of this box is uncertain; possibly 1890 when the line was doubled. Originally called Appleby West, it was renamed as Appleby Station in 1909 and then as Appleby East in 1951. This photograph was taken in 1969, some five years after closure. Good surviving examples of this design can be seen at South Bank, Cargo Fleet Road, and Hopetown.

R. D. Foster

Plate 195 (above) This **Type N1** box at How Mill was inspected on 28th January 1875.

M. Marshall

Plate 196 (right) According to BR records, the **NE Type N2** box at Milton (near Brampton Junction) was built in 1893.

M. Marshall

Plate 197 (right) Alnmouth, an **NE Type N3** box of 1907. Because of its size this box has a 'panelled' base, but these were rare on the Northern Division.

H. G. E. Wilson

135

Special designs were used on some lines, notably the **Alnwick & Cornhill** Type of 1886/7 (stone gabled boxes with small eaves brackets), and the **Carrhouse** Type of 1896.

Type N4 covers the gabled boxes of the late 1900s and 1910s, several of which had semicircular-arched locking room windows as shown in **Plate 198**. Prior to this, gabled boxes had been extremely rare.

The Northern Division built an unusually large number of overhead boxes from the late 1890s (**Type N5**). The cabins on these were mostly to the design shown in **Plate 92**, although those at Newcastle were more elaborate. A report of 1911 recommended that 'the Northern Division practice of gantry boxes is not to be encouraged, and this type of box should only be used where unavoidable'.

The **Eden Valley Railway** had one or two interlocked boxes prior to its take-over by the Stockton & Darlington Railway (**vide Plate 34**), and the **Stockton & Darlington** itself had built a few boxes before passing to the NE. **The Blyth & Tyne Railway** was 62 per cent interlocked when it passed to the NE in 1874, but in none of these cases is there any photographic evidence to help establish box designs.

Plate 198 NE Type N4 box, probably of 1912, at Bedlington North. This style of roof vent was common on the North Eastern.

H. G. E. Wilson

Midland

Of the major companies, the Midland had the most peculiar signalling history. It never bought locking frames from the signalling contractors, it used the same basic box design from 1870 right through to the Grouping, and it carried out in later years a resignalling programme so thorough that most pre-1890 boxes had gone by 1923. This latter fact has naturally impeded the study of early Midland signalling.

We saw in **Chapter 1** how the Midland resisted the Board of Trade's attempts to impose interlocking at new junctions in the early 1860s. Not until 1866 was the idea of interlocking accepted, and then only grudgingly. Rather than purchase from the contractors, the Midland designed a primitive locking frame of its own,

with up to three levers in each slot and only very crude interlocking between levers in different slots. With frames of this type, it is clear that boxes would not have been very long. Until 1870 most or all box structures were put up by building contractors, and the prices confirm that they must indeed have been very small. The lowest tender for 'three signalmen's huts for the Mangotsfield and Bath line' in 1868 was £68 14s., and the 25 additional signal boxes required for the introduction of block working between Bradford and Wigston were costed in 1864 at only £16 each! Even the more important junction boxes were poor things by national standards; compare the £49 for Long Eaton Junction, £54 10s. for Erewash Junction, and £74 10s. for Beighton Junction (all in 1864) with the £95 spent by the GN on the by no means large box at Newark Crossing. We have no idea of what these boxes looked like, although it is unlikely that such cheap huts would display any decorative features. Poor photographs do, however, exist of what were, given their location, probably the finest signal boxes built by the Midland in the 1860s, the St. Pancras boxes of 1867/8. These were hipped boxes with decorative valancing and decorative window framing. By 1871 there were 'signal boxes' at most stations on the more important lines, although many of these would have been non-interlocked huts.

In the spring of 1870, authority was given for the building of a new signal works near the north end of Derby Station, and it appears that it was from this date that the Midland began to erect its own box structures from prefabricated sections made in the signal works, as described below. A new type of locking frame — an early version of the 'tumbler' frame — was produced from around the same date.

During the 1870s, block working was extended to the majority of routes, and new interlocked boxes were built in connection therewith. In 1880 the Midland had 730 interlocked boxes, and 180 locations where there were either non-interlocked boxes or no boxes at all. Overall, 86 per cent of points were interlocked, a figure which had increased to 95 per cent by 1889. There were still a few lines without block working in 1889.

In March 1890, a sum of £150,000 was voted for the purpose of fulfilling the interlocking requirements of the 1889 Act. The size of this sum is surprising in view of the claimed interlocking figures; the most likely explanation would seem to be that the Midland decided that the earlier frames still in use at this date were not in fact satisfactory, either from its own viewpoint or, perhaps, from the Board of Trade's. What is certain is that a much-accelerated programme of renewing old boxes began in April 1890. An average of twenty or so straight renewals (i.e. cases where no track alterations were involved) was authorised each year in the 1890s and 1900s, on top of which there were as many or more renewals necessitated by a heavy programme of quadruplings and other expansions. So it was that the majority of pre-1890 boxes disappeared. In circa 1892, the 'tumbler' frame went through its last significant redesign, producing the version still to be seen in many boxes.

The well-known prefabricated Midland box design was in use from circa 1870 to 1929. Throughout that lengthy period, the basic timber structure and hipped roof remained largely unaltered, the only important changes being in window size and pane pattern, and in the type of boarding used. These major changes occurred in 1884, 1900, and 1906, dividing Midland boxes into four main types, as described below. All Midland boxes were built wholly of timber, except for the STF box at Cudworth Station South Junction (1900), the brick boxes at Trent Station North Junction and Trent Station South Junction (1893), the BTF box at Spondon Station (1918), and possibly a few others. Many other Midland boxes were of course bricked up in later years. The reasons for the choice of non-standard construction in these cases are not known except in the case of Spondon Station, which also had concrete corner posts, and was a deliberate experiment with new materials. The experiment was not followed up because W. B. Worthington, the company's Chief Engineer and the proponent of concrete, retired and was replaced by James Briggs, who did not care for it.

The prefabricated 'panels' or 'flakes' which formed the walls of the Midland box were made up in the signal shops in standard lengths of 10ft., 12ft., 12ft. 10in. and 15ft. (but with varying window or door arrangements, depending on which facade of the box they were intended for), transported to the desired location on special wagons together with the posts and roof, and bolted together on site. On prepared foundations this could be done in a single day. Indeed, in a special test on 1st June 1920, the wagon crew erected the new box at Souldrop in 85 minutes, complete except for the roof slates. In earlier decades the corner and inter-mediate posts extended down into the ground, but in later years concrete bases were introduced instead to prevent timber rot, with the posts mounted on a 12in. by 4½ in. sill, secured on to bolts pre-set in the concrete. Many earlier boxes were subsequently under-pinned with new concrete bases, or with brickwork.

Both 10ft. and 15ft. panels were used throughout the life of the Midland box design. 12ft. 10in. panels were in use, to give an intermediate size, by 1890. 12ft. panels first appeared in 1900 and effectively superseded the 12ft. 10in. panels, which were used in only a handful of boxes after 1905.

Most boxes were one 10ft. panel in width, but there were a few 12ft. 10in. wide boxes in the 1890s, and during the 1900-1909 period the majority of boxes were built 12ft. wide (see below for the reasons for this). Oddities were the 15ft. wide Marple, and the 'double' boxes at St. Pancras Passenger (two 12ft. wide boxes back-to-back) and Bedford South (two 10ft. boxes back-to-back with an extra portion in between). Widest of all, however, was Sheffield 'B' platform box, built some 30ft. wide in order to give a view round both sides of the island platform buildings.

TABLE 25

Widths of Midland Boxes

Panel	Total External Width	Percentage of boxes of width concerned, by box type			
		1	2	3	4
10ft.	11ft. 4in.	100	95	28	95
12ft.	13ft. 4in.	-	1	72	5
12ft. 10in.	14ft. 2in.	-	4	-	-
		100%	100%	100%	100%

TOTAL SAMPLE: 530 boxes

Widths are measured at operating floor level.
Boxes built of non-standard panels due to site constraints are excluded.
Boxes more than 12ft. 10in. wide are excluded: these are mentioned by name in the text.

TABLE 26

Lengths of Midland Boxes

Panels	Total External Length	Percentage of boxes of length concerned, by box type						
		1	2a/2b	3a	3b	4a	4b/4c	4d/4e
10ft.	11ft. 4in.	29	2	2	-	4	-	5
15ft.	16ft. 4in.	43	46	46	-	33	3	23
10ft. + 10ft.	21ft. 11in.	14	33	52	13	52	11	32
12ft. + 12ft.	25ft. 11in.	-	-	-	-	4	11	18
12ft. 10in. + 12ft. 10in.	27ft. 7in.	-	6	-	10	-	4	-
10ft. + 10ft. + 10ft.	32ft. 6in.	14	9	-	40	7	39	13
10ft. + 15ft. + 10ft.	37ft. 6in.	-	-	-	-	-	14	3
12ft. + 12ft. + 12ft.	38ft. 6in.	-	-	-	10	-	4	-
12ft. 10in. + 12ft. 10in. + 12ft. 10in.	41ft. 0in.	-	1	-	3	-	-	-
10ft. + 10ft. + 10ft. + 10ft.	43ft. 1in.	-	1	-	17	-	11	4
15ft. + 15ft. + 15ft.	47ft. 6in.	-	1	-	3	-	-	-
12ft. + 12ft. + 12ft. + 12ft.	51ft. 1in.	-	-	-	2	-	-	1
10ft. + 10ft. + 10ft. + 10ft. + 10ft.	53ft. 8in.	-	-	-	-	-	-	1
15ft. + 15ft. + 15ft. + 15ft.	63ft. 1in.	-	1	-	2	-	-	-
12ft. + 12ft. + 12ft. + 12ft. + 12ft.	63ft. 8in.	-	-	-	-	-	3	-
		100%	100%	100%	100%	100%	100%	100%
Sample size for each type:		7	206	48	40	27	28	77

TOTAL SAMPLE: 433 boxes

This table shows the lengths of boxes as originally built, ignoring subsequent extensions. Lengths are measured at operating floor level. Other lengths found on one or two boxes only are 12ft., 15ft. + 15ft., and 12ft. + 10ft. + 12ft. Additionally, a very few boxes had to be built of non-standard panels due to site constraints.
The contemporary Types 3a and 3b are shown separately to demonstrate the correlation between length and type in this case; the same applies with Types 4a and 4b/4c.

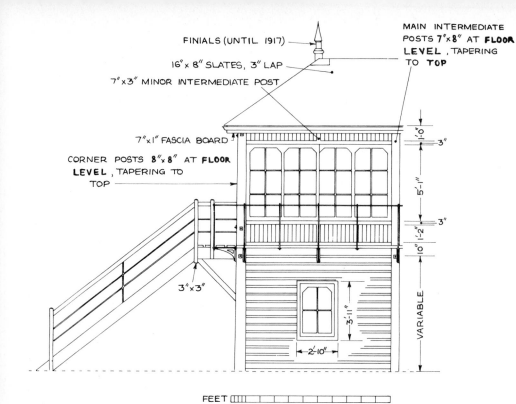

FINIALS (UNTIL 1917)

16" x 8" SLATES, 3" LAP

7" x 3" MINOR INTERMEDIATE POST

MAIN INTERMEDIATE POSTS 7" x 8" AT **FLOOR LEVEL**, TAPERING TO **TOP**

7" x 1" FASCIA BOARD

CORNER POSTS 8" x 8" AT **FLOOR LEVEL**, TAPERING TO TOP

3" x 3"

FEET

PANEL WITH 5'-1" WINDOWS

10'-0" PANEL SHOWN, AS IN FRONT OF TYPE 4a BOX, WITH 3½" BOARDING ON UPPER PART OF BOX AND LAPPED BOARDING ON LOWER PART. CAST IRON SUPPORT BRACKETS FOR WALKWAY.

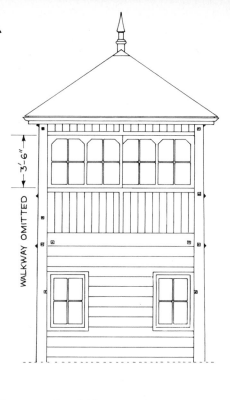

PANEL WITH 3'-6" WINDOWS

10'-0" PANEL SHOWN AS AT NON-DOOR END OF TYPE 2a BOX, WITH 6" BOARDING ON UPPER PART OF BOX AND WEATHERBOARDING ON LOWER PART.

STAIRCASE

DOOR IS NORMALLY PLACED AT THE END OF THE BOX WHICH FACES ONCOMING TRAFFIC ON NEAREST LINE (BUT MANY EXCEPTIONS: ALSO A NUMBER OF BOXES HAVE THE DOOR IN THE BACK).

STAIRCASE IS NORMALLY SINGLE FLIGHT, PARALLEL TO TRACK.

11" x 2" TIMBER STEPS, 2'-0" LONG, WITH 8" RISE.

ARRANGEMENT OF 10' PANEL AT DOOR END
(TYPE 3a BOX SHOWN WROUGHT IRON SUPPORT BRACKETS FOR WALKWAY)
IN THE CASE OF TYPE 4 BOXES WITH REAR FRAMES, THE OPERATING FLOOR DOOR IS NORMALLY 2'-6" NEARER THE FRONT, AND THE STAIRS ARE NORMALLY 2'-6" NEARER THE REAR.

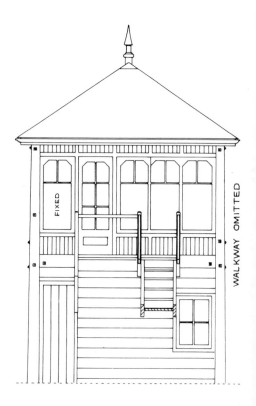

ARRANGEMENT OF 12' PANEL AT DOOR END
(TYPE 3b BOX SHOWN.)

138

THE MIDLAND RAILWAY SIGNAL BOX

BOARDING ON UPPER PART OF BOX

UNTIL 1892/3, 6" VERTICAL BOARDING, FLUSH JOINTED
FROM 1892/3, 3½" VERTICAL BOARDING, V-JOINTED:

- 17 BOARDS ON EACH HALF OF A 10' PANEL
  OR THIRD OF A 15' PANEL
- 15/14/15 BOARDS ON THE THREE SECTIONS
  OF A 13' PANEL
- 20 OR 21 BOARDS ON EACH HALF OF A
  12' PANEL

BOARDING ON LOWER PART OF BOX

UNTIL 1906, 8"-8¼" COVER WEATHERBOARDING
FROM 1906, 6" COVER/7" NOMINAL LAPPED BOARDING

LENGTH OF SLIDING SASH WINDOW SECTIONS (NON-DOOR END)

IN 10'-0" PANEL : 5'-1" + 5'-1"
" 12'-0" " : 6'-1" + 6'-1"
" 12'-10" " : 4'-5" + 4'-4" + 4'-5"
" 15'-0" " : 5'-1½" + 4'-11½" + 5'-1½"

IN 10'-0" AND 12'-0" PANELS THE LEFT-HAND SASH IS SET IN FRONT:
IN 12'-10" AND 15'-0" PANELS THE CENTRE SASH IS SET IN FRONT.
ALL SASHES ARE MOVEABLE BUT IN PRACTICE ONLY THOSE ADJACENT
TO THE FRONT CORNER-POSTS ARE MOVED IN MOST BOXES.
APPROX. 1¾" OVERLAP BETWEEN SASHES, AND APPROX. ½" BEADING
BETWEEN POSTS AND SASHES.

"LOCKING ROOM" WINDOWS

ON WEATHERBOARDED BOXES SET IN THE ENDS, ALWAYS 2 PANES BY 2
(EXCEPT WHERE NECESSARILY SMALLER ON A LOW BOX).
ON LAPPED-BOARDED BOXES SET IN THE FRONT : 2 PANES BY 2 ON 10'-0"
PANELS ; 2 UP x 3 ACROSS ON 12'-0" & 12'-10" PANELS ; 2 UP x 4 ACROSS
ON 15'-0" PANELS.
USE OR NON-USE OF CORNER-PIECES ON LOCKING ROOM WINDOWS
IS ERRATIC AT ALL PERIODS.

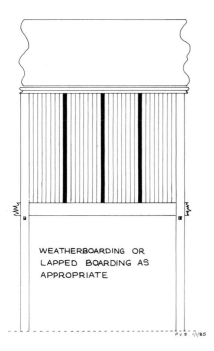

WEATHERBOARDING OR
LAPPED BOARDING AS
APPROPRIATE

P.V.S 17/1/85

REAR - ALL TYPES (SHOWN AS INTERMEDIATE 10' PANEL)

UPPER PART OF BOX

STANDARD ARRANGEMENTS :
10'-0" PANELS DIVIDED INTO 4 SECTIONS
12'-0" " " " 5 "
12'-10" " " " 5 "
15'-0" " " " 6 "
BOARDING (FROM 1892/3):
8 VERTICAL 3½" BOARDS IN EACH
DIVISION (EXCEPT 7 IN 12'-0" PANELS)
ABNORMAL ARRANGEMENTS :
A FEW 10' PANELS DIVIDED INTO
3 SECTIONS AND A FEW 12' AND
13' PANELS DIVIDED INTO 4
SECTIONS.

SOME BOXES HAVE WINDOWS OR
DOOR AT REAR, ACCORDING TO
SITE.

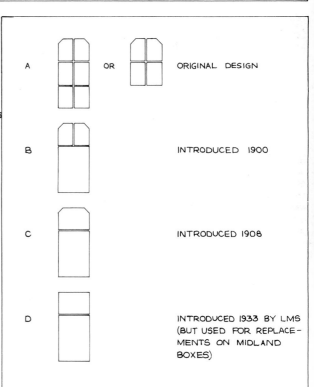

A	OR	ORIGINAL DESIGN
B		INTRODUCED 1900
C		INTRODUCED 1908
D		INTRODUCED 1933 BY LMS (BUT USED FOR REPLACEMENTS ON MIDLAND BOXES)

OTHER TYPES OCCUR INFREQUENTLY AS REPLACEMENTS
OR ON SPECIAL BOXES.
THE TIMBER "CORNER PIECES" ON DESIGNS A, B AND C
ARE PLACED BOTH INSIDE AND OUTSIDE THE GLASS.

MIDLAND & LMS STANDARD WINDOW DESIGNS

Plate 199 The Midland Railway signal box. Nameboard, downpipes, stovepipe, and other minor fittings are omitted for clarity.

SCALE: 4mm = 1 foot

P. V. Starling

The most common lengths were always 15ft., 10ft. + 10ft., and 10ft. + 10ft. + 10ft. Other panel combinations for the length of boxes varied over time, with 12ft. 10in. + 12ft. 10in. (Types 2 and 3) giving way to 12ft. + 12ft. (Type 4); and 12ft. 10in. + 12ft. 10in. + 12ft. 10in. (Types 2 and 3) giving way to 12ft. + 12ft. + 12ft. (Type 3) and then to 10ft. + 15ft. + 10ft. (Type 4). It will be seen that the introduction of 12ft. panels in place of 12ft. 10in. enabled a better spread of lengths in the middle of the range (21ft. 11in. — 25ft. 11in. — 32ft. 6in. — 38ft. 6in. — 43ft. 1in., instead of 21ft. 11in. — 27ft. 7in. — 32ft. 6in. — 41ft. 0in. — 43ft. 1in.). Prior to the introduction of the 10ft. + 15ft. + 10ft. combination, panels of different lengths had not normally been mixed in the same box.

The Midland had a 'small box' policy, with only about 9 per cent of its boxes more than 33ft. long (compared with 16 per cent on the LNW). This was achieved, in spite of the use of frames with 6in. lever centres, by the provision of very few spare levers, the use of combined point and facing point lock levers, and by building a large number of boxes at complicated locations. Until the early 1890s, there were very few Midland boxes with more than 36 levers, although much larger frames appeared subsequently. The largest Midland box, St. Pancras Junction, was just over 80ft. long, probably as the result of an extension.

As noted in **Chapter 3**, all types of Midland frame had above-floor locking, and were supported on the operating floor joists. The term 'locking room' is therefore strictly not accurate in the case of Midland boxes, but will be used for convenience.

The extent to which the Midland reused material from abolished boxes is unknown. There are several references in the Minutes to boxes being reused whole. The ability to reuse individual parts is one of the advantages of prefabrication, and as there was always a good number of fairly new boxes being abolished, one suspects that individual panels were frequently reused as well.

Plate 200 The 15ft. long **Midland Type 1** box at Dale Street (Burton-on-Trent) was probably built in 1882 when the crossing was widened. Final design was less standardised during the Type 1 period; on Types 2, 3 and 4, finials were as identical as was practicable, given that they had to be hand-turned. The double-length locking room window, and its location in the front of the box, were unusual; many Type 1 boxes had the locking room windows in the end as Type 2. The walkway is a later addition, and the nearer end of the box has been reboarded in part with 3½in. boarding.

R. Newman

Plate 201 The 10ft. + 10ft. long **Midland Type 2a** box at Settle Station. The building of this box was authorised on 2nd May 1890, at a cost (including signalling work) of £235. Note the inconsistent width of the boarding on the upper part of the box. The sashes in the left-hand front panel have been left the other way round to normal practice. The walkway is of the pre-1899 type, with wrought iron brackets, and with the railings attached to the front of the planks. Here, however, it does not extend the full length of the box, as it would otherwise be foul of the structure gauge, due to the presence of the siding which diverges to the left. According to local staff, the box nameboard was never returned after being removed during World War II. This box was abolished on 13th May 1984.

R. D. Foster

Plate 202 The 10ft. + 10ft. long **Midland Type 2b** box at Stamford. The renewal of the box and signalling at Stamford was authorised on 16th March 1893, for the comparatively large sum of £985, and the box was opened on 19th November 1893. One might have expected a walkway on a box of this height. Stamford was abolished on 15th May 1984.

R. D. Foster

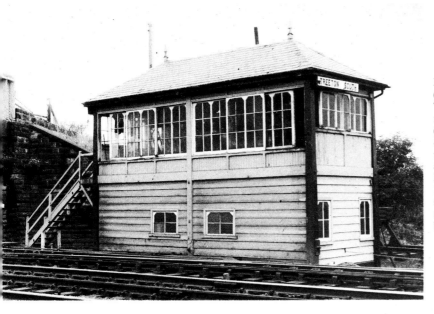

Plate 203 The **Midland Type 2b** box at Treeton South (built 1899) was 12ft. 10in. + 12ft. 10in. long. On Types 2 and 3 boxes there were normally two locking room windows in the non-door end (as here), and one (plus the locking room door) at the door end **(Plates 202 & 206)**. Treeton South had additional locking room windows in the front, as did many of the longer Type 2 and 3 boxes, but they were rarely placed 'sideways' as here. The photograph was taken on a warm day in July 1981, and so illustrates the point that in most boxes only the sashes adjacent to the front corner posts were ever moved in practice. Again there was no walkway. This box was abolished on 3rd October 1982.

R. D. Foster

Plate 204 Stourton Junction was a 12ft. 10in. wide **Type 2b** box, built in 1893. The length of 10ft. + 10ft. + 10ft. + 10ft. was the result of a 1903 extension. A new frame was fitted in the rear in later years; hence the stovepipes in the front. Ridge tiles were added by BR (NER) and the finials were removed. The photograph was taken shortly before the abolition of the box, which took place on 5th July 1981. Now, none of these 12ft. 10in. wide boxes remain.

R. D. Foster

Full details of the component parts of Midland boxes, and their dimensions, are given in **Plate 199**.

Turning now to the historical development of the different types of Midland box, the first version, **Type 1** (circa 1870-1884) had 3ft. 6in. deep Design A windows in the ends and in the front, with 6in. (approx.) vertical boarding above operating floor level, and weatherboarding below. Type 1 boxes were 10ft. wide, and few were more than 10ft. + 10ft. long. Few survived into recent decades, the last (Junction Road Junction) closing in November 1985. A gabled Type 1 box (so far unique) is known to have existed at Coalville Crossing.

Type 2a (1884-93) introduced deeper (5ft. 1in.) Design A windows in the front, retaining the 3ft. 6in. windows in the ends. **Type 2b** (1892-1901) was similar, but omitted the 3in. post between the windows at the door end (cf. **Plate 202** with **Plate 201**). Also in circa 1893 the 6in. boarding on the upper part of the box was changed to 3½ in. boarding (a handful of the last Type 2a boxes in fact had 3½ in. boarding). Over 500 Type 2 boxes were built, and some 50 are still in use.

The width of the locking mechanism on the 'tumbler' frame increased with the length of the frame and, with the average frame size increasing all the time, the Midland began to find in more and more cases that 10ft. was somewhat cramped as an internal width. A dozen or so of the larger Type 2b boxes were accordingly built 12ft. 10in. wide instead (**Plate 204**). This was of course the 'next size up' if standard panels were to be used, but it was perhaps felt that this was too wide, and in 1900 the 12ft. panel was introduced instead and was made the normal width for all except the smallest boxes. Only two of the very last Type 2b boxes, Westerleigh North (1901) and Wath North (1901), were built 12ft. in width.

A few Type 2 boxes had 5ft. 1in. windows at one of the ends as well as on the front. In most cases (e.g. Elstree North, Loughborough, Cudworth South Junction) this was the result of later extensions, but where it occurred at level crossings (e.g. Pinxton, Attenborough) it could have been an original feature.

Type 3 (1900-06) had 5ft. 1in. windows in the ends and in the front. The smaller boxes retained the Design A pane arrangement (**Type 3a**); about half of these were 10ft. wide, and half were 12ft. wide. Boxes more than 10ft. + 10ft. long (plus a few of that length) had a new window pane arrangement (Design B) with fewer glazing bars, to give the signalmen at these — the busier — boxes a less cluttered view. These **Type 3b** boxes were all 12ft. wide except in a few cases where the site enforced a lesser width. A good example of the choice between Types 3a and 3b was the new Heaton Mersey to New Mills line of 1903, where the larger boxes (New Mills South Junction, Cheadle Heath South, Cheadle Heath North) were all Type 3b boxes, and the smaller boxes (Heaton Mersey Station Junction, Hazel Grove, Disley) all Type 3a.

Plate 205 (left) Fiskerton, a 10ft. wide (and 15ft. long) **Midland Type 3a** box. The resignalling here was authorised on 2nd May 1902 at a cost of £250. Small locking room windows of this type were often found on the lower Midland boxes, but the presence of a walkway was unusual for such a low box.

R. D. Foster

Plate 206 (right) The 10ft. + 10ft. long **Type 3a** box at Sherwood Colliery Sidings South, built in 1904, was 12ft. wide, and the extra width is clearly evident in this photograph by comparison with **Plate 205**. The 12ft. and 12ft. 10in. wide boxes had sliding sashes in the door end windows.

R. Newman

142

In 1906 came **Type 4** with lapped boarding instead of weatherboarding on the lower part of the box. Another change, circa 1907, was in the walkway brackets (for the four different types of walkway brackets and railings on Midland boxes see the photograph captions). As with Type 3, the smaller boxes (up to 10ft. + 10ft. long) retained the Design A pane arrangement (**Type 4a**, 1906-17). The larger boxes were, for a year or so, given Design B windows (**Type 4b**); Morecambe (1907) and Lawrence Hill Junction are the only examples of this type. However, in 1908, a further new window design (Design C) was introduced, and this was thenceforth used for the larger boxes (**Type 4c**, 1908-15). With only a single horizontal glazing bar, this resulted in a further improvement of the signalman's view at the busier boxes.

In 1910, the tumbler frame was replaced by a new tappet frame which did not require such a wide locking space for the larger frames. Accordingly, there was no longer any need for the larger boxes to be 12ft. wide, and all boxes from 1910 were built 10ft. wide. Prior to 1910 the larger Type 4 boxes had been built 12ft. wide as with Type 3, although it so happened that almost all boxes of 1906-09 were small ones, so that only five 12ft. wide Type 4a/b/c boxes are actually known. Another change made was that from circa 1908, many Midland boxes had rear frames. This was in accordance with national trends, although on the Midland over half the new boxes built after this date were still in fact given front frames, and no pattern can be traced in the choice between front and rear.

Plate 209 The 10ft. + 10ft. long boxes of the 1908-15 period were mostly given Design A windows, but a minority had Design C windows, as here at Settle Junction. This **Type 4c** box was opened on 14th September 1913, replacing a box of 1892 which had itself replaced the original box of 1874. The walkway is of the 1907-13 type, identical to the post-1913 type, except for the fact that the top handrail and the verticals are joined with a much smaller clamp.

R. D. Foster

Plate 210 The 10ft. + 10ft. long **Type 4d** box at Swadlincote Junction. The Type 4 designs look very well when in good repair and recently repainted, as here. This box closed on 16th June 1969. Another Type 4d box can be seen in **Plate 41**.

R. Newman

Between 1908 and 1915, the Types 4a and 4c designs were (as noted above) used in parallel, for the smaller and larger boxes respectively. In 1915, however, the production of Design C windows ceased. The reason is unknown, but it may be that the heavier plate glass became difficult to obtain because of the war. The wartime shortages of skilled labour and materials brought another casualty in 1917 when the use of finials had to be given up. **Type 4d** is the designation of the finial-less boxes with Design A windows, built 1917-28. Those built after 1925 had the new LMS 'REC' type frame.

The last 'Midland' box design was the **Type 4e** of 1928/9, still finial-less but now with Design C windows (resurrected after a 13 year gap, and used subsequently on the first LMS design boxes until 1934). A few of these Type 4e boxes were built 12ft. wide instead of 10ft. From 1928, the LMS also built a few Midland-type boxes with brick bases, as part of the experimentation leading to the LMS standard box (for which see **Chapter** 8).

A number of non-standard boxes were built at conspicuous lo-cations in the period 1889-96. Bradford (1890) and Manningham Junction (1889) had 5ft. 1in. deep windows on both front and ends, arranged in 5ft. long sashes, with two vertical and one horizontal glazing bar. They also had decorative eaves brackets. Another box with eaves brackets (but otherwise a normal Type 2 box) was Gloucester Passenger Station (1896). Hendon (1890) had similar windows to those at Bradford, but no eaves brackets, and Barton Street Crossing (Gloucester) (1894) had similar windows, but with two horizontal glazing bars (and again no eaves brackets).

There were platform boxes within the island platform buildings at Nottingham (still standing) and Leicester, and a freestanding platform box of special design at Derby 'A' (**Plate 97**). However, at Sheffield, the two platform boxes were freestanding structures made up of the standard components.

For small crossing huts and ground frame huts the Midland had a standard timber hut with curved canvas roof (**Plate 213**). Once widespread, only a handful now survive.

Plate 211 Hall Lane Junction (Barrow Hill) was a 12ft. + 12ft. long **Type 4e** box, and shows the 3-panes-across locking room windows used in 12ft. panels on Type 4 boxes, here without corner pieces. The rear frame of this box is clearly seen. Hall Lane Junction opened in 1929 and was abolished on 16th November 1981.

R. D. Foster

Plate 212 This special design box at Bradford was built in 1890 to replace three earlier boxes. It was 15ft. + 15ft. + 15ft. + 15ft. long, and 10ft. wide. This view shows the rear. The lapped boarding is not original and has been placed over the outside of the corner and intermediate posts. The finials have been cut off. This box closed on 21st October 1984.

R. D. Foster

Plate 213 The standard Midland ground frame hut is illustrated here by Morton Crossing. A signal box (Fiskerton Junction) was provided at the same crossing in 1928, but the crossing hut was retained for the working of the main line running signals by a crossing keeper, at times when the signal box was switched out. A preserved hut of this type can be seen at Damems Station (second-hand from Earby).

R. D. Foster

The **London, Tilbury & Southend Railway** was, from 1854, worked on a 21 year lease by the contractors Peto, Brassey and Betts. When the company took over the running of the line in July 1875, the signalling was in a desperately primitive condition, with a minimal amount of interlocking. A programme of improvement was soon put in hand under the energetic control of a new Engineer, Arthur Stride. The important junctions at Stanford (Thames Haven Jn.) and Barking (West Jn.) were interlocked in 1875 and 1876, this work being carried out by Stevens, one guesses with Stevens-design boxes. During 1877/8, the block system was introduced over the whole network, and during 1880-1 all the stations were interlocked.

The 1880-1 work was given to Easterbrook, as was other LT&S work, subsequently, until the demise of the Easterbrook company in 1885. The boxes were hipped, and of timber (with vertical boarding) or brick construction (**Plate 129**). As noted in **Chapter 5**, it seems likely that Easterbrook rather than the LT&S was responsible for their design. Unfortunately none lasted into recent years, and no really detailed photographs are known of any of them.

From the late 1880s to 1912, all LT&S signalling work was done by the RSCo. Boxes were built to the RSCo design, without lower windows (**Plate 42**). Most also had larger-than-normal locking room windows. After 1900, a large number of new boxes were built in expansion schemes, notably the Campbell Road Junction to Barking quadrupling. RSCo boxes still in use are West Thurrock Jn. (1892), Woodgrange Park (1894), Grays East (1900), and Dagenham Dock (1901).

'Special' boxes were built around the turn of the century at Leigh-on-Sea and Southend Central. These were brick-built hipped boxes with decorative ridge tiles.

The Midland took over the LT&S in 1912, but there were no significant new works until the early 1920s, when several Midland Type 4d boxes were built (**Plates 41 & 307**). Of these, Rainham, Purfleet, and Low Street are still in use.

The 1850s' signal huts at Southend Central and Tilbury East Jn. both stood in derelict condition for many decades after their replacement.

The **Severn & Wye Railway** interlocked the major part of its lines in 1875, prior to the introduction of a passenger service. Most stations had only open ground frames, but there were a few cabins. The only information as to the signalling contractors responsible is that the Serridge Junction to Drybrook Road section was carried out by the Crumlin Viaduct Co., Lydbrook Junction by S&F, and Lydney Junction Station by McK&H. The **Severn Bridge Railway**, opened in 1879, was signalled by the GWCo, with GWCo boxes (the GWCo also built some of the station buildings on this line). The two companies amalgamated in 1879, and in the early 1890s two new boxes were built, at Upper Lydbrook and Coleford Jn., to replace earlier installations. These boxes were to a local design. In 1894 the company was taken over by the Midland and GW jointly, together with the Midland's Sharpness branch, and became the **Severn & Wye Joint Railway**. At first, the signalling of the whole line was a GW responsibility, but from 1906 the Midland took over south of Coleford Jn. By 1912, almost all the pre-1894 boxes had been replaced. Accordingly, the boxes in use in later years were mainly of GW Types 5 and 7 and Midland Type 4. All have now gone.

The **Clifton Extension Railway**, a Midland and GW Joint line which opened from Ashley Hill to Sneyd Park Jn. over the period 1874-7, originally had four McK&H Type 1 boxes. In 1890 it took over the **Bristol Port Railway & Pier Company's** line, which seems to have still been in primitive condition. New boxes from the 1890s were built by the Midland, and one of these, Avonmouth Dock Junction, remains in use.

Cheshire Lines Committee

The CLC acted independently of its owning companies in signalling matters. At first it relied on the contractors, primarily Stevens but with some S&F and McK&H work also known. All passenger lines were interlocked by 1881 except for the five stations Ashley to Lostock Gralam, which were not dealt with until 1885/6. Around 1885, the CLC began manufacturing locking frames and other signalling equipment itself at Warrington Works, and from 1886 it seems to have relied solely on this in-house manufacture. The CLC frame was basically to the Stevens pattern.

Some early boxes were built to contractors' designs; a dozen or so non-standard Stevens boxes from circa 1875-1886 (**see Chapter 5**), and an S&F Type 8 box of circa 1875 at Hale. However, the

Plate 214 Central Cabin (Northwich), a **CLC Type 1a** box. The date of this box is unknown, but it was in existence prior to 1886 when the new box at Sandbach Junction was built. On most CLC boxes (as here) there were sliding sashes by the front corner posts only. Note the splendid CLC nameboard here. This box was abolished on 2nd April 1980. Type 1a boxes still in use are Mouldsworth Jn. and Skelton Jn.; Mobberley is the only surviving Type 1b box.

R. D. Foster

Plate 215 Trafford Park Station, a **CLC Type 2a** box. Built to serve the new passenger station, this box was inspected on 15th January 1904. Identical boxes were built in 1906 at Trafford Park Jn., Throstle Nest South Jn., and Flixton Station.

R. D. Foster

Plate 216 The **CLC Type 2c** box at Bewsey, opened on 5th July 1930. The embankment site, which led to the choice of timber construction here, is evident, but the use of vertical boarding to the Type 1 pattern was a curious reversion after 27 years of horizontal boarding.

R. D. Foster

very standardised **CLC Type 1** design was used for most boxes from around 1873, and all from 1886 to 1903. These boxes were hipped, with fixed 'upper lights' above the three-panes-deep main operating floor windows. Almost all were of timber construction, with vertical boarding, and 2-panes-by-2 locking room windows. Most (**Type 1a**) had no eaves brackets, but some boxes of 1879-87 (**Type 1b**) had a greater roof overhang and large eaves brackets.

From 1904, all CLC boxes were gabled, and less standardised. **Type 2a** (1904-6) had horizontal boarding, 3-panes-deep operating floor windows, plain bargeboards, small finials, 2-panes-by-2 gable windows similar to those in GC boxes, and 2-panes-by-2 locking room windows (**Plate 215**). **Type 2b** (from 1907) introduced unusual 4-panes-deep operating floor windows with sliding sashes (provided by the front corner posts only) in the lowest three panes only. Bargeboards were plain in some cases (e.g. Brookfold) and similar to the GC Type 5 pattern in others (e.g. Glazebrook West Jn.); otherwise Type 2b was similar to Type 2a. The CLC continued its independent existence after the Grouping, and **Type 2c** covers six boxes of 1928-34, of brick-to-roof construction (except for the timber Bewsey) without gable windows, with plain bargeboards, and again with 4-panes-deep windows with sliding sashes in the lowest three panes only.

In 1930 the LMS took over control of CLC engineering, but it was not until the 1940 Risley boxes that standard LMS box designs appeared on the CLC.

The **Southport & Cheshire Lines Extension Railway**, worked by the CLC, provided itself with RSCo boxes for its opening in 1884.

London & North Western

The LNW ordered its first interlocked frames from Saxby in December 1861 (**Table 1**) and came to a sole-contract agreement for system-wide supply in 1862. The LNW work was very important to S&F in the 1860s. The contract was renegotiated, with reduced prices, in 1867 and again in 1871. No contractor other than S&F is known to have supplied locking frames to the LNW proper, but some work was done by other contractors on LNW Joint lines, as described below.

With its general policy of in-house manufacture, the LNW began to look askance at the large sums of money being paid to S&F for signalling work, and in 1872 the decision was taken to begin the

manufacture of locking frames and all other signalling equipment at Crewe Works. George Edwards, a former S&F employee, was appointed as Signal Superintendent in July 1873, and it was anticipated that the company would do all its own work from the expiry of the then-current S&F contract on 31st December 1873. In the event, however, Crewe took several years to build up production of signalling equipment (and particularly of locking frames) to the required level. At the end of 1875, S&F were still carrying out 20 per cent of the LNW's signalling work, and they were still doing a little even in the early 1880s. Edwards did not fit in well with the LNW hierarchy and soon left to join the GWCo. His later career is described in **Chapter 5**.

Until the end of 1873, the signal box structures were normally built by S&F and to S&F designs — Type 1 until circa 1869, then Type 2a on the southern part of the LNW network and Type 6 on the northern part. (In *LNWRS* the S&F Type 2 design was referred to as 'LNW Type 2', and the S&F Type 6 design as 'LNW Type 1'. This was done for compatibility with earlier published works, but the present classifications are more appropriate bearing in mind that these were not LNW designs. However, we have retained the designations 'Type 3', 'Type 4', and 'Type 5' for the true LNW designs, in order to avoid confusion). From circa 1867, brick or BTF construction was normal. The only pre-1874 boxes not to standard S&F designs were some of those on the Chester & Holyhead (*LNWRS Plate 9.2*) and Lancaster & Carlisle (*LNWRS Plate 9.3*) sections. It seems likely (although final proof is lacking) that in these cases the box structures were built by the LNW.

From January 1874, the box structures were normally built by the LNW, even in those cases where the signalling equipment was still supplied by S&F. However, a few boxes were still built by S&F until circa 1876; for example Milnthorpe (the only known S&F Type 8 box on the LNW) and, more significantly, the S&F Type 2b boxes for the Willesden to Bletchley quadrupling of 1874-6, the work for which was let to S&F on a 'special contract' basis to relieve the strain on Crewe.

When the LNW began the general building of its own boxes in 1874, it decided to adopt BTF construction as the norm, with timber construction used only where the site demanded it (about 10 per cent of boxes in all). This policy was retained throughout the LNW's life, as was the use of lapped boarding on the timber portions of boxes, and the use of S&F type locking room windows in BTF boxes. The timber components, and even the bricks, were manufactured at Crewe Works, and all boxes were built to standard sizes (*LNWRS Figure 10.3*). Indeed, LNW boxes were more standardised than those of any other major company. Moreover, there were only three basic design variations between 1874 and the 1920s.

Plate 217 An **LNW Type 3** box at Fossway Crossing (Lichfield), showing the brick chimney. This is a Size C box, the smallest standard size, and was built in 1875. Although already closed in this 1974 photograph, it still stands. Type 3 boxes are still in use at Narborough, Betley Road, and Monks Siding (Warrington).

R. D. Foster

Plate 218 (right) The **LNW Type 4** box at Lichfield Trent Valley Junction was built in 1897. It is of Size K. Note the alternate bays of fixed glazing. Various unusual bonds were used for the brickwork of LNW boxes; most commonly three courses of stretchers followed by one course of alternate headers and stretchers (best seen here in the end wall).

R. D. Foster

Plate 219 (below) Ellesmere Port No. 4, a 1924 **LNW Type 5** box of Size N. Like most large LNW boxes, this box had 'panelled' brickwork for extra strength (9½ in. in the recessed sections and 13in. elsewhere). Some years after this 1968 photograph it was burnt out, and a new BR (LMR) top was built on the old base.

R. D. Foster

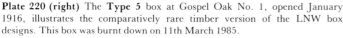

Plate 220 (right) The **Type 5** box at Gospel Oak No. 1, opened January 1916, illustrates the comparatively rare timber version of the LNW box designs. This box was burnt down on 11th March 1985.

M. Christensen

The first design, **Type 3** of 1874-6, had a hipped roof and 4ft. 6in. deep windows. **Type 4** boxes of 1876-1904 were similar to Type 3 below eaves level, but had gabled roofs, with bargeboards set directly over the boarding and finials inset into the boarding. Open hearths and brick chimneys were provided in Type 3 and the earlier Type 4 boxes, but from the 1880s stoves and stovepipes were installed instead; many earlier boxes were so converted subsequently. The glazing in some bays of Type 4 boxes was all fixed and impossible to clean from inside so, from circa 1880, walkways were provided to assist cleaning from outside. These did not have outer railings except on the very tallest boxes. The LNW Type 4 was one of the most widely-reproduced of all box designs, and about a hundred are still in use.

From 1898 a few boxes, where improved vision was required,

were fitted with 6ft.-deep windows. One such box was Shrewsbury Severn Bridge Junction, illustrated in **Plate 40**. From 1904, however, these 6ft. windows were used for all boxes, and this, coupled with a change in the roof style to give a greater overhang at all sides, and more conventional 'free' bargeboards, produced the **Type 5** design. At the same time, it was decided to provide sliding sashes in every bay, so enabling all windows to be cleaned from inside, and removing the need for a walkway.

Like the Midland, the LNW had a special design of hut for ground frames and very small boxes. This was introduced in 1880 and was gabled with vertical boarding, with an 8ft. x 8ft. plan (**Plate 106**). These huts were also used (with fewer windows) for non-signalling purposes.

For further information on LNW signalling the reader is referred to *LNWRS*.

The major **LNW/GW Joint lines** — the Shrewsbury & Hereford, Shrewsbury & Wellington, Shrewsbury & Welshpool, and Birkenhead — were all jointly owned prior to the coming of interlocking. Until 1885, the signalling of these lines was under the control of a Joint Lines' Engineer's Office in Birkenhead, acting independently of the two owning companies. Interlocking began around 1869 on the Birkenhead section, and around 1872 on the Shrewsbury lines. Signalling work was let on a competitive tender basis; most was done by S&F, but Stevens, GWCo, and RSCo contracts are also recorded. The known boxes were all to the same two designs, which must therefore have been specified by the Joint Lines Engineer, although both designs owed a good deal to contemporary S&F practice.

The **LNW/GW Joint Type 1** design (1869-late 1870s) was based on the S&F Type 1 design, but with the additional decorative features of a string course at operating floor level, a splay stone course immediately below the operating floor windows, and curved fram-

ing at the head of the operating floor windows. All were built of brick, and many were very wide. Chester No. 5 box additionally had McK&H type parachute finials, and one therefore assumes that it was McK&H-built, although there is no written evidence.

The more developed **Type 2** design of the early 1880s could be regarded either as the S&F Type 5 design without the curved framing of the sashes and upper lights, or as the S&F Type 9 design without the lower windows; the string course and splay course were, however, retained. The Type 2 design was used for English Bridge Junction at Shrewsbury, for four boxes at Wellington in 1881, and for four boxes at Hereford in 1884.

In 1885, the LNW took direct control of the signalling of these joint lines, and LNW Type 4 boxes soon began to appear. However, in 1904 responsibility for all except the Birkenhead was transferred to the GW. In 1909, the Shrewsbury & Wellington reverted to the LNW; after that there was no change until nationalisation.

The **Whitehaven, Cleator & Egremont Railway** purchased from Stevens in its independent days, and the boxes were built to the Stevens standard design *(LNWRS Plate 17.21)*. In 1877 the line became LNW property, and from 1878 LNW & Furness Joint, with the LNW responsible for the signalling side and the Furness for the telegraph side. All boxes from 1877 were therefore to the LNW designs, but until the mid-1880s they were fitted with (LNW-purchased) S&F frames or, in the case of two boxes, RSCo frames. For further details of this line see *LNWRS pages 253 & 254*.

Plate 221 (left)   **LNW/GW Joint Type 1** box at Church Stretton on the Shrewsbury and Hereford line. Nine boxes of this type are still in use, all on the Shrewsbury lines. With a width of 13ft. 7½in., this was one of the narrowest of these boxes. The locking room windows in boxes of this type were 2ft. 8½in. deep, 2½in. deeper than the standard S&F version.

P. V. Starling

Plate 222 (right) Ayleston Hill (known simply as 'Hereford' since a 1973 resignalling) is the last **LNW/GW Joint Type 2** box in use. This box is 15ft. 5½in. wide. The 1884 resignalling of Hereford was carried out by the RSCo for £2,950, but the frames were made to the S&F 'rocker' design.
P. V. Starling

The **North London Railway**, with its dense suburban traffic, was necessarily quick to adopt the improved signalling technologies of the 1850s and 1860s. Absolute Block working was in use from 1855, and the line was fully interlocked before the first Board of Trade returns in 1873. There must accordingly have been many boxes built in the 1860s, of which we know nothing. Many further new boxes were then built from 1870-5, when the line was quadrupled from Kentish Town (the present Camden Road) to Broad Street. In this early period, the NL put signalling work out to competitive tender, and Stevens, S&F, McK&H, and Easterbrook contracts are known. Easterbrook claimed in 1870 that they were completing a contract for signalling 'the whole of the North London Railway', but this would seem to have been an exaggeration. In 1878, however, the NL began to manufacture its own locking frames at Bow Works. The LNW tumbler design was used at first, but was superseded around 1890 by a new NL tappet design.

Some of the early boxes were to contractors' designs — definite cases of this were the McK&H Type 2 boxes at Canonbury Junction and Bath Road (Hammersmith) — but the majority, in the 1870s at least, seem to have been NL-designed. However, there was very little standardisation, except for the fact that all had hipped roofs. These early NL boxes have been classed **Type 1**.

Plate 223 (above) The early NL hipped box (**NL Type 1**) at Canonbury Station (Canonbury No. 2 in the days when there were two boxes here). This box was probably opened late in 1870 when the station was resited in connection with the quadrupling. The design was similar to that of Dalston Junction No. 1 (1871) and No. 2 (1872). It is possible that Canonbury once had valancing, like the Dalston boxes. Vertical boarding was used for the timber portions of NL boxes at all dates (the weatherboarding on Dalston Junction No. 2 as seen in *LNWRS, Plate 17.14* was not original). This photograph was taken in June 1970 and the box was burnt out on Christmas day 1973. It was officially abolished on 6th January 1974 when a new temporary box opened.

M. A. King

Plate 224 (left) Acton Central, a brick **NL Type 3a** box. The locking room windows are bricked up. The photograph was taken in 1983 shortly after abolition, hence the removal of the nameboard.

P. Kay

Plate 225 (right) The **NL Type 3b** box at Kew East Junction. Although the box is basically of BTF construction, the centre front is entirely of timber, to allow the provision of the large removable locking room windows. The centre sash of each three-sash set in the locking room windows is normally bolted shut along the bottom inside edge. When unbolted it can be lifted forward and then removed entirely. The two side sashes (which are normally held in place by the centre sash) can then also be removed entirely. The roofing material is not original.

P. Kay

After the NL started carrying out its own signalling work, box design became more standardised. **Type 2** boxes of the 1880s had hipped roofs and 2-panes-by-2 operating floor window sashes, with vertical boarding between windows and eaves. **Type 3a** (1890-5) was a gabled version of Type 2. These designs were built in timber, BTF, or brick form. After the tappet frame was introduced, many boxes were given the very large removable locking room windows seen in **Plate 225**: the purpose of these was to facilitate access to the locking mechanism, which on these frames was to the front as well as the rear. **Type 3b** (1895-1909) introduced a new operating floor window design, with two horizontal glazing bars only, but was otherwise the same as Type 3a.

The NL was responsible for signalling the North & South Western Junction Railway.

The LNW had always exercised a close control over the NL, and in 1909, when the NL was suffering a disastrous loss of traffic to the new trams and tubes, the LNW took over its management and engineering directly. Along with the other NL officers, the Signal Superintendent, Henry J. Pryce, was retired. From 1909, signalling equipment came from Crewe, and the couple of boxes built after this were to the LNW Type 5 design.

On the **Manchester South Junction & Altrincham Railway** (LNW & MS&L Joint), the contracts appear to have been let by the Joint Committee until 1904. S&F were used when the line was generally resignalled from 1877-82, with boxes built to the S&F Type 9 design (except for the unique structure at Brooklands). From 1886 to 1903, the RSCo was used, with RSCo-design boxes. From 1904, the LNW and GC took direct signalling responsibility for rotating three-year periods, but as it turned out the three new boxes built between then and the Grouping were all built by the LNW to the LNW Type 5 design.

Lancashire & Yorkshire

The L&Y had a good number of interlocked boxes in the 1860s, but few were ever photographed. It is likely that they were S&F or Stevens-built (**Plate 21**). Interlocking was virtually completed by 1880. Until 1889, the L&Y purchased all its signalling equipment from the contractors, with all boxes being built to the contractors' designs. **Table 27** shows the contractors used in the 1870s and 1880s. It will be seen that the majority of the work went to S&F until 1879, after which the GWCo predominated until 1881. In October 1880, the L&Y Engineer was asked by his Directors to investigate the possibility of the company setting up its own signal works, but the decision went against the idea at this time. Instead, the L&Y invited tenders in June 1881 for a 3 year signalling contract. This contract was won (as apparently the L&Y intended all along that it should be) by the new RSCo, who then did most of the L&Y's work from late in 1881, and all of it from 1883. Further information on the L&Y's dealings with the GWCo and RSCo is given in **Chapter 5**.

The L&Y displayed a greater variety of contractors' box types than any other railway company (for examples see **Plates 108, 118, 119, 120, 130, 132, 133, 135, & 137**).

It was decided to incorporate a signal works within the company's new Horwich Works, and after this opened in 1889 the L&Y undertook all its own signalling work. H. Raynar Wilson was appointed as Signal Superintendent. The RSCo frame design and the RSCo box design were adopted. However, **L&Y** Type boxes differed from RSCo-built boxes in that they had plain bargeboards, stovepipes instead of the brick chimneys found on many RSCo boxes, and a different window arrangement for 'Size 3' boxes (**see Table 19**). All L&Y-built boxes appear to have had the 'lower windows', as did all GWCo and RSCo boxes on the L&Y. BTF and timber construction were about equally preferred. The box structures were prefabricated at Horwich.

TABLE 27

The L&Y's Signalling Contractors, 1870-1891

The figures represent the number of boxes built by each contractor (ground frames have been excluded), and not the number of contracts let. The figures are based on an L&Y list of boxes existing at 1919. They therefore under-represent the total number of boxes built during the period 1870-91, but they should give a reasonable idea of the split of the work between the various contractors. Errors in the L&Y list have been corrected if known, but a few probably still remain undetected.

	Stevens	S&F	Yardley	GWCo	RSCo
1870	-	2	-	-	-
1871	1	-	-	-	-
1872	-	1	1	-	-
1873	1	12	1	-	-
1874	6	19	6	-	-
1875	1	28	12	-	-
1876	1	25	2	-	-
1877	-	17	3	-	-
1878	-	29	7	-	-
1879	-	10	-	10	-
1880	1	6	-	16	-
1881	-	3	1	7	1
1882	-	-	1	2	2
1883	2	-	-	-	8
1884	-	-	-	-	12
1885	-	-	-	-	8
1886	-	-	-	-	25
1887	-	-	-	-	25
1888	-	-	-	-	11
1889	-	-	-	-	15
1890	-	-	-	-	4
1891	-	-	-	-	1

A variation to the standard L&Y design was the use of steep-pitch hipped roofs on a few boxes, mostly oversailing or overhead boxes and mostly in the 1904-06 period. Birkdale is a surviving example of this **L&Y hipped** design. Similar hipped roofs were used for the special electro-pneumatic boxes at Bolton West (1903), Southport Station (1917) — **Plate 227** — and St. Luke's (1918).

After the L&Y's amalgamation with the LNW in 1922, the LNW Type 5 box design became the normal type for new boxes on the ex-L&Y lines, but the locking frames were still made at Horwich, to the L&Y pattern. There were also several new boxes built to the L&Y design until around 1926.

The **Bury & Tottington District Railway** was signalled by the GWCo, one contract of £1,500 being let by the railway company itself in March 1880, and another of £3,000 by the contractors building the line in June 1881. The line opened in 1882 and the company passed to the L&Y in 1888.

The **West Lancashire Railway** was equipped with McK&H Type 3 boxes for its opening in 1882-4, but used the RSCo for the little additional work required subsequently. Its offshoot, the **Liverpool, Southport, & Preston Junction Railway** of 1887, had RSCo boxes. Both companies were taken over by the L&Y in 1897.

Plate 226 (left) The well-preserved **L&Y** Type timber box at Clayton West Junction, still with its L&Y nameboard. This Size 9 box was built in 1915. Compare this with the RSCo design in **Plate 136**.

R. D. Foster

Plate 227 (right) The L&Y power box at Southport Station was equipped with an 87-lever Westinghouse electro-pneumatic frame. The ground floor of this three storey box housed the compressors which provided the power to work the points and signals, and the first floor contained the relay equipment. Note the special design of the operating floor window sashes.

R. D. Foster

North Staffordshire

The North Staffs was one of the most advanced companies so far as progress with interlocking was concerned. All but a handful of locations had been dealt with by 1876, and the last station, Alton, was completed in 1880. All known signalling work on the NS was done by McK&H on a schedule basis.

Nothing is known of the design of pre-1870 boxes. From circa 1870 to 1875, boxes were built to the McK&H Type 1 design (**Plates 124 & 125**), but after that the standard McK&H box designs were not used. The **NS Type 1** design of 1876-85 could, perhaps, be regarded as a special version of the McK&H Type 3 design; it had McK&H-type locking room windows, and small gable window/vents similar to those on some McK&H Type 3 boxes. It was also closely related to contemporary GN boxes in Nottinghamshire, where much of the work was also done by

McK&H. About half the NS boxes of the 1876-85 period were to the version of the Type 1 design depicted in **Plate 228**, with 'flowing' bargeboards and 4-panes-up, 2-across operating floor window sashes. The remainder were not dissimilar in outline but varied considerably in detail, some having different bargeboard and locking room window arrangements, and some having 3- instead of 4-panes-deep windows. All boxes of this period were of brick construction.

In contrast, the **NS Type 2** design used from circa 1885 until the Grouping was extremely standardised, and owed nothing to any other design. These boxes were all of BTF construction, with the brick base (in English bond) built wider than the weatherboarded superstructure and topped by one course of splay bricks. The locking room windows were set in the very top of the brick base. The roofs were steeply-pitched, and the bargeboards, plain apart from one roundel at the foot, were unusual in that they extended out at

Plate 228 (left) Sudbury was one of the last **NS Type 1** boxes built. The contract for resignalling this station was let to McK&H on 25th November 1884 for £685. Compare **Plate 166** for the close relationship with contemporary GN boxes.
R. Newman

Plate 229 (below) This **NS Type 2** box was originally known as Harecastle Kidsgrove Junction, and was built twice as long as it is now. It was shortened and reduced to ground frame status in 1966; the original door end was moved back to what had been the centre of the box. There were originally two locking room windows and the remaining one is acentral to the new length. Operating floor windows in Type 2 boxes were three panes deep, with sliding sashes by the front corner posts only. Another NS Type 2 box can be seen in **Plate 85**.

M. A. King

the foot beyond the fascia board. A gabled porch was provided.

The **Macclesfield, Bollington & Marple** Railway (GC & NS Joint) was signalled to NS standards. The original boxes were to the McK&H Type 1 design, but the later (probably 1890s) boxes at Macclesfield Goods Junction and Rose Hill were to a special **GC&NS Joint** design, of brick construction with McK&H-type locking room windows, but with a superstructure similar to contemporary GC boxes.

Wirral

Opened in part as early as 1866, this line was a very ramshackle affair in its early days. Originally the Hoylake Railway, the line was owned from 1881 by the **Seacombe, Hoylake & Deeside** company. There was little interlocking until 1888, when a general resignalling of the existing Birkenhead North to West Kirby line was carried out by the RSCo. At the same time, a new branch was opened to New Brighton, again signalled by the RSCo. Also, in 1888, the **Wirral** Railway opened its line from Birkenhead North to Birkenhead Park. In 1891 the SH&D and Wirral amalgamated to form a new company under the **Wirral** name. All known SH&D/Wirral boxes were to the RSCo design, of timber construction and without the lower windows. Four are still in use.

Mersey

Opened in stages between 1886 and 1892, the Mersey Railway originally had nine signal boxes on its small network. All the signalling work was done by the RSCo. Most of the boxes were to a special **Mersey** design of very distinctive appearance, although with some basic features in common with the RSCo standard design (**Plate 230**). The Liverpool Central boxes of 1892 were,

however, built wholly of standard RSCo components. The boxes in the tunnel sections had flat roofs; those in the open had hipped roofs. The two 'intermediate' cabins at River and Adelphi Street were squeezed into openings in the tunnel walls. They were open in rush hours only and were closed at an early date, although the structure at River lasted in situ until 1983, and that at Adelphi Street is still there. From around 1920, the cabins were lettered. Birkenhead Central (Cabin E) is the only one now in use.

Plate 230 The **Mersey** box design is exemplified by James Street, a flat-roofed underground box situated at the end of the station platform.

R. D. Foster

Furness

The Furness bought its signalling equipment from a variety of contractors. By 1879 Easterbrook predominated, but from 1882 the RSCo was the main supplier. There was, however, also some EOD work around 1900 and an Atkinson contract in 1907. Several huts and small boxes were built out of standard RSCo components — amongst them Devonshire Bridge of 1883, now enjoying a second life as a pavilion in a Barrow park — but all full-size boxes were built to Furness designs. In some cases the box structures were certainly included in the signalling contracts (**vide Table 8**), but in others they were separate building jobs.

Until the late 1890s, stone or STF construction was most common (although there were also many timber boxes) and there was no standardisation of design. Indeed, the Furness at this period was concerned, more than any other railway company, to make its signal boxes accord with the materials and style of nearby station buildings. From 1896, however, a fully standard box design was used, and brick construction became usual. All Furness boxes had hipped roofs and, like the boxes of the other Cumbrian railways, they were closer in spirit to the boxes of the Scottish companies than to designs elsewhere in England.

The oldest Furness boxes known are Drigg, Bootle, and Ravenglass, which date from circa 1871-74. These **Type 1** boxes had

Plate 231 The **Furness Type 1** box at Drigg. Drigg, Bootle, and Ravenglass were all given new RSCo frames in 1882, and it is not known which contractor provided the original equipment. Note that the stone base is bigger than the timber superstructure. It would be rash to assume that the present boarding is to the same pattern as the original. Note also the peculiar practice, adopted by the LMS on the Furness section, of placing the nameboard above eaves level.

R. D. Foster

Plate 232 Meathop represents the **Furness Type 2** design, here in STF construction. The signalling work at Meathop was noted as being 'in hand' in January 1879. In contrast to the GE and LSW boxes, these Furness boxes mostly remained with inside boarding only into BR days. The disadvantages of providing only one layer of boarding can be seen here, where two of the boards have fallen out leaving the signalman exposed to the elements. Meathop has been demolished since this 1969 picture was taken. The brick box at Haverthwaite is the best surviving example of the type.

R. D. Foster

Plate 233 Park South (**Furness Type 3 design**) was opened on 18th June 1883 and is still in use. The stonework here is unusually regular. Note the wooden shutters, which were provided in several of these boxes instead of opening windows. Other Type 3 boxes included St. Bees, North Lonsdale, Ramsden Dock, and Dalton Station.

R. D. Foster

Plate 234 Ulverston West (**Furness Type 4** design) was opened at 5p.m. on Sunday, 16th December 1900, directly to the east of its predecessor, the disconnection of which had begun at 1p.m. on the previous day.

R. D. Foster

'upper lights' similar to those of the contemporary S&F Type 2 designs, and main windows with no horizontal glazing bar.

The majority of boxes of the 1875-95 period have been classified **Type 2**. They shared many features despite the lack of overall standardisation, notably the absence of a fascia board, the provision of inside boarding only, and operating floor windows with no horizontal glazing bar (often also with a boarded section in the centre of the box front). Several boxes of the same period were, however, built instead to the rather more splendid **Type 3** design (**Plate 233**) with sloping bases, steeply-pitched roofs, and sub-divided upper panes in the operating floor windows. There were also several 'one-off' boxes.

From 1896, all boxes were built to the **Type 4** design. **Plate 234** shows the most common version of this, with 'panelled' brick base, brick stairs, 2-panes-deep operating floor windows, fascia boards, and terracotta finials. Variations on this were the retention of the Type 2 features of no horizontal glazing bars and no fascia board on two early examples (Broughton (1897) and Salthouse Junction (1898)): timber staircases on the later examples (Askam Iron Works (1910), Shipyard Junction (1912), Lakeside (1913), Sellafield (1918), Silecroft (1923)): no finials at Sellafield and Silecroft: and a non-panelled base at Sellafield. Two otherwise-standard boxes, Arnside and Sandside, were built of stone.

Maryport & Carlisle

Although the M&C did not introduce Absolute Block working until 1890-1 (it was the only English company of any significance to have no block working on a main line at 1889), it was reasonably forward with interlocking. Most stations were dealt with in the 1870s, and only six locations remained to be done at 1889. Stevens were the favoured contractors. All the known 19th century M&C boxes were to the same design (**Plate 235**). The last M&C box built, Carlisle No. 8 of 1918, was however to an entirely different gabled design (**Plate 236**), and, following the demise of Stevens, had a Tyer frame. The diagonal asbestos tiles used on this box were also applied to some of the earlier boxes, such as Bulgill and Brayton, in replacement of the original slates. Over half of the M&C's boxes had been abolished by 1931, and only one (Aspatria) now remains.

Plate 235 A typical **M&C** type box at Dalston. The opening date is unknown, but the late 1870s would seem most likely. Closure came on 3rd June 1973.

R. D. Foster

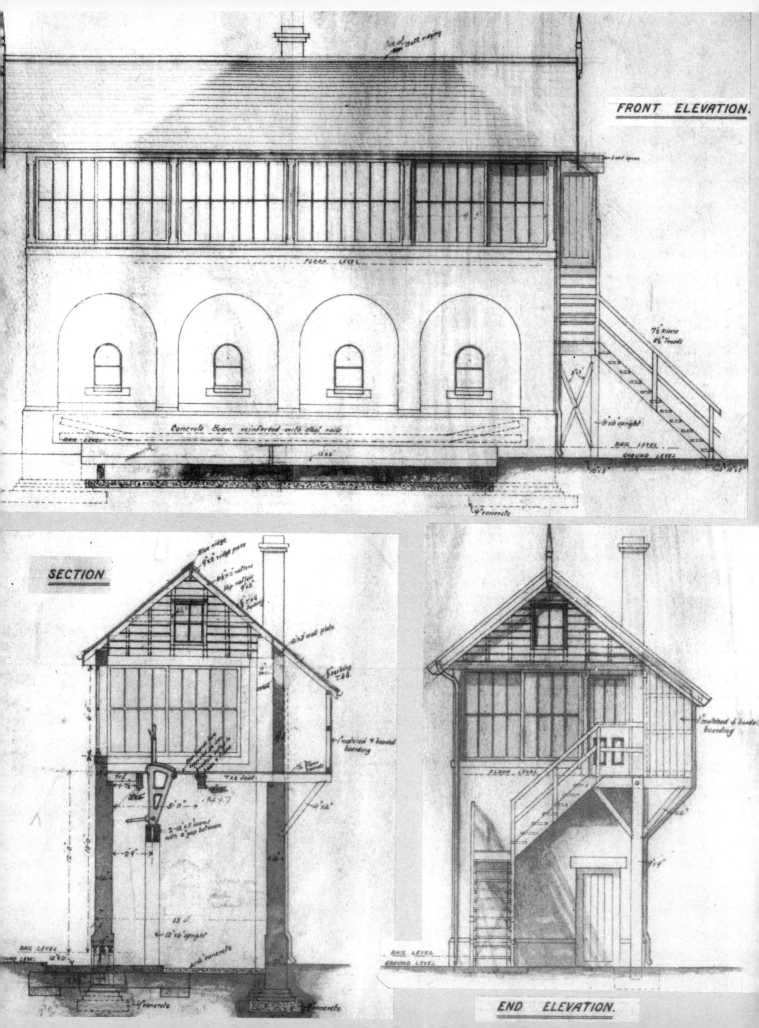

FRONT ELEVATION.

Concrete Beam reinforced with steel rails

Concrete

SECTION

END ELEVATION.

Cockermouth, Keswick & Penrith

In August 1873 (at which date Redhills Junction seems to have been the only existing box) the CK&P Board asked its Engineer, John Wood, to report on signal arrangements. Following this, the whole line (except Cockermouth) was interlocked and resignalled by S&F in 1874. S&F Type 6 boxes were built at Troutbeck, Penruddock, Keswick, and Bassenthwaite Lake; at the other four 'roadside' stations only ground frames seem to have been provided. Block working was introduced in 1875 and, following discussions with the LNW, Cockermouth was interlocked in 1875, so enabling the company to claim 100 per cent interlocking in its return at the end of that year.

Additional or replacement boxes were built at Threlkeld (1894), Penruddock (1896), Blencow (1900), and Redhills Junction (1900), in connection with the doubling of parts of the line; and in 1910 Bassenthwaite Lake box was 'rebuilt'. These boxes had Tweedy frames, but the box structures would appear to have been designed by Wood, whose signature appears on a drawing of Threlkeld. The four boxes differed in detail. All were built of brick, with the upper part (in later years at least) rendered, and most were without fascia boards. Blencow (**Plate 237**) and Penruddock were very similar, except that the latter had a peculiar half-hip roof. Threlkeld had a steeper pitched roofed to match the station buildings with which it was integrated, and Bassenthwaite Lake had deeper (3 panes deep) operating floor windows.

Although the line is now wholly lifted, the boxes at Troutbeck and Threlkeld still stand in derelict condition.

Cleator & Workington Junction

The contract for the signalling of the initial section of this line (which opened in October 1879) was given to Tweedy on 13th December 1878 for £4,000, but the box structures were erected by building contractors; one James Stewart was paid £300 in December 1879 for part of this work. The 1879 boxes, and those on the 1880s extensions, were mostly to a similar outline, but as on the CK&P no two were really identical. All were of brick construction, and all except Oatlands were gabled. Most had 2-panes-deep operating floor windows, and most had no fascia boards.

Plate 237 The **CK&P** type box at Blencow, pictured in April 1968. A peculiarity of the CK&P box design was the provision of only one sliding sash in the front of the box (instead of the more normal two, one by each corner post). In common with the other remaining boxes on the line, Blencow was closed on 3rd December 1967 when one-train-working was introduced.

R. D. Foster

In 1913, the C&WJ were still referring to Tweedy's successors, Tyer, as 'our signalling contractors'; but there was also a fair amount of RSCo and Stevens work, mostly reframings and alterations rather than new boxes. There are now no C&WJ boxes standing.

Plate 238 The **C&WJ** box at Distington Joint Junction (opening date uncertain). In later years this box had a Stevens frame. Note the provision of buttresses to support the structure after subsidence.

Cumbrian Railways Association

Plate 236 (left) The contract drawing made by the M&C for Currock Junction box in 1918. The draughtsman clearly had artistic pretensions, as he has drawn in the shadows (most noticeably by the stairs). The box, as shown here, is 36ft. x 13ft. x 12ft., and a note at the side of the drawing estimates that 30,000 bricks would be needed to build it. The exact dimensions of the box as built are not known, but the two central bays were each 8 panes across, instead of 7 as in the drawing. The drawing itself has undergone several alterations. The end elevation shows the closet roofed with a physically impossible continuation of the main gable (in fact it was built with an independent gable).

SCALE: 4mm = 1 foot

Knott End

The Garstang & Knot End Railway opened from Garstang to Pilling in 1870. There was no interlocking until the company's hand was forced by the 1889 Act. Gabled timber shacks were then erected to serve as signal boxes at Nateby and Garstang Town, the latter an extension of the station buildings. The company's name was changed in 1898. In 1908 it at last reached Knott End; small RSCo boxes were provided on this extension.

Stratford-on-Avon and Midland Junction

The SMJ company existed only from 1909 to 1923. In this period signalling work was done by the RSCo, and three new RSCo boxes were built, at Towcester, Stratford-on-Avon, and Blisworth.

Of the SMJ's constituents, the **Northampton & Banbury Junction** presents the greatest problems, since not only have the company's records been lost, as is also the case with the other three constituents, but also the N&BJ's few boxes had all been replaced by 1923. All that is known is that there was a £110 contract given to the GWCo in 1880, and that the 1897 box at Blisworth was built by Stevens.

The major constituent, the **East & West Junction** Railway, was opened over the period 1871-3, but the boxes, all of which were to the RSCo design, were not built until later, probably in 1884 when passenger services were resumed.

The **Evesham, Redditch & Stratford-on-Avon Junction** Railway opened in 1879, and was signalled by the GWCo. A covered ground frame was provided at Binton, and a full-size GWCo box at Stratford.

The **Stratford-on-Avon, Towcester & Midland Junction** Railway of 1891 was signalled by the RSCo. Originally there were three RSCo boxes, at Stoke Bruern, Roade Junction, and Salcey Forest, but all had been replaced by ground frames by 1918.

Great Western

The GW possessed a signal works at Reading from 1859, and began making locking frames to its own design from 1863. The Directors, however, were not enthusiastic about interlocking in the 1860s, and for some time the GW remained one of the most backward of the major companies in this respect. As late as 1872 there were only two interlocked boxes (at Whitland) on the whole of the South Wales main line west of Grange Court. But from the mid-1870s a consistent, if unspectacular, progress was made with interlocking. The last area to be dealt with was Cornwall, in the mid-1890s, after elimination of the broad gauge.

In the 1860s and 1870s signalling was in the hands of the Divisional Engineers, and Reading Works met only a small proportion of the GW's signalling requirements. The rest of the work went to the contractors; primarily S&F south of Gloucester/Oxford and McK&H to the north of this, with both firms sharing the work in South Wales.

Where signalling work was done by the contractors, the boxes were built to the contractors' designs. Most S&F boxes on the GW (none of which survive) were to the S&F Type 2a design, as for example the Pembrey boxes in 1873 and the Swindon boxes in 1874. Additionally there were a couple of boxes to a version of the S&F Type 3 design (**see Chapter 5**). Reading seems to have undertaken most of the new work for the southern part of the network from as early as circa 1876, and as a result there are only two known S&F Type 5 boxes — St. Ives (1877) and West Drayton Loop (1884) (**Plate 114**).

All three of the McK&H designs are known on the GW (**Plates 81, 126 & 127**). Reading does not appear to have undertaken much work for the northern part of the system prior to 1885.

During the period 1878-82, the GW acquired a number of GWCo boxes. Most of these (for example, Swindon K, Wolfhall Junction, and Bourton-on-the-Water) were cases where new junctions with the GW were being made by other companies which were using the GWCo, and where the other company was bearing the cost of the works. However, the GWCo minutes also record the GW ordering a box (probably that for Lydney Jn.) on its own account in December 1877.

By April 1885, production at Reading Works had reached a sufficient level for the Engineering Committee to decide that all new work should in future be done in-house unless otherwise authorised. In practice, no contractors' work is known on the GW after 1885.

Turning now to the GW's own box designs, the earliest GW boxes known from photographs were of the gabled brick-to-roof **Type 1** design of circa 1869-circa 1875. Examples were Steventon, Challow, Wootton Bassett, Foxes Wood, Grange Court West, and (**Plate 239**) Bullo Pill East. (The Type system used for GW boxes is that previously set out by J. P. Morris and M. R. L. Instone in the Signalling Record Society Newsletter. Although this system is on a different basis from that used elsewhere in this book, it was thought best to retain it as it has now gained acceptance. In most cases, GW timber boxes are given a type number 20 higher than that of the corresponding brick boxes).

Plate 239 Bullo Pill East was the last surviving **GW Type 1** box. It was built shortly after June 1873, when the GW informed the Board of Trade that boxes at Bullo Pill were 'already provided for' (i.e., planned), and it closed on 2nd June 1969, four weeks after this photograph was taken.

M. A. King

Plate 240 The **GW Type 2** box at Par was, in all probability, built in 1879. It was 17ft. 8in. long when new, but was extended to 38ft. in 1893. The right-hand end is the original, and the join can be seen just to the right of the 'P' nameboard. The few surviving Type 2 boxes have all been significantly altered in one way or another.

P. Kay

Type 2 of circa 1875-80 was a plain hipped design, of BTF construction (but with brick to the eaves at the rear, and a brick chimney) and with vertical boarding. A very few timber examples (**Type 22**) are known. Operating floor windows were normally 3 panes deep and in sashes 3 or 4 panes across. Locking room windows were segmental-arched with fixed glazing (2 or 3 panes up, 3 or 4 panes across) in a cast-iron frame. These characteristics were also shared by the operating floor and locking room windows of Type 3, 4c, 5, and 6 boxes.

Type 3 (1880-89) saw a reversion to gabled roofs. Construction was BTF on all facades; again, there were a very few timber examples (**Type 23**). Vertical boarding was used. Distinguishing features were the small curved eaves brackets at 2ft. centres, and the 7-louvre vents in the gable ends. Type 3 boxes were once quite numerous, but only two (Ferryside and Johnston) now remain in recognisable form.

Plate 241 The **GW Type 3** box at Sarnau was opened circa 1885 and closed on 25th March 1979, after which it was moved for preservation to Scolton Manor Museum. Note the unusual method of supporting the landing and porch, on brick walls. In this instance the porch appears to be an original feature, but many Type 3 boxes did not have porches.

J. P. Morris

Plate 242 GW Type 4c box at Cradley East. Opened in 1888 as 'Cradley B', it was renamed 'Cradley Heath and Cradley East' in 1901. Part of the nameplate has been painted out following the contraction of the station name. Unusually for Type 4, this box is of BTF rather than brick construction, leaving no room for the normal segmental-arched locking room windows. Other surviving Type 4c boxes are Rowley Regis (timber) and Blakedown (brick): Type 4b boxes can be seen at Ascott-under-Wychwood and Moreton-in-Marsh.

R. D. Foster

Types 1, 2, and 3 boxes were built only on the southern parts of the GW network. When GW-built boxes eventually began to supplant McK&H boxes on the northern parts in the 1880s, they were not built to the Type 3 design but to different designs (**Type 4**), which owed a good deal in appearance to the contemporary McK&H boxes. Type 4 boxes had gabled roofs (mostly steeply pitched) and large finials — the first appearance of finials on GW boxes. The gable vents had 4 louvres. Horizontal weatherboarding was used instead of the vertical boarding of earlier types; all subsequent GW designs (except Type 28a) also had weatherboarding. The major versions of Type 4 were **Type 4b**, used for the interlocking of the Oxford to Worcester line circa 1883, and **Type 4c**, used on the Kidderminster to Rowley Regis section in 1887-8. Both these versions had a large porch-plus-closet; on Type 4b this was supported on iron brackets, on Type 4c it was supported on a brick pillar incorporating a coal store at ground level. Type 4b boxes had a brick pillar supporting the landing instead.

After Reading took over full responsibility for GW signalling, a system-wide box design was evolved for the first time. Used from 1889 to 1897, with a few later examples up to 1902, the **Type 5** design was derived from Type 4, but with a roof of lesser pitch. A very large number were built, in the final burst of interlocking following the 1889 Act. Most were of brick, and a few (**Type 25**) of timber. Many had the operating floor door set back to give a 'porch' within the main outline of the box, with a closet entered by a door to the left, and no landing (**Plate 243**). But some boxes of 1889-92 had a large gabled external porch-plus-closet supported on a brick pillar as Type 4c, and a few boxes had a similar external porch-plus-closet on iron brackets *(GWS, Plate 84)*. In circa 1893 the 'rocket' ridge vents were introduced, but the 4-louvre gable vents were still included. Also around 1893 the well-known cast-iron nameplates appeared, instead of the former large screw-on letters which had been fixed directly on to the boarding on timber or BTF boxes, and on wooden nameboards on brick boxes. Type 5 was also the first GW box design to be built to standard sizes.

Plate 243 The **GW Type 5** box at Tirydail Station was built in 1896 and is 30ft. 5in. long and the standard 12ft. in width. Like most Type 5 boxes it is in Flemish Bond. Here there are sliding sashes in every bay, but some boxes of Types 2 to 6 had fixed glazing in the centre bays at the front (despite which, no type of GW box was ever provided with a walkway as standard). Tirydail was reduced to ground frame status on 13th March 1966, and all signals and connections were removed. Confusingly, the station has been renamed 'Ammanford'. At the 'real' Ammanford Station, at the other end of town, one can see the last surviving GW Type 6 box.

J. P. Morris

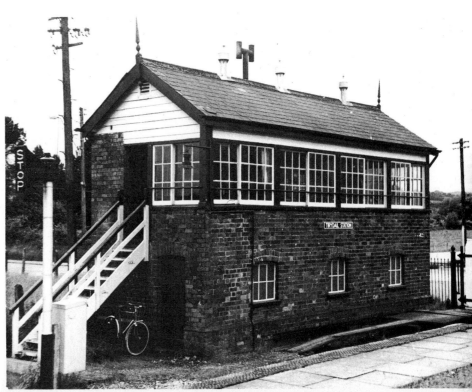

Type 6 was a narrow (9ft. 6in. wide) and finial-less version of Type 5 for small branch line stations. Most were low boxes built on the station platforms, but there were one or two taller examples.

In 1896 a radically new design, **Type 7**, made its appearance. This was to become the best known and most widely-reproduced GW box design, with several dozen still in use today. A hipped roof was adopted again, with large decorative eaves brackets, and a new design of operating floor window with fewer glazing bars (3-up, 2-down pattern) to improve the signalman's view. Brick boxes were mostly built of red bricks, which were much brighter than those used previously — similar bright red bricks were also adopted for GW stations at this period — offset, in all except a few early examples of the type, by Staffordshire blue bricks for the plinth, the quoins, and the door and window surrounds. The segmental arches of the locking room windows were formed of specially-shaped bricks. Timber boxes (**Type 27**) were weatherboarded and had a single large locking room window with the old 3-panes-deep sashes rather than the '3-up, 2-down' design of the operating floor windows. With Types 7/27, the GW began for the first time to build timber boxes regularly, and not just when site constraints required timber construction.

On Type 7/27 boxes, the door at the top of the stairs led into an internal porch, with a second door on the right into the operating room, and another door on the left into an inside toilet. There was no landing. Many later Type 7/27 boxes, however, had inside stairs instead; these became more common with subsequent designs.

The design was used until 1925 (Type 7) and 1927 (Type 27), and various changes were made during its 30 years' currency. Taking the brick boxes first, the earliest ones (**Type 7a**) had lead flashing along the ridge and hips, terracotta finials, brick chimneys, and cast-iron locking room window cills. In circa 1900, ridge tiles and wrought-iron hip-hooks replaced the lead flashing and finials, making **Type 7b**. In circa 1904, stoves and stovepipes replaced hearths and brick chimneys (**Type 7c**); and in 1906 the cast-iron locking room window cills gave way to two courses of Staffordshire blue splayed plinth bricks (**Type 7d**). Timber boxes went through fewer changes. The earlier boxes with brick chimneys (in most cases) and lead flashing and finials have been classified **Type 27a**. Later boxes with stovepipes, ridge tiles and hip-hooks are **Type 27c**.

Plate 244 A **Type 7a** box at Lavington. This box opened in 1900 and closed on 22nd January 1979. It measured 25ft. x 12ft. x 8ft. This was one of the few boxes without Staffordshire blue bricks. Early Type 7 boxes were in English Bond, as here, but some later ones were in Flemish Bond. Type 7/27 boxes had opening windows in every bay. A Type 27c box can be seen in **Plate 78**.

J. P. Morris

Plate 245 This GW drawing of a **Type 7** box is shown with 'Dawley' on the nameplate, but the box in the drawing measures 25ft. x 12ft. x 8ft., whereas that actually built at Dawley (between West Drayton and Hayes) in 1897 measured 29ft. x 12ft. x 11ft. The box is shown with both finials and ridge tiles, a combination unknown in practice; but it is not unusual for box drawings to show detail features that were not actually adopted in practice.

SCALE: 4mm = 1 foot

Authors' Collection

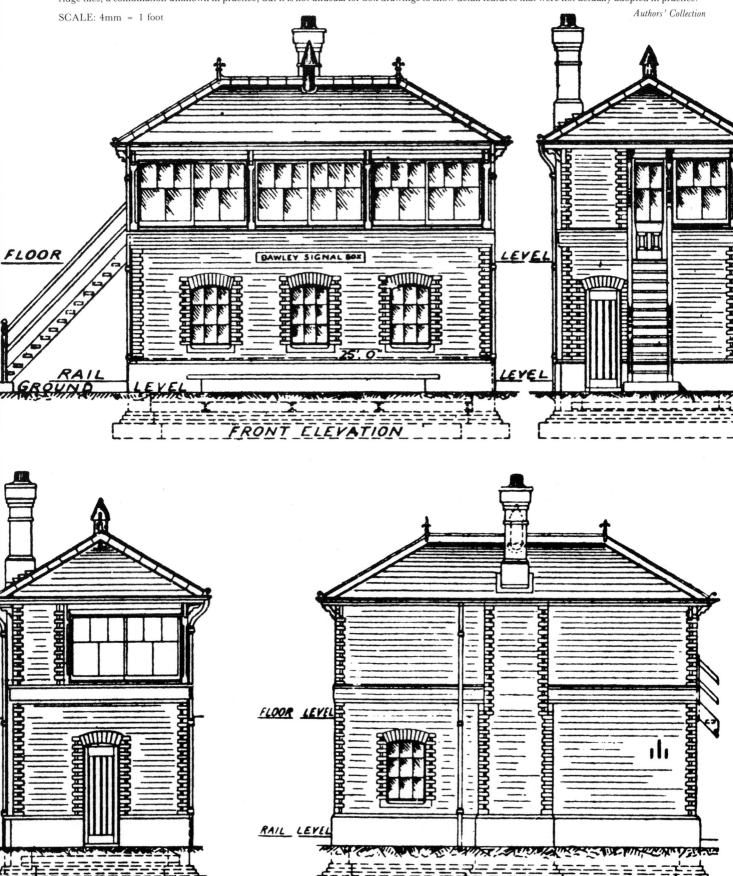

FLOOR

LEVEL

RAIL

GROUND   LEVEL

LEVEL

DAWLEY SIGNAL BOX

25' 0"

FRONT ELEVATION

FLOOR LEVEL

RAIL LEVEL

27' 6"

Plate 246 Henley-in-Arden, a 38ft. x 13ft. x 8ft. **Type 7d** box, opened with the North Warwickshire line on 9th December 1907. Type 7d boxes had an additional locking room window at the door end.

J. P. Morris

Very soon after the introduction of Type 7/27, a gabled version, Type 28, was introduced in order to facilitate the erection of temporary timber boxes. Along with post-grouping GW boxes, this is dealt with in **Chapter 8**.

Two types of standard timber crossing hut/ground frame hut were to be found on the GW. **Type 21** had vertical boarding — 8ft. x 10ft. and 7ft. x 11ft. were the most common sizes. **Type 29**, even smaller, had weatherboarding — 5ft. x 7ft. was the normal size (**Plate 103**).

The pre-grouping GW was unparalleled in the extent to which much of its route mileage remained in the hands of independent (or quasi-independent) companies until a sufficiently late date for interlocked signal boxes to have been built prior to the GW acquiring the lines concerned. The GW inherited a large number of contractors' and other boxes from these constitituents.

The **Bristol & Exeter**, taken over on 1st January 1876, was perhaps the foremost of the GW's pre-grouping constituents. The B&E had been worked on the Absolute Block system since 1866/7 and, by the date of take-over, was also virtually fully interlocked. The B&E's signalling work was (except for the installation of a Poole frame at Langport) carried out by S&F, and in most cases the

boxes were built to S&F designs. There were a few S&F Type 2a boxes — Norton Fitzwarren Junction (1870), Clevedon, and Bleadon & Uphill are known — but the major interlocking programme was carried out from 1874-6, using the S&F Type 4 design (**Plate 113**).

A few boxes were, however, built to the railway company's design, perhaps because it was inconvenient for S&F to undertake the building work at the particular times and locations concerned. Five of these B&E type boxes are known. They had several common features, all being gabled and of brick-to-roof or stone-to-roof construction, but were not identical. Weston-super-Mare (**Plate 49**) was the plainest and probably dated from 1866. Cowley Bridge Junction (1871, gable-to-track), Tiverton Junction (1874), Williton (1875) (**Plate 247**), and Yatton West (by 1877) (*GWS, Plate 110*) were the others. The last three had decorative bargeboards of a type found also on many B&E station buildings.

The **South Devon** Railway, taken over on 1st February 1876, was another S&F customer. The first interlocked box on the SD, at Totnes in 1873, was built to the S&F Type 2a design; but as with the B&E the majority of the network was interlocked during the period 1874-6, with boxes to the S&F Type 4 design. The last SD

Plate 247 The **B&E** type box at Williton. This box was inspected on 22nd February 1875. The porch, nameplate and rocket vents are later GW additions. For a close-up of the bargeboards see **Plate 62**. Closed by BR on 4th January 1971, this box is now in use again in the hands of the West Somerset Railway. It is an interesting reflection on the longevity of signal boxes, by comparison with other features of the railway scene, that a box like this, which began life controlling broad gauge trains with disc-and-crossbar signals, should still be in use today.

J. P. Morris

boxes in use were Dainton Sidings and Marsh Mills, both of which were abolished in 1965.

The **Cornwall** Railway was leased from its opening to the GW, B&E, and SD jointly, and thereby came under sole GW control from 1876. Although it claimed a large amount of interlocking in its 1870s returns to the Board of Trade, there were, in fact, hardly any full-size boxes. Early boxes of a primitive hipped design existed at St. Austell, Bodinnick (near Burngullow), and Westwood (near Doublebois), but their origins and exact dates are unknown. More definite history starts in 1874 when the Committee ordered two S&F Type 2a boxes for the interlocking of Truro Station. One of these boxes still stands at the west end of the station in use as a hut. In 1876 the Cornwall contributed to the interlocking of Plymouth by having an S&F (probably Type 4) box built at Devonport Junction. After this, boxes were built by the GW (**Plate 240**), although little work was done prior to the Cornwall Railway's formal absorption into the GW in 1889.

The **West Cornwall** Railway was under GW/B&E/SD control from 1866, and under sole GW control from 1876. There was virtually no interlocking prior to 1876.

The **Cornwall Minerals** Railway opened from Fowey to Newquay in 1874, and for passengers in 1876. The line was fully interlocked prior to the opening for passengers, but it is not known how many locations had full-size boxes. The only original box known from photographs is Bugle, a plain hipped structure. Part at least of the signalling work was done by Stevens. The GW took over the working of the line from October 1877.

The **Liskeard & Looe** Railway had an early box at Looe, about which nothing is known, and two S&F Type 12b boxes of 1901 at Coombe Junction and Liskeard Station. There was also a stone box of local design at Moorswater, which may have belonged to the associated Liskeard & Caradon Company rather than the L&L. The GW worked both companies' lines from 1909.

The **Bridport** Railway had two signal boxes. That at Bridport Station was of uncertain origins. West Bay, on the 1884 extension, was a stone box designed (as were the station buildings) by William Clarke, the company's engineer: it had a GWCo frame. The company was absorbed by the GW in 1901.

The **Abbotsbury** Railway, opened in November 1885, had three RSCo boxes.

The **Bristol & Portishead Pier & Railway Co.** (line opened 1867) had several interlocked boxes prior to its absorption into the GW in 1884. The two boxes known from photographs, Clifton Bridge and Pill, were hipped and to a local design, with inside boarding and exposed struts.

The **Bristol & North Somerset** Railway, a child of the GW, opened in 1873 and had McK&H Type 1 boxes. The GW absorbed it in 1884.

The **Banbury & Cheltenham Direct** Railway was worked by the GW but arranged its own signalling contracts. The initial Cheltenham to Bourton section, opened in 1881, had GWCo boxes; the GW contributed part of the cost of Bourton box. Of these GWCo boxes, none outlasted the 1930s, although Bourton box still exists in use as a garage. The Chipping Norton to King's Sutton section, opened in 1887 but largely completed in 1884-6, had RSCo boxes. Chipping Norton East survived until the end. The GW absorbed the B&CD in 1897.

The **Worcester & Hereford** Railway had an interlocked box built at Worcester (Shrub Hill) in 1860, although a few days before the junction concerned opened, the W&H was taken over by the West Midland Railway, which itself passed to the GW in 1863.

The **Didcot, Newbury & Southampton** Railway had GWCo boxes on the Didcot to Newbury section, which opened in 1882, and the unique S&F Type 11 boxes on the 1885 Newbury to Winchester section. The latter were very small structures; the instruments were kept in the station offices. Although it was worked by the GW from the start, the DN&S remained independent until the

Grouping. However, the GW carried out the signalling work in later days. The 1909 box at Kingsworthy was a GW Type 27 box. During 1942/3, all the remaining S&F boxes were replaced by GW ARP boxes in connection with war works.

The **Leominster & Bromyard** Railway provided the GWCo with an unhappy experience! In November 1881, a £173 contract was agreed and a signal box built at Steens Bridge, but the railway company could not find the money to pay, and the GWCo retained possession of the box. In February 1884, the GWCo heard that the GW, who were to work the line (then about to open), had 'taken possession' of the box, but in May the Leominster & Bromyard Railway were still only promising to pay 'as soon as possible'. Later boxes were GW-built.

The **Golden Valley** Railway was another less than ideal customer. The GWCo provided both the signalling and the timber station buildings for the Pontrilas to Dorstone section, opened in 1881, but had to stop work at one time as the railway company ran out of money. Eventually the GWCo had to be satisfied with debentures in settlement. When the line was extended to Hay-on-Wye in 1889, the signalling work was carried out by S&F. During 1897/8, the company ran out of money again and had to close the line; they then sold out to the GW, who reopened the line in 1901. There were no signal boxes at any time.

The **Newent** Railway (very much a GW protégé) opened the Over Junction to Dymock line in 1885. It was signalled by McK&H. No photographs of the boxes are known, but one guesses that they were to the McK&H Type 3 design.

The **Monmouthshire Railway & Canal Co.** is likely to have had a number of interlocked boxes prior to the GW taking control in 1875. Nothing is known about them, although S&F and McK&H are known to have supplied to this company.

The **Pembroke & Tenby** Railway had no interlocking at all until 1893/4, when McK&H Type 3 boxes were built at every station. It was absorbed by the GW in 1896.

The **Whitland & Cardigan** Railway had McK&H Type 3 boxes. Those on the Crymmych Arms to Cardigan section were built for its opening in 1886; the others were somewhat earlier. The GW absorbed the company in 1890.

The **Manchester & Milford** Railway had no boxes until 1893, when a McK&H Type 3 box was built at Pencader Junction. The rest of the line was interlocked in 1895, with S&F Type 12b boxes (**Plate 123**). The GW leased the M&M from 1906 and purchased it in 1911.

The **Maenclochog** Railway was provided with McK&H Type 3 boxes for its opening in 1876. After a period of disuse it reopened in extended form in 1895 as the **North Pembrokeshire & Fishguard** Railway, with Dutton Type 3 boxes on the new section. It passed to the GW in 1898.

The **Rhondda & Swansea Bay** Railway was worked and signalled by the GW from 1906, although it remained independent until the Grouping. Between 1885 (when the first section of the line was opened) and 1906 some 40 boxes were built, all to the McK&H Type 3/TV design, but with the additional variant of segmental-arched locking room windows in the brick boxes.

The **South Wales Mineral** Railway had no boxes when the GW assumed responsibility for its signalling in 1908; three boxes were subsequently built by the GW.

The **Port Talbot** Railway, too, was independent until the Grouping, but was worked and signalled by the GW from 1908. Of its dozen pre-1908 boxes, most, unusually for a South Wales company, were RSCo boxes, but there were also a couple of McK&H boxes.

The **Weymouth & Portland** Railway was a GW/LSW Joint line, but most boxes were built by the GW. However, the **Easton & Church Hope**, its extension of 1900, had an EOD type box at Easton.

Cambrian

In the 1870s and 1880s, the Cambrian's signalling work seems to have been carried out by McK&H. However, there were very few interlocked signal boxes prior to the 1889 Act, although many stations were interlocked after a fashion with ground frames. Known pre-1889 boxes existed at Dovey Junction (type unknown), Penpontbren Junction (McK&H Type 1, built 1872 but, like the ill-fated line it served, probably never used), Talerddig (McK&H Type 1, 1874, still in use, although with a rebuilt roof), Oswestry (type unknown), and Welshpool (two early boxes of an unknown type which were replaced by two LNW Type 4 boxes in 1887).

Accordingly, the Cambrian had to carry out a vast amount of work in 1890-95. At the Grouping, 90 per cent of the boxes existing on the Cambrian dated from these years. Almost all this work was carried out by Dutton, with boxes built to all four Dutton designs (**Plates 141, 80, 142 & 143**). However, there was a McK&H Type 3 box of 1893 at Buttington North. The Cambrian continued to use Dutton/Pease until Pease ceased trading in 1901.

After 1901, most of the Cambrian's work went to Tyer, who supplied many ground frames, and also built five boxes to (it seems) their own design (**Plate 134**). There was also some McK&H work, including the 1907 box at Pwllheli West which was built to the Dutton Type 2 design. Although the boxes varied in design, locking frames and other signalling equipment after 1901 were all made to Dutton patterns, irrespective of whether they were Tyer or McK&H-supplied.

The **Tanat Valley Light** Railway was built and worked by the Cambrian on behalf of the owning company. The story of its signalling sheds an interesting light on the problems that could arise when lines were promoted by quasi-independent companies. The signalling contract for the TVLR was let by the Cambrian to Tyer in August 1903 for £2,326 5s. 6d. (the other tenderers were S&F, McK&H, and Sykes). Signal boxes were built at Porthywaen, (Llany)Blodwell Junction, and Nantmawr Junction, and open frames at other stations. The line opened in January 1904 but the Cambrian refused to pay Tyer, saying that they must look to the Tanat Valley company for payment. Tyer sued the Cambrian, and won their case in the High Court in February 1906 and in the Court of Appeal in July. However, this episode did not prevent Tyer from subsequently taking other Cambrian contracts. The TVLR became Cambrian property in 1921.

The **Vale of Rheidol** Railway was equipped with Pease ground frames for its opening in 1902. An additional loop at Aberffrwd in 1905 was worked from a Tyer ground frame.

The **Welshpool & Llanfair** Railway had 15 small Tyer ground frames when it opened in 1902, probably ordered by the Cambrian. In 1907 a small signal box was built by Tyer at Castle Caereinion to break the line into two sections. This was used in the summer only (with the points being reconnected to ground frames in the winter) but the signalman was removed as early as 1911. However, the structure is still standing.

Alexandra (N&SW) Docks & Railway Co.

The known boxes on this railway were to the McK&H Type 3 design. Some were built for the **Pontypridd, Caerphilly & Newport** Railway of 1884-6, which was not absorbed until 1897.

Brecon & Merthyr

The B&M was somewhat slow with interlocking until a burst of activity from 1883-5, after which it again rested on its laurels until forced to complete the task during 1892/3. McK&H were the major contractors, but the B&M tended to put work out to competitive tender (unlike most of the other South Wales companies, which preferred to have a single supplier), and some GWCo and S&F work is also known. Early McK&H Type 1 boxes are known at Dowlais Top, Dowlais No. 1, and Dowlais No. 2, but most boxes were to the McK&H Type 3 design. The main S&F contract was for the Bassaleg to Machen doubling in 1883/4, where the boxes were built to the S&F Type 12b design. One of these, Rhiwderin, is now preserved at the Caerphilly Railway Centre and is the only extant B&M box.

Rhymney

All the Rhymney's signalling work was done by McK&H, and all the known boxes were to the McK&H Type 3 design, the majority of them built of stone. The only survivor is Ystrad Mynach South, illustrated in **Plate 89**.

Taff Vale

The TV completed its interlocking programme as early as 1881, but little is known about the early boxes, as most were replaced in pre-grouping days. The only known boxes from the early 1870s, Porth and Aberaman, were very plain gabled boxes (brick and timber respectively) of local design.

McK&H carried out the Taff Vale Railway's signalling work in the 1870s and 1880s, and from circa 1876 boxes were built to a special version of the McK&H Type 3 design. This **McK&H Type 3/TV** type had special decorative bargeboards, decoration on the fascia boards, cockscomb ridge tiles, and terracotta finials. (R&SB and Swansea Harbour Trust boxes were also built to this design).

Around 1895, a new box design was introduced. This **TV Type** was still based on the McK&H Type 3 outline, but the operating floor windows had much larger panes with only a single, horizontal, glazing bar. The decoration on the fascia boards was retained, but the cockscomb ridge tiles and terracotta finials were replaced by plain ridge tiles and timber finials. This design was used until the Grouping. McK&H continued to carry out the greater part of the Taff Vale's work in later years, but a little went to other contractors, notably Dutton and the RSCo.

Plate 248 PC&N Junction (south of Pontypridd) illustrates the **McK&H Type 3/TV** design. This box was probably built in 1884 when the Pontypridd, Caerphilly & Newport line was opened. Only two boxes of this type now exist on the Taff Vale, the derelict Roath Branch Junction (brick), and Abercwmboi (timber).

M. A. King

Plate 249 A timber **TV** Type box at Gyfeillon Upper. The timber boxes of this type retained the small panes in the locking room windows; the brick boxes had segmental-arched locking room windows. The fascia board decoration is just visible here. This box was abolished in 1984; the surviving TV Type boxes (Llandaff Loop Jn., Walnut Tree Jn., Pontypridd Jn., and Radyr Quarry Jn.) are all of brick construction. *J. P. Morris*

Plate 250 The **Barry Type 1** box at Barry Station was built around 1897. The rear of the box is shown here; it is glazed all round (except for the chimneys) due to the presence of sidings to the rear. Most unusually, this box has a hearth in the locking room, with its own chimney, but both chimney stacks have been removed. The veranda is not a standard feature of the type. Note the two EOD maker's plates, above the bricked-up locking room windows.

J. P. Morris

Cardiff

All known boxes were to the McK&H Type 3 design. Many were built in 1909 when the main line was opened, but there were earlier and later boxes in the docks.

Barry

The Barry network was opened between 1888 and 1901. Signalling work was done by S&F until 1895, then by EOD from 1895 until 1903, then by S&F again but with EOD pattern frames. Boxes were built by the signalling contractors to Barry designs.

The **Barry Type 1** design (**Plate 250**), used for most boxes, owed so much to the GE Type 5 design that one must postulate some connection. Shared features were the division of the uppermost panes into four, the 'rusticated' woodwork in the gable ends, and the bargeboard design (similar rather than identical).

A different design, **Barry Type 2**, was used for the 1897 Vale of Glamorgan line only (**Plate 251**).

Plate 251   Barry Type 2 (Vale of Glamorgan) design box at Aberthaw East. On this type, the uppermost window panes are divided into two only, and on the ends of the box they are not divided at all.   The bargeboards are also to a different design.   The two boxes illustrated here are the only surviving Barry boxes.
J. P. Morris

Neath & Brecon

The N&B had fifteen boxes built altogether. The earliest was the 1873 McK&H Type 1 box at Colbren Junction, and for most of its life the N&B remained a McK&H customer, with boxes to the McK&H Type 3 design. But about half the boxes were in fact built during 1894/5, when the N&B completed interlocking under the pressure of the 1889 Act; and this work went to Dutton with boxes to the Dutton Type 2 design.

Swansea Harbour Trust

SHT boxes were to the McK&H Type 3/TV design. Three of them were in fact built in 1895 for the R&SB and subsequently sold to the SHT, together with the section of line concerned. The other SHT box, King's Dock Junction, was built in 1908, and is still in use.

Llanelly & Mynydd Mawr

The L&MM had only one box, to control the swing bridge at North Dock; it was not a block post. Apparently an EOD box, it still stands in altered condition in private use. The main section of the L&MM line was not signalled until 1959-62, when three BR (WR) Type 37 boxes were built; all three were closed during the period 1966-8.

Burry Port & Gwendraeth Valley

The BPGV had no boxes until the start of passenger services in 1909. Six boxes were built from 1909-14, four with Tyer frames and two with RSCo frames. All were huts of crude design.

Gwendraeth Valley

This company had no boxes.

Corris

The three interlocked boxes on the Corris Railway (Machynlleth, Maespoeth Jn., and Corris) were almost certainly built in 1883 when passenger services began. McK&H were the contractors. The boxes were huts of local design.

Cleobury Mortimer & Ditton Priors Light

This company had no boxes.

Midland & South Western Junction

Although it passed to the GW at the Grouping, the MSWJ in pre-grouping days was closely linked with the LSW. Indeed, the later MSWJ boxes were built to the LSW design — a unique occurrence.

The **Swindon, Marlborough & Andover** Railway, opened in 1881-2, was signalled by the GWCo. Contracts to a total value of £5,248 were let between January 1881 and July 1883. The company had some difficulty in finding the money to pay for this work in 1882. The boxes were built to the GWCo design and all were originally of timber construction. The **Swindon & Cheltenham Extension** Railway, opened from Swindon to Cirencester in 1883, was also signalled by the GWCo, at a cost of £1,915. Again there were timber GWCo boxes.

The two companies amalgamated to form the MSWJ in 1884. In 1891 the line was extended to Andoversford Junction, and this section had four Dutton Type 1 boxes.

Finally, ten new boxes were built from 1900-5, for the new Tidworth branch and for a series of improvements elsewhere. Two of these, Cerney (1900) and Chedworth (1902), were brick boxes built to a kind of Dutton-EOD-esque design, with Dutton type bargeboards, EOD type windows, and additional lower windows. Their construction was generally of an unsophisticated appearance and it may be that they were built by the MSWJ itself. Indeed, the MSWJ Minute Books record that all work 'other than signalling' at Cerney was to be done by 'the company's own workmen'.

The other eight of these boxes (Ludgershall, Perham, and Tidworth in 1901; Wolfhall MSW Jn. in 1902; Swindon A, Swindon B, and Rushey Platt in 1905: Wolfhall MSW Jn. replacement box in 1905), were built to the LSW Type 4 design, some of brick and some of timber construction.

Signalling contracts in later years went to Pease until 1901, then EOD until 1903, then Sykes during 1904/5, the changes being necessitated by the demise of the Pease and EOD firms.

London & South Western

There were many boxes on the LSW by the late 1860s, but the impression given by the LSW Minute Books is that they were mostly small timber huts. Although a good way behind its neighbour the LBSC, the LSW had installed the block system on most of its network by 1876, and made steady progress with interlocking, effectively completed in the mid-1880s.

Most LSW signalling work was carried out by Stevens, but there was also a fair amount of S&F work. A number of Dutton and McK&H contracts are known in the 1890s, and the RSCo carried out a great deal of work from the 1880s, and probably most in later years. By the late 1880s, the LSW was specifying that all frames were to be made to the Stevens pattern, irrespective of the supplier.

Contractors' box designs were used in a few cases in the earliest years. There were S&F Type 2a boxes on the Kingston to Wimbledon line of 1868; Malden Crossing survived until 1979. The 1881 box at Gunnersbury East was made up from a second-hand S&F Type 2a top on a new base. A Stevens design box was built at Aldershot North Junction as late as 1879, but this box may have been ordered by the SE for whose benefit the junction was installed.

A standard LSW box design was in use by 1871 (**see below**), but about 25 per cent of LSW boxes in the 1870s, and some subsequently, were built to non-standard designs. In particular, a number of boxes, mostly of 1868-74, were built of brick-to-roof construction (**Plate 252**), some with hipped and some with gabled roofs. However, there were also many timber, BTF, and STF boxes built to 'one-off' designs, mostly with hipped roofs but too varied to describe in detail here.

The LSW standard box designs described below all had hipped roofs, with slates and lead flashings (ridge tiles and hip-hooks on some Type 4 boxes). BTF (or, west of Salisbury, STF) construction was usual for Types 1-3, and brick construction for Type 4. Locking room windows generally were segmental-arched, although some Type 1 boxes do not appear to have had any locking room windows at all. There were, of course, necessarily a few timber boxes as well.

The LSW **Type 1** design (circa 1871-circa 1880) was very common, dating from the period when most of the interlocking programme was carried out. The timber superstructure of these boxes measured 4ft. 0in. up to the bottom of the window cill, and 3ft. 0in. thence to the eaves. The window sashes were 2 panes up, and 3 or 4 panes across. Most boxes were 11ft. 0in. wide. Brick chimneys were normal. Originally there was inside boarding only, with exposed struts (**Plate 253**), but most boxes had exterior weatherboarding (always six boards) added before the Grouping (**Plate 254**). Valancing was provided originally, but has long since disappeared in most cases. One or two boxes had finials.

Type 2 (1878-84) brought much deeper (4ft. 3in.) operating floor windows, 3 panes up and each sash 2 or 3 panes across. In addition there were 1ft. 0½in. deep upper lights, but these were largely obscured by the valancing. The valancing was of a different design to that of Type 1 boxes, omitting the holes in the centre of each board. Many Type 2 and Type 3 boxes had walkways, with outer railings, as the sashes were now too large to clean from inside and the longer boxes had fixed glazing on the front except at the corners. Vertical boarding was used on the superstructure, although a few boxes seem to have originally had interior boarding only. Stovepipes were normal on this and later LSW designs.

Continued at page 173

Plate 252 The early LSW brick-to-roof box at Salisbury Tunnel Junction. The date of building is unknown, but was probably circa 1870 when the block system was put in. The photograph was taken in 1980 and the box was abolished on 17th August 1981. Other brick-to-roof boxes were Winchester City (1869, gabled); Broadstone (hipped); Wimborne (1880?, hipped); Buriton Siding (gabled); and New Kew Junction (1873?, hipped). For photographs see *Southern Signals, Plates 115, 117 and 119*; and *Southern Stations, page 130*. For a particularly splendid BTF box of the same period see the photograph of Milford Goods (originally Milford Junction) in *Southern Signals, Plate 110*; this box was authorised on 8th October 1868.

R. D. Foster

Plate 253 This view of Dean Station in LSW days shows the **LSW Type 1** design in its original form. Dean box was probably built circa 1875 for the start of block working. Note the relieving arches in the brickwork, and the absence of a locking room window.

Lens of Sutton

Plate 254 In contrast, this 1970s view shows the normal state of **Type 1** boxes in later years, with weatherboarding added and valancing removed. The ridge vent is of a type common on LSW boxes. Dean closed on 9th September 1980. Of the once-numerous Type 1 boxes, only Pinhoe, Crediton West, Instow and Alresford can now be seen; the last retains its valancing.

J. P. Morris

Plate 255 (left) The **LSW Type 2** box at Bollo Lane Junction. The box was probably built in 1878 when the junction was opened. It measures 15ft. 4½ in. x 11ft. 7½ in. over the base and 14ft. 11½ in. x 11ft. 2½ in. over the superstructure. It had a 19-lever Stevens frame but this has now been replaced by a panel. The crude finials are not a standard feature. The locking room window has been bricked up; the nameplate is a BR (SR) enamel replacement. Raynes Park (1884) is the only other surviving Type 2 box.

R. D. Foster

Oxshott Station.

Plate 256 (right) Oxshott, an **LSW Type 3a** box on the 1885 Guildford New Line, where all the stations had boxes of this type. Type 3a boxes were also to be found in large numbers on the new lines of 1885-8 in the Bournemouth area. Oxshott closed on 9th September 1974 under the Feltham resignalling. There was no walkway due to the lowness of the box. Surviving Type 3a boxes are Bournemouth West Junction, Effingham Junction (disused), and Petersfield Junction.

Lens of Sutton

Plate 257 (left) The **Type 3b** box at Umberleigh, inspected in December 1890, and of STF construction. The new Wimbledon Park (1889) and Lydford to Devonport (1890) lines had boxes of this type. Extant examples are East Putney, Wimbledon Park, Hamworthy Junction, and Bere Alston (disused). Type 3c boxes are known only on the North Cornwall line, and there are none left.

D. Collins

Plate 258 Haslemere is the best-preserved of the eleven remaining **Type 4** boxes. It was built in 1895. The locking room windows are protected by bars to prevent damage, as on many platform boxes. Note also the dowels in front of the sliding sashes of the operating floor windows.

P. Kay

Type 3 was similar in outline to Type 2, but the main windows were now 4 panes deep, and the sashes usually 3 panes across. Valancing was abandoned (only one Type 3 box, Petersfield Junction, is known to have had it). **Type 3a** (1884-8) had vertical boarding, as Type 2. **Type 3b** (1889-92) had horizontal weatherboarding, and instead of 'upper lights' had boarding between the head of the main widows and the eaves. **Type 3c** (1892-5) also had weatherboarding, but, curiously, reverted to glazed upper lights.

During 1894/5, there was a complete rethink of box design. The new **Type 4** design, used from then until circa 1928, owed nothing to its predecessors. Most Type 4 boxes were of brick, with a brick pillar interrupting the operating floor glazing at the centre front — an unusual development at a time when most companies were maximising the area of glazing. The sashes were distinguished by curved framing at the head. They were always two panes deep, and two (occasionally three) panes across. Every other sash was sliding and, coupled with the smaller area of glazing, this rendered a walkway unnecessary. All in all this was an unfussily stylish and distinctive design. It was used also on the S&DJ (in some cases in gabled form) and the MSWJ. Some of the later Type 4 boxes omitted the brick pillar. A further variation was that a few boxes had the curve of the sash framing extended over two panes instead of one.

A characteristic of the multi-track section between Waterloo and Clapham Junction was the several overhead boxes on gantries spanning the full width of the layout. Most famous were the Waterloo 'A' boxes built successively in 1867, 1874 (extended 1878), and 1892 (extended 1911, abolished 1936). The two overhead boxes still in use, West London Junction (1911) and Clapham Junction 'A' (1905), consist of little more than a series of sheds on the gantry.

Other interesting LSW survivors are the original 1898 boxes at Waterloo (W&C) and Bank — the former now the only mechanical box on a British 'tube' line.

LSW ground frame huts were built to varied designs, but most common were weatherboarded timber huts with lean-to or gabled roofs.

There are now less than 30 LSW boxes in use.

Somerset & Dorset Joint

The Somerset & Dorset Railway was taken over by the Midland and LSW jointly in November 1875. The LSW, which had been closely associated with the S&D previously, assumed responsibility on the take-over for engineering and signalling; but S&DJ boxes were not built to wholly standard LSW designs until 1895.

The new owners inherited a fairly ramshackle selection of signalling, especially on the older section of line from Highbridge to Wimborne, where there was little interlocking. The 1874 Bath Extension had necessarily been fully interlocked in order to obtain Board of Trade approval for opening, but the 'boxes' were only huts. They had S&F frames, but no photographs have yet been found of the structures.

A long list of improvements was authorised on 8th November 1876. This included the building of nine interlocked boxes at stations on the older section, the 'enlargement' of many of the Extension boxes, and, curiously, the removal of the interlocking at Midford and Masbury, of which the Board of Trade would hardly have approved! With the LSW in charge, S&DJ signalling equipment now came from Stevens.

The first S&DJ boxes were built to a design very much influenced by contemporary LSW practice. This S&DJ **Type 1** design (1876-9) had the same hipped roof with lead flashings, and valancing of the same pattern, as LSW Type 1 boxes, but the operating floor windows were 3 panes deep. The original style of boarding is uncertain. Some examples had small ball-and-spike finials. Bailey Gate, Shillingstone, Sturminster Newton, Wincanton, Cole, Pylle, and Highbridge 'B' survived into BR days.

Between 1885 and 1894, a large programme of doubling and other improvements was carried out, necessitating many new boxes. These were built to the **Type 2** design (1878-95), the most characteristic of the S&DJ box designs. This design bore no relation to LSW practice, but was rather similar to the standard Stevens design. However, the decorative bargeboards and the 'valancing' at the foot of the gable end boarding were unique to the S&DJ. BTF or STF construction was normal, with vertical boarding on the superstructure.

Plate 259 (right) The idyllic scene at Pylle, on 2nd June 1963. This **S&DJ Type 1** box was apparently built in 1877. The Minutes refer to the submission of a plan for 'alterations needed at Pylle . . . including interlocking apparatus' on 9th March 1877. Further alterations were carried out here in 1891 when the passing loop was installed. Pylle box was reduced to ground frame status from 8th December 1929, and closed completely on 21st June 1964.

C. L. Caddy

Plate 260 (below) The STF **S&DJ Type 2** box at Binegar was built in 1885 when the Binegar to Chilcompton section was doubled. It was fitted with the S&F frame from the 1874 box, the transfer of which was effected on Sunday, 27th July 1885. The 1874 boxes were all replaced by Type 2 boxes during the 1885-94 doublings, but no other case is known of the old frame being reused in this way. Porches like this were standard on Type 2 boxes. The bricking-up of the superstructure of this box was carried out in about 1960, and this photograph was taken in May 1965. Binegar was one of the boxes that lasted until the end of the S&DJ on 6th March 1966.

C. L. Caddy

SCALE OF FEET

WELLOW SIGNAL BOX

Drawn by P.V. Starling from
Measurements & Photographs
Taken in April 1983

Plate 261 A drawing of the BTF **Type 2** box at Wellow. Opened in 1892 and closed in 1966, this is the only S&DJ box now standing.

SCALE: 4mm = 1 foot

175

P. V. Starling

Plate 262 The brick **LSW Type 4 gabled** box at Moorewood. Note the rear frame and stovepipe at the front. Opened in 1914, this was the last but one box to be built on the S&DJ. The photograph was taken on 19th May 1965, and the box closed on 5th July.

C. L. Caddy

From 1895, S&DJ boxes were built to the new LSW Type 4 design, at first with the standard hipped roof (Highbridge 'A', Shapwick, Glastonbury and Stalbridge), but from 1905 with a gabled roof for cheapness (Stourpaine, Radstock West, Corfe Mullen, Blandford Forum, Morewood and Evercreech New). Evercreech New in 1920 was the last new box ever built on the S&DJ network.

Lynton & Barnstaple

The L&B's signalling work was let to EOD in February 1897 for £2,024, and the line opened in 1898. The line was fully interlocked, but only the largest box, Barnstaple, was to the EOD design, and even that was a very small structure. The 'signal boxes' at the other main stations, Chelfham, Bratton Fleming, Blackmoor, Woody Bay, and Lynton, were small gabled huts of local design. That at Lynton was replaced by an LSW-style lean-to hut in 1925, after the L&B had sold out to the Southern Railway.

London, Brighton & South Coast

Much reference was made in **Chapter 1** to the early signalling history of the LBSC. It was on the LBSC that the signal box as we know it was developed by John Saxby from 1857-63. The LBSC was way ahead of other companies with interlocking in the early 1860s, and achieved the 100 per cent figure in 1880.

When Saxby and Farmer left the LBSC's service during 1862/3, their new company was given a monopoly of the LBSC's signalling work. The only known exception prior to 1898 was the granting of a contract to Stevens for the resignalling of Three Bridges Junction in June 1866. In April 1869 the LBSC Minutes record that legal advice had been received that 'the use of S&F locking apparatus was binding on the company'. For many years all boxes were built to S&F designs; Type 1a until 1863 (**Plates 15, 16 & 17**), Type 1b 1863-71, plus one or two until 1876, (**Plates 18, 19, 109**), Type 2a 1868-74 (**Plate 110**), Type 2b 1874-5 (**Plate 111**), Type 5 from 1876 (**Plates 44 & 115**), and the scattering of Type 3 boxes (**Plate 112**) at various dates between 1872 and 1878. However, from 1880, an increasing proportion of boxes began to be built to LBSC designs instead.

The first LBSC design (**LBSC Type 1**) was evolved in special circumstances. The lavishly-built new lines of 1880-3 (Hailsham to Eridge, Chichester to Midhurst, East Grinstead to Barcombe/ Haywards Heath) were provided with elaborate half-timbered station buildings, and the signal boxes were designed by the same architect (Myers) to form a harmonious ensemble (**Plate 95**). There were 27 of these Type 1 boxes in all, as several stations had two boxes. The boxes would have been built by the same building contractors as the station buildings; the signalling equipment was provided by S&F as normal. Although the boxes were much less elaborate than the station buildings — the small 'crosses' in the panels above the windows were in fact the only purely decorative feature — their design was charming enough. Most were of BTF construction, and a few were of timber. The operating floor windows were 3 panes deep, except on some of the lowest boxes where they were 2 panes deep. All these boxes have now been demolished except for Horsted Keynes South on the Bluebell Railway. The Type 1 design was not used outside of the new lines mentioned.

Plate 263 The **LBSC Type 2a** box at Bedhampton Crossing.

R. Newman

Plate 264 Opened in 1896, Oxted was one of the last **LBSC Type 2c** boxes built. It has an S&F-type vent rather than the large iron type. The surviving Type 2 boxes, other than the two illustrated here, are Littlehampton (2a, brick); Plumpton (2b, brick); Hampden Park (2b, brick); Seaford (2c, timber); and Uckfield Shunting (2c, a small BTF box).

R. D. Foster

The **Type 2** design for system-wide use also first appeared around 1880. These boxes had frames of a new design developed from the S&F 'Rocker'. It is thought, but is not certain, that these frames were still made by S&F; it is not known who built the box structures. Type 2 boxes were hipped, with, in most cases, a splendidly-large iron roof vent. Brick and BTF boxes had segmental-arched locking room windows; timber boxes had horizontal lapped boarding and square 2-panes-by-2 locking room windows. Operating floor windows were 2 panes deep, the sashes 2 (sometimes 3) panes across. There were three versions of the Type 2 design. **Type 2a** (circa 1880-7) had valancing of a type found also on contemporary LBSC station buildings, and eaves brackets, largely obscured by the valancing. **Type 2b** (1888-93) omitted the valancing. **Type 2c** (1894-6) omitted the eaves brackets as well, and had a less overhanging roof to correspond. During the Type 2 period about half the LBSC's boxes continued to be built to the S&F Type 5 design, with standard S&F 'Rocker' (or, from 1888, 'Duplex') frames.

At the end of 1895, W. C. Acfield, previously a draughtsman with S&F and a subscriber when the Limited Company was formed in 1893, was appointed Assistant Signal Superintendent of the LBSC. Whether by result or coincidence, 1896 saw the end of the LBSC Type 2 box design and its corresponding frame design. Instead, the eight known new boxes of the 1896-8 period were all to the S&F Type 5 design with 'Duplex' frames, but this was the last burst of purely S&F boxes and frames on the LBSC.

A new LBSC box design (**Type 3**) was introduced in 1898. This had a gabled roof with small eaves brackets, large finials and, with a few exceptions, plain bargeboards. Type 3 boxes came in BTF or timber form, with lapped boarding as previously. **Type 3a** (1898-9) had 3-panes-deep operating floor windows, in sashes 3 panes across: **Type 3b** (1899-1915 or later) had 2-panes-deep windows, in sashes 2 panes across.

At the same time as the Type 3 box design was introduced, a new frame design, a version of the Stevens tappet frame, was also adopted. From 1898 to 1901 the LBSC's signalling work was let variously to S&F, the RSCo, McK&H, Dutton, and EOD (but not to Stevens) all of them making the frames to the same pattern. However, from 1st January 1901, a new five-year monopoly agreement with S&F came into force. This lasted in the event only to the end of 1904, when S&F asked to be released from it as they were sustaining a loss on the prices charged. Under these 1898-1904 contracts the box structures were built by the signalling contractor; the prices from the 1901 S&F contract are quoted in **Table 8**.

Plate 265 Four **LBSC Type 3a** boxes were built by the RSCo for the new station at Stoats Nest in 1899. This box was originally 'Stoats Nest Shunting' but, like the others, suffered three changes of name along with the station, ending up as 'Coulsdon North Shunting' from 1923 until closure in October 1983. The original boarding in the gable-end was replaced with the vertical boarding shown here. One of the walkway brackets on this box bore the lettering 'LB&SCR Dutton & Co. Ltd. Worcester'; it was probably a refugee from the contemporary Dutton-built box at Sutton West. The other brackets had RSCo markings, as one would expect.

P. Kay

Plate 266 An official drawing of the BTF version of the **LBSC Type 3b** design.

SCALE: 4mm = 1 foot

Authors' Collection

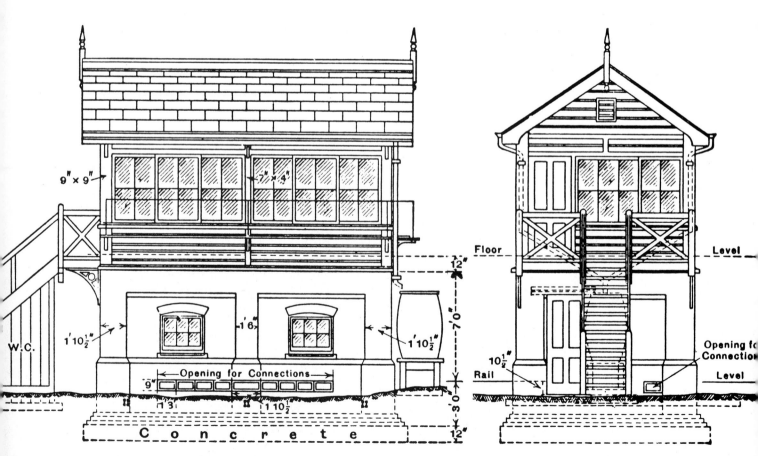

FRONT ELEVATION.

END ELEVATION.

178

Plate 267 The timber **LBSC Type 3b** box at Hassocks was opened on 25th May 1913, replacing an S&F Type 2b box of 1875. See **Plates 59 & 60** for details of this design.

P. Kay

From 1905, until the late 1920s, a further new frame design was used. These frames do not have contractors' markings, and according to one source they were assembled at the LBSC's Cold Blow (New Cross) signal shops. However, the frame for Birchden Jn. in 1914 was certainly made by the RSCo.

Just before the Grouping, the LBSC evolved a new box design (**Type 4**). Only two examples are known — Bromley Junction and Itchingfield Junction, both built in 1920. These boxes were of brick construction and had hipped roofs with small eaves brackets. The operating floor windows were 2 panes deep, and the locking room windows segmental-arched. For the first time on the LBSC internal stairs were provided. A photograph of Itchingfield Junction can be seen in *Branch Lines to Horsham* (Middleton Press).

Isle of Wight

The IoW's stations were fully interlocked at various dates between 1875 and 1893. Ryde St. John's Road South (1875), and Brading Quay, St. Helens and Bembridge (1882) were Stevens boxes. Ventnor (1877) and Brading (1882) were to the IoW design shown at **Plate 268**. Sandown (1893) and Shanklin (1892) were S&F Type 12b boxes.

Plate 268 The **IoW** Type box at Brading. It is likely (although one cannot be certain) that these boxes at Ventnor and Brading were designed by the railway company and erected by builders; both had Stevens frames. Brading box was inspected on 25th August 1882; its construction had been necessitated by track alterations in connection with the new Bembridge branch. Note the curious arrangement of splay bricks below the windows.

M. Christensen

Isle of Wight Central

The IoWC was an 1887 amalgamation of the **Ryde, Newport & Cowes** and the **Isle of Wight (Newport Junction)** Railways. These lines were partly interlocked prior to the amalgamation, but no details are known. The IoWC itself was a RSCo customer, and RSCo boxes are known from photographs at Newport North, Mill Hill, Cowes, and Shide. In 1913 the IoWC absorbed the **Newport, Godshill & St. Lawrence** Railway, which had been signalled by the RSCo, with RSCo boxes at Merstone and Whitwell (1897), and Ventnor West (1900).

Freshwater, Yarmouth & Newport

When it opened in 1889, the FY&N had five boxes, one at each station. These were small lean-to huts with vertical boarding; the signalling contractor is not known. In 1913, an additional box was built at the new Newport FY&N station; this was a RSCo box. The structure of this Newport FY&N box is now preserved at Wootton on the Isle of Wight Steam Railway, having been, in the interim period, a second box at Freshwater (1927-53) and then a bus shelter!

The remaining section of railway on the Isle of Wight, the LSW/LBSC Joint Ryde Pier line, had LSW Type 2 boxes, built for its opening in 1880.

The Southern Railway carried out a great deal of work on the Island in the 1920s, abolishing some boxes altogether to cut costs, but improving facilities elsewhere. Most notably there were new loops controlled from new combined Booking Office/Signal Boxes at Haven Street and Wroxall, an additional box at Smallbrook Junction, and a new box at Ryde St. John's Road, to replace the two original boxes. Only five boxes survived the closures of the 1950s and 1960s, and only three (Ryde St. John's Road, Brading and Sandown) are in use today.

South Eastern & Chatham

The **South Eastern** was notable for introducing 'Absolute Block' working by telegraph on all its lines in the 1840s. At most stations a hut for the signalman and instruments was erected at the end of the station platforms; these were gabled timber structures of a standardised design (**Plate 4**). By the 1850s there were also a few elevated signal boxes at junctions, for example at Surrey Canal Junction and Greenwich Junction (= North Kent East Junction) between London Bridge and New Cross, and at Strood (**Plate 12**). The most important locations were interlocked in the 1860s; notably, of course, the termini at London Bridge (**Plate 20**), Cannon Street and Charing Cross. However, the SE proceeded very slowly with interlocking in the 1870s and 1880s, so much so that, of the major companies, only the GNoS and the Cambrian showed a worse return in 1889 than the SE's 70 per cent. Accordingly, the SE had to carry out a crash programme of interlocking between 1892 and 1895.

At first, the SE bought its signalling equipment from S&F and Stevens, and boxes were built to the contractors' designs. But in 1867 the South Eastern's Engineer Francis Brady patented a locking frame of his own design, and from that date the company began to meet an increasing proportion of its signalling needs from in-house manufacture (the SE signal shops were at Angerstein). From 1884, it was able to meet all its needs itself. Where the company did its own work, it built the boxes to the same design that it had used for the less distinguished of its station buildings ever since its beginnings in 1842. The SE was the only company to use the same design for signal boxes and station buildings on such a widespread basis but, as noted in **Chapter 4**, this was not done for architectural harmony since there were very few stations where both the box and the station buildings were to this design (East Farleigh was one). However, the design was certainly in tune with the Kent vernacular tradition. This **SE** box design appeared in timber and BTF form, with weatherboarding, 2-panes-by-2 vertical sash windows, and hipped roofs with lead flashings.

Plate 269 The **SE** Type box at Battle. Note the non-symmetrical arrangement of the windows, and the small doors at centre front for access to the locking. **Plate 61** shows in detail the vertical sash windows of these boxes. Nine SE Type boxes are still in use.

P. Kay

Because of the increasing in-house manufacture, the number of contractors' boxes on the SE was much reduced in the 1870s and early 1880s. A dozen Stevens boxes are known, and there was an S&F Type 5 box built at Ash in 1879. One Stevens box, Grain Crossing of 1882, is still in use. From 1884 there was no contractors' work at all for several years. However, the 1892-5 crash interlocking programme involved far more work than the SE was capable of carrying out from its own manufacture, so there was a reversion to the use of contractors from 1892. Many S&F Type 12a (**Plate 122**), McK&H Type 3, and RSCo boxes were accordingly built from 1892-5, plus a couple of Dutton boxes (to a special design, as noted in **Chapter 5**). No other railway company was acquiring such a variety of contractors' boxes at this late date. In the late 1890s, the volume of work was still such as to require outside assistance, but now the SE turned to EOD instead. EOD boxes appeared most notably on the Tattenham Corner (1897-1901) and Bexhill West (1902) branches, with a dozen or so elsewhere (**Plate 144**). Additionally, a few SE Type boxes of 1903-6 had EOD frames (by this date, of course, purchased from S&F).

The SE continued to carry out some of its own work throughout these years, still using the same box design. A revised frame design with tappet locking was used from 1889.

Developments subsequent to the formation of the Joint Committee are described below.

The **London, Chatham & Dover** Railway was well-signalled from an early date, despite its impoverished finances. Absolute Block working was universal from the early 1870s, and interlocking was completed in 1879. At first, all work was carried out by Stevens and S&F, with both frames and boxes built to the contractors' designs. A few S&F Type 1 boxes are known, many S&F Type 5 boxes from 1876, and a good number of Stevens boxes up to 1881 (**Plate 107**).

Around 1878, however, an LCD pattern locking frame was introduced, and within a few years this became universal for new work. It is not yet established whether these LCD frames were manufactured in-house, or purchased from S&F or some other contractor. A few boxes of the late 1870s were built to the plain gabled **LCD** design shown in **Plate 270**, with vertical boarding and 2 or 3-panes deep operating floor windows. From around 1880, however, most boxes on the LCD were built to the S&F Type 5 design (in the case of the 1892 Catford Loop, to the S&F Type 12a design), but fitted with LCD frames.

To further confuse the picture, the Maidstone to Ashford line of 1884 had S&F Type 10 boxes (**Plates 46 & 121**) with standard S&F frames, and Gravesend Station in 1886 was given a RSCo box.

A joint Signal Department seems to have been formed within a few years of the establishment of the South Eastern & Chatham Joint Committee in 1899. A new **SEC** box design was also introduced around 1900 (**Plate 271**). This was a development from the S&F Type 5 design, omitting the curved framing of the sashes and upper lights, and with a different type of eaves bracket with a convex section in the strut. Several boxes were built to this design on the ex-LCD lines, and at least one, Dunton Green, on the ex-SE lines. However, the SE Type box design was also still used for several new boxes on the ex-SE lines at least until 1906. In 1920 a gabled version of the SEC box design was introduced, but as all but one example of this type were built after the Grouping, it has for convenience been classified SR Type 11a, and is described in **Chapter 8**.

Between 1899 and 1906, new boxes on the ex-LCD lines seem to have been fitted with LCD pattern frames, and new boxes on the ex-SE lines with SE or EOD pattern frames. In 1907, W. R. Sykes and the SEC's Signal Superintendent, E. R. F. Hallam, patented the 'SEC new pattern' frame, used thereafter as standard. The place of manufacture of these post-1907 frames is not known.

Plate 270 (above) Shepherdswell, an **LCD** Type box, probably of 1878 when other stations on the Canterbury to Dover section are known to have been interlocked. This is the only box of the type left.

J. Hinson

Plate 271 (right) Gillingham was resignalled in 1913 when a new up loop was provided. Two new boxes, 'A' and 'B', were built, to the **SEC** design. They were inspected on 6th May 1913. Note that the upper lights in this SEC box design are given either a vertical glazing bar above each vertical bar in the main windows or, as here, more bars than in the main windows; whereas in S&F Type 5 boxes, the upper lights have a bar only above the join between one main sash and the next. Gillingham 'A' box, shown here, has now been abolished, but Gillingham 'B' is still in use. Canterbury East, Dover Marine, and Margate are the other surviving boxes of this type.

D. Collins

North British

The NB was slow in the introduction of interlocking, with only 30 per cent of its stations dealt with at 1880. Stevens was the NB's main signalling contractor right up until the Grouping, but there was also some RSCo and S&F work. Only a handful of boxes were built to a contractor's design — the RSCo type boxes at Broomlee, Dolphinton, certain level crossings on the Peebles Branch, and at stations on the Anstruther & St. Andrews Railway.

NB-designed boxes were built of brick, except where site conditions dictated timber construction, with brick chimneys; and almost all had hipped roofs. Little is known about the earliest boxes, as few survived into recent years. The various standard box designs of the period up to 1908 had vertical sash windows but, after this, the more conventional sliding sashes were used. NB boxes were not particularly standardised in detail, and there is no room here to mention the less important variations. There were also special designs on some lines, as described below.

NB **Type 1** boxes (circa 1878-circa 1884) had 2-panes-by-2 operating floor windows, fixed except for vertical sashes at either end of the front elevation. Above the windows there was panelled woodwork with diagonal boarding. The locking room windows in most examples had segmental arches. This design was used most notably on the Arbroath to Kinnaber Junction line during 1880/1, and on the Edinburgh Surburban line in 1884.

Plate 272 (left) The **NB Type 1** box at Montrose North. This line opened on 1st March 1881, and this box, and those at Montrose South and Inverkeilor, are still in use.

D. Collins

Plate 273 (right) Opened on 28th August 1893, Kincardine Junction box was to the **NB Type 2a** design. A rear view of this box is in **Plate 48**. It was abolished on 8th April 1981. The Edinburgh resignalling in the late 1970s exacted a heavy toll on surviving NB boxes, and only two Type 2 boxes are now left in use (Tay Bridge South and Cambus Junction). There are no surviving Type 3 boxes.

F. Alexander

Plate 274 The typical **NB Type 4** box at Westerton, built around 1900. The single storey relay room structure at the left was added at the time of electrification when the box's control area was extended. **Plate 88** shows another Type 4 box.

E. S. Nicoll

The distinctive brick-to-roof **Type 2** boxes were once very common, as this design was in use from around 1873, and the last known example was not built until 1903. The operating floor windows and the (large) locking room windows had segmental arches. **Type 2a** boxes (**Plate 273**) had 2-panes-by-2 vertical sashes at either end of the front elevation, but the remainder of the operating floor windows had fixed glazing with a special pane pattern. **Type 2b** boxes had 2-panes-by-2 vertical sash operating floor windows throughout. A good number of Type 2 boxes had their windows altered in later years in order to improve the signalman's view; large oriel windows were added in several cases. Timber and BTF

boxes of the same period were conceptually similar to Type 2, but have in this instance been given a separate classification (**Type 3**) due to the very considerable difference in their external appearance! Type 3 boxes had vertical boarding and the operating floor windows all had 2-panes-by-2 vertical sashes (*LNERS, Plates 313 & 317*).

The final standard vertical-sash design, **Type 4** of circa 1890-circa 1908 (but with most examples built in the 1900s), had somewhat deeper operating floor windows, 4 panes up by 2 across and all with vertical sashes. The locking room windows on this design had stone lintels.

Plate 275 Rannoch, a typical West Highland Line platform box (**NB Type 6a**). These West Highland boxes are being swept away with the conversion of the line to radio working in 1985/6.

R. Newman

183

Turning now to the special designs of the 1880s-1900s period, **Type 5** covers the boxes built for the interlocking of the Northumbrian lines. These were of stone construction with steeply-pitched hipped roofs and finials. The operating floor windows had large panes with only a horizontal glazing bar, but details varied considerably. **Type 6a** covers the majority of the West Highland line boxes of 1894. These were small (11ft. 6in. x 11ft. 6in.) platform-level structures located on the island platforms to provide cover for the lever frames; the signalling instruments were placed in the station offices. They had 3-panes-by-3 operating floor windows, and a hipped roof with no fascia board. At Fort William, Mallaig Junction, Corrour, Gorton, and Glen Douglas there were taller free-standing boxes, with round-arched locking room windows and subdivided panes in the head of the operating floor windows (**Type 6b**). All these West Highland boxes were designed to harmonise with the station buildings. The signalling equipment for the line was provided by S&F.

The West Highland Extension of 1901 was signalled by the RSCo and the boxes were built to a special version of the RSCo design as shown in **Plate 140**. The **Invergarry & Fort Augustus Railway** of 1903, then unconnected with the NB, was also signalled by the RSCo, with the boxes built to this same RSCo/West Highland Extension design.

The years around 1900 also produced a crop of 'special' designs for individual stations. In connection with the enlargement of Edinburgh (Waverley) from 1895-8, large new East and West boxes were built, gabled with cross-gables as well; and subsidiary North and South boxes bracketed out from the curtain walls (**Plate 99**). The important suburban termini at Leith Central (1903) and Corstorphine (1902) were deemed worthy of special boxes, with large curved eaves brackets similar to those on Caledonian Southern Division boxes. At Dumbuck (1896) and Dalmuir Park (1897) there were gabled brick-to-roof boxes with semicircular-arched operating floor and locking room windows.

Type 7 was the standard design of 1908-18. These boxes had sliding sashes in the operating floor windows, and segmental-arched locking room windows. The operating floor windows were in fact subdivided into a wholly-fixed upper portion, and a main section which had sliding sashes by the front corner posts (plus, in the case of a few long boxes, at centre front) and fixed glazing elsewhere. There were several window pane arrangements; the three most common versions are shown in **Plates 52, 276 & 277**. The few timber Type 7 boxes had horizontal boarding.

Type 8, the final NB design, used from 1919 to 1935, was a development of Type 7, with horizontal boarding below the eaves instead of Type 7's fixed upper glazing, and undivided plate glass in the remaining window area. Again, there were sliding sashes by the front corner posts only.

Plate 276 Monktonhall Junction, an **NB Type 7** box, opened on 15th December 1912. It had small panes in the head of the operating floor windows, as found in about half the known Type 7 boxes. The locking room windows are typical of the type. Closure, under the Edinburgh resignalling scheme, came on 1st August 1977.

F. Alexander

Plate 277 One of the last **NB Type 7** boxes built was at Grantshouse, opened on 7th April 1918, and closed on 27th February 1978. Rear frames were installed by the NB in many post-1915 boxes, hence the chimney in the front. The locking room windows have bars to protect them, as the box was originally on the station platform.

F. Alexander

Plate 278 The **NB Type 8** box at Dundee Central. Note the very large bricked-up locking room windows.

E. S. Nicoll

Great North of Scotland

The GNoS was the slowest of all the major British companies in interlocking. Only seven locations, all but two of them around Aberdeen, had been interlocked by 1879. A vast amount of work still remained to be carried out after the 1889 Act, and much of it was not in fact done until 1894-8. Many GNoS stations had two boxes, one being the main block post and the other, known by the GnoS as the 'minor box', controlling the connections at the other end of the siding or loop.

Stevens was the GNoS's main supplier, but the RSCo also carried out some work. No Stevens design boxes are known, but two boxes were built to the special RSCo hipped typed shown in **Plate 139**.

The first GNoS box design, **Type 1**, was hipped, with 3-panes-deep operating floor windows. Timber, BTF, and STF examples are known. The design was in use by the late 1870s. The last example dated from 1903, but the later ones were probably second-hand structures, as the GNoS was fond of reusing boxes.

Type 2, introduced around 1884, was basically a gabled version of Type 1. However, almost all Type 2 boxes were of timber construction. Most had brick chimneys, often encased within the main box outline as in **Plate 281**. Multiple small locking room windows were provided. The bargeboards were plain and in most cases were placed closely over the weatherboarding. Over half the total number of GNoS boxes were to the Type 2 design, which was in general use until circa 1900; there were a couple built after 1900 but these, again, were probably second-hand.

Hipped roofs came back again for the more stylish **Type 3** design, introduced at Lossiemouth in 1896 and reproduced at Craigellachie (Main box) (1900), Inverurie (1902), Fraserburgh (1904), Keith Junction (1905), and Aberdeen North (1914). A new operating floor window design was used. The timber examples retained the same type of locking room windows as Type 2 boxes, but the boarding above operating floor level was arranged into 'panels' as shown. Several boxes had cockscomb ridge tiles and terracotta finials.

Plate 279 Kittybrewster South (**GNoS Type 1** design) was one of the earliest GNoS boxes. Built in the late 1870s, it was closed on 25th May 1967. It was of STF construction with granite ashlarwork, and vertical boarding above (the latter may not have been original as most Type 1 boxes had weatherboarding). Dyce South, of 1880, is now the only surviving Type 1 box.

D. Collins

Plate 280 The **GNoS Type 2** design is illustrated by Elgin West. This box, opened on 1st May 1888, was renamed Elgin Centre in 1934, and closed on 11th November 1973; but it still stands in good condition, as shown, in use as staff accommodation. Note the hatches under the locking room windows, which could be lifted up for better access to the cranks, etc. Insch and Huntly South are the last remaining Type 2 boxes in signalling use.

J. Hinson

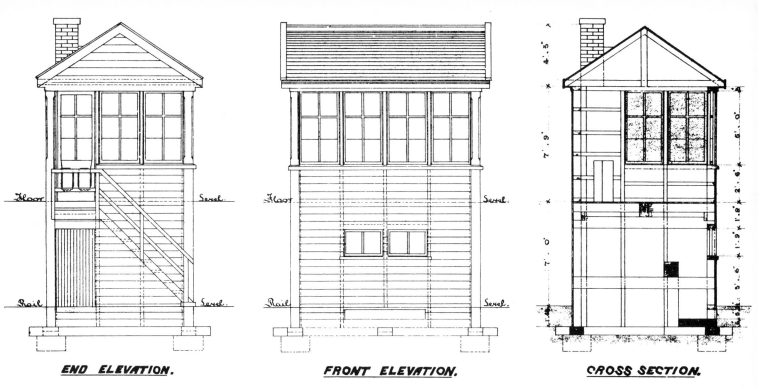

END ELEVATION. FRONT ELEVATION. CROSS SECTION.

—G.N. of S. [BUCKIE EXTENSION] RAILWAY.—

—SIGNAL CABIN—

AT

—URQUHART—

Plate 281 This GNoS drawing shows the **Type 2** box for Urquhart, which opened on 12th August 1884.

SCALE: 4mm = 1 foot

Scottish Record Office

Plate 282 The **Type 3** box at Inverurie was opened on 10th February 1902 as 'Inverurie New Station', but soon became known by the shorter name. The layout here was heavily reduced in 1970 and a new 30-lever frame was installed, but the box is still in use, as is Keith Junction.

J. Hinson

Caledonian

The Caledonian was far in advance of the other Scottish companies with its interlocking programme. At first it acquired its signalling equipment from the contractors, with much Stevens and S&F work up to the 1900s, and some RSCo work. From the 1890s, in-house manufacture of locking frames, to the Stevens pattern, was undertaken at St. Rollox. Signal boxes were all built to Caledonian designs, and in most cases were built by building contractors. All Caledonian boxes had hipped roofs. Box designs varied between the Northern and Southern Divisions, the boundary being at Castlecary.

Northern Division boxes were very standardised, and most were of brick construction. **Type N1** of circa 1870-circa 1889 was a very plain design, with 3-panes-by-3 sashes and no fascia board. Most do not seem to have had any locking room windows. The few timber examples had vertical boarding, as did most other Caledonian timber boxes. **Type N2**, introduced circa 1889, was also plain but had a more 'finished' appearance, with fascia boards now provided, and with semicircular-arched locking room windows. The operating floor windows were still 3 panes deep, but each section was now 2 panes across. Sliding sashes were provided by the front corner posts only. **Type N3** of 1902-8 was more decorative. The roof had ridge tiles and terracotta finials, and a 'tilting piece' at the foot. The operating floor windows were 3 panes across, and had a single horizontal glazing bar set towards the head. The locking room windows were semicircular-arched, but larger than those on Type N2 boxes, with an arched pane pattern (**Plate 75**). From 1908, new boxes were built to the Type N2 design again, this design having been dormant during the Type N3 period.

The **Southern Division** had several box designs in simultaneous use in the 1870s, and there was also considerable variation within the types. **Type S1** covers the boxes built on the Carlisle to Car-

stairs line in the early 1870s, and a few elsewhere. These were plain brick or stone boxes with 3-panes-deep windows, rather similar to Type N1 but much less standardised. Some had low-pitched zinc roofs, and others slated roofs; some had large timber or iron finials; some had fascia boards, and others did not; and locking room windows also varied. Types S2 and S3 were similar in outline to Type S1, but had more decorative operating floor window designs, **Type S2** having curved timber framing added on the outside of the normal window frames, and **Type S3** having a special pane pattern with subdivided upper panes.

Type S4 was by far the most numerous Southern Division type. This design was already in use by 1870, and from the late 1880s through till the Grouping it was the only design used. The distinctive features were the overhanging eaves and large curved eaves brackets, and the operating floor windows with only a single horizontal glazing bar placed near the head. About 40 per cent of these boxes were built of timber, with vertical boarding. Brick examples normally had segmental-arched locking room windows, but some of the 1895-1910 period had semicircular arches instead. Other details too naturally varied somewhat over the long period in which the design was used. Some early boxes had a large iron grille and other decorative ironwork on the roof (**Plate 289**). Other early examples had more widely-spaced eaves brackets with a vertical glazing bar in the windows between each bracket. Some of the later boxes had ridge tiles and terracotta finials, and 'tilting pieces' at the foot of the rafters, as Type N3.

Type S5 was a variant of Type S4 used on the Clarkston to Lugton line of 1903, with two equally-spaced horizontal glazing bars in the operating floor windows, and semicircular-arched locking room windows.

The Motherwell resignalling in the 1970s saw the removal of large numbers of Southern Division boxes, and the only survivors today are half a dozen Type S4 boxes.

Plate 283 A typical **Type N1** box at Fordoun, probably built in 1876 when the block system was introduced on this line. Most Type N1 boxes were of this length. Fordoun closed on 5th October 1975, but ten boxes of this type are still in use at various locations between Stirling and Aberdeen.

E. S. Nicoll

Plate 284 (right) Dalmally, a **Type N2** box of 1896. Nine Type N2 boxes remain in use.

P. Kay

Plate 285 (below) The **Type N3** box at Oban was opened on 23rd June 1904, and closed on 5th December 1982. The photograph was taken in 1983, after all fittings had been disconnected and the walkway and walkway brackets had been removed. Five boxes of this type survive.

P. Kay

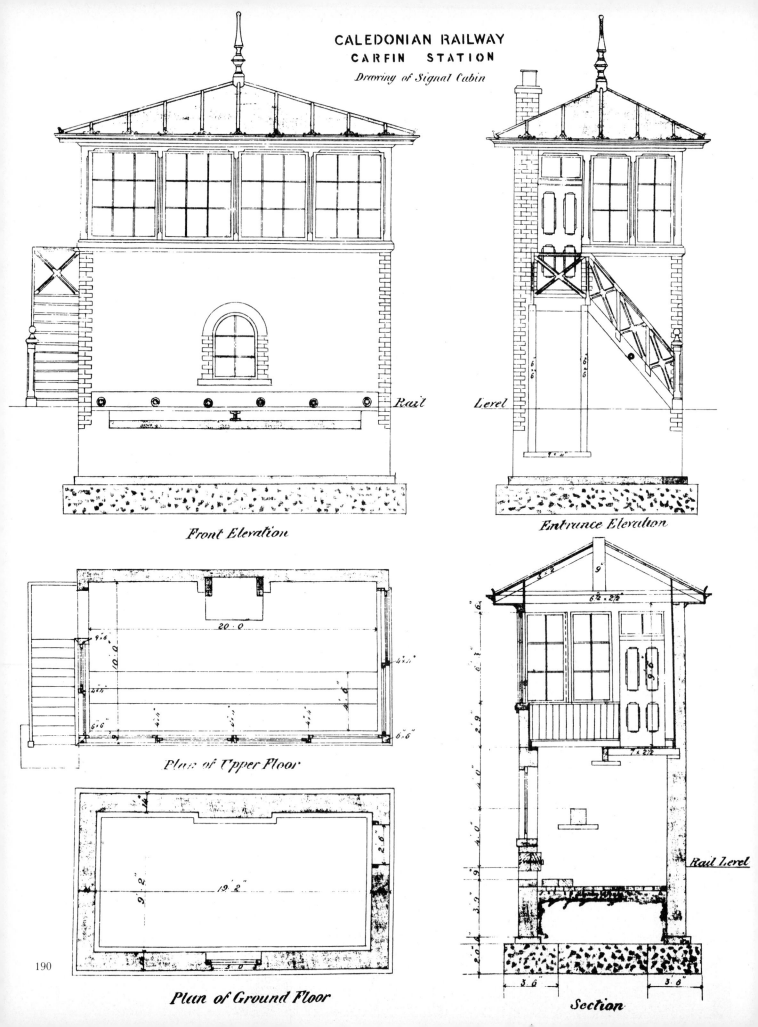

CALEDONIAN RAILWAY
CARFIN STATION
Drawing of Signal Cabin

Front Elevation

Entrance Elevation

Plan of Upper Floor

Plan of Ground Floor

Section

Rail

Level

Rail Level

Plate 286 (left) This drawing of Carfin Station box shows one version of the **Type S1** design. This box was opened on 1st June 1880 and was subsequently renamed Carfin Junction, and ' then Holytown Junction. The drawing is entitled 'Caledonian Railway. Carfin Station. Drawing of Signal Cabin. Contract Drawing No. 5'. Under the title is written 'This is one of the plans referred to in and signed as relative to contract entered into and executed by and between the Caledonian Railway Company, of the first part, and Robert McAlpine, Builder, Hamilton, of the second part, dated twelfth and twenty-ninth November Eighteen hundred and seventy nine'. The drawing also includes a complete written specification. This written material has had to be omitted here for space reasons. The semicircular-arched locking room windows shown here are unusual for Type S1. The roofing material is specified as 'best 24oz. zinc'. Another Type S1 box with a zinc roof, and basically the same as Carfin, can be seen in **Plate 43**.

Scottish Record Office

SCALE: 4mm = 1 foot

Plate 287 The **Type S3** box at Benhar Junction, built in the 1870s and abolished on 29th June 1981. The clumsy walkway and the brick portion of the stairs are later additions. This box design was used on the lines to Edinburgh.

E. S. Nicoll

Plate 288 Lockerbie was a typical **Type S4** brick box of later years. It was opened on 18th January 1892 and closed on 29th April 1973.

R. D. Foster

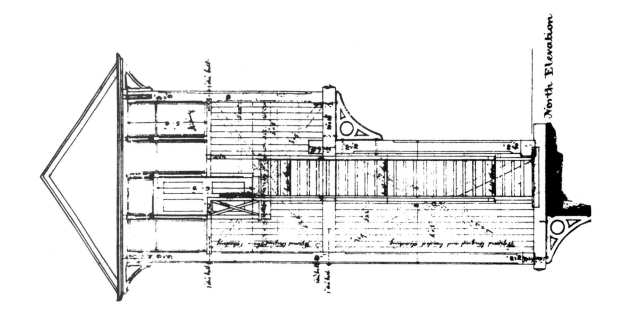

North Elevation

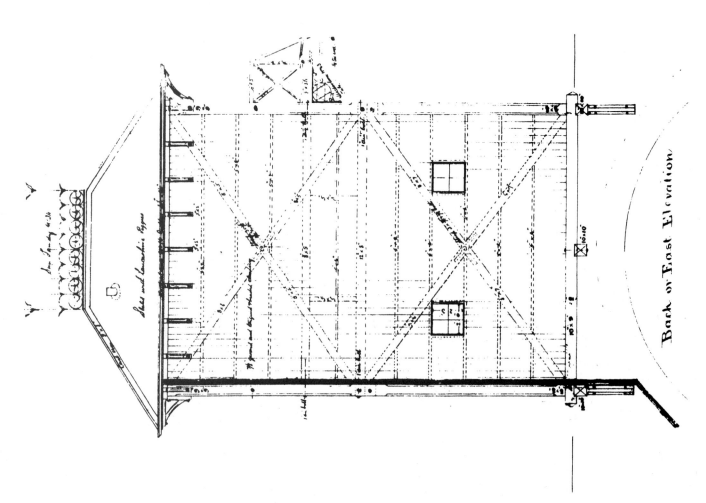

Back or East Elevation

192

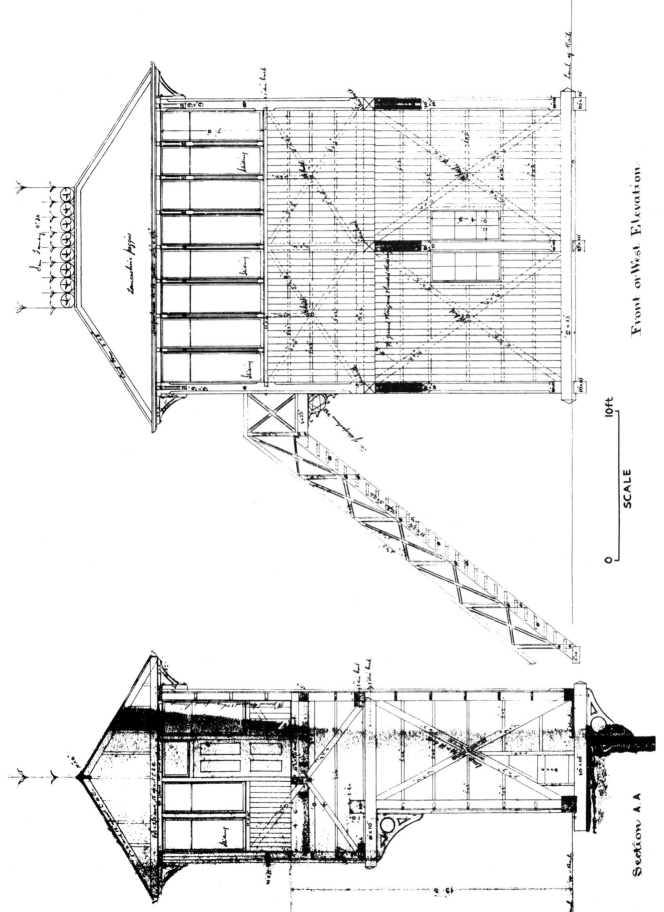

Section A.A

SCALE: 4mm = 1 foot

SCALE 0 _____ 10ft

Front or West Elevation

Scottish Record Office

Plate 289 Part of the contract drawing, dated August 1875, for Rutherglen Loan Junction box, showing the exuberant ironwork of some early **Type S4** boxes. This box was built on a difficult viaduct site, the rear being bracketed out from the viaduct wall, and the operating floor oversailing the front. In fact, less than half the operating floor width actually rests on terra firma! The written notes specify the iron grille on the roof as 'Sun Foundry No. 34', and the landing brackets as 'MacFarlane's No. 63'. The vertical boarding is specified as '7/8in. tongued & grooved & beaded'.

Glasgow & South Western

The GSW purchased from Stevens at first. In later years frame components were still apparently bought from Stevens, but frames were assembled at the GSW's Irvine Signal Works, with GSW locking.

All GSW boxes were built to GSW designs. In many ways GSW boxes were reminiscent of the Midland; most were of timber construction (but with a few courses of brickwork to prevent rot), all had hipped roofs, and the major changes over the years related to the operating floor window arrangements.

The **Type 1** design (circa 1875-circa 1887) had small 2-panes-deep operating floor windows, interrupted at the front centre by a boarded section. The main part of the structure had horizontal weatherboarding, as was also usual on later types, but between the windows and the eaves there was closely-spaced vertical boarding. The eaves overhung some distance, and fascia boards and eaves plates were provided. Stoves and stovepipes were the usual heating equipment. There were no locking room windows.

Type 2 covers a handful of 1880s boxes similar to Type 1, but with deeper (3 panes deep) operating floor windows.

The **Type 3** design of circa 1885-circa 1904 had 5ft. 8in. (approx.) deep operating floor windows, which now extended right up to the eaves. They had two horizontal and no vertical glazing bars. Most boxes did not have a boarded section at front centre, but some did. Fascia boards and eaves plates were again provided. Most boxes now had hearths and brick chimneys. Small locking room windows were included in some cases.

Type 4 was concurrent with Type 3, being used circa 1891-circa 1900. The operating floor windows extended up to the eaves as with Type 3, but included vertical glazing bars, each sash being 3 panes up and 2 across. Instead of fascia boards and eaves plates, Type 4 featured exposed rafter-ends. Brick chimneys were usual, as with Type 3.

The later Types 5, 6 and 7 also featured exposed rafter-ends, but reverted to the Types 1 and 2 practice of having a section of 4in. vertical boarding between the head of the windows and the eaves. The major differences between Types 5, 6 and 7 lay in the operating floor window designs. The comparatively few **Type 5** boxes of circa 1904/5 had the same window pattern as Type 3 (two horizontal and no vertical glazing bars). **Type 6** boxes of 1901-06 had undivided plate-glass operating floor windows, and **Type 7** of circa 1905-23 had windows with a single horizontal glazing bar set near the head. In the early 1900s, the GSW flirted with brick construction, and all Type 6 and one or two Types 5 and 7 boxes were built of brick, with large arched locking room windows. Timber boxes of Type 7 had much larger locking room windows than earlier types, usually 3 panes up and 5 to 9 across.

Around 1905, the GSW adopted rear frames as standard. At the same time stoves and stovepipes were readopted, and as these were now necessarily placed in the front on the box, the boarded section at front centre became virtually ubiquitous in post-1905 boxes. Types 5 and 6 boxes had variously front frames (with brick chimney at the rear) or rear frames (with stovepipe at the front), according to the date of construction, but virtually all Type 7 boxes had rear frames.

At present, there are several surviving examples of all the GSW box designs, but many will disappear under the current Ayrshire resignalling.

In their independent days, the **Wigtownshire, Portpatrick and Girvan** and **Girvan and Portpatrick Junction** railways acquired their signalling equipment from various contractors (**as noted in the Tables in Chapter 5**). Such boxes as existed were probably to contractors' designs, but with the exception of Challoch Junction (**Plate 131**) they all disappeared at an early date, and photographs are unknown. When the **Portpatrick & Wigtownshire Joint Committee** was established in 1886, the Caledonian and GSW agreed to take alternating periods of responsibility for signalling, but as it happened all the known boxes were built during GSW periods. Further information on the signalling of these lines can be found in D. L. Smith's *The Little Railways of South West Scotland* (David & Charles, 1969).

Plate 290 The tall **GSW Type 1** box at West Kilbride was built for the opening of the line, and was inspected on 24th April 1878. It closed on 25th January 1981. Some Type 1 boxes had vertical boarding above the windows on the ends only, as here; others also had it above the front windows.

E. S. Nicoll

Plate 291 The **GSW Type 3** box at Kilkerran, built probably in 1895, when the line was doubled.

E. S. Nicoll

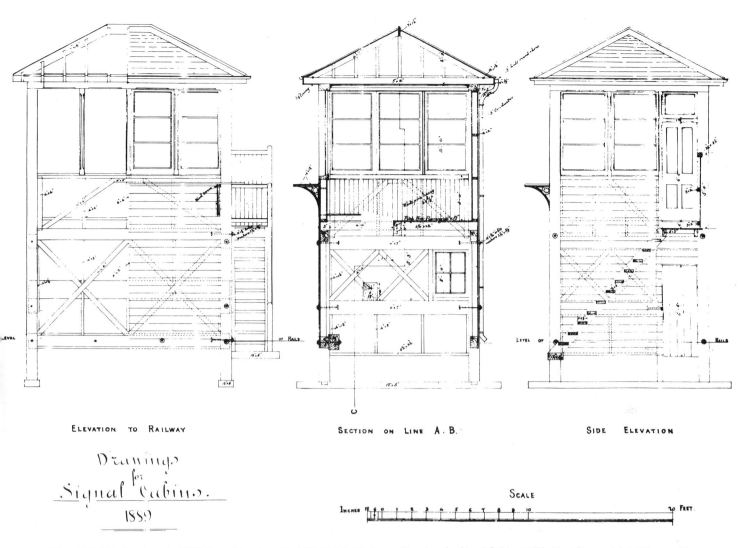

ELEVATION TO RAILWAY   SECTION ON LINE A. B.   SIDE ELEVATION

Drawings
for
Signal Cabins.
1889

SCALE

INCHES 12 6 0 1 2 3 4 5 6 7 8 9 10 .... 20 FEET.

Plate 292 This drawing of a **GSW Type 3** box is entitled 'P&W Joint Railways Drawings for Signal Cabins 1889'. Most Portpatrick & Wigtownshire stations were still not interlocked at this date, and most were indeed provided with boxes to this design shortly afterwards. The drawing does not show any heating or chimney arrangements.

Scottish Record Office

Plate 293 Corkerhill No. 1 box was built to the **GSW Type 4** design, and opened on 15th March 1896. As the photograph clearly shows, it was extended at the near end in 1922. The brick base dates from the time of the extension.

E. S. Nicoll

Plate 294 (right) The **GSW Type 6** box at Brownhill Jnct., opened on 1st June 1905. The remains of a chimney on the left suggests that this box originally had a front frame; the present frame in the rear is certainly a replacement. The clumsy boarded section would most likely have been added on reframing, when the stove was installed in the front. Some of the present window sashes are also clearly not original.

E. S. Nicoll

Plate 295 (below) Dalrymple Junction, a typical rear-framed **GSW Type 7** box. It survived long enough to receive these new BR nameboards, but succumbed on 28th October 1973. **Plate 90** shows another box of this type.

E. S. Nicoll

Highland

The Highland Railway was, as one might expect, slow to adopt improved signalling methods. There were only about twenty interlocked locations at 1880, and the network was still only 50 per cent interlocked at 1889, so necessitating a heavy interlocking programme in 1890-4. The Highland was very much the odd man out amongst the Scottish companies in signalling matters. McK&H were the favoured contractors (also Dutton in the 1890s), rather than Stevens, and contractors' box designs were used generally until the turn of the century. On the single track lines which formed the greater part of the network many stations had two small boxes, one near each end of the loop, which were worked as ground frames with the signalling instruments kept in the booking office. As the signalman at such stations spent most of his time in the station buildings, the boxes had no stoves or other comforts. This system remained in use on the Dingwall-Kyle of Lochalsh and Dingwall-Georgemas Jn sections until 1984 and 1985 respectively, and is still in operation at Nairn.

The McK&H and Dutton boxes on the Highland Railway were built to the normal outline but had vertical battened boarding (found also on many Highland station buildings) and corrugated-iron roofs. Most had porches formed by an extension of the rear part of the main box roof, with valancing over the entrance.

Little is known about the earliest Highland boxes, but it is likely that the **McK&H Type 3/Highland** design was used from 1876. This became the most widely-reproduced Highland box type. Although some of the larger boxes of this type had the 3-panes-deep windows found on standard McK&H Type 3 boxes, most had smaller (3ft. 8½in. deep) 2-panes-deep windows. To some extent this can be attributed to the lowness of most of the Highland boxes, but not wholly so, as some reasonably tall examples (e.g. Forres East) also had 2-panes-deep windows. At Inverness, four boxes were built in 1898 to a specially-decorative version of the McK&H Type 3/Highland design. These were Ness Viaduct, Rose Street, Welsh's Bridge and Millburn (the last now at Murthly). They had slated roofs, decorative bargeboards similar in appearance to GC practice, curved framing in the heads of the sashes, and fascia board decoration similar to that on McK&H-built GE boxes of the 1880s.

Dutton Type 1/Highland boxes all had the standard 3-panes-deep windows. There were (until 1985) many of these boxes on the Invergordon to Georgemas Junction line, which was resignalled by Dutton in 1894. Some were built with stone walls at the ends up to operating floor level. Two **Dutton Type 3/Highland** boxes were built (i.e. with roofed landing and the revised window design), Stromeferry West and Kyle of Lochalsh of 1897. The two boxes at Brora can be classified **Dutton Type 4/Highland**, as they were virtually identical (except for the special Highland features) to the Cambrian examples of this type; and several others, such as Georgemas North and Invershin, were similar but had plain bargeboards.

From the 1900s, the contractors' box designs were replaced by a new **Highland** design. Boxes were now mostly built of brick, with 'panelled' bases, but the vertical battened boarding was retained in the gable ends, and there were also timber examples at Pitlochry and Lentran. Most boxes of this type had slated roofs with no fascia boards, plain bargeboards and stumpy finials, and very small gable window/vents divided into four panes. Operating floor windows were either 3 panes deep, or 2 panes deep with boarding between windows and eaves.

Plate 296 (above) A typical **McK&H Type 3/Highland** box, Blair Atholl South. The two-panes-across gable window/vents are found in all Highland boxes of this type, although only a few of the standard McK&H Type 3 boxes elsewhere had them.

E. S. Nicoll

Plate 297 (right) Detail of Rose Street box, Inverness, showing the various decorative features referred to in the text.

P. Kay

Plate 298 (right) This view of one of the 1894 boxes at Rogart illustrates the **Dutton Type 1/Highland** design.

R. D. Foster

Plate 299 (below) The brick **Highland** type box at Ballinluig North was built in 1919.

D. Collins

The Signal Box from the 1930s to the 1980s: 'Modern Architecture' and Modern Electronics

The Introduction of 'Modern Architecture'

The influence of the architectural 'modernists' spread to the design of signal boxes on a large scale in the 1930s, but there were a few hints of it earlier.

Perhaps the most obvious feature of the new style was the use of flat roofs, normally of reinforced concrete (although in some cases of timber). Reinforced concrete had been available as a roofing material since the 1890s, but took some time to catch on. The weight of a reinforced concrete roof is such that any signal box provided with one had necessarily to be built of brick-to-roof construction (or, increasingly, steel-framed with brick or other material used as cladding only). Boxes which, for site reasons, had to be of timber construction therefore had to have a timber flat roof instead, if a 'modern style' appearance was desired; and some brick boxes too were given timber flat roofs.

As noted in Chapter 3, flat roofs had in the 19th century been used only for a very few boxes which were located under station canopies or in tunnels, and which did not therefore require the normal protection from rail. The first use of flat roofs for boxes in normal exposed locations was on the District Railway in 1905, where the many new boxes provided for the resignalling of the line were so built. The first use of *reinforced concrete* flat roofs as a standard feature was on the Metropolitan, from 1924.

The upper surface of a flat roof in normal exposed locations is not horizontal, but has a slight slope (about 5 per cent) so that rainwater can drain off, and is covered with a waterproof material-asphalt, bitumen, asbestos or felt. Usually the roof overhangs a little to provide better rain protection for the structure, and sometimes a canopy (usually of reinforced concrete in the 1930s-1950s) was provided as well. Nevertheless, subsequent experience has proved that many flat roofs do not provide such good weatherproofing as a traditional hipped or gabled roof!

As far as signal boxes were concerned, the other main features of the 'modern style', as it emerged in the 1930s, were as follows:
— Steel-framed windows, with plate glass, with few glazing bars. Casement or hopper windows were common, but sliding sashes also remained popular. Some 'modern style' boxes also still had timber-framed sliding sashes.
— Cills and lintels of concrete.
— External stairs of brick, with steel handrails, or of prefabricated-concrete sections, or of steel. An increasing number of boxes were given internal stairs.
— The rendering of brickwork for decorative purposes. For example, many SR boxes had the brickwork between the head of the windows and the eaves rendered with 'snowcrete' to match the concrete roof; they also had a rendered 'waistband' (**Plates 300 & 345**). Some boxes were rendered all over (**Plate 304**).
— The casting of the box name in large letters within a concrete block (primarily on the SR).

The 'modern style' was very well established on the London Underground railways by the time the London Passenger Transport Board was set up in 1933, and was used by them for all subsequent signal boxes. The main line companies were rather slower to adopt the new style, and varied considerably in their enthusiasm for it. The SR was keenest, building virtually all new boxes in the 'modern style' from 1935. The LNER came next, adopting the new style for new boxes in the North Eastern Area from around 1933, then in Scotland from around 1936, and in the Southern Area from around 1939. However, there was little standardisation on the LNER, and many of its boxes were given steep-pitched hipped roofs or timber flat roofs rather than reinforced concrete flat roofs. The other two companies remained generally committed to 'traditional' box designs. The LMS had 'modern style' boxes built at Manchester Victoria in 1929 and Manchester Central (CLC) in 1935, but made no use of the new style subsequently except for its ARP boxes (for which **see below**). The GW, despite having experimented with advanced steel-frame and concrete-block-infill con-

Plate 300 The photographs on this page and page 200 show three 'modern style' boxes, typical of the designs of the 1930s and 1940s. Here is the SR mechanical box at Deal, opened on 14th May 1939, with overhanging roof and stylish rounded ends. None of the other companies' designs had quite the same 'Odeonesque' chunkiness as did the Southern boxes of the 1930s.

P. Kay

struction in the 1920s, built no 'modern style' flat-roofed boxes other than the large power boxes at Bristol, Paddington and Cardiff in 1933-5 (and, again, its ARP boxes).

One effect of the spread of the 'modern style' was that it made signal boxes look more like other contemporary buildings than they had previously, as the basic aims of the new style — functionalism and maximum window space — were exactly what had always been required in the case of signal boxes. It was also the case, however, that as box structures became larger and also began to incorporate staff accommodation, the design of signal boxes began to come more often into the hands of the railway companies' architects, rather than the Signal Engineers' Departments; and the architects would of course be more familiar with the latest trends in architectural fashion.

Plate 301 (above) The LNER's panel box at Northallerton, built in 1937 and opened in 1939, shows that company's preference for steep-pitched hipped roofs on some 'modern style' boxes. Northallerton was opened on the day war broke out, and the windows were all wholly bricked-up for the first years of its life.

R. Newman

Plate 302 (right) Copmanthorpe box opened on 12th November 1950, and was built to the LNER standard design of 1944. Note the 'splay corners' at the front.

R. Newman

'ARP' Designs: Signal Boxes and World War II

The coming of World War II, and the general expectation that this would involve air raids on civilian targets, brought new requirements for signal box design. By giving a new purpose to the reinforced concrete roof, the war also gave the 'modern style' a boost, forcing its adoption by those companies (the LMS and GW) which had not previously looked favourably upon it for ordinary mechanical boxes.

The railway companies were already giving serious consideration to the war by 1938. The LT boxes of 1938/9 were built to ARP (Air Raid Precaution) specifications, with double reinforcement of the roof and steel shutters for the windows; and in February 1939 the LMS began work on replacing the vital, but tall and vulnerable, LNW boxes at Crewe North and Crewe South with new boxes to ARP specifications. The two new boxes, which were brought into use during August/September 1940, had reinforced-concrete walls 15in. thick, and reinforced concrete roofs no less than 18in. thick.

By the end of 1939, the four main railways had evolved new ARP box designs for general use. The LMS and GW versions were the most standardised, and were all the more noticeable as they had not previously made much use of the 'modern style'. The first of the LMS ARP boxes, Crewe Coal Yard, opened on 10th December 1939, and over fifty boxes were built to the design between then and 1950, plus several more to a slightly different design in Scotland. The first of the GW ARP boxes was North Acton, ordered on 19th September 1939 and opened on 25th August 1940; some 45 examples then appeared until 1945. The SR also had a fairly standardised ARP design, with some thirty built between 1940 and 1949, but the LNER's few ARP boxes were not standardised (except in Scotland); indeed, the LNER built surprisingly few new boxes at all during the war years.

Some ARP boxes were (like the two at Crewe already mentioned) built to replace existing boxes where the equipment would not have needed replacing in normal circumstances, but where the structure was felt to be particularly vulnerable to air raid damage. In particular, the LMS replaced, during 1939/40, a number of overhead boxes, such as Windsor Bridge No. 1, Acton Grange Junction, Camden No. 1, Polmadie Bridge, and Wakefield West. But most ARP boxes were built as additional boxes to serve new sidings for military depots, airfields, etc. (Many such new works had also been provided in World War I, but the boxes built then had not been to special designs). There were also many on routes where additional tracks or loops were provided for war traffic, as on the West Highland and the DN&S. These extra facilities were in many cases of little use after the end of the war, with the result that many ARP boxes had a very short life. A correspondingly small number survive in use today; none from the GW, two from the SR (Point Pleasant Jn. and Crabtree Crossing), two from the LNER (Skelton and Heatheryknowe), and a dozen from the LMS. However, because of the comparative difficulty of demolishing an ARP box, many disused examples still stand, such as Ardmore East and Lochailort on the West Highland, Woodhay, Highclere and Burghclere on the DN&S, and Burton Dassett and Broom West on the SMJ.

ARP boxes were not designed to survive a direct hit by a bomb (except for small incendiaries — the LMS box, for example, was designed to resist penetration by a 1kg. incendiary bomb), but rather to minimise the effects of blast and debris from bombs landing nearby. The walls of ARP boxes were of 14in. brickwork, and the reinforced-concrete roofs were around 12in. thick (the two Crewe boxes were exceptional!). In most cases there were no locking room windows and no roof overhang or canopy, as these might have been broken off by blast. Timberwork was kept to a minimum (block shelf and instruments, and other furnishings) in order to make boxes as fireproof as possible.

By no means all new boxes of the war years were built to ARP specifications. The GW and LMS in particular continued to build boxes to 'traditional' designs and without any special protection at those locations which were considered less important or less vulnerable, even in some cases on lines built specially as war works, as at Hawkeridge (Westbury). Also, timber boxes were built where urgent construction was required.

As well as building new ARP boxes, a large amount of work had to be carried out during 1939/40 to provide protection for existing boxes. Timber boxes were obviously at most risk, and many were 'bricked up' to operating floor or window level. Generally, this was done in an inelegant fashion, but sixteen of the more important Midland boxes in the London area were bricked up in a more stylish fashion, with 'panelled' brickwork and pebbledash in the inset sections (**Plate 307**). An alternative to providing a new brick base in this way was to leave the timber box structure as it was, and build an independent 14in. brick wall around it up to window level. This approach was particularly favoured by the SR (**Plate 308**), and by the LNER in the Sheffield area.

Less needed to be done with brick boxes. The LMS considered converting all brick boxes to 14in. brickwork, but rejected the idea as impracticable. The locking room windows of many brick boxes were either bricked up or covered, inside and out, with steel plates, in order to protect the locking apparatus and also any persons who might be sheltering in the locking room during a raid. This, of course, made the locking room permanently dark, so that a Tilley lamp had to be provided where electricity or gas was not installed. The LMS, as an example, recorded that it had bricked up 910 locking room windows and fitted 12,950 with steel plates. The steel plates were mostly removed after the war, but those locking room windows which had been bricked up were generally left so.

A few boxes of major importance were given new reinforced-concrete roofs in place of their original hipped or gabled roofs. This was done at Glasgow St. Enoch and (as an 'umbrella' over the existing roofs) at Manchester London Road Nos. 1 and 2 boxes.

Steel shelters were provided for the signalmen in many boxes in the areas most subject to air raids. Other changes arising from the war were the removal of box nameboards, the permanent painting out of parts of the operating floor windows, and the fitting of reduced lighting. A 100 per cent blackout was not possible (except when a raid was actually in progress and rail traffic had stopped), as the signalmen had to be able to look out to observe trains, and some lighting had to be provided. In some boxes, the operating floor windows were protected at night by putting up wire mesh on the inside, with small peep-holes at either end of the box to observe the trains.

Only a few boxes were actually destroyed beyond repair by bombing. Amongst those were Tulse Hill, Yarmouth South Town, Castle Cary, St. Budeaux West, West Kensington East and Liverpool Exchange Station Junction. Sometimes destruction came by indirect means; Turnchapel box, for example, was burnt down when nearby Admiralty oil tanks were hit and the burning oil flowed on to the railway. However, there was an unending task in repairing damaged boxes.

Plate 305 (above)The GW ARP box (**GW Type 13**) at Beechgrove (Warminster) opened on 11th April 1944 to serve Army sidings. This 28-lever box measured 24ft. 2in. x 12ft. x 8ft. It closed as early as 13th December 1949 but still stands in good condition, as shown. Many of the GW ARP boxes did have locking room windows. They also had timber-framed operating floor window sashes (of the '3-up, 2-down' pattern).

J. P. Morris

Plate 303 (above left) Illustrated in **Plates 303-306** are ARP designs from each of the main railway companies. Acton Grange Junction, opened on 5th April 1940, was a standard LMS ARP box (**LMS Type 13**) with prefabricated concrete staircase components. The common red facing brick used for most of the structure of these boxes was relieved by a blue brick base, and by two bands of blue bricks near operating floor level. In most cases, each of these two bands was of three courses, but in some cases (as at Acton Grange) it was of single bricks set on edge. The pre-cast reinforced concrete roofs of these boxes were a proprietary product made by Messrs Evanstone of Riddings. An Evanstone roof had been spotted by W. F. Hardman of the LMS Signal Department at the Co-op Bakery in Crewe, when he was looking for a suitable roofing for the new ARP box design. The roofs used on the boxes were 13in. thick at the front and rear, with a 6in. fall from either side to a drain in the centre; the waterproofing was effected by a covering of bitumen, two layers of felt, asbestos, and chippings on top. The floor of the operating room was also of 'Evanstone beams', but these were not visible externally. The 4ft.-deep operating floor windows had concrete cills, mullions, and lintels, and the galvanised steel window frames (another proprietary product) had a small sliding section in the centre. The LMS ARP boxes were very standardised for the most part, but the three Wigan boxes, and the box at Sefton Junction (*LMSA, Plates 581 & 549*) had smaller operating floor windows, and the 1946 boxes at Mold Junction and Carlisle No. 12 were given locking room windows. For the Scottish version see **Plate 330**.

R. D. Foster

Plate 304 (left) The LNER Scottish Area ARP box (**LNER Type 14**) at Dunbar West was opened on 22nd March 1942. Note the chimney at the front.

E. S. Nicoll

Plate 306 Finally, we see the Southern Railway's **Type 14** ARP box at Gomshall & Shere, opened on 26th October 1941. The windows at the corners are steel-framed, but the others are timber-framed. The rendered 'waistband' has decayed at the corners revealing the brickwork underneath, thereby proving the point that it is only a decorative add-on.

P. Kay

Plate 307 This view of Barking East shows the style of bricking-up applied to certain Midland boxes in the London area, here extended up to roof level at the rear. This brickwork was 14in. below operating floor level (9in. in the inset 'panels'), and 9in. above operating floor level. A Midland Type 4d box, Barking East had been built around 1919 on the foundations of the 1908 RSCo box which was burnt down in an arson attack. This would account for the evident abnormal width. The nameboard also appears to belong to the 1908 box.

C. H. Betts

Plate 308 The SE Type timber box at the very important junction at Redhill 'B' was provided with this independent anti-blast wall. A more extreme example of this practice can be seen in *Southern Signals, Plate 23*. In one case (Point Pleasant Junction) the SR went so far as to build a whole new ARP 'box' around the outside of the existing box.

P. Kay

Plate 309 The majority of London Transport boxes were very heavily bricked-up during the war. Here is the GW Type 7 box at Hammersmith (H&C), with the locking room windows bricked up, and the original operating floor windows entirely removed and replaced with much smaller windows. The photograph was taken in February 1951, shortly before this box was replaced by a new LT-design box.

London Transport

Modern Electronics: The 'Panel' Box

As noted in **Chapters 1 and 2**, a small proportion of new boxes after 1898 were fitted with power frames (with miniature levers or slides) instead of purely mechanical frames, but this had little effect on the external appearance of boxes, except for reducing their length. However, from 1930, developments began in signalling technology which were to make a fundamental impact on the functional requirements with which the signal box architect was faced, and which in due course were to bring about the end of the 'signal box', as such, altogether.

Up until 1928, all power frames had retained mechanical interlocking, and it had therefore remained necessary for the levers to be placed in a continuous row with the locking below or behind them. But as installations grew larger, the difficulties of fitting the mechanical locking became ever greater. Very considerable difficulties were experienced in completing the interlocking of the 311-lever box at London Bridge (SR) in 1928, and it came to be realised that an alternative form of interlocking was required if larger areas than

this were to be controlled from one box. This was the inspiration for the introduction of electrical interlocking by lock magnets, first used in this country at North Kent East Junction in 1929. This box was built with the miniature lever frame arranged in a single row as previously, but a single row was no longer inevitable, and the 225-lever frame in the new Brighton box of 1932 was arranged in three sections, with the two outer sections placed at 45 degrees to the central section, in order to reduce the length of the box and assist communication between the operators.

In 1933, however, an even greater leap forward was made with the introduction of 'relay interlocking', working entirely through electrical relays. With relay interlocking, there was no need for 'levers' at all; all that was needed were small switches or buttons mounted on a 'panel', taking up far less room than a miniature lever frame. Relay interlocking was pioneered by the LNER's North Eastern Area under A. E. Tattersall, in co-operation with the various power signalling contractors. Tattersall was one of the first signal engineers to realise that, with relay interlocking and track circuiting, there would soon be no limit to the area that could

Plate 310 An early power frame with mechanical interlocking. This is the pneumatic (when installed) frame at the GC's Ashburys West Junction box, supplied (along with thirteen others) by the British Pneumatic Railway Signal Co. Ltd. for the 1903-6 Ardwick to Newton resignalling. These frames have slides which pull out horizontally, instead of the miniature levers which were more common in British power signalling practice. The interlocking mechanism is behind the wooden casing, and the sliding doors in the front give access to it. By 1929, frequent failures were being experienced here and at Fairfield Junction due to defects in the outside air pipes, and it was decided that the cheapest way to remedy the problem was to convert to electro-pneumatic operation (this change did not affect the frame itself). Further changes came in connection with the electrification of the line in the early 1950s; the illuminated diagram and (to its right) block instruments shown here date from that period. The train describer to the left of the block shelf was fitted when Ashburys West became a fringe box to the new London Road panel box.

R. D. Foster

be controlled from one signal box. (Until the 1960s, however, direct wires were needed from the box to each signal, and the economic limit remained around 10 miles). The first, experimental, panel was installed in Goole Swing Bridge box (**Plate 102**) early in 1933. It was followed later in that year by a much larger installation in a new box at Thirsk. The operating room at Thirsk had a floor area of 300sq. ft., against an estimated 1,300sq. ft. if a miniature lever power frame had been used; but the ground floor relay and equipment rooms were much longer than the first floor operating room, as was also to be the case with most subsequent panel boxes. Thirsk was followed by Leeds West in 1937, and Hull and Northallerton (**Plate 301**) in 1939. With much larger schemes at York and Liverpool Street in progress, the LNER was now in the van of world progress; but these schemes were stopped by the outbreak of the war, and in the event they were not completed until 1949-51. Small panels were installed in existing boxes by the LMS at Brunswick Goods (CLC) in 1939, and Kilburn No. 1 circa 1944, and by the SR at Bank (Waterloo & City) in 1940; but with these

exceptions there were no panel boxes outside of the LNER North Eastern Area until BR days.

These early panel boxes were provided with full glazing in the operating room (or, as it was now to become known, the 'control room'), but the signalmen were not expected to observe passing trains, as the provision of full track circuiting made this unnecessary. Hot axle boxes, shifted loads, open doors, etc., would be seen by the signalmen at the adjacent mechanical boxes which were, in the case of most of the early panel boxes, less than a mile away. However, when control areas began to expand and panel boxes were built supervising automatic signals over lengthy stretches of open line, some signal engineers came to the view that it was desirable for the signalmen to observe passing trains, which might otherwise go unobserved for ten miles or more. Some boxes, therefore, such as Tweedmouth in 1961, were built with the panel arranged in such a way that the signalman could observe trains without leaving his seat; but this was not to be the course of the future.

Plate 311 Temple Mills West was opened in 1958 and conveys an impression of the interior of a medium-sized panel·box. The panel shown here is actually a replacement of 1969, installed when the box's area of control was extended to cover the Lea Valley line. Many panel boxes of this era had venetian blinds to further reduce the amount of direct sunlight getting into the operating room.

R. D. Foster

Plate 312 Another medium-sized panel box of the late 1950s was the Southern Region's Rainham, opened on 26th April 1959 as part of the Kent Coast electrification and resignalling scheme. It has an oversailing steel-framed operating room; venetian blinds are again provided.

P. Kay

By 1960, the 'panel' had superseded the power frame as the normal choice for large resignalling schemes on all BR regions. Moreover, the implementation of the 'Modernisation Plan' meant that the number of large resignalling schemes being undertaken increased very considerably from the late 1950s. In the late 1950s and early 1960s many new panel boxes were fitted with large louvred canopies, or with large 'sun baffles', in order to keep direct sunlight out of the control room. The aim was to maintain an even intensity of light to facilitate the signalmen's observation of the illuminated train and route indications on the panel, which would have been difficult to see in strong sunlight. However, the alternative course was soon adopted of providing only a minimal window area in the control room, and working by artificial lighting, with the panel placed in the rear of the room well away from any stray sunlight. In a few cases, such as Leeds in 1967, panels were located in buildings where no view of the railway was possible at all. However, it became recognised that the provision of some window space with a view on to the railway was psychologically desirable, even if technically unnecessary.

The general adoption in the 1960s of the entrance-exit ('NX') system of panel switches, in place of the previously more common one-control switch (OCS) system, brought about a considerable reduction in the size of panel needed to control a given layout. At the same time, developments in electronic remote control systems were rapidly increasing the area that could economically be controlled from a single panel box. 'Satellite interlockings' were now possible, located in relay rooms at the major locations remote from the controlling box. Control areas increased from 15 route miles at Wilmslow in 1959, to 59 at Rugby in 1964, and 114 at Bristol in 1970-2, with some boxes controlling more than a dozen satellite interlockings. At Saltley and Trent, in 1969, a reversion was made to locating all the relay interlocking equipment in the main box, but this has not been repeated. With such large control

areas, there could now be no question of signalmen observing trains. Hot axle box detectors were placed at intervals along the line to enable trains with a hot box to be identified and stopped, but it cannot be said that this solved every problem, and there have been several cases in recent years where trains have been derailed due to defects which would probably have been spotted in time to avoid a serious accident under mechanical signalling. However, the demise of the traditional freight train is now minimising this problem.

In some resignalling schemes, 'emergency panels' have been fitted in the remote relay rooms to enable local control in an emergency. In the East Coast Main Line resignallings in the mid-1970s, many of the relay rooms were built adjacent to level crossings, and had a control room mounted on top with a panel, acting as a block post in the initial stages of the scheme, and subsequently as a gate box only but with (in some cases) the facility for full local control in an emergency.

With control areas becoming larger, it was natural that the box structures themselves became larger, albeit that the ever-developing miniaturisation of components has acted in the opposite direction. By the 1960s, the larger new panel boxes were often of three storeys. Typically, the ground floor would contain a boiler room, ventilation plant, workshops, and mess rooms; the first floor the relay room; and the second floor (shorter than the others) the control room. By the mid-1970s, the very term 'signal box' was becoming inadequate, and the largest recent installations at Motherwell (1972), London Bridge (1975), Edinburgh (1976), Victoria (1980), and Three Bridges (1983), have been described instead as 'Signalling Centres'. The larger panel boxes have always been built to individual architect-produced designs, although naturally, boxes built on the same region at the same time have usually been to similar designs.

Plate 313 Willesden, a large panel box of the 1960s. The control room has only a small amount of window space, but a large canopy is still provided.
R. D. Foster

Plate 314 The Southern Region's Three Bridges Signalling Centre, opened in 1983, shows the 1980s' style — anonymous rather than positively ugly! The photograph was taken a few weeks before opening, and provides evidence of the point that signal box structures were, and are, often built by building contractors.

P. Kay

New Building Materials: Signal Box Design Under British Rail

The 1948 railway nationalisation had little impact on signalling practices or signal box design, as the new British Railways Regions (Eastern, North Eastern, London Midland, Western, Southern, and Scottish), to which responsibility for signalling was delegated, were largely the same as the pre-1948 companies (or, in the case of the LNER, Areas). The Scottish Region, however, was new, and was a merger of the LNER and LMS organisations in Scotland, both of which had always been fairly independent of their companies' main organisations in England.

The London Midland and Western Regions at last adopted the 'modern style' of architecture for general use in 1949. Accordingly, the majority of new signal boxes on all regions in the early and mid-1950s were of brick-faced construction, with flat reinforced-concrete roofs and steel window frames. A number of the boxes built up to about 1953 had actually been designed in the 1938/9 period, but not then proceeded with due to the war. During the 1950s, designs became 'lighter' in appearance as the ARP influence waned. For some years around 1955, the box designs of the various regions were quite similar (**Plates 320, 331, 339, 346 & 349**), but subsequently they diverged again.

From the late 1950s, the reinforced concrete roof fell out of favour. For the smaller mechanical boxes, new, less costly, designs appeared, of 'traditional' construction generally but with flat timber roofs (although the North Eastern Region reverted to gabled roofs). For larger boxes, new plastics-based cladding materials were becoming available to form the walls of a steel-framed structure. The aesthetic nadir came in the 1960s with the use of prefabricated concrete panels as a cladding material. The London Midland's Edge Hill (1961) and Manchester Victoria East Junction (1962) were perhaps the ugliest signal boxes ever built. On the Eastern there were four concrete-clad boxes at Tinsley during 1964/5, and on the Southern Region several boxes were built to the 'CLASP' system (**Plate 348**). Fortunately, however, some other boxes of the 1960s stuck to brick and timber as facing materials.

Design quality improved somewhat in the 1970s, and brick has now been re-established as the normal cladding material for steel-framed structures (**Plate 314**). The recent panel boxes at Cambridge and Chester were even built with gabled roofs.

The Last Years of the Mechanical Signal Box

The number of signal boxes in use had already begun to fall by the 1923 Grouping, with the relaxation of Board of Trade limits on the distance at which points could be worked enabling a reduction from two boxes to one at many locations, and with the first rationalisations of little-used facilities. Power resignallings also usually resulted in one box taking control of an area previously controlled by several; for example, the installation of colour-light signalling between Coulsdon and Brighton in 1932 resulted in 24 boxes being abolished. The decline in numbers continued through the Grouping period (but with a respite during the war years) and accelerated with the 'Modernisation Plan' in the late 1950s and with the mass line closures of the 1960s. Even on those lines which remained open and mechanically signalled, large-scale abolitions of boxes took place as sidings were closed and block sections were extended. By 1970, only some 4,000 boxes were left in use, and each large new panel box scheme was resulting in the disappearance of a hundred or so old boxes.

Nevertheless, new mechanical boxes continued to be built in large numbers until well into British Railways days. Many, however, were to have working lives as short as those of contemporary steam locomotives. An extreme example was the Salisbury to Exeter line, where many new mechanical boxes were built in 1957-61 to replace the original and cramped 1870s boxes, but where a rationalisation and further resignalling in 1965-7 resulted in several of the new boxes being closed. Partly in anticipation of short lives, and partly to reduce costs generally, the London Midland and Western Regions, which were building more new mechanical boxes than the other Regions, evolved, in 1954 and 1957 respectively, new standard mechanical box designs in BTF or timber form intended for easy dismantling and reuse. The Southern Region ceased building new mechanical boxes in the mid-1960s, and 1972 was the last year in which a significant number of new mechanical boxes were built in the country as a whole. **Table 28** lists the few mechanical boxes built since 1972. Most of these were either made up from second-hand parts, or were undistinguished ground-level huts.

No new mechanical frames were bought by any BR Region from the contractors after the early 1960s, and the in-house manufacture

TABLE 28

The Last Mechanical Signal Boxes

This table lists all mechanical boxes opened since 1st January 1972
(except temporary boxes)

Box	Region	Date of Opening	Date of Closure
Hungerford	W	19.3.1972	17.7.1978
Kirkby Summit	LM	2.4.1972	-
Letterston Junction	W	30.7.1972	-
Whitland	W	2.9.1972	-
Norton	LM	3.9.1972	-
Waterloo Colliery Sidings	E	10.9.1972	28.6.1981
Astley	LM	17.9.1972	-
Crow Nest Junction	LM	1.10.1972	-
Midge Hall	LM	5.11.1972	-
Penyffordd	LM	17.12.1972	-
Warrington Central	LM	11.11.1973	-
Norbury Crossing	LM	1.1974	-
Dovecliffe	E	10.3.1974	18.4.1982 (As Block Post)
Twenty Feet River	E	31.3.1974	27.11.1982
Kirkby Stephen	LM	21.10.1974	-
Ravenhead Junction	LM	2.1978	-
Uttoxeter	LM	28.1.1981	-
Porth	W	31.3.1981	-
Dubbs Junction	Sc	8.11.1981	-
Maryhill Park Junction	Sc	Built 1984 but not opened	-

of new mechanical frames ceased in around 1964 on the Scottish Region, around 1966 on the Western, and around 1970 on the London Midland, later work on these and the other Regions being carried out with second-hand or reassembled frames. During the 1970s, it became gradually more common for life-expired mechanical frames in existing boxes to be replaced by a 'panel' instead of by a replacement mechanical frame. It is now unlikely that any further mechanical reframings will occur on the Eastern, London Midland, Western, or Southern Regions. At the time of writing, the Scottish Region is still carrying out mechanical reframings, the latest being Carnoustie in 1984. Since the mid-1970s the 'panel' has effectively become the norm for all resignallings, instead of just for the larger schemes as previously. In addition to the mechanical boxes listed in **Table 28**, a number of new small panel boxes have been built in recent years to the same designs.

By mid-1980, the total number of signal boxes in use on BR was down to 2,000 as block posts, plus another 350 as gate boxes and shunting frames. Of these, about 10 per cent were pre-grouping boxes to the signalling contractors' designs, 60 per cent were pre-grouping boxes to the railway companies' designs, 13 per cent were to the designs of the grouped companies, and 17 per cent were to BR designs. In addition to these boxes in BR use, there were, in mid-1980, some 120 boxes in use on London Transport, industrial, and preserved railways, plus some 500 disused boxes still standing in various conditions ranging between loving care and total dereliction. Mechanical signalling has already been wiped out in sizeable areas of the country; and by the turn of the century the mechanical signal box will, at present levels of change, be largely a thing of the past.

Plate 315 The new box at Uttoxeter under construction in August 1980. In the foreground is the NS box called Pinfold Crossing (**see also Plate 124**) which this box replaced. Uttoxeter proved to be the swansong of large new mechanical works on the London Midland Region, as regional policy was changed in 1983, and it was decided to build no further mechanical boxes. As a result, a scheme for a new box at Wrexham was cancelled.

R. D. Foster

CHAPTER EIGHT

Signal Boxes of the Post-Grouping Railway
Companies and British Railways

London & North Eastern Railway
British Railways (Eastern Region)
British Railways (North Eastern Region)

The **LNER** was split into three 'Areas' — Southern, North Eastern, and Scottish. Until 1943 each of these was responsible for its own signalling, but in that year A. E. Tattersall was appointed Assistant Chief Engineer (Signals) with overall responsibility for the signalling of the whole of the LNER. On nationalisation, the Southern and North Eastern areas retained their identity as the BR Eastern and North Eastern Regions respectively; the Scottish Area went into the BR Scottish Region and is dealt with at the end of this chapter.

In the **Southern Area** some frames (mainly for the larger new boxes) were purchased from Westinghouse and the RSCo, and also, in a few cases, from Tyer and British Power. However, most 'new' mechanical frames, whether for new boxes or reframings, were made up in the ex-GE Leyton Works from old frames and old and new parts. BR(ER) continued with this policy, but again ordered a good number of new frames from the RSCo as well (until the mid-1960s) plus a few from Westinghouse from 1957-61. Leyton Works closed in 1983, its mechanical work in later years having been largely in the making up of ground frames for both the BR(ER) and other BR Regions.

The **North Eastern Area** bought new frames from Westinghouse (to the McK&H pattern, following NE practice) until 1924/5 only. After that, it seems to have made up all 'new' frames itself in the York S&T shops, using reconditioned parts from old frames, plus a large quantity of new parts obtained from Westinghouse, Tyer, and Henry Williams. Unlike Leyton, which produced frames to many designs depending on what was available, all frames produced at York were to the same McK&H pattern. BR(NER) continued the same practice after 1948. Between the 1920s and the 1950s, the majority of the non-McK&H frames in existing NE boxes were replaced by new frames made up in this way. York Works is still open, but it is some years now since any 'new' mechanical frames were assembled.

The **Scottish Area** bought Stevens-pattern frames from the RSCo for most new boxes, but also made up frames from reconditioned parts at Ladybank Shops, especially for reframings.

A number of new power frame boxes were built by the LNER, notably at Cambridge (1926), King's Cross (1932), Fenchurch Street (1935), Edinburgh (1936 and 1938), and Darlington (1939). In addition, there were the 'panel' boxes referred to in **Chapter 7**. LNER contracts for power work went variously to Westinghouse, British Power, Siemens, and the General Railway Signal Co.

Turning now to box designs, most **Southern Area** boxes of the period 1924-41 were built to a new design (**LNER Type 11**), evolved from the GN Type 4b design. All Type 11 boxes had plain bargeboards and (in most cases) short finials as with the GN boxes; but they had concrete lintels over the locking room windows, instead of the GN boxes' segmental arches, and the arrangement of the operating floor windows varied considerably. In the 1920s, most had 2-panes-deep windows (**Type 11a**); but in the 1930s, 3-panes-deep (**Type 11b**) and 4-panes-deep (**Type 11c**) windows were more common. Windows 5-panes-deep were used at Parkeston West and Parkeston Goods Junction in 1934 (**Type 11d**), and a few other varieties are also known. There were differences in pane

sizes as well as in the total depth of the windows. A further complication was that from circa 1930 most boxes were built with a boarded (in a few cases, brick) section at the centre front, by the stove. However, all Type 11 boxes had rear frames right from 1924. Most Type 11 boxes were of brick construction.

Until about 1930, some (but not all) boxes on the GC lines were still built to the GC Type 5 design, with GC-pattern frames. Amongst these were Thoresby Colliery and Ollerton Colliery in 1926, Firbeck Junction A in 1927, and Harworth Colliery in 1929. In these cases, the box structures were erected by the signalling contractor (Westinghouse for some, the RSCo for others) — one of the last-known instances of this practice anywhere in the country. Normal LNER practice was for the box structures to be put up by building contractors.

Also, some boxes up to 1931 were (as noted in **Chapter 6**) built to the pure-GN Type 4b design; for example, Welwyn Garden City in 1926 and Blankney in 1928.

From 1939, a few Southern Area boxes were built to non-standardised 'modern architecture' designs to ARP specifications. Examples were Rotherwood (1939), Woodford No. 1 (1941), and Yarmouth South Town (1943). These have been classified **Type 13** along with contemporary NE Area boxes (**see below**).

In the **North Eastern Area**, new boxes continued to be built to NE designs until around 1933 when the 'modern style' took over. The 'modern style' boxes of the period 1933-44 showed no standardisation; those with steep-pitched hipped roofs (**Plate 301**) have been classified **Type 12**, and those with flat roofs (**Plate 318**) **Type 13**. The later ones were to ARP specifications.

In the **Scottish Area**, the NB Type 8 design was used for all new boxes up to 1935, including the one new box (Maud Junction, 1935) built on ex-GNoS lines in this period. A few non-standardised 'modern style' boxes then appeared, notably the flat-roofed power boxes at Edinburgh Waverley West (1936) and East (1938), and the hipped Galashiels (1937) — classified Types 13 and 12 respectively. However, the Scottish Area, unlike the others, did have a standardised ARP box design; a dozen or more boxes were built from 1941-3 to the **Type 14** design illustrated in **Plate 304**.

After Tattersall was appointed to take overall control in 1943, a system-wide box design appeared for the first time. This **LNER Type 15** design (**Plates 302 & 319**) was notable for the 'splay' corners at the front (and, where the rear was glazed, at the rear also). The canopy too had splay corners. The first box of this type was Brunthill, brought into use on 16th July 1944. The design was continued in use by the BR Eastern, North Eastern, and Scottish Regions until 1954. A few boxes of this period were however to non-standard designs, in some cases because they had been designed prior to 1944 but delayed by the war.

To conclude with the post-nationalisation box designs, the **BR(ER) Type 16a** design of 1955-9 (**Plate 320**), and the **BR (NER) Type 16b** of 1955-6, were very similar flat-roofed designs. The BR(NER) version differed only in having exposed canopy supports, and an additional horizontal glazing bar near the head of the operating floor windows. Also very similar was the BR(ScR) Type 16c (**see end of Chapter**). The BR(NER) then reverted to low-pitched gabled roofs for its last mechanical boxes of 1957-67. These boxes, classified **Type 17**, were not standardised in design, but most were of brick construction with vertical boarding in the gable ends. BR(NER) panel boxes, of which there were a fair number from 1958, all had flat roofs. Most distinctive were Tollerton, Pelaw, Tweedmouth, and Belford of 1959-62, where the steel-

Plate 316 Ely North Junction had a new box to the **LNER Type 11a** design in 1926, when the Sugar Beet Factory sidings were opened. It was built by Messrs Ekins & Co. for £1,295, of which the Sugar Beet company contributed £150. The locking frame was a second-hand McK&H frame of 1890. The locking room windows have been bricked up.

R. D. Foster

Plate 317 Chesterton Junction, built during 1930/1 to the **LNER Type 11c** design. The name of the builder is not known, but the mechanical and electrical work was let to Westinghouse in July 1930 for £5,249 6s. 3d. A 50-lever Westinghouse A2 frame was fitted.

R. D. Foster

Plate 318 The North Eastern Area **LNER Type 12** box at Barton Hill was opened in 1936. Unusually, it had a front frame. This box was paid for by the County Council who wanted a box at the level crossing.

R. D. Foster

Plate 319 One of the last **LNER Type 15** boxes built was that at Fountainhall on the 'Waverley Line', opened by the BR (ScR) on 2nd May 1954. It is seen after closure, which took place on 6th January 1969. Another box of the type can be seen in **Plate 302**.

E. S. Nicoll

framed control rooms had their walls inclined outwards at 8½ degrees, in order to eliminate reflections. The North Eastern Region was abolished in 1967, and the area was incorporated into the Eastern Region.

BR(ER) mechanical boxes of 1959-61 were built to various 'one-off' flat-roofed designs; examples were Dodworth (1959), Quarry Junction (1960), Netherfield Junction (1960), and Hubberts Bridge (1961). Ware (1960) was to the Type 18 design (**see below**). Standardisation made a comeback with Pasture Street (1961), Seymour Junction (1963), Gainsborough Trent Junction (1964), and Dovecliffe (built 1966, but opened 1974), all of which were built to the **Type 19** design with brick base, plate-glass windows, a slightly overhanging horizontally-boarded section above the windows, and a flat roof. With the exception of the gabled Twenty Feet River of 1974, the few mechanical 'boxes' built after 1966 were little more than huts.

BR(ER) panel boxes of the period 1959-65 were to the striking and semi-standardised **Type 18** design. They had a very large 'sun baffle' of green tinted 'maintenance-free polyester resin reinforced with glass fibre'. The later large panel boxes at King's Cross (1971), Peterborough (1972), Sheffield (1973), Scunthorpe (1973), Doncaster (1979), Cambridge (1982), and Colchester (1983) varied in design, although all were brick-faced. Standardisation was, however, manifested in the eight new small panel gate-boxes built in the 1970s East Coast Main Line resignalling. These (**Type 20**) consisted of a horizontally-boarded control room with plate-glass windows, mounted on a brick relay room. Further boxes to this design were Morpeth (1978) and Norton (1980).

Plate 320 The **BR (ER) Type 16a** box at Sleaford South, opened on 30th December 1957. Some of these boxes had continuous glazing in the front. This was one of the best-proportioned and best-finished 'modern style' box designs.

R. Newman

214

Plate 321 Milford South, a **BR (NER) Type 17** box built in 1957. The design could hardly be called attractive, the windows being particularly ungainly. Internal stairs are provided.

R. Newman

Plate 322 The **BR (ER) Type 18** panel box at Hackney Downs. This box was brought into use on 28th May 1960, replacing the original McK&H Type 1 box of 1872. The photograph was taken on a sunny June afternoon, and shows a partial success for the 'sun baffle'.

P. Kay

Plate 323 Barnby, one of the **BR (ER) Type 20** panel boxes. This opened on 10th July 1977 as a block post, replacing the GN box, but on 2nd February 1980 the control of signalling in this area was passed to the main panel box at Doncaster, leaving Barnby as a gate box only. Unlike some of these boxes, Barnby does not now have a switch for taking over control of signalling in an emergency. Note the lifeless appearance of the stretcher bond brickwork.

R. Newman

London Midland & Scottish Railway
British Railways (London Midland Region)

The LMS in England and Wales continued to build boxes to pre-grouping designs until 1929/30. On the **Midland Division**, the Midland Type 4d (until 1928) and 4e (1928/9) designs were used; and on the **Western and Central Divisions**, the LNW Type 5 design. Because the divisions did not wholly correspond with the pre-grouping companies' boundaries, there were some cases of boxes being built on the 'wrong' line for the type; but there were also cases where the new Divisional policies were not followed either, for example the Midland boxes built at Aughton Road and Eastbourne Road in Southport in 1928, and the LNW box built at Lloyds Sidings North (Corby). There were also several L&Y-type boxes built until circa 1926. The **Scottish Division** is dealt with later. The LNW and L&Y boxes were fitted with standard LNW and L&Y pattern frames, but the Midland boxes were, from 1925, fitted with the new 'REC' type frame. This was a modified version of the Midland tappet frame which the national Railway Executive Committee had proposed in 1921 as the future standard locking frame for all British railways, but which in the event was never used outside of the LMS. The first REC frame was that installed in the existing Market Harborough No. 3 LNW box in 1925. With 4½in. lever centres, the REC frame enabled LMS-built boxes to be significantly shorter than boxes with the 5½in. LNW and L&Y and the 6in. Midland frames had been.

The development of a standard LMS box design was dependent on some compromise between the Midland and LNW signal departments, whose views on box design were very different. The first sign of change came in 1928 with the appearance of several Midland-type boxes with brick bases — in some cases (Cynghordy and Northampton Down Sidings) with only a few courses of brickwork, in others (Rufford Colliery, Exhibition Junction and Northampton No. 4) of full BTF construction. Then, in 1929, the LMS created a separate S&T Department, and drawings were made for a new standard LMS box design. This was to be based on the Midland system of prefabricated parts, but with a gabled roof, and of BTF construction except where the site dictated a timber box. The first boxes to be built to this new **LMS Type 11** design were Madeley and Market Harborough No. 2, both authorised in 1929.

Panels of 10ft., 12ft., and 15ft. were used in the construction of the new Type 11 boxes, as had been the case with the later Midland boxes. The Type 11 boxes, unlike Midland boxes, often had 10ft. and 12ft. panels used together in such combinations as 12ft. + 10ft. + 12ft. 10ft. + 12ft. + 10ft., and 10ft. + 12ft. + 12ft. + 10ft.; and non-symmetrical combinations, such as 10ft. + 12ft., 10ft. + 15ft., and 12ft. + 15ft. were also now used. Where non-symmetrical combinations were used for a BTF box, an untidy appearance was created, as it made the upper part of the box unrelated to the symmetrical brick base. Type 11 boxes were mostly one 10ft. panel in width, but a good number were one 12ft. panel in width. All new boxes were now given rear frames, so the operating floor door was normally placed 2ft. 6in. from the front of the box, with the landing extending towards the rear (as had also been the case with rear-framed Midland boxes). The brickwork of BTF boxes was 'panelled' following LNW practice, except in the case of small or low boxes. Timber boxes had lapped boarding below operating floor level as with the Midland Type 4 designs. Bargeboards were completely plain, and there were no finials. On most boxes the roof ridge had mastic joints following Midland practice, but some boxes had cockscomb ridge tiles. Whether through poor materials or poor craftsmanship, most LMS boxes had an unhappy appearance compared with their Midland predecessors. Over 200 Type 11 boxes were built altogether.

A few of the smaller pre-1935 boxes had Design A windows (**Type 11a**) — see **Plate 199** for the various window patterns — but most boxes of 1929-33/4 had Design C windows (**Type 11b**). In 1933, a new window design (Design D) was introduced, omitting the Midland 'corner pieces', and this was used for the later boxes of the period 1933-54 (**Type 11c**). From around 1940 the majority of Type 11 boxes built were of timber construction, as the Types 13 and 14 designs were used for brick boxes. A few Type 11c BTF boxes of the war years were built with 14in. brickwork throughout.

Continued at page 221

Plate 324 The **Midland Type 4d** box with brick base at Rufford Colliery Sidings, opened in 1928, and closed on 29th November 1981.

R. D. Foster

Plate 325 A 15ft.-long **LMS Type 11a** box, (unusually) of STF construction. Keswick No. 1 box closed on 3rd December 1967, and is pictured in April 1968.

R. D. Foster

Plate 326 The 12ft. + 12ft. long timber **LMS Type 11b** box at Hickleton Main Colliery Sidings, opened on 1st April 1933. The locking room windows have been boarded up here. Locking room windows in timber LMS boxes were less consistent than in Midland boxes. Those in 10ft. panels were always 2 panes up, 2 across; those in 12ft. panels were either 2 up, 2 across, or 2 up, 3 across; and those in 15ft. panels 2 up, 3 across, or 2 up, 4 across.

R. D. Foster

Plate 327 A BTF **LMS Type 11c** box. Elmton & Cresswell is 10ft. + 10ft. + 10ft. long and 12ft. wide, and opened in 1946. It has the cockscomb ridge tiles which were supposed to be a standard fitting, but which in fact most boxes never had. The locking frame in this box is an experimental type made in 1938, and kept at Crewe until the scheme could be resumed at the end of the war; no further frames were ever made to this pattern.

R. D. Foster

FRONT ELEVATION

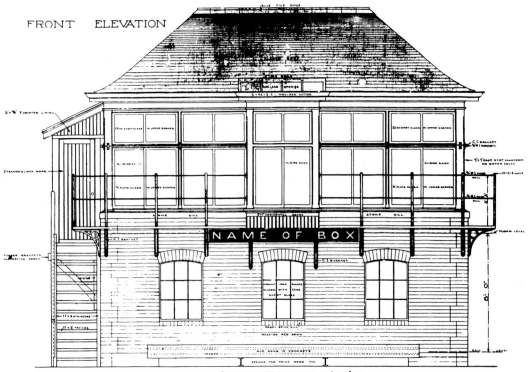

N A M E   O F   B O X

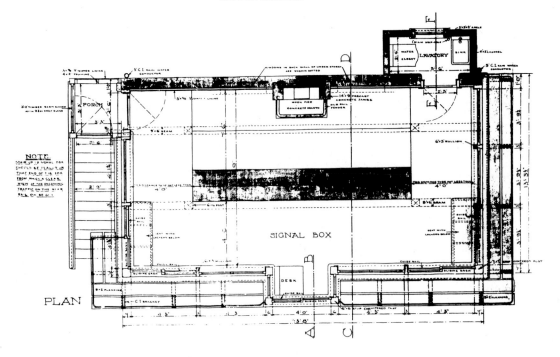

PLAN

SIGNAL BOX

Plate 328 This is the very detailed official standard drawing of the **LMS Type 12** design. Here a Stevens-pattern locking frame is shown (in the rear of the box) but boxes built from 1929 had an altered arrangement of joists and supports, in order to accommodate REC-pattern frames instead.

Scottish Record Office

SCALE: 4mm = 1 foot

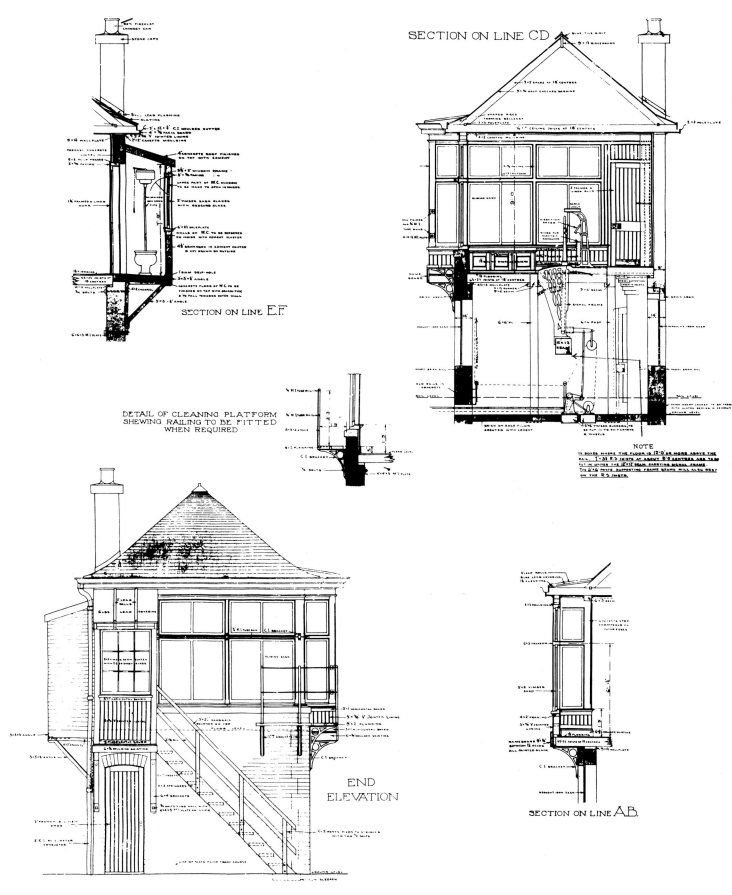

SECTION ON LINE E.F.

SECTION ON LINE CD

DETAIL OF CLEANING PLATFORM
SHEWING RAILING TO BE FITTED
WHEN REQUIRED

NOTE

END
ELEVATION

SECTION ON LINE AB.

Plate 329 (left) The **Type 12** design in practice — Longforgan, opened in 1929. This box has an LMS-made Stevens pattern frame, 'made up from second-hand material' according to the installation drawing.

E. S. Nicoll

Plate 330 (below) The Scottish Division ARP box at Stevenston No. 1, opened on 16th June 1947. This box has the only known RSCo-made REC-pattern frame in Scotland.

E. S. Nicoll

From 1929, all new LMS mechanical boxes in England and Wales had REC pattern frames. The manufacture of frames, other signalling equipment, and box parts was shared between Crewe and Derby until 1932, but in 1932 the closure of Derby Signal Works was authorised, and thereafter all the work was done at Crewe. A few complete frames, and rather more parts and outdoor equipment, were however obtained from the RSCo. For the most part, the LMS remained unadventurous in signalling matters, with all but a handful of new works being carried out on a mechanical basis. Such power work as there was mostly carried out by Westinghouse, the General Railway Signal Co., and British Power.

The LMS **Type 13** ARP box design of 1939-50 is fully described in **Chapter 7 (Plate 303)**.

The only non-standard boxes built on the LMS in England and Wales were the three 'modern style' Manchester Victoria power frame boxes of 1929 (*LMSA, Plate 583*), and similarly the new Manchester Central power frame box of 1935.

The **Scottish Division** enjoyed a certain degree of independence. Until 1929, Stevens-pattern frames were used, made in the ex-Caledonian St. Rollox Works and assembled in the ex-GSW Irvine Works. From 1929, new boxes were fitted with LMS (REC) frames made in Crewe, but the in-house manufacture of Stevens-pattern frames was continued for the reframing of old boxes, as substantial structural alterations would have been needed in order to support an REC frame in older boxes designed for a Stevens frame. Two cases are also known of the Scottish Division acquiring frames from the RSCo.

Box designs in Scotland were entirely different. The Type 11 design was not used in Scotland, except for a handful of Type 11c timber boxes erected in emergencies during the war years — for example, at Symington where the Caledonian box was destroyed by fire in 1945. Instead, a new Scottish Division standard box design made its appearance as early as 1925. Used until the late 1930s, this **Type 12** design was more reminiscent of the Caledonian Type S4 design than of any of the other pre-grouping constituents' designs. All Type 12 boxes were of brick construction, and all had an oriel window at the centre front. The hipped roofs had a 'tilting piece' at the foot, as on some Caledonian boxes. The operating floor windows were fixed in the upper portion, and had sliding sashes by the front corner posts, and in the oriel, in the lower portion.

The 1939 box at Coupar Angus South was built to a different and cheaper-looking design, with 2-panes-by-2 operating floor windows interrupted by a brick pillar at the centre front. If this was intended to be a new standard type, the war intervened to prevent it. Scottish boxes of the period 1940-7 were built instead to ARP designs. These Scottish ARP boxes were less standardised variants of the **Type 13** design (**Plate 330**).

The **London Midland Region** of British Railways continued LMS practice by manufacturing its own locking frames and signalling equipment at Crewe (some equipment was bought from the RSCo, but no frames). From 1948, frames were made to the so-called 'LMR Standard' or 'LMS post-1943' design, a revision of the REC frame. The first years after nationalisation were marked by a dispute between the Signal Department and the regional architects, over which should be responsible for signal box design. One of the last ARP boxes built, Liverpool Lime Street, opened on 25th January 1948, included some mess accommodation for shunters on the ground floor. When this came to the notice of the architects, they complained that the Signal Department should not be designing such structures, as they were not qualified architects. The architects' view was upheld, and from 1948/9 to 1954/5 all new brick signal boxes were designed by the architects. Timber boxes, however, were still built to the LMS Type 11c design.

The architects, not unexpectedly, preferred brick structures with flat reinforced-concrete roofs. Their boxes, classified **BR (LMR) Type 14**, were individually designed, and varied somewhat in window pattern, and in the position of the canopy. A feature shared by most was a large extension at the door end, housing the WC, etc.

Plate 331 Rockcliffe Hall, a **BR (LMR) Type 14** box, opened in 1953 to serve the sidings for the adjacent power-station.
R. D. Foster

As will readily be imagined, these architects' boxes were rather more expensive to build than prefabricated structures in the Midland/LMS tradition. In 1954, the Signal Department reasserted itself and won back the right to design box structures (other than large panel boxes). W. F. Hardman, who had also been responsible for the Types 11 and 13 designs, produced the new **BR(LMR) Type 15** design, to which over 150 boxes were built between 1954 and 1983. This was a further development in the tradition of prefabrication. The most obvious changes from Type 11 were the flat timber roof and canopy with 'splay' corners, and the different operating floor window design. The roof sloped towards the rear and was covered with one layer of roofing felt and one layer of rubberoid; the canopy was of timber on steel joists. The operating floor was of wood boards but with steel joists below to support the locking frame. A steel staircase was provided, leading directly to the operating floor door without a landing. Behind the door was an 'internal porch' and a second door into the operating room. There was no walkway as the windows could all be cleaned from inside. About 65 per cent of the Type 15 boxes have been of BTF construction, and about 35 per cent of timber. The brick bases of the BTF boxes broke right away from the LNW/LMS tradition, being of 14in. English Bond brickwork with concrete-framed locking room windows. The top four courses of the brickwork were inset 2in., and covered with a 2in. thick band of rendering (some boxes, however, had ordinary brickwork here instead). The bases of timber boxes retained lapped boarding but had small square locking room windows instead of the Midland type.

New panel sizes were used — 8ft., 10ft., and 12ft. 6in. The last was used in width only, except that a few ground frame huts were 12ft. 6in. long. 3½in. vertical boarding was used on the superstructure, as with Midland/LMS boxes, with 13 boards in each half of an 8ft. panel, 16 or 17 in each half of a 10ft. panel, and 21 in each half of a 12ft. 6in. panel. At the rear, the panels were (as previously) divided by intermediate verticals, into three sections in an 8ft. panel and four in a 10ft. panel. The panel combinations used for box lengths are shown in **Table 29**. Boxes of 10ft. +

10ft. or lesser length were normally one 10ft. panel in width, those of 8ft. + 8ft. + 8ft. or greater length normally one 12ft. 6in. panel in width. The corner posts were 8in. x 8in. throughout, instead of tapered, and the intermediate posts were 6in. instead of 7in. The later Type 15 boxes were constructed of parts recovered from closed boxes. The last mechanical Type 15 box to be built was Uttoxeter, opened in 1981 (**Plate 315**), and the use of the design was abandoned as a result of the decision taken in 1983 to cease new mechanical work; although a number of small panel boxes were also built to the Type 15 design, including Llandudno Junction which was the last ever Type 15 box to be built (completed July 1983 and opened February 1985).

Large panel boxes remained the architects' responsibility. Over 30 large panel boxes have been built since 1958. As far as architectural design is concerned, the following groups are identifiable, the remaining boxes being to one-off designs:

Manchester London Road, Wilmslow, and Sandbach (all 1959) — steel-framed with blue plastics-based cladding.
Edge Hill (1961), Manchester Victoria East Junction (1962) — steel-framed with concrete-panel cladding.
Coventry (1962), Nuneaton (1963), Watford (1964), Rugby (1964), Willesden (1965) (**Plate 313**), Bletchley (1965), Walsall (1965), Wolverhampton (1965) — bricked-faced lower storey, and large canopy above the control room. Some have an additional ground floor with workshops, etc.
Derby (1969), Saltley (1969), Trent (1969), Preston (1972), Warrington (1972), Carlisle (1973) (**Plate 334**) — brick-faced lower storey, control room with smallish windows at the corners only, large canopy above. These boxes were built with flat roofs but were fitted with new hipped roofs around 1980 to provide better weather protection.
West Hampstead (1979), Chester (1984) — 'post-modern' designs with brick facing all over.

Future BR(LMR) boxes will either be large architect-designed structures, or 'Portakabins'.

TABLE 29

Standard Sizes of BR (LMR) Type 15 Boxes

Size Number	Panel Arrangement	Total Exterior Length	Number of Levers
1	8ft. + 8ft.	17ft. 10in	10
2	10ft. + 8ft.	19ft. 10in.	15
3	10ft. + 10ft.	21ft. 10in.	20
4	8ft. + 8ft. + 8ft.	26ft. 4in.	25 or 30
5	8ft. + 10ft. + 8ft.	28ft. 4in.	35
6	10ft. + 8ft. + 10ft.	30ft. 4in.	40 or 45
7	8ft. + 8ft. + 8ft. + 8ft.	34ft. 10in.	50 or 55
8	10ft. + 8ft. + 8ft. + 10ft. or 8ft. + 10ft. + 10ft. + 8ft.	38ft. 10in.	60 or 65
9	8ft. + 8ft. + 8ft. + 8ft. + 8ft.	43ft. 4in.	70 or 75
10	8ft. + 8ft. + 10ft. + 8ft. + 8ft.	45ft. 4in.	80 or 85
11	8ft. + 10ft. + 8ft. + 10ft. + 8ft. or 10ft. + 8ft. + 8ft. + 8ft. + 10ft.	47ft. 4in.	90
12	10ft. + 10ft. + 8ft. + 10ft. + 10ft.	51ft. 4in.	95 or 100
13	10ft. + 8ft. + 8ft. + 8ft. + 8ft. + 10ft.	55ft. 10in.	105 or 110
14	10ft. + 8ft. + 10ft. + 10ft. + 8ft. + 10ft.	59ft. 10in.	115 or 120
15	8ft. + 8ft. + 8ft. + 8ft. + 8ft. + 8ft. + 8ft.	60ft. 4in.	125

Plate 332 The 10ft. + 8ft. + 10ft. long/12ft. 6in. wide **Type 15** box at Victoria Park on the North London line. This box controlled lines on both sides, and therefore had windows and a canopy on all facades. Note the water tank! Another BTF box of this type is illustrated in **Plate 315**, and an interior in **Plate 38**.

R. D. Foster

Plate 333 The timber **Type 15** box at Tile Hill was opened on 4th July 1966 in connection with the resignalling carried out on electrification. It was 10ft. + 8ft. long and 10ft. wide, and it too had a canopy on all sides. It closed on 1st July 1979 when control of the level crossing was transferred to Coventry panel box, via CCTV.

R. D. Foster

Plate 334 The BR (LMR) panel box at Carlisle, photographed in July 1972 before it was brought into use (it opened on 17th February 1973).

R. D. Foster

Great Western (from 1922)
British Railways (Western Region)

The Grouping had no significant impact on GW signalling practices. The story of GW box designs is taken up here from **Chapter 6**.

Type 8/28 was a gabled cheaper version of Type 7/27. At first, from 1900, this design was used only for temporary timber boxes and small break-section boxes; some of these had vertical boarding (**Type 28a**) but most had horizontal boarding (**Type 28b**). From 1921 to 1933, however, this design was widespread, and appeared also in brick form (**Type 8a**). However, most GW boxes of the 1920s were in fact of timber construction — the only period during which this was the case. A few boxes of this type were given finials, and have been classified **Type 8c/28c**.

Standardisation went somewhat to the wall in the 1920s and 1930s. Reference was made in **Chapter 3** to the GW's experiments with steel frame and concrete block construction at Waltham Siding

in 1923-5. This led to the **Type 9** design of 1927-33, which was effectively a Type 7 box, but built of these new materials. Type 9 boxes had no eaves brackets. Some were rendered, others not. A few had non-standard operating floor window arrangements, but most had the normal 3-up, 2-down variety (*GWS, Plates 103 & 107 and GWA, Plates 518 & 519*).

Other efforts were then made to find a cheaper alternative to the Type 7/27 design. **Type 11/31** of 1931-40 was simply a Type 7/27 box without eaves brackets and without the Staffordshire blue bricks. However, from 1932, the GW began a complete break away from the Type 7/27 outline. Solihull, Knowle & Dorridge, and Lapworth (all of 1932) were in a class of their own (**Type 10**), with steeply-pitched hipped roofs and concrete lintels over the locking room windows, but still with 3-up, 2-down operating floor windows. Then came **Type 12/32** of 1935-46, again with concrete lintels, but with a new pane arrangement for the operating floor windows, and, in most cases, asbestos instead of slated roofs. These boxes were not very standardised, most (**Type 12a/32a**) having gabled roofs (**Plate 337**), but some (**Type 12b/32b**) having hipped roofs.

Plate 335 (above) The **GW Type 28b** box at Heywood Road Junction, opened on 1st January 1933 to control the eastern junction of the new Westbury avoiding line. This box measured 25ft. 2in. x 12ft. 2in. x 8ft. It was abolished in May 1984. Note the bricking-up of the lead-off space.

J. P. Morris

Plate 336 (below) Taunton West Station box, a **GW Type 11** box, opened on 20th December 1931 and measuring 61ft. long x 12ft. wide. The locking room windows have all been bricked up.

J. P. Morris

Plate 337 The **GW Type 12a** box at Haverfordwest Station. This was the third successive box here and was opened on 12th September 1938.

J. P. Morris

In the meantime, the GW had turned to the 'modern style' for its first larger power boxes; two at Cardiff in 1933/4, two at Paddington in 1933, and three at Bristol *(GWS, Plate 121)* in 1934/5. These **Type 18** boxes had 14in. brickwork, steel-framed operating floor windows, and reinforced concrete flat roofs. A similar outline was used for the GW's ARP boxes (**Type 13**) of 1939-45 (for which see **Chapter 7** and **Plate 305**), but these reverted to the older timber-framed 3-up, 2-down operating floor windows.

Type 14/34 of 1947-50 was basically similar to Type 12a/32a, but the operating floor window design was again altered. It was not until after the advent of the **British Railways Western Region** that flat-roofed designs became ubiquitous. **Type 15** of 1949-55 was a brick design with a reinforced concrete roof and brick chimney. The operating floor windows were to the same design as with Type 14/34. **Type 16** (1955-9) was of a much less 'heavy' appearance, and had a steel framework roof. The full-height steel-framed operating floor windows tended to make these boxes excessively hot in summer. There were no locking room windows in these boxes, or in subsequent BR(WR) designs.

The final BR(WR) mechanical box design was introduced in 1957. For this, the operating floor windows were reduced in depth, and a louvred instead of a solid canopy was provided, hung from steel brackets. Eight of the earlier examples were of brick construction (**Type 17**), but most (and all after 1961) were of timber, with vertical boarding (**Type 37**). The timber boxes were built from 6ft. long prefabricated panels in order to facilitate reuse, and indeed all those opened after 1969 were made up from reused parts. The last Type 37 boxes were opened in 1972. Porth, the only mechanical box built since then, is a ground-level timber structure.

The GW over the period 1922-47, and the BR(WR), made virtually all their own mechanical locking frames and other mechanical equipment at Reading Signal Works (which closed in 1983). Power equipment in the 1922-47 period came from Westinghouse, Siemens, and the General Railway Signal Co.

Thirteen large panel boxes have been built by BR(WR) since 1960.

Plate 338 Fosse Road box (on the main line south of Leamington Spa). This **Type 14** box opened on 28th September 1950, and closed on 28th November 1976. It was built in Stretcher Bond (indicating cavity walls), and had the asbestos roofing found on most Type 12/32 and Type 14/34 boxes, and a nameplate of the type introduced around 1948 to replace the GW cast-iron version.

M. Christensen

Plate 339 (below) Carmarthen Junction, a **BR (WR) Type 16** box, opened on 5th February 1956.

J. P. Morris

Plate 340 Rossett, a **BR (WR) Type 37** box, opened in February 1960, on a line which has since become part of the LMR. This box is made up from five 6ft. panels, with an overall length of 32ft. The standard width of Type 37 boxes was 13ft., and the standard height 9ft. Many of them had operating floor doors in both end panels (the end panels being so constructed so that they could be reused at any location) but with one blocked off. The later Type 37 boxes, in fact, had internal stairs.

J. P. Morris

Plate 341 The BR (WR) panel box at Gloucester, opened in 1968. Cardiff (1966), Old Oak Common (1967), Swindon (1968), and Bristol (1970) were to very similar designs.

M. Christensen

Southern Railway
British Railways (Southern Region)

SR boxes of the 1920s were all of similar outline but showed Divisional variations, each of the three versions contriving to show resemblances to its pre-grouping predecessor design. All were built of brick, with segmental-arched locking room windows and 2-panes-by-2 sashes in the operating floor windows.

Type 11a (1920-9) on the Eastern Division in face pre-dated the Grouping, and was simply a gabled version of the SEC design, with the same glazed upper lights and curly eaves brackets. Type 11b (1924-30) on the Central Division had panelled boarding above the main operating floor windows instead of glazing, and no eaves brackets. The bargeboards on Types 11a and 11b boxes normally had a concave curve at the foot; finials were either very small or not provided at all. However, the Western Division's Type 11c (1924-8) retained the LSW practice of hipped roofs, and was very similar to the LSW Type 4 design, except for the absence of the curved framing at the head of the window sashes. Some had a brick pillar at the centre front, but others did not.

Plate 342 (above) The SR Type 11a box at Ramsgate, opened in 1926 when the present station was built.

M. Christensen

Plate 343 (right) A new box to the SR Type 11b design was built at Reigate in 1929. It was fitted with a new Westinghouse frame. This box is unusual in having 'upper lights' (some with 'hopper' openings), instead of boarding above the windows as on all other Type 11b boxes. The front windows, which face due south, have been provided with venetian blinds.

P. Kay

Type 12 of 1929-35 was a gabled design similar in outline to Types 11a/11b, but now with concrete lintels over the locking room windows, and a new operating floor window design with the horizontal glazing bar set near the head (reminiscent of EOD practice). The space between the windows and the eaves was boarded. Most examples had small solid eaves brackets, but Hastings and Minster had SEC-type curly brackets. St. Helier (1929) was a timber Type 12 box with corrugated-iron cladding.

In the early 1930s, the SR carried out a programme of replacing the signal boxes at some of the quieter branch line stations with a locking frame and signalling instruments in the booking office, so that the separate post of signalman could be abolished. Often, this meant an extension to the booking office on the platform side to give a view of the line (**Plate 100**). In a few cases an open frame was installed on the platform (*SS, Plate 138*).

In 1935, the SR adopted the 'modern style' for signal boxes. The first two boxes so built, Millbrook and Southampton Central, were to a conventional rectangular plan and had two horizontal glazing bars in the operating floor windows. But at Surbiton in 1936 there appeared the first example of the **Type 13** design, one of the most striking of all 20th century box designs, with rounded corners to the structure and plate-glass (but still timber-framed) operating floor windows. The larger boxes, some of which had mechanical and some power frames, had a ground floor with equipment and staff accommodation space much longer than the operating room (**Plate 345**), but the smaller mechanical boxes had a locking room of the same length as the operating room (**Plate 300**). The rear corners were not always rounded if there were no lines behind the box. More than a dozen boxes had been built to this design by 1940.

From 1940 to 1945 almost all new boxes were built to the **Type 14** ARP design (**Plate 306**). Few new boxes were built in the late 1940s; amongst them were Wimbledon A (1948), a Type 13 box but with steel-framed windows, and Crabtree Crossing (1949), a Type 14 box but similarly fitted with all steel-framed windows.

In the first few years of the **British Railways Southern Region**, energies were concentrated on the resignalling of the LBSC main lines in the London area. The new boxes built for this scheme, classified **BR(SR) Type 15**, were an updated version of the Type 13 design, with steel-framed windows, a canopy immediately above the windows instead of at roof level, rather less exposed concrete, and a generally lighter appearance. All had power frames. All have recently been closed under the London Bridge, Victoria, and Three Bridges resignalling schemes.

Type 16 covers the flat-roofed brick boxes of the period 1953-61. These reverted to a rectangular plan and, although not standardised in detail, shared the common features of a concrete canopy at roof level, steel-framed operating floor windows with a short fixed section at the head, and no locking room windows. Most had a brick pillar at the centre front. Around 1955 cavity walls were introduced and stretcher bond replaced English bond.

The Southern's first panel boxes opened in 1959, in the resignalling of the ex-LCD lines. These boxes (**Type 17**) had a brick-faced lower storey, and tinted cladding in the walls of the oversailing operating room (**Plate 312**). There was a canopy at roof level. A development of this design was **Type 18** of 1961-66 (**Plate 347**), with the operating room built directly over the ground floor, and with a louvred canopy immediately above the windows (or, in some cases, no canopy at all). The panel boxes built for the resignalling of the SE main line in 1962 were to the Type 18 design, as were the BR(SR)'s last mechanical boxes in the early 1960s.

Panel boxes of 1966-70 (Guildford, Eastleigh, Basingstoke, Portsmouth, Surbiton, and Dartford) (**Type 19**) were built to the 'CLASP' system of prefabricated concrete panels, also used for BR(SR) station buildings of that period. Since then, there have been only the four large panel 'Signalling Centres' at Feltham (1974), London Bridge (1975), Victoria (1980), and Three Bridges (**Plate 314**) (1983).

Until around 1929, pre-grouping preferences were continued in respect of locking frames. After that, the SR and BR(SR) acquired the majority of the new mechanical frames they required from Westinghouse, but many of the smaller new boxes were fitted with second-hand frames instead. Power frames also were bought from Westinghouse.

Plate 344 Dover Priory, an **SR Type 12** box, opened on 16th November 1930. It was fitted with a new Westinghouse frame, No. 10579, which can be seen in this 1978 photograph. In 1980, the frame was replaced by a panel, during the installation of which the operating floor windows were all replaced to a different pattern. Note the dowels in front of all the windows.

M. Christensen

Plate 345 The large mechanical **SR Type 13** box at Horsham, brought into use on 24th April 1938. This design has become colloquially known as the 'Glasshouse'.

R. D. Foster

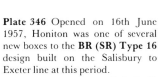

Plate 346 Opened on 16th June 1957, Honiton was one of several new boxes to the **BR (SR) Type 16** design built on the Salisbury to Exeter line at this period.

C. L. Caddy

Plate 347 The **Type 18** panel box at Sevenoaks was opened on 4th March 1962.
P. Kay

Plate 348 A rear view of the **Type 19** 'CLASP' panel box at Guildford, opened on 17th April 1966.

P. Kay

British Railways (Scottish Region)

As noted above, the LNER Type 15 design was used for new BR(ScR) boxes until 1954 (**Plate 319**). However, most post-nationalisation examples in Scotland (including two, Kelty and Oakley, on ex-LNER lines) had LMS pattern frames! The **BR (ScR) Type 16c** design of 1955-61 was very similar to the contemporary Eastern and Northern Eastern Region designs, but had a deeper concrete framing around the operating floor windows. The few mechanical boxes built after 1961 all had flat roofs, but were less standardised. From 1954, the Scottish Region, freed again from the influence of Crewe, gave up using LMS-pattern frames, and reverted to the pre-1929 LMS Scottish Division practice of making new Stevens-pattern frames itself, at St. Rollox and Irvine, for new boxes as well as for reframings. However, new boxes on ex-Highland lines were given reconditioned McK&H-pattern frames. In recent years all 'new' frames have been made up from reconditioned old frames and parts rather than new manufacture. The last frame prepared at Irvine Works was in 1982, since when work has been done locally.

Fifteen panel boxes have been opened since 1959, to very varied designs.

Plate 349 (right) The standard BR (ScR) Type 16c box at Kincardine Station, built in 1960.

E. S. Nicoll

CHAPTER NINE

Signal Boxes of London Transport and Constituents

Metropolitan

The Metropolitan was fully interlocked and worked on the Absolute Block system from its opening in 1863. Few illustrations are known of the original boxes on the central sections. Those which are known are Farringdon and Farringdon Junction of 1866 (full-size boxes in the open, built to 'special' designs), and Bayswater of 1868 (a small box on the end of the platform, for which see *Plate 16 in London Railway History by H. P. White*). There were also several 'hole-in-the-wall' intermediate boxes in the tunnels. Reference was made in **Chapter 5** to the 1875 box at Liverpool Street, which shows some McK&H characteristics. But most of the Metropolitan Railway's signalling equipment in the early period came from S&F, and when the main line 'extension' northwards from Finchley Road commenced in 1879, the boxes were built to the S&F Type 5 design. The last box to this design was Pinner in 1885.

In the years 1889-96, most boxes were fitted with frames of a somewhat crude design not known elsewhere, which would seem most likely to have been manufactured in-house, although there is as yet no documentary evidence of this. One of these 'Met' frames is still in use at Great Missenden. However, there was also some RSCo work, and the 1904 Uxbridge line was a Sykes contract. Irrespective of frame type, all Metropolitan boxes from 1887 were built (often by building contractors) to various standard Met. designs instead of to signalling contractors' designs. The first of these designs (**Type 1**) was based on the S&F Type 5 design, but had no glazing in the upper panels, no vertical glazing bars in the operating floor windows, a different type of locking room window, and diagonal boarding (except in the central section of each facade, where horizontal boarding was used). All Type 1 boxes were of timber construction, with brick chimneys. This design was used on the extension from the Rickmansworth section in 1887 through to the very end at Verney Junction in 1896, and of course for a number of replacement boxes elsewhere. Great Missenden box is still open, and disused examples can be seen at Chorleywood and Chesham. At Verney Yard and Winslow Road there were small ground-level gabled boxes instead.

Plate 350   A typical **Met Type 1** box at Amersham. It was inspected on 16th August 1892, and the line opened on 1st September.

London Transport

Plate 351 The **Met Type 3** box at Watford. The Watford branch was a Met/LNER Joint line, but the works were under the Metropolitan's control. Three new signal boxes were required, at Watford Junction, Croxley Green, and Watford. It was intended, at one time, to have these boxes built to a more elaborate brick design, but at £828, the cheapest tender for the first of them, Watford Junction, was way over what had been budgeted. (Drawings of this original design do not survive, but one suspects it was a version of the Type 4 design, which had been evolved during the latter part of 1923). In April 1924, Selbie, the Company Secretary, accordingly asked the Engineer to prepare new drawings for timber boxes and go out to tender again. This was done, and on 21st July the contract was given to Messrs Logan and Hemingway, who were in fact the contractors for building the line. Their tender was of £584 for Watford, £340 for Croxley Green, and £436 for Watford Junction. The signalling work, which also included a new frame for Rickmansworth box, was done by Westinghouse. Watford box had a 42-lever Westinghouse A2 frame, No. 9436. It was abolished on 27th September 1958. With their horizontal lapped boarding, 2 panes by 2 operating floor windows, and small solid eaves brackets, these boxes were very reminiscent of the LBSC Type 3b design.

London Transport

For the Harrow & Uxbridge line of 1904, another variant of the S&F Type 5 design was evolved. These Metropolitan **Type 2** boxes (Rayners Lane, Ruislip and Uxbridge) were of BTF construction with S&F-type locking room windows, diagonal boarding, and 'pendant' eaves brackets. They did have vertical glazing bars in the operating floor windows. Ruislip is still standing.

From 1907, the Metropolitan began to install automatic signalling, a process which it completed on all except the northern end of the extension prior to its absorption into LT. Signalling work was now carried out by the McKenzie, Holland & Westinghouse Power Signal Co. (after 1920, by Westinghouse). Westinghouse all-electric power frames were installed at Aldgate (1908), Praed Street Junction (1908), Baker Street (1913), Baker Street (new box) (1924), Edgware Road (1926) and Wembley Park (1932); but elsewhere the resignalling was carried out using full-size mechanical frames, with power-worked signals but mechanically-worked points. The signalling work for the Metropolitan Railway's last two new boxes, Farringdon and Aldersgate (both of 1932), was con-

tracted to the British Power Railway Signal Co. instead of to Westinghouse.

From 1908 or so, new boxes seem to have been built with gabled roofs and 2-panes-deep windows (**Type 3**), although no exterior photographs are known of many boxes of this period. The Watford line boxes of 1925 are however well documented (**Plate 351**). In its final years, the Metropolitan adopted the 'modern style', with the flat (reinforced concrete) roofed **Type 4** design (**Plate 352**). The first of these was Baker Street, opened in 1924. It was built as a result of a series of fires in the electrical equipment in the old box early in 1923. Although only minor in themselves, these were put down to the fact that the old box did not really provide a satisfactorily weatherproofed and spacious housing for the power frame and associated equipment, and it was felt best to replace it, before any worse incident occurred, with a new structure purpose-designed for modern electrical equipment. The Type 4 design was used also for the later power boxes at Edgware Road, Wembley Park, Farringdon, and Aldersgate.

Plate 352 The **Met Type 4** box at Wembley Park, photographed in 1936. This box was built in connection with the Wembley Park to Harrow quadrupling. The 95-lever Westinghouse all-electric frame was ordered in October 1930, and the box opened on 3rd January 1932. Later in 1932, in an unprecedented development so far as British practice was concerned, the new Stanmore line opened, controlled entirely from this box on 'Centralised Traffic Control' principles. Most of the windows in these Type 4 boxes were bricked up for ARP purposes, and have not been reopened subsequently. Wembley Park box is still in use and still sports the original black-on-white enamel nameplates, seen here. The limewhiting of the exterior brickwork is another original feature of all Type 4 boxes.

London Transport

Metropolitan District

The District, like the Met., was fully interlocked and worked on the Absolute Block system from the opening of the first sections of its network in 1868-72. Photographs of early boxes are rare, but it seems that most signalling work was done by S&F, and there were some S&F Type 2a boxes. The Ealing, Putney Bridge, and Hounslow lines of 1879-84 had S&F Type 5 boxes, of which Boston Manor (1883) still stands.

Underground Electric Railways Co.

In 1901 the District fell into the control of the American financier C. T. Yerkes. Yerkes' company, known from 1902 as the Underground Electric Railways Co. of London Ltd., also took over during or prior to their construction three tube lines, the Baker Street & Waterloo, the Great Northern, Piccadilly & Brompton, and the Charing Cross, Euston & Hampstead. Although these four companies retained their legal independence for some years, the operation and engineering of the 'Underground' group was under central control from the start, this including the apppointment of a single Signal Engineer.

The 'Underground' group immediately undertook the electrification of the District, and the replacement of the old mechanical signalling with automatic signalling, to enable an increased train frequency. It was decided to adopt the Westinghouse electro-pneumatic system, which was already in use on the Boston Elevated Railway in the USA. To test this system out in England, the Westinghouse Brake Co. Ltd. was asked to install it on the Ealing & South Harrow Railway, a District protégé whose line had been completed in 1899 with mechanical signalling supplied by EOD (and with EOD design boxes), but which had never been opened to public traffic. H. G. Brown, Signal Engineer of the Boston Elevated Railway, was brought over to England to superintend this work. Brown was to stay in England, becoming Chief Engineer and subsequently Managing Director of the McKenzie, Holland & Westinghouse Power Signal Co. Ltd., and eventually overseeing the creation of the Westinghouse Brake & Saxby Signal Co. Ltd. in 1920, as described in **Chapter 2**. The Ealing & South Harrow opened at last in 1903 with the new automatic signalling in use, and, its reliability having been proven, the resignalling of the whole of the District followed in 1905-6. Most of the old boxes were abolished. At thirteen of the most important locations new boxes were built (**Plate 353**), fitted with electro-pneumatic power frames supplied by the Westinghouse Brake Co. Sixteen of the old mechanical boxes were retained in the outer areas, but here too the signals were converted to electro-pneumatic operation. Between the boxes there were long stretches of automatic signalling.

The new District boxes were built of brick with flat roofs, this being the first use of flat roofs for a normal outdoor box design in this country. They had 3-panes-deep operating floor windows plus 2 or 3-panes-deep upper lights. The same design was used for the later mechanical box at Hounslow Central (Cabin WT).

The new tube lines were equipped with electro-pneumatic signalling from the start. Signal boxes, with Westinghouse power frames, were provided only at stations with pointwork, with automatic signals elsewhere. The BS&W, opened during 1906/7, had five boxes; the GNP&B, opened in 1906, also had five; and the CCE&H, opened in 1907, had six. Golders Green was an open-air box similar to those on the District, but most of the boxes were of course in the tunnel sections, built on the ends of the station platforms. They were tiled for much of their height in the same way as the platform walls, but some glazing was provided. Some were quite large structures with flat roofs, others no more than a walled-off area with the walls continuing up to the tunnel crown. All these original boxes have now been replaced, but those at Hyde Park Corner, Covent Garden and Holborn lasted in use until 1979 and still exist, as does Mornington Crescent.

The 'Underground' group's 1920s extensions resulted in new open-air boxes at Brent and Hendon (1923), Colindale and Edg-ware (1924), and Morden (1926). These were built to a new design, Hendon even sporting a hipped roof. The Edgware line boxes were fitted with Westinghouse electric instead of E-P frames, but E-P frames were reverted to for all later work. Also at this period, a number of new boxes were opened in the tube sections of the C&SL line and its Morden extension.

The last boxes built by the 'Underground' group were during 1932/3 for the Piccadilly Cockfosters extension (Arnos Grove, Oakwood, and Cockfosters) and the quadrupling to Acton Town (Hammersmith, Turnham Green, and Acton Town). These had reinforced-concrete roofs and minimal window space. This box design was also used for post-1933 boxes (**see below**), as the railway side of the new London Passenger Transport Board was based on the 'Underground' organisation.

We have not attempted to give type numbers to the 'Underground' box designs.

Plate 353   West Kensington West Cabin WC in the District's new box-lettering system (for which see **Chapter 3**), was opened in October 1906. It was built on a steel gantry over the Piccadilly tracks, at the point where they emerge from the tunnel. The brickwork is rendered in this photograph, but this was not a normal feature of this box design. The photograph was taken in 1962, in which year the box was replaced by an Interlocking Machine Room, controlled from Earls Court.

London Transport

City & South London

This pioneer tube line of 1890 had mechanical signalling, supplied by Dutton, with boxes at the platform ends (two boxes at the split-level stations). The 1900-1 extensions were signalled by EOD. In 1913, the company passed into the 'Underground' group, and in the early 1920s automatic signalling was installed in place of block working, and the whole line was reconstructed.

Central London

Opened in 1900, the CL had mechanical signalling supplied by EOD. There were originally 16 boxes (2 each at the three split-level stations), with block working; but during 1912/13 automatic signalling was installed by the McKenzie, Holland & Westinghouse Power Signal Co., and most of the boxes were abolished. The CL passed into 'Underground' control in 1913. One of the original platform-end boxes, Marble Arch, is still in use.

Great Northern & City

The GN&C, opened in 1904, was the first tube line to have automatic signalling, provided by Spagnoletti & Co. However, 'boxes' with full-size mechanical frames (manufactured by the RSCo) were built at every station, in rooms between the platforms. At Finsbury Park, Drayton Park, and Moorgate, where there was pointwork, the boxes were fully staffed, but at the intermediate stations the signals worked automatically in the normal circumstances, the staff merely observing the passage of trains. The original Drayton Park 'box' was later replaced by a larger freestanding hipped box with a concrete-blocks base. The GN&C was taken over by the Met. in 1913.

London Transport

The London Passenger Transport Board (hereafter referred to as LT, to avoid having to go into the several changes of name that have occurred since) was established in 1933 and took over all the above railways. Mechanical signalling was by 1933 already a thing of the past for new works on LT lines, and all new boxes built by LT were fitted with Westinghouse electro-pneumatic frames (from 1952, push-button desks). Some mechanical ground frames were however installed.

The 'New Works' programme resulted in a large number of new boxes being built in the late 1930s, notably on the Metropolitan Line between Finchley Road and Uxbridge, on the northern extensions of the Northern Line, and on the eastern and western extensions of the Central Line (where, however, the new installations were not brought into use until after the war). The Bakerloo Line was also resignalled in 1939, but here the 'boxes' were rooms in the underground stations.

As noted above, the first LT boxes were built to the same design as the last 'Underground' group boxes. The 1939 Northern and Central Line boxes were given canopies with a greater overhang and placed immediately above the windows, but were otherwise very similar. The few post-war boxes showed greater variations, and the last two local signal boxes built by LT, Upminster in 1957 and Amersham in 1960, were to completely different 'one-off' designs. No type-numbering has been attempted for LT boxes.

In the 1940s, remote control operation was developed, at Shoreditch, Harrow North and South, Ruislip Gardens, North Acton Junction, and Grange Hill. Here the boxes had 'slave' lever frames which were remotely operated from another box in normal circumstances, but which could be operated locally in emergencies. This was followed in the 1950s by the 'Interlocking Machine Room' and 'Programme Machine' operation, under which remote interlocking machines are normally controlled automatically by a programme machine according to the booked timetable, but under the supervision of a central 'Control Room' where control staff can intervene if problems arise. An interesting feature of this otherwise very advanced system is that the 'interlocking machines' themselves are still Westinghouse electro-pneumatic installations with mechanical interlocking, this choice being due to the fact that this apparatus had proved so reliable in many decades of LT use. Most 'Interlocking Machine Rooms' are new windowless single-storey structures, but in some cases the former signal boxes have been converted to serve as IMRs. The whole of the Northern Line, and most of the District and Piccadilly lines, have now been converted to programme machine operation, with Control Rooms at Earl's Court and Coburg Street; and the Victoria Line was so controlled from its opening. In fact, the 'signal box' as such has already disappeared from most of the LT network. Future resignalling schemes, including those currently under preparation for the Central and Jubilee lines, will be based on solid state (computer) interlocking instead of 'interlocking machines'.

An attractive feature of the LT network is the survival of a number of long-abolished boxes in good condition. Mention was made above of those dating from the various LT constituents; in addition there are several GE and GN boxes (**Plate 161**).

Plate 354 Rayners Lane was the first box built by LT. It was built in 1935 after the previous mechanical box was demolished by a runaway ballast train, and had a 35-lever Westinghouse electro-pneumatic frame. Closer examination of the brickwork shows that the bottom half of the box is in Stretcher Bond, the next quarter in English Bond, and the top quarter has two courses of stretchers for each course of headers!

London Transport

CHAPTER TEN

Signal Boxes of Minor and Industrial Railways

Many of the minor railways excluded from the 1922/3 Grouping were Light Railways, and had no signal boxes. Interlocking was required on such lines, but a small open ground frame sufficed in many cases. Some of the minor railways, however, did have boxes. These are listed in **Table 30**. The boxes on these minor lines were variously to the signalling contractors' designs or to local designs.

Additonally, there were many boxes on military (**Table 31**), dock companies' (**Table 32**), and colliery and other industrial railways (**Table 33**). These were often to fairly crude local designs, but here too the contractors' designs were used in some cases.

Finally, some of the preserved railways have, in recent years, built small new signal boxes, notably the Ffestiniog, Tal-y-llyn, Welshpool & Llanfair, Torbay & Dartmouth, and Ravenglass & Eskdale. More often, however, the preserved lines have reopened existing boxes or acquired second-hand box structures from BR.

TABLE 30

Minor Railways (Companies Excluded from the 1922/3 Grouping) with Interlocked Signal Boxes

Company	Boxes	Date	Signalling Contractor	Box Design
Bideford, Westward Ho! & Appledore (Light)	Westward Ho! Causeway Crossing	1901 circa 1905	S&F S&F	Local S&F Special
Campbeltown & Machrihanish (Light)	Lintmill Crossing	1906	Not known	Not known
Festiniog	Three boxes at Blaenau	1880	McK&H	McK&H Type 3
Isle of Man	Douglas	1890	Dutton	Dutton Special
Liverpool Overhead (see footnote)	Several boxes	1893-1905	RSCo	Local
Manx Northern	St. Johns	circa 1886	Stevens	Local
	(Also Stevens ground frames at St. Johns, Waterfall, and Foxdale)			
Mersey — see Chapter 6	(Company was excluded from the Grouping but nationalised in 1948)			
Nidd Valley (Light)	Pateley Bridge	1907	J. B. Saunders	Local
	(The other stations had open ground frames on the platforms)			
North Wales Narrow Gauge	Boxes at most stations	1877-8	McK&H	McK&H Type 3
	(Also some work done by GWCo in 1881)			
Romney, Hythe & Dymchurch (Light)	Hythe New Romney Dymchurch	1927	Made in-house (Greenley designs)	Local
	(Hythe and New Romney still in use)			
Shropshire & Montgomeryshire (Light)	Kinnerley Jn.	1911	Not known	Covered GF
Snowdon Mountain	Hebron Halfway Clogwyn Summit	1896	RSCo (frames to Stevens pattern)	Block huts with outside frames.
	(Equipment still in use but some of the huts are replacements)			

Liverpool Overhead: When opened in 1893, this railway had automatic signalling based on Timmis' system of contacts patented in 1891. There were boxes at the terminal stations only. The Electric Construction Co. Ltd. of Wolverhampton were the contractors, but the signal work was subcontracted to the RSCo. The boxes were to local designs. The subsequent extensions of the line were also signalled by the RSCo. In 1920, the line was resignalled by the McKenzie, Holland & Westinghouse Power Signal Co., who installed colour-light signals worked by track circuits.

Plate 355 Douglas Station was enlarged in 1890, and new signalling was supplied by Dutton. Although the box is to a 'Special' design, it has sufficient Dutton characteristics to suggest that the signalling contractor was responsible for its erection.

R. D. Foster

Plate 356 The old and new boxes at Graven Hill on the Bicester Military Railway, photographed on 31st March 1979 shortly before the new box opened. The locking frames for the two new boxes on this line were ordered from Westinghouse in 1977.

M. Christensen, reproduced by permission of the Commandant COD Bicester

TABLE 31

Signal Boxes on Military Railways

Bicester Military Railway

Interlocked signal boxes built 1949 at Graven Hill ('A' Cabin) and Arncott ('B' Cabin), with Westinghouse frames. Both were replaced during 1978/9 by new boxes built adjacent, again with (new) Westinghouse frames **(Plate 356)**.

Cairnryan Military Railway

Built in 1942. Signal boxes with Westinghouse frames at Leffnoll South and Leffnoll North. Additional block posts at Aird, Construction Jn., School Sidings South, School Sidings North, and Deep Water Quay.

Shropshire & Montgomeryshire

This line was taken over by the War Department in 1941, and new signalling was provided. It remained under Military control until 1960.
Small signal box with LMS (REC) pattern frame at Kinnerley. Block huts (War Department standard design) with outside ground frames (Tyer pattern) at Hookagate East, Hookagate West, Ford & Crossgates, Quarry, and Nesscliffe.

Woolmer Instructional Military Railway/Longmoor Military Railway

Signal boxes with inside frames at Bordon (1925), Longmoor (four consecutive boxes in 1923, 1931, 1941, and 1950), Woolmer (two consecutive boxes), and No. 2 Range. Block huts with outside ground frames at several other locations. Owing to the many alterations made to the line, it is impossible to summarise usefully the full history.

Only the two 1978/9 Bicester boxes are now in use, the other lines being closed

TABLE 32

Signal Boxes on Dock Companies' Railways

(Excludes those Railway and Dock companies which were included in the 1922/3 Grouping)

East & West India Dock Co.

Four boxes in West India Docks (1867-71). West India Dock Jn. **(Plate 79)** was an S&F Type 2a box, the others of unknown design/contractor. Two boxes in Tilbury Docks (1886); signalling work carried out by RSCo, boxes built to 'Special' design similar to contemporary GE boxes.
These railways were owned by the Port of London Authority from 1909.

London & St. Katharine Dock Co.

Eleven boxes built in 'Royal' Docks at various dates 1880-87. Some or all the signalling work was done by S&F. The three boxes of which photographs are known were very similar to the GE Type 2 design. These railways were owned by the Port of London Authority from 1909.

Millwall Dock Co.

One box (1871); no details known. To Port of London Authority in 1909.

Manchester Ship Canal

Boxes at Aubrey Street and Chester Road (local hipped design). Another box (with flat concrete roof) was built later at No. 2 Swing Bridge, Salford; this had an LMS-pattern frame made by the RSCo.

Mersey Docks & Harbour Board

RSCo box at Liverpool Riverside; this box is now at Steamtown, Southport.

Tyne Commissioners

About nine boxes. Most signalling work done by McK&H.

All these boxes have been abolished.

TABLE 33

Signal Boxes on Colliery and Other Industrial Railways

Only the major systems are listed here. Many other colliery and industrial lines had gate boxes at public road crossings **(e.g. Plates 358 & 359)**. All these boxes were to local designs.

Ashington Collieries
The largest colliery system. Around eight boxes altogether. Still in use are Ashington No. 1 Loop (McK&H frame), Ashington Colliery (1943, Westinghouse frame), and the later NCB boxes at Lynemouth (1956) and Alcan (1973).

Lambton Collieries
Several boxes. McK&H and Westinghouse frames known. Burnmoor Colliery box is still in use.

South Shields, Marsden, & Whitburn Colliery Railway
Three boxes (Westoe Lane, Mowbray Road, Lighthouse). Signalling work carried out by the RSCo in 1888.

Wemyss Private Railway
Box at Denbeath Jn. (Stevens knee frame).

Beckton Gas Works
Fourteen boxes. S&F and Westinghouse frames known.

British Steel (and constituents)
Several boxes. A box is still in use at Scunthorpe.

Derwent Valley Water Board (Bamford & Howden Railway)
Four boxes built in 1903. Equipment supplied by the Midland Railway, but box structures to local design with corrugated-iron cladding and lean-to roofs.

Rowrah & Kenton Fell Mineral Railway
Box at Sherriff Gate Junction.

Oxfordshire Ironstone Railway
Boxes at Wroxton and Horley. Equipment supplied by McK&H **(Plate 357)**.

Lever Bros. (Port Sunlight)
Box at Port Rainbow.

Bass & Co. (Burton-on-Trent)
Box at Station Street ('modern' flat-roofed design).

Worthington & Robinson (Burton-on-Trent)
Box at High Street (built in 1870s, and copy of the Midland Type 1 design).

Ind Coope (Burton-on-Trent)
Box at Station Street (built in 1860s, local hipped design originally unglazed).

Allsopp's (Burton-on-Trent)
Box at Horninglow Street (local hipped design).

Most of the signalling equipment on the Burton Brewery lines was supplied by the Midland Railway.

Plate 357 The Oxfordshire Ironstone box at Wroxton. The two boxes on this line were both at level crossings, and each had a 3-lever frame and a gate wheel. The board on the front of this box gives details of locomotive duties. The crude construction is typical of industrial lines.

C. H. Betts

Plate 358 The small gate box at Rawdon Colliery (near Moira) is still in use. It is quite elegant by industrial standards, and may (given the bargeboards) have been built by the RSCo. It contains an RSCo gate wheel. The signals (one of which is seen here attached to the box) are of the 'traffic lights' type, common on NCB lines.

R. D. Foster

Plate 359 One of the most peculiar signal boxes anywhere was this gate box on the Holly Bank Colliery Company's line at Bursnip Road in Staffordshire. The signalman's 'turret' appears to have been added to an existing building (which housed the Colliery Company's offices). The signal (supplied by McK&H) was worked by rod, and the barriers by chains. The line is now closed but the structure still exists.

C. H. Betts

Index

Notes on Index

Bold type indicates the major references (in cases where a large number of references are given).

Plates, Figures and Tables are indexed under page numbers.

Individual signal boxes and locations are not indexed except where they are of especial historical importance.